COMPUTATIONAL COLLECTIVE INTELLIGENCE

WILEY SERIES ON PARALLEL AND DISTRIBUTED COMPUTING
Series Editor: Albert Y. Zomaya

Parallel and Distributed Simulation Systems / Richard Fujimoto

Surviving the Design of Microprocessor and Multimicroprocessor Systems: Lessons Learned / Veljko Milutinović

Mobile Processing in Distributed and Open Environments / Peter Sapaty

Introduction to Parallel Algorithms / C. Xavier and S. S. Iyengar

Solutions to Parallel and Distributed Computing Problems: Lessons from Biological Sciences / Albert Y. Zomaya, Fikret Ercal, and Stephan Olariu (*Editors*)

New Parallel Algorithms for Direct Solution of Linear Equations / C. Siva Ram Murthy, K. N. Balasubramanya Murthy, and Srinivas Aluru

Practical PRAM Programming / Joerg Keller, Christoph Kessler, and Jesper Larsson Traeff

Computational Collective Intelligence / Tadeusz M. Szuba

Parallel and Distributed Computing: A Survey of Models, Paradigms, and Approaches / Claudia Leopold

Fundamentals of Distributed Object Systems: A CORBA Perspective / Zahir Tari and Omran Bukhres

Pipelined Processor Farms: Structured Design for Embedded Parallel Systems / Martin Fleury and Andrew Downton

COMPUTATIONAL COLLECTIVE INTELLIGENCE

Tadeusz M. Szuba
University of Kuwait
Kuwait City

A WILEY-INTERSCIENCE PUBLICATION
JOHN WILEY & SONS
New York • Chichester • Weinheim • Brisbane • Singapore • Toronto

This book is printed on acid-free paper. ♾

Published simultaneously in Canada.

For ordering and customer service, call 1-800-CALL-WILEY.

Library of Congress Cataloging-in-Publication Data:

Szuba, Tadeusz M.
Computational collective intelligence / Tadeusz M. Szuba.
p. cm.—(Wiley series on parallel and distributed computing)
"A Wiley-Interscience publication."
Includes bibliographical references and index.
ISBN 0-471-34966-6 (cloth : alk. paper)
1. Computational intelligence. I. Title. II. Series.

Q342 .S98 2001
006.3—dc21 00-047772

Printed in the United States of America.

10 9 8 7 6 5 4 3 2 1

This book has been accomplished thanks to the constant help with language supervision and correction of Linda Raye Sue

CONTENTS

PREFACE

We live and work with the term *intelligence*, but when it is necessary to take a closer look, the real problem is to determine what *intelligence* really means. An encyclopedia[1] gives the following definition for this term:

> *Intelligence*, capacity to learn or to understand. It is generally synonymous with intellect but is usually differentiated from intellect in practice to emphasize ability or efficiency in dealing with concrete situations and in profiting intellectually from sensory experience. In psychology, *intelligence* is somewhat more narrowly defined as the capacity to acquire knowledge or understanding and to use it in novel situations. Under experimental conditions, the success of a subject in adjusting his or her behavior to the total situation or in meeting the challenge of the specific situation may be studied and, to some extent, measured in quantitative terms.
> Psychologists believe that the capacities measured in testing or laboratory situations are also significant in everyday life, in which individuals analyze or apprehend new sensory and mental data so as to direct their actions toward desired goals. Psychologists still differ, however, as to a precise definition of the comprehensiveness and functions of *intelligence*; one school of thought considers it as a sum of specific abilities best displayed in specific situations.
> In the formulation of *intelligence* tests, most psychologists tend to adopt an eclectic concept, according to which *intelligence* is treated as a general ability operating as a common factor in a wide variety of special aptitudes. It is observed and measured by techniques focused upon these aptitudes singly or in combination.

If we go deeper into analysis of this term, the perception of *intelligence* gets split and fuzzy, and it is found that there are at least two independent types of *intelligence*: one is the *individual intelligence* of beings and the other one, which is fast growing as a scientific and industrial discipline is the *machine or artificial intelligence* (AI). The latter has been boosted by recent rapid progress in vision systems, manipulators and effectors and computer technology. These two disciplines are linked but are growing almost independently. Individual *intelligence* is (now) mainly a psychology domain that targets biologic *beings*, whereas AI targets computerized machines and is a domain of computer science.

Both research disciplines are now well established, with extensive libraries of theoretical and practical works. However, there is one more kind of *intelligence*, which seems to be something separate but is highly related to individual

[1] *Microsoft® Encarta® 97 Encyclopedia.*

intelligence: *collective intelligence* (CI). This term is well known, but its scientific (journal articles, books) reference base is surprisingly poor however, the following teams are good exceptions:

- The McMaster University team led by William Sulis and I. Trofimova, who is the administrator of the CIlab (Collective Intelligence Lab.). The 'credo' of their laboratory is '*to study the dynamics, capabilities, limitations and applications of systems composed of embodied, strongly situated, weakly coupled agents interacting without hierarchical control*' with the focus on the psychological facets of the problem.
- The NASA Ames team led by David Wolpert. They focus on distributed systems of reinforcement-learning-based agents, each with an associated personal utility function that works on maximizing.

Due to the importance of their work, a list of their papers will be presented at the end of the bibliography to allow the reader to have direct access and review of them. Competitive terms such as *distributed intelligence, synergy, swarm intelligence*, and so forth have also been coined.

There are convincing manifestations of *collective intelligence* on almost all levels of life. We can observe cooperating groups of beings express powerful *collective intelligence* in solving their common problems, even if some group members have mutually conflicting goals and points of interest.

For example, we are often caught unawares by the *collective intelligence* of ants that are able to get through barriers to our food.

Even in a human environment, I have often observed and been surprised at how life or research problems become almost immediately eased, if not solved, by a cooperating group, for example, during free, relaxed discussion such as at a party or a conference.

Collective intelligence can also be observed on the much lower level of a bacterial colony fighting for survival under threat of antibiotics.

The common factor here is that a collective sum of agents of any nature, even with low *intelligence*, can often create a more powerful (compared to a single being), *collective intelligence*. The term *sum* has been used instead of synergy or cooperation because surprisingly, as is demonstrated in this book, *collective intelligence* can emerge,[2] even if beings are in conflict to some extent.

The lack of significant research results on *collective intelligence* can probably be explained by a widespread, unconscious fear of scientists that *collective intelligence* must surely be something much more complex and complicated than individual *intelligence* is. Many believe that *collective intelligence* a priori represents a higher level than that of the individual. In the past some more formal research considerations have led scientists to this conclusion.

[2] More examples can be given of "what we consider as an artifact of human *intelligence*," which can also emerge spontaneously in nature. In 1972 (72) in the area of today's Gabon Republic, at a site called Oklo, fossils of a natural nuclear reactor have been found.

An example is the conclusion of A. Newell (considered as one of the founders of *artificial intelligence*), who raised an objection to the notion of *collective intelligence*, arguing[3]:

> A social system, whether a small group or a large formal organization, ceases to act, even approximately, as a single rational agent.
> This failure is guaranteed by the very small communication bandwidth between humans compared with the large amount of knowledge available in each human's head.
> Modeling groups as if they had a group mind is too far from the truth to be useful scientific approximation very often.

This conclusion seems a logical result of certain a priori–assumed models of computations, which could artificially impose such a fear.

However, if we drop the assumption that a deterministic model of computations[4] must be used and take a careful look into this problem, a paradox will be found in that the evaluation of the *collective intelligence* of social structures of humans, ants, and so forth can be easier than the evaluation of the IQ of a single being.

The missing link is the assumption of proper, specific quasi-chaotic models of computations with mathematical logic, such as the Random PROLOG Processor. This model shows reasonable results when applied to *collective intelligence*.

A being's individual *intelligence* is evaluated on the basis of external results of behavior during the processes of perception, problem-solving, and output of the answer. Researchers are still far from a comprehensive understanding and thus from satisfactory modeling of the neuropsychologic processes responsible for perception and problem-solving in the brain. At this point, it is necessary to use models of *intelligence* that are still hypothetical proposals (1).

With humans, we can make contact, for example, for IQ tests, even if we face language or culture incompatibilities (2), but with ants or bees we cannot make contact directly. We can only observe external symptoms of their intelligent activity.

In contrast, many more elements of collectively intelligent activity can be observed, measured, and evaluated in a social structure because we can penetrate the social structure. We can observe displacements and actions of beings, exchange of information between beings (e.g., the language activity of humans or the ant's pheromone communication system[5]). During cooperative problem-solving, individual *intelligence* and behavior are mainly scaled down as a factor to accidental, local, and probabilistic processes.

This book emerged as a result of research on the Random PROLOG Processor and application of this tool to the problem of *collective intelligence*. This has allowed a successful, formal definition of the *collective intelligence* phenomenon

[3] Newell A.: *Unified Theories of Cognition*. Harvard University Press, Cambridge, MA, 1990.

[4] Based on the Deterministic Turing Machine.

[5] Understanding of pheromone-based communication systems is still at an early research stage (73).

and a reasonable formal definition that allows efficient assessment of the *collective intelligence* measure (IQS). This brings us in "research mountains" to a certain "viewpoint", where many "research tales" related to *collective intelligence* start to be sharply visible, whereas others go out of focus. The definition of *collective intelligence* results in further generalization of prior *intelligence* concepts and subsequently makes changes in the hierarchy of *intelligence*-related problems.

This book is expected to be the first attempt to deal with *collective intelligence* based on formal theory.

There will be a specific focus on *collective intelligence* as we merge several related topics taken selectively from psychology, sociology, *artificial intelligence*, the theory of computations, and so forth. Until now, *collective intelligence* has escaped any attempt to be described in a satisfactory formal way; thus this book must start with a broad review of such topics. This should provide the reader with a basis for the formal *collective intelligence* definition and justify the approach applied in this book.

The first major part of the book (after the introduction) will discuss the issue of *intelligence*, because now we come to point where there are several types of *intelligence*: individual, collective, and artificial, and perhaps in the future, some other types will be discovered or defined. The *intelligence* types mentioned here are discussed in a different order: individual, artificial, and finally *collective intelligence*, because AI should be considered as a projection of research results on "how the human brain works" in computer applications. While considering *collective intelligence*, we must take into account not only humans but also animals. Even simple beings can be collectively intelligent, and in this way, they can even surpass beings of higher individual *intelligence*. Thus, *collective intelligence* should be discussed type by type, from bacteria to humans. This also forces us to discuss the important functions of social structure and how it impacts *collective intelligence*.

The next major part of the book takes us into the problem of possible models of computations. It is relatively easy to make a formal definition of "what kind of property" *collective intelligence* is for a given social structure, but to measure and simulate *collective intelligence*, it is necessary to have a specific model of computations. The model we are looking for is not very apparent; thus, a comparative presentation of all theoretically possible models of computations (including even the analog model of computations as related to neural networks) are given in the book. After that, the most important section of this part is devoted to the presentation of the Random PROLOG Processor, which is the essential tool suggested here for *collective intelligence* modeling and evaluation.

In the fourth section of the book, the concept and definition of a *collective intelligence* quotient (IQS) emerges naturally on the basis of previous considerations — from the formal definition of *collective intelligence* given in Section 3.1 and the Random PROLOG Processor model of computations. Some theoretical considerations on IQS are also presented.

The fifth part of the book analyzes the consequences, which brings the emergence of the formal *collective intelligence* theory and definition and how to measure the IQS. It is surprising that computational *collective intelligence* can be used as a tool to draw some interesting conclusions in other disciplines — seemingly far from its point of focus. These conclusions are presented in this part of the book. Moreover, as a tool, the IQS measure takes us directly to the emergence of *collective intelligence engineering* (CIE), which could be an essential future tool from the point of view of restructuring private companies and even governments. Probably, even some historical events could be explained by analyzing related IQS changes, but this domain is not incorporated into this book.

Finally, the book concludes with an analysis of what has been done and what the future perspectives are. A rich bibliography related to *collective intelligence* is also provided.

TADEUSZ (Ted) SZUBA

Kuwait City, December 1998–December 2000

The above book has required the surveying of a wide spectrum of research disciplines, which are seemingly unrelated, but relevant from the point of view of *collective intelligence* theory.

This unfortunately implies that despite a concentrated effort, attention, caution, and the help of friends who reviewed parts of this book, some errors or misuse of words may have occurred.

I apologize for this and will appreciate any constructive criticism regarding the contents or improvement of this book.

I also apologize if some researchers are working on *collective intelligence*, but are not cited, or cited insufficiently, because I was not able to detect them, or their approach has been found far from the one presented in the book.

ACKNOWLEDGMENTS

Writing such a book is a grueling process, during which you live under the heavy stress of a deadline and are constantly alarmed by recurring discoveries of lack of knowledge to write chapters that suddenly appear to be key.

In addition, the requirements of everyday life, university duties, and so forth also never seem to go away. In such an environment, there are always a few people who are unfailingly supportive.

First, I want to express my appreciation to Dr. Waldemar Koczkodaj at Laurentian University, Dr. Jan Zytkow at the University of North Carolina at Charlotte, and Dr. Albert Zomaya at University of Western Australia for lighting the fire in me to write this book.

I would especially like to express gratefulness to my wife and son for their patience and understanding during this time. They have provided really firm family support for me without which it would have been so much more difficult.

I also want to express appreciation to Ms Linda Raye Sue, who began to work with me around 1993 as an English language proofreader for my publications. She quickly became a scientific referee as well and was able to point out technical and even theoretical problems, sometimes even in mathematical formulas. I have frequently been impressed with the speed of her work, the quality of proofreading, and the fact that for this book she has moved aside her other work several times.

Special words of appreciation should be given to my friend and research colleague Dr. Robin H. Meakins[1]. During our research discussions, he guided me and helped me to understand animal life and their ways of thinking. He has also reviewed and improved the sections on individual and *collective intelligence* of animals. Dr. Bader Al-Ansari from the Department of Psychology at Kuwait University reviewed the section on the individual intelligence of humans. Dr. Anton Cerny and Dr. Peter Neubert from the Department of Mathematics and Computer Science at Kuwait University have made suggestions on models of computations and their complexity problems. I also want to thank Dr. Hans Loeper from the Department of Mathematics and Computer Science for providing me with significant organizational help at the beginning of the project.

[1] Formerly in the Zoology Department of Kuwait University.

Last but not least, Virginia Hamilton at Mississippi State University was the first reviewer of the complete manuscript of this book. Her enthusiasm, besides all her technical advice, about it has been a real help to me.

T. Szuba

ABOUT THE AUTHOR

Dr. Tadeusz Szuba earned his M. Sc. degree (1974) in the area of Computer Science, with a thesis on the problem of computer languages used to control industrial processes. His Ph. D. dissertation (1979) was in the area of applied *artificial intelligence* and was entitled "Application of Robinson's Resolution Method for Construction of Programs in Automatic Program Synthesis of Numerically Controlled Machine Tools." Both degrees were earned at the oldest technical university in Poland, the University of Mining and Metallurgy (AGH) in Kraków (Cracow).

Dr. Szuba began the teaching of AI courses at AGH on the M. Sc. level. He has also written a university textbook on computer languages for symbolic computations.

Continuing the research direction started with his Ph. D. thesis, and during the period from 1985 to 1989, he was the founder and head of a research grant sponsored by IPPT PAN (a branch of the Polish Academy of Sciences) to design and model a fully autonomous, intelligent robot excavator. This research focus resulted in a spectrum of publications ranging from computer graphics (3-D modeling of intelligent robot activity), PROLOG programming for AI, designing of an on-board network computer for an intelligent robot, and man–machine interaction to the problem of "consciousness" of intelligent robots. The results of this research resulted in a second book on intelligent autonomous machines published by AGH Press.

In late 1991 he moved to Kuwait to participate in the reconstruction of Kuwait University after the Gulf War in 1991. His teaching activities there have included courses on Expert Systems at the M. Sc. level and teaching of undergraduate courses in *artificial intelligence*.

In Kuwait, he started to work on the problem of abstract molecular, quasi-chaotic models of computations, which resulted in the design of the Random PROLOG Processor. This computational model has allowed the successful formalization of *collective intelligence*.

Recently, Dr. Szuba has been engaged in research on the theoretical aspects of *collective intelligence* and the exciting prospects of *collective intelligence engineering* applications.

Collective intelligence touches different areas of research and life: Dr. Szuba is engaged in cooperation with a range of researchers from biology, psychology, networking, and so forth and participates in other areas of scientific development that can profit from the *collective intelligence* approach.

CHAPTER 1

Introduction

Starting our journey into computational *collective intelligence*, accepted methods of perception, comprehension, and evaluation of prevailing computational processes will be challenged.

Our entire world is a strange combination of chaos and order. We are always trying to impose individual or group order on our behavior, thinking, work (production), and so forth, but eventually almost everything gets chaotic. Finally, we try (or we convince ourselves) to be fully or partially satisfied with the results of the actions we take. However, reviewing past actions, we are often confused or even angry at how many elements were not taken into account during the planning stage and how far our success was dependent on "a bit of luck."

Any attempts to exclude chaos appear in the end to be too costly or even dangerous, as the Marx-Lenin concepts of centrally governed life in the former communist countries were. The free market economy, in fact quasi-chaotic, appears to be much more effective.

Even on the level of a single, private company, if the structure of the company becomes excessively rigid, formal, or rule-based, the probability of crisis and collapse rapidly increases.

Even if we look at the military, which should be a pattern of discipline and order, the situation is similar. Top-quality units like special forces, paratroopers, and so forth never apply rigid organization or tight schedules of action. Rather, they behave quasi-chaotically, situation-dependent, cooperative-based, focusing on the final goal. Almost everybody in such a unit has an officer rank.

If we look into our thinking (even dreaming), the vector (or point of interest) of our inferences is constantly changing from one topic to another, sometimes very distantly related. We are able to concentrate on certain topics only for a few minutes. There are rare exceptions to this situation. It seems that quasi-chaotic thinking is embedded in our nature as individuals. It is obvious that this phenomenon allows and perhaps forces us to think in parallel about many aspects of daily life. This seems like the familiar "time sharing" in computer science, but it probably is much more complicated from a neuropsychological point of view because sometimes long-awaited solutions to problems emerge from our subconscious at unexpected moments.

In general, we observe that real live beings make parallel, quasi-chaotic inferences rather than the ordered ones of digital processors. Taking into considerations all of these observations, there arises a fundamental question:

> Why do ordered inferences demand discipline and training, while parallel, quasi-chaotic inferences come easily to us and are in fact basic inferring patterns for both individuals and social structures?

Certainly this is an alternative solution for governing computational processes, just as a propeller is an alternative to wings. So why don't living beings prefer regular inferring processes, and what are the domains in which quasi-chaotic behavior prevails over routine, well-organized life?

But as Shakespeare's Hamlet said: "*There is* (must be) *a method in this madness*."

As researchers, we should suspect that perhaps with this approach there are undiscovered systems and algorithms more powerful or more convenient from an implementation point of view for solving some of these difficult problems.

If we look at this problem from another perspective (computer-oriented), we may see why live beings and groups of beings are not organized like our personal computers (PCs) or multiprocessors of, for example, "any abstract hypercube form" or even like networks of computers. Several reasons for this can be suggested.

Early PCs were equipped with nice, small operating systems like those of the DOS family. They allowed us to see how they work and even to make small improvements.

Even for PCs we now have monster systems like Windows '98, UNIX, LINUX, and so forth, which are big and complicated because they have to serve all possible requests of computers and users in a stable way, even those that could emerge in the future.

As a result, most user programs look small compared to their operating systems, so we can conclude with a bit of irony: "*a mountain is built to supervise mice*," and finally we might ask *what size of operating system is really needed*?

Someone could argue here that distributed operating systems are coming, and what about the Internet? Is it a single deterministic computer system with a distributed operating system or a quasi-chaotic informational structure? Presently we cannot even imagine the number of active nodes in the Internet system (new ones are constantly being set up, others are being disconnected, while still others are being reconfigured). We cannot say what the flow of information is, how much data processing there is, and so forth. The Internet is a computational process; everybody will agree with this, but it is a quasi-chaotic system with a very fuzzy shape of hardware. There are Internet rules and protocols but certainly no central control.

There is another problem with operating systems. We have to remember the philosophical consequences of Gödel's Theorem (3) "*its own unprovability*." An operating system, no matter how big and sophisticated, cannot always get us on-line or ensure that the proposed or executed actions are correct.

It is a very disappointing situation that in various ways we pay a lot for such supervision, for example, royalties, reduction of computational resources, time delays for operating system activity, and so forth—and even then there is no guarantee of accuracy. Thus, what is the value of determinism without provability? Why not go to some form of restricted chaotic (quasi-chaotic) computations where the operating system becomes redundant and is replaced only by mechanisms internally stabilizing the computational and streaming processes into the goal of computations?

Another disappointing element of deterministic computations is the problem of implementation of parallelism. Even in a basic computer course it can be demonstrated that an increase in the number of processors in the system will not increase the computational power at the same rate.[1] Amdahl's law gives the following estimation for this phenomenon:
If we define speedup $S(n)$ as the ratio of the total execution time $T(1)$ on a sequential computer to the corresponding execution time $T(n)$ on a parallel computer with n processors $S(n) = T(1)/T(n)$, then $S(n) = n/[1 + (n-1)f]$ where f is interpreted as the fraction of nonparallelizable operations or instructions (4).

The conclusions in Figure 1-1 are clearly disappointing. It is clear that an increasing number of processors will not provide the expected speedup and that even this speedup will depend (can be significantly reduced: see $f = 0.01$ and $f = 0.1$) on the percentage of nonparallelizable operations in a specific program. It should also be remembered that there is a narrow domain of applications when all processors can be fully utilized. Additionally, programming difficulties are mounting, while at the same time, the programmer has to write a code to solve a problem and to synchronize the involved computational processes.

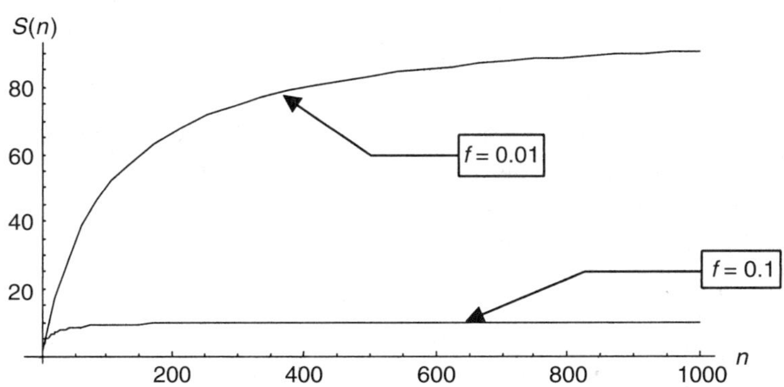

Figure 1-1. Amdahl's law.

[1] Surprisingly, the counterpart of Amdahl's law can be found when analyzing the efficiency of social structures (see Section 2.2.3.1). The so-called Riegelmann effect is related to *social loafing*. However, cooperating beings are much more complex than the cooperating processors discussed above; thus, the hidden nature of the Riegelmann effect is yet to be formally described.

Compilers able to automatically (partially) parallelize the source code are rare and expensive.[2]

Another important consideration is that Amdahl's law is derived for processors that take a fixed position in the structure (nodes), and the "only moving element" is the information that flows between processors during the computational process.

We should concur with *real life* that this really does not support our human way of organizing computational processes.

Let us take a look at what is available in any research disciplines to support our quest for a quasi-chaotic, parallel computational process that would be suitable for *collective intelligence* modeling and evaluation.

Significant progress has recently been made in the area of nondeterministic bioinspired computations:

- In 1994, Adleman (5) demonstrated his famous model of a DNA computer, which should be able to solve NP-complete problems in polynomial time (6). In this computer, DNA agents react quasi-randomly because the rendezvous in the solution are random; however, the matching (sticky ends) of DNA is deterministic.
- Genetic algorithms (7,8) are making significant research progress.
- Cooperating colonies of simple beings like ants are attracting research attention (9,10) because it can be demonstrated that as a sort of *computational system*, they are even more efficient than genetic algorithms (11).

All bioinspired computational systems share a common concept: there are agents of some nature that, in parallel and quasi-randomly, move, are born and expire, and infer according to imposed logical diagrams.

The general (and psychological) problem for researchers working with this approach is "the resistance of the computer society" against nondeterministic computations. The concept of deterministic computations is doing so well that no computer company will suddenly change policy and invest billions to build a DNA computer. Almost six years have passed (5), and there is still no commercial successor of Adleman's computer available on the market.

In addition, regular computer users are proud of the deterministic power provided to them by workstations, mainframes, or even PCs. I once heard an opinion that "today's proof" of the power of the deterministic approach to computations is the ability to stop underground nuclear tests and to replace them by simulated explosions on high-end super-computers.

To advocate a quasi-chaotic concept of computations we either have to somehow build such a computer *and* prove that it can be better than the existing processors or find an application, for example, computational *collective intelligence*, in which this model is the only one we can use. The latter is probably

[2] The author has written a simulation model of the Random PROLOG Processor on an 8-processor SGI 480 VGX using a parallel version of C (Power C) with the CaseVision debugger, under UNIX.

much more easily achieved. A secondary issue of this book, after research topics related to *collective intelligence*, is to convince the *computer world* that *collective intelligence* could be such a *breakthrough* application. Computational *collective intelligence* may be the gateway to lucrative future applications, that is, in *collective intelligence engineering*.

Now let us discuss how to do this, that is, how to design quasi-chaotic computations to work efficiently for our purpose.

First, we should agree or assume that quasi-Brownian movements and mathematical logic should be used for such a model of computations. There are several important reasons for this.

QUASI-BROWNIAN MOVEMENTS

We can easily observe the Brownian movements (see Fig. 1-2) of the bigger particles suspended in a gas or liquid because such particles undergo random bombardment by much smaller (not visible) molecules in the environment (gas or liquid) (12,13). The same is true with beings in a social structure.

In a social structure, beings behave and move randomly because needs and opportunities of real life force them to do so. From a computational point of

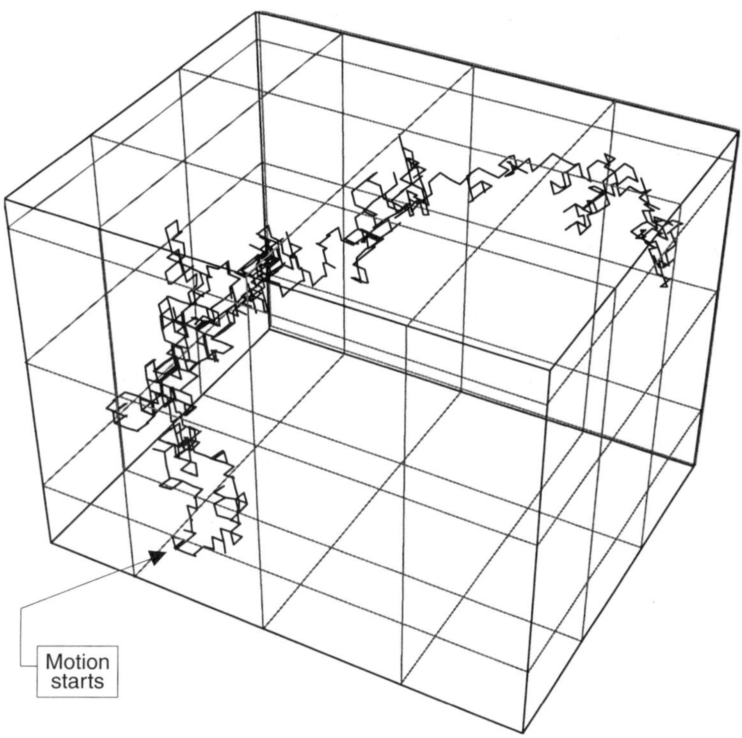

Figure 1-2. Random walk of a single *information molecule* in an abstract 3-D lattice of *computational space*.

view, when we start to consider a social structure or even a single being, there is no predictable method to count all such influences. Rather it is necessary to use some statistical approximation of behavior for a being and a whole group.

It can be observed that inference processes are made randomly, starting when there is a need, or when higher level needs are temporarily not disturbing a given being, or when there is a chance to make inference(s).

Most inferences are not finished at all. This makes the similarity to Brownian movements almost striking.

Thus, the Brownian motion "tuned" by restrictions of structured *computational space* and individual characteristics of displacements can be used as the driving force for the whole process in our model of computations.

The use of the concept of Brownian motions is key here, especially because the concept of operating systems has been rejected.

In a digital computer, the operating system is the driving force for computations, deciding which subcomputational process will be executed, where it will be allocated, and so forth.

With Brownian movements, information exists as *information molecules*, which also act as the *processor*. This is the next step toward general unification between the data, program, and now the processor. In a digital processor, there is unification only between data and program—that is, we cannot differentiate between them. Data can be program as well. Examples of this can be given both on a binary level, and on, for example, LISP language level. Such a processor is more dependent on the "program," that is, the set of *information molecules*, than present processors depend on loaded software.

However, ATTENTION, please! *Information molecules* as processors can *only* process data closely related (matching) to the information they carry. In our model of computations they are not general-purpose processors—rather simple automata carrying *active information*!

Use of the concept of Brownian movements removes the problem of allocation of information because memory and processor are unified in *computational space* (*CS*). Information is allowed to move itself, to have multiple copies, to be born and to expire, and the concept of address is no longer necessary.

When using this approach, based on Brownian motion, the computational process takes place ("fires" using the terminology of Expert Systems) (14) when two (or more) *information molecules* rendezvous. This is the opposite of what we have in a digital processor where the operating system points to the process to be executed next, that is, decides which piece of code and which data will be taken into L1 code or data cache inside a processor. This is a key issue for parallelism because the quasi-chaotic processor allows as many parallel processes to be executed at the same time as probability of successful rendezvous will allow, not just the few allowed by the hardware of V-, U-, and FPU-pipes in, for example, a Pentium processor.

As mentioned at the beginning of this chapter, chaos is an inevitable element of our activity, but it is highly moderated by our planning and predicting. Thus, in our concept of a model of computations, the term *quasi-chaotic Brownian movements* is used. Chaos can be restricted by some fundamental elements:

- The probability function that governs random displacement can be adjusted. For example, *information molecules* that have acquired specific properties can migrate to specific locations in *computational space*.
- *Information molecules* can be equipped with a kind of attracting or repelling, within short-distance vector fields, similar to Van der Waals forces (15). This is to increase the probability of the required number of rendezvous and inferences, and such an approach is not inconsistent with what we see in real life.
- *Computational space* is never open space. There are always some soft or hard barriers that direct displacements. In the case of human social structures, there are many such structures, either natural or artificial, for example, bridges, meeting points, and so forth. With these structures (membranes) *computational space* can be configured to some extent as the computer designer plans, for example, layout of PC motherboard. This problem is discussed in Section 3.4.4.2.

MATHEMATICAL LOGIC

The second important element of a quasi-chaotic model of computations, as proposed for *collective intelligence* modeling and evaluation, is formal mathematical logic, which is used for the following important reasons:

- The mathematical logic of predicate calculus is now the fundamental tool for inferring systems such as Expert Systems. For our purposes, the concepts of Expert Systems can be also used to create "black boxes," simulating intelligent behavior of beings in a specific environment.
- Mathematical logic is discrete, that is, knowledge can be partitioned and defined in terms of clauses of facts, rules, and goals, which fits well with the concept of *information molecules* as carriers of information in *computational space*. When using mathematical logic, the most basic elements carrying information can be easily defined in every expression, that is, *terms* and *unit clauses* (16).
- There are no contradictions to having elementary (atomic) logic objects, for example, single facts in the same *computational space*, with complex structures of any level, for example "black boxes" simulating beings, which emit or absorb other, for example, atomic logic objects. Thus, we can create and efficiently maintain all the different levels (components) of intelligent life, that is messages, beings, social structures, and so forth, with one common mathematical formalism.
- Mathematical logic allows building inference systems that allow different diagrams of inference, (e.g., 17), which can consecutively and efficiently simulate most "methods of thinking" observable in real life.

- Mathematical logic has been very successfully implemented with PROLOG systems. This provides the domain of *collective intelligence* with plenty of tools and methods (18). This is especially important when trying to estimate a *collective intelligence* measure through simulation models of a given social structure.
- On the basis of PROLOG it is obvious how easily we can introduce parallelism of inference (19–21), and so forth as well as "programmer-controlled" nondeterminism into logic systems.
- With mathematical logic, formulas and their interpretations can be separated. If we want to have a computational model for a universal theory of *collective intelligence* appropriate for ants, bees, humans, and so forth, a system must be used that is culture independent. In predicate calculus we have *wff* (the "well-formed formula") of facts, rules, and goals that can be used for inferences, without considering interpretation (16). We can, for example, assign such logic formulas (or logic systems) to observable elements of intelligent ant behavior, without communicating with them to get their interpretation. This approach has been successfully applied to the concept of Expert Systems (14). The kernel there is the so-called *shell* of the Expert System, able to process facts, rules, and goals for inference, without regard to whether it is used with medical applications (e.g., MYCIN) or geology (e.g., PROSPECTOR) (14). Systems defined in terms of predicate calculus are easy to modify. This property is essential for our purpose because we can start building a simulation system for *collective intelligence* with only entry-level approximations of activities in a given social structure. Later such a system can be easily improved, as observation of, for example, when foraging ants will deliver more information about the logic of their behavior.

The following elements of the *collective intelligence* theory proposed in this book are the direct consequences of the assumption of quasi-Brownian movements, but they are important, and we should keep them in mind.

COLLECTIVE INTELLIGENCE IS DISTRIBUTED, INCONSISTENT, AND DYNAMIC

If we look from a logical point of view into a being's behavior, its production process, and its inferences we can find the following:

- Information is spread around among beings in unpredictable ways. Education and cultural heritage provide a social structure with multiple copies of facts, rules, and goals; however, the utilization of a specific logic component depends on an unpredictable number of factors. A secondary result of this is that in some cases in a socially cooperating structure it is difficult to differentiate thinking and nonthinking beings (abstract logical beings must be introduced to describe some situations, e.g., messages). The same being can be fact, data, or goal from the point of view of different inferences.
- It is a well-known paradox that social structures use inconsistent sets of facts, rules, and goals. It will be demonstrated here that such logic systems

can work and produce successful conclusions, provided some stabilizing measures are present.

- In a social structure, information exists dynamically, that is, is permanently created ("asserted" in PROLOG terminology), removed (retracted), and changes location because of the quasi-Brownian behavior of beings.

It can be observed that sequences of inferences are started, stopped, or suspended, where there are opportunities or needs. Multiple inferences cross (through use of common elements) sometimes even without the conscious knowledge of the involved beings.

PROBABILITY SHOULD BE USED FOR MEASURING *COLLECTIVE INTELLIGENCE*

When a single being is evaluated by an IQ test, such as the Stanford-Binet test (22), the direct use of probability is difficult.

The reason is that a being is usually separated from his environment for the testing period, and the test cannot be repeated several times to get an "experimental or statistical measure for probability" because the being can learn a test, and the result will depend on the repetition. Moreover, the test itself has a huge impact on the behavior of the being. Thus, probability could be used for a single being if a battery of reliable equivalent tests were available.

For these reasons, IQ measures for individuals are scalars or vectors (22,23,24).

Working with social structures of beings, we find that the situation is different. First, it seems to be difficult to take a social structure to an "in vitro" environment. Second, it can be easily assumed that the social structure will not notice or learn that it is under investigation. However, the same test repeated later will most probably give a different result because of constantly changing sets of factors.

A social structure of humans usually is such a robust dynamic object that it will not be affected at all by any simple test. In the case of social insects, if we do not change their natural environment, we (as the analyzing layer) will also not be perceived by them.

Another reason to use probability for *collective intelligence* evaluation is that it can be measured indirectly through a set of statistical properties of a given social structure. The displacements, contacts, and informal unification between beings are basic. On this basis, analytically or through simulations, the probability of certain situations can be estimated.

The *collective intelligence* measure proposed in this book is given by the *probability of successful termination of inferences of a certain type*.

At the end of the introduction to our concept of *collective intelligence* and its proposed measure, some concepts must be discussed. Later they will be more precisely justified, but now they must be presented to differentiate our approach from standard "beliefs" that could be *destructive* for our general perception of *collective intelligence*.

Let us look at the following examples referring to the problem of synergy or cooperation for *collective intelligence*.

In every medieval city there were streets with only, for example, shoemaker shops. Nobody forced them to put their shops on such a street, but they gravitated to one area. They did this because the large number of benefits (as a weighted sum) gained from this overwhelmed the disadvantages, even losses, for example, of some customers who decide to buy shoes from their competition, having another shop just in front of them.

The benefits can be small (even difficult to define) and devious, for example, to have the possibility of spying on techniques used by other shoemakers.

In such an example of a social structure of shoemakers, some of them could even be enemies.

Collective intelligence emerges in this situation (in most cases) without any doubt. It is obvious just looking at the high quantities and quality of shoes produced on such a street, compared with shoes produced even by the best shoemakers when all the shoemakers worked far away each other, were spread around the country, such as those working separately in small villages. However, *collective intelligence* will not emerge or might even vanish after a certain time if shoemakers "fight too much" instead of producing shoes.

In general, it is a well-known paradox that technological progress is fastest during wars (e.g., during World Wars I and II), when the level (sum) of global synergy or cooperation is significantly decreased.

Thus, it seems that we cannot assume willful cooperation for *collective intelligence*; if we did, the definition of cooperation would have to be very vague. In fact, it will be demonstrated that cooperation is not necessary for *collective intelligence*; however, it is a *very important optimizing factor*. Starting at a certain level of *collective intelligence* development, cooperation *must* be applied.

Our research on *collective intelligence* has also brought us to the point that the assumption that the beings are alive is not essential for *collective intelligence*. Let's explain this briefly in advance. First, there is no precise definition available as to *what life really is*. Thus, we must distance ourselves from this issue any way in our formal approach to *collective intelligence*. There are also other observations supporting this concept. Bacteria and viruses also cooperate through exchange of genetic information; they are *collectively intelligent* against drugs, but the question is whether they are alive during the entire process.

Thus, the assumption about the existence of live agents must also be dropped from the formal definition of *collective intelligence*. In the course of the book, it will be demonstrated that a definition of *collective intelligence* can be given without the assumption of live beings and/or *cooperation*.

CHAPTER 2

Intelligence — Our Present State of Understanding

"The ability to perceive, reason, and act," a slightly modified version of the definition of *artificial intelligence* given by Winston (25) is proposed here as one that is also accurate for the general concept of *intelligence*.

An attempt to understand what *intelligence* really means could entail an approach taken from the theory of control. This theory says that if a given process or phenomenon can be observed, it is labeled as *observable*, and (not necessarily at the same time) if it can be measured in any way, it can be labeled as *measurable*. This is a very convenient approach because certain individuals can be intelligent in a specific way but are not appreciated by others for various reasons — and thus are not labeled as intelligent. People often start to consider them intelligent after specific test(s) are done or after a specific event occurs that demonstrates their *intelligence*.

We face the same problem with *collective intelligence*. Most probably there are frequent and numerous occurrences of this phenomenon in our own and other species and processes, but they have not been acknowledged or labeled as certain types that could be evaluated.

However, with *intelligence*, as our knowledge about the real world grows, we are increasingly aware that only part of this phenomenon is observable, like an iceberg in the polar seas, where only about 10 percent appears above the surface of the water.

This book provides another argument to confirm that the largest part of the domain of *intelligence* is not yet efficiently observable and not at all measurable — by demonstrating that it is possible to formalize and evaluate at least one more type of *intelligence*, that of a social structure (CI).

Certainly *intelligence* as a phenomenon is observable; this is even historically acknowledged because old Latin texts use almost exactly the same (label) term *intelligens* $\approx$ *intelligent*. This term most probably was used long before Latin, as the problem of *intelligence* was analyzed and discussed in the past.

For example, in *De Anima*[1] (*On the Soul*) by Aristotle (384–322 B.C.) we can find the following text applicable to this book, where he speaks about the

[1] *De Anima* (*On the Soul*) by Aristotle translated by J.A. Smith is available on-line at http://members.aol.com/elvers/deantpag.html

intelligence of both humans and animals:

> What Anaxagoras says ... it is found, he says, in all animals, great and small, high and low, but mind (in the sense of intelligence) appears not to belong alike to all animals, and indeed not even to all human beings.

Going back to the roots of human understanding of *intelligence* and analyzing how this concept emerged and developed, we ask if the Romans were able to measure *intelligence*. When we look into existing quotes derived from Latin documents, their approach was probably like this:

> AN INTELLIGENT ≈ INCORPOREAL BEING, ESPECIALLY AN ANGEL
> INTELLIGENCE ≈ THE PRIMAL, ETERNAL QUALITY OF GOD[2,3,4].

If we try to measure *intelligence* perceived in this way, another Latin judiciary sentence immediately comes to mind here: *causa finita est*, that is, this case is closed, at least from a scientific point of view ... nothing can be measured here by humans when speaking about God(s); this is an example of the very practical approach of ancient Romans.

It is well known that sophisticated concepts like *intelligence* emerged and developed in parallel in different civilizations around the world a long time ago. For example, in works of Confucius, who lived in China from 551 to 479 B.C.; in his *Analects* (or sayings), we can find the sentence:

> One can acquire intelligence but not stupidity.

This fits well with our present knowledge of how *intelligence* displayed by tests is affected, for example, by education and environment.

Thanks to the courtesy and help of Mr. Li Zhu from the East Asian Library at the University of Minnesota in Minneapolis, we can here summarize the development of intelligence concepts and intelligence tests as follows.

> The Chinese definition of intelligence from the earliest time is from Confucius' concept of "Five Virtues": Ren (Benevolence), Yi (Righteousness), Li (Respect), Zhi (Intelligence or Wisdom), and Xin (Trust). The fourth virtue, Zhi, is more about wisdom one accumulates during one's lifetime.
> In about 165 B.C. a system of recommendation and examination, laying emphasis on moral excellence, was instituted in the Han Dynasty. The system developed throughout the ages, and emperors used it to select officials. In the Tang Dynasty (618–907 A.D.), for example, for the final examination, there were the following requirements:

[2] Ohtfrid's letter to Liudebert. about A.D. 870.

[3] *Ergo est aliquid intelligens, a quo omnes res naturales ordinantur ad finem: et hoc dicimus Deum.* Thus, there is something intelligent, by which all natural things are ordered to an end: and we call this God. *Summa Theologica*, Part I, question 2, article 3, Saint Thomas 1225–1274.

[4] This perception of *intelligence* is still referred to as theological in Microsoft Encarta Encyclopedia'98.

(a) five essays on current events,
(b) essays on the Confucian classics and history,
(c) an original poem and a composition in rhythmic prose called "fu."

> Special examinations were also held, covering a great variety of topics, including mathematics and law.
> Beginning in 1066, the examinations in the national capital and the accompanying tests in the palace were held every three years. By the opening of the Ming period (1368–1644 A.D.) the system was set up so that one who passed the examination in a district was known as a "Xiu-cai," one who passed at the provincial capital, a "Ju-ren," and one who was successful at the national capital, a "Jin-shi," the three honors corresponding roughly to the Western system of B.A., M.A., and Ph.D. degrees. One could scarcely become a prime minister unless one had a "Jin-shi" degree. The system was abolished in 1905. The system described here was nothing like the intelligence tests that the Westerners have in mind.

The problem with such texts is that they were copied so many times, and all these languages have changed, or we are translating from "dead languages," so that now we cannot be sure of what was the original text and intention of the ancient authors. Moreover, even now we are not clear about the term *intelligence*.

In the Arab culture around 1130 A.D. we can find the following understanding of the phenomenon of intelligence:

> Meaning of intelligence: quality of interpretation process that takes place in a short un-negligible amount of time, so that the intelligent being knows the intended meaning of a statement after hearing it.
> It has been said that the amount of intelligence of someone is based on the speed and/or the sharpness of his/her understanding. Thick mindedness is an indication of a low speed or vagueness of their understanding.[5]

The "mechanistic" approach to the concept of *intelligence*, which can be claimed as taking us directly to the present concept of *machine (artificial) intelligence*, can be dated from the epoch of Descartes. In "Discourse on Methods," the Fifth Part, by René Descartes (1641), the following sentence can be found regarding animal *intelligence*:

> ... Nature makes them behave as they do according to the disposition of their organs; just as a clock, composed only of wheels and weights and springs can count the hours and measure the time more accurately than we can with all our intelligence ... .

On the other hand, it is also obvious from this sentence that at least philosophers of that age were considering animal *intelligence* as observable.

[5] This text was found by Dr. Abu-Bakr and translated by Dr. Almulla (from Kuwait University) from the book *Intelligent Beings* by author, "Al-Hafiz Gamaluddeen Abu-Faraj Abdul-Rahman Ibn El-Gawzy Al-Quarashi Al-Baghdadi".

In the nineteenth century the general progress of civilization, especially the introduction of a universal, standardized elementary school system, created an organizational base and has provided a reference (common perception, reasoning, and acting in the unified environment of the school) for comparing the *intelligence* of human beings.

It is remarkable that at the same time in the nineteenth century, a strong demand for a reliable evaluation tool for human skills, to serve tasks of growing complexity emerged worldwide. Fast-developing and increasingly advanced industry and military establishments were looking for ways to measure *intelligence*.

Together these factors have provided an appropriate environment for rapid progress in the domain of assessing *intelligence* through tests.
However, ancient China (27) provided the emergence of the first IQ tests in:

1. Testing to select bureaucrats emerged approximately 200 B.C. Earliest tests were in the form of written tests.
2. During the Ming dynasty (1368–1644 A.D) "work samples" for tests were elaborated.

In such a favorable environment of rapidly developing Western industrial societies of the nineteenth and twentieth centuries (after the decided success of the Binet *intelligence* test), progress in the area of *intelligence* testing grew very fast. We can mark the following milestones (2,22):

- 1869 Francis Galton — measured IQ with sensorimotor tasks
- 1890 James M. Cattell — mental test
- 1895 Alfred Binet and Victor Henri — measured successful performance in school. *Intelligence* tests should be based on memory, mechanical and verbal comprehension, distance judgment, mental imagery, reasoning, judgment, and imagination.
- Binet-Simon test to detect retardation
- Test to rate normals, mental age (Binet)
- Revision of IQ testing (30 items, standardized on 50 children ages 3–11)
- Stern used IQ concept: IQ = mental age/chronological age $*$ 100.
- 1916 Terman — transformed Binet-Simon scale into Stanford-Binet test; restandardized to 90 items.
- 1937 Terman and Merrill restandardized it to 129 items; two forms L & M; 20 age levels from 2 years to superior adult
- 1939 Wechsler-Bellview — standardized on patient population later modified to 1949 WAIS (Wechsler Adult *Intelligence* Scale), WISC (Wechsler *Intelligence* Scale for Children)
- Terman and Merrill — IQ equation eliminated, restandardized; tests verbally loaded

Let us look at how this iceberg of *intelligence* is now perceived, at least for humans.

In 1986 R.J. Sternberg and D.K. Detterman asked a group of 24 scientists working in psychology how they conceive *intelligence*. Later they compared results with the answers of 14 other scientists questioned in 1921. Table 2-1 shows how the perception of *intelligence* changed in a period of 65 years (28).

The conclusion is unequivocal — even specialists are not sure how to define *intelligence*.

There is another "floating point" in our perception of the iceberg of *intelligence* that should be discussed here, the so-called "Flynn effect" (26). J.R. Flynn has discovered that since IQ testing started, there has been a steady worldwide rise in *intelligence* test performance. More precisely, there has been a +3 IQ points per decade shift of scored results.

Various researchers have suggested possible explanations:

- Cultural development resulting in an *increased complexity of mental abilities*; that is, the human mind is changing rapidly
- Better nutrition
- Incorrectly defined *intelligence*
- IQ tests are weak when correlated with real *intelligence*, if such exists.

Thus, the attempt to understand *intelligence* through measurement is also a bit risky because measurements are not constant. For example, in the Netherlands in 1952 only 0.38 percent of these tested had an IQ over 140, but in 1982 scored by the same norms 9.12 percent had a score over 140 (>140 is considered outstanding). A similar increase in "geniuses" is nowhere to be seen.

TABLE 2-1. Shift in perception of intelligence, 1921–1986

Properties of intelligence	1921	1986
Reasoning, problem solving (higher cognitive processing)	57%	50%
That which is valued by culture	**0%**	**29%**
Executive control processes	7%	25%
Sensing, perceiving, attending (lower cognitive processing)	21%	21%
Knowledge	7%	21%
Successful or effective response to novel situation	21%	21%
Monitoring one's processing (metacognitive processes)	7%	17%
Ability to learn	29%	17%
Spatial, verbal, auditory (specific abilities)	7%	17%
Ability to solve problems in all domains (general ability)	14%	17%
Not easily definable	14%	17%
Adapting to the demands of the environment	29%	13%
Psychological mechanisms	**29%**	**8%**
Speed of mental processing	14%	13%
Integrating processes and knowledge	**0%**	**17%**

Let us look at *intelligence* from a communication point of view.

It has almost always been assumed "by default" that "it is us" (i.e., humans) who decide "who is *intelligent*, and who is not." Even in personal human–human relations, this egocentric approach prevails. This personal and ethnic egocentric human approach has mainly been based on the ability to communicate on the subject of *intelligence testing*, which ultimately depends on ability to communicate efficiently between participants in the test.

Moreover, the previously given definition of *intelligence*: "the ability to perceive, reason, and act," in connection with our egocentrism imposes and strengthens by default our human way of perceiving, our way of reasoning, and finally our way of acting. Even between humans, if another person cannot understand us, or think as we do, and finally act as we wish, our scoring of the respondent's *intelligence* is lowered.

The situation is even worse with animals where the issue of their *intelligence* is concerned. Animals use different communication systems (ants, dolphins, etc.); they are equipped with different effectors because of their different environments, and finally "how they reason" is concluded today only from research theories. However, if an animal *intelligence* test is applied to the solution of a common problem in that animal's daily life (e.g., to find a path in a maze), their results can often outperform those of humans if measured in the same way. Nevertheless, people assume a huge superiority over animals.

A partial solution to this problem has come from the field of computers.

The rise of computer technology after World War II can be considered a real breakthrough in the human comprehension of *intelligence* for two basic reasons:

1. The ascension of *machine intelligence* or *artificial intelligence* (MI or AI) has provided researchers working on the problem of *intelligence* with similar, but seemingly new kinds of *intelligence*. AI is similar to human *intelligence* because in fact it is a projection of our methods of thinking onto the deterministic hardware of digital computers. The best known example of this approach (projection) is the general problem solver (GPS) system of A. Newell, J.C. Shaw, and H.A. Simon (29,30). Progress in AI is very human-oriented, which is especially obvious in the progress in perception systems, which apparently target humanoid systems. This is not strange; the best help in most cases is another human, even a "mechanical one." Methodology of AI is not discussed further here because section 2.1.3 is devoted to this issue.
2. A significant theoretical step ahead in better comprehension of what *intelligence* is has been made on the basis of computer communication technology. First, researchers came up with the *complexity theory*, which provided a common measure and ordering of problems that could be given to beings (31,32), etc.

   Another key factor for our perception of *intelligence* that has been proposed is the so-called *Turing test*, which was originally proposed by the mathematician Alan Turing, one of the founding fathers in computing.

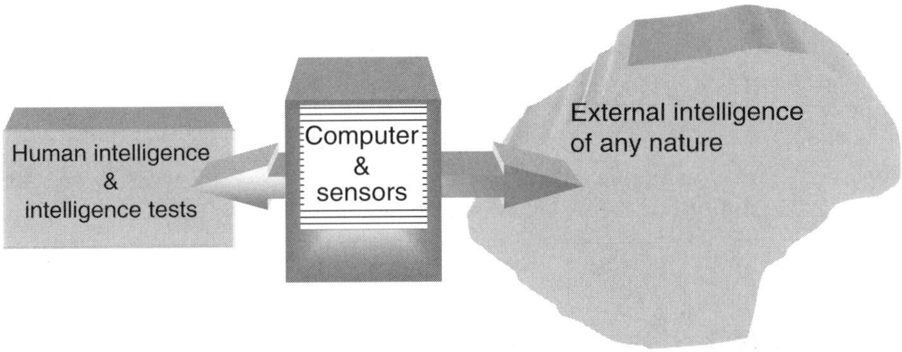

Figure 2-1. Turing test for interfacing intelligence.

> He assumed that "it is a behavioral approach to determining whether or not *a computer system* is intelligent." Turing argued (33) that conversation was the key to judging *intelligence*. In the *Turing test*, a judge has conversations (via computer terminal) with two systems, one a human and the other a *computer system*. The conversations can be about anything and proceed for a set period time (e.g., an hour). If, at the end of this time, the judge cannot distinguish the *computer system* from the human on the basis of the conversation, Turing argued that we would have to say that the *computer system* was intelligent.

Observe that with this revolutionary approach to *intelligence*, not only *a computer system*, but also any other *being* or *system of any nature* could be analyzed with the condition that the computer provide an interface with that *being* or *system*. An example is when the computer can translate the language of ant pheromones into human language. Thus, the definition of the Turing test has created at least a theoretical link (interface) between different types of *intelligence*.

Additionally important is the fact that the *being* or *system* investigated for *intelligence* can hide his nature behind that interface; thus, any human psychological prejudices will be removed.

The relation between our *intelligence* and the *intelligence* of a questioned *being* or *system* can be defined formally by so-called *weak equivalence* (sometimes called Turing equivalence) (34).

DEFINITION 1: WEAK EQUIVALENCE

Weak equivalence is a relationship between the outputs of two systems that are being compared. If these systems are only weakly equivalent, we can say that they are computing the same function (or generating the same external behavior) but that they are using different procedures to do so. For example, human chess players and computer chess players are weakly equivalent in the sense that they both play the game of chess, but they use very different procedures to decide which move to make next in a game.

For symmetry let us also give a definition of strong equivalence. This could be important if intelligence is related to learning ability. For example, when we evaluate the ability of a being or system to acquire a strong equivalence to the instructor's ability over a certain domain of problems.

DEFINITION 2. STRONG EQUIVALENCE

If two systems are strongly equivalent:

1. They compute the same function; that is, they are weakly equivalent.
2. They use the same program to compute this function.
3. This program is written in the same programming language; that is, the two systems have the same functional architecture.

From the point of view of this book, and probably also in future research with (as yet undiscovered) *intelligence* types, the *Turing test* may be found much more important than the emergence of AI itself, which can be considered as only a specific (digital computer–based) manifestation of *intelligence* in our environment.

Now let us discuss another bias in our comprehension of *intelligence*. Looking back into the historical roots of the term *intelligence*, it was assumed that *intelligence* was one of God's blessings to us; thus, it was OK that we were intelligent.

Now in the twentieth century more people agree than in Descartes's time that (to some extent) animals are also intelligent, for example, our pets (dogs, cats), horses, dolphins, and perhaps even ants.

However, when the DeepBlue IBM computer beat Garry Kasparoff as the top human representative in chess play, even most academic folks would say: "... this machine is not intelligent ... it is only crunching numbers so fast that Kasparoff lost ... ."

If the next day somebody (e.g., from a zoology department) informed them that (after long research) his dolphin, equipped with, for example, special computer communication interface had also beaten Kasparoff, nobody would deny that this dolphin could be intelligent.

Thus, we come to the conclusion that our perception of *intelligence* is closely related to the property of "*being alive*." Later in this book it will be demonstrated that certain assumed formal definitions of *collective intelligence* have established certain formal ordering (relationships) between *life* and *intelligence* itself.

However, the theoretical result differs from the common-sense understanding of this dependency in a somewhat surprising way.

Discussing our comprehension of *intelligence*, the following is a current list of different types of *intelligence*:

- Individual human *intelligence*, which also bifurcates, according to Gardner's theory of multiple intelligences (35):
  1. Linguistic (related to linguistic skills)
  2. Logical-mathematical (mathematical and quantitative skills)
  3. Spatial (e.g., used by artists to manipulate and recreate objects)
  4. Bodily-kinesthetic (dexterity of body and handling objects)
  5. Musical
  6. Intrapersonal (understanding the behavior of others, e.g., through reading, moods, desires, intentions)
  7. Interpersonal (understanding one's own feelings and behavior)
- Artificial or machine *intelligence*
- Animal *intelligence*
- *Collective intelligence*

Perception of *collective intelligence* and an ultimately clear distinction of this term has been "masked" for a long time by the existence of other terms overlapping the concept of *collective intelligence*. For example, if we observe a group of wolves collectively hunting for deer during the winter, and we say "this temporary social structure is collective intelligent in catching deer," most probably some will object saying: "they are only cooperating or displaying synergy to catch deer."

To define specific properties of *collective intelligence*, it is important to list some of the overlapping[6] terms of *collective intelligence*:

$\cong$ Cooperation, i.e., shared effort by individuals or groups for the common benefit of the group

$\cong$ Synergy, i.e., the action of two or more substances, organs, or organisms to achieve an effect of which each is individually incapable

$\cong$ Group behavior

$\cong$ Even altruism, i.e., devotion to the welfare of others

As a result, even now in most encyclopedias the term *collective intelligence* is not available. In this book, we try to demonstrate that *collective intelligence* is a generalization of the preceding terms.

[6] This is why the symbol of "inexact equivalence" $\cong$ is used now.

At the end of this discussion, let us summarize what affects our present state of comprehension of the term *intelligence*.

1. There are many possible types of *intelligence*, with a very high probability that some new ones are on the horizon.
2. Most terms used for defining *intelligence* are themselves vague and are changing, for example, comprehension of the terms *perceive, reason*, and *act*. Any attempts to formalize these terms will further affect understanding of the term *intelligence*.
3. Our comprehension of *intelligence* is highly egocentric, even on an interpersonal level.
4. Common-sense understanding of *intelligence* is "synchronously changing" with changes in our environment. The required skills evaluated for *intelligence* change periodically. The length of this period (when similar skills are necessary) is currently shortening (to just years) with increasing speed from that of several centuries ago.

2.1. INTELLIGENCE OF INDIVIDUALS

Analyzing the problem of *intelligence*, we face a specific dualism of nature. The being or object (agent) under investigation appears to us in two dynamically interleaving and interacting forms:

- as a product of its (biologically inborn) abilities, and
- as a product or even an "*input/output terminal*"of a particular civilization that has a very high level *collective intelligence*.

Even biological abilities (e.g., of muscles) can be amplified or reduced depending on use or nutrition, and on the educational, cultural, environmental facilities, or even on doctrine.

Depending on the temporary problem and state of the environment, one of these components can prevail, or they may interact in specific ways. As a result, *intelligence* evaluations will differ. There is a famous example of this with the literary character, Robinson Crusoe, fighting for survival after being stranded on an uninhabited island. His previous technological education plus high individual *intelligence* allowed him to survive. Later he even succeeded in some incredible situations that became very complex.

This problem is well recognized and is the topic of much research activity, attacking it from many different directions. As examples, studies can be given on twins, (e.g., D.T. Lykken et al. (36)), cross-cultural comparisons, (e.g., R.B. Cattell (37)), nature-nurture studies (e.g., R. Plomin and R. Rende (38)), and so forth.

From the point of view of this book, this dualism is one of the most important elements to be discussed because *collective intelligence* eventually manifests its presence through the actions of individuals and the result of those actions as a whole.

If we look at human history in different epochs and at social, business, or military systems, either individualism or collectivism has prevailed. Individualism required higher individual *intelligence* (e.g., the self-made businessman). Collectivism (e.g., army, former communist systems, etc.) acted to reduce individualism; high individual *intelligence* could even be a disadvantage.

Examples can also easily be found where variable behavior is required when the ratio of individualism to collectivism is rapidly changing based on the situation and its requirements.

To illustrate this problem, a three-dimensional (3-D) space can be constructed (see Fig. 2-2) where different species are assigned (approximate) different spatial positions on the basis of the different proportions between subordination of their successful existence to individual *intelligence* and/or more reliance on the existence of *collective intelligence*. In this book, we claim that there is no formal difference between the evaluation of individual *intelligence* and *collective intelligence*; however, proper scaling for Figure 2-2 has not been yet done, and it will probably take several years to finish this picture with an appropriate scale. Thus, Figure 2-2 should be considered as only a type of ordering for now.

Probably the lowest level in 3-D space would be biological cells creating tissues or simple microorganisms, which according to biological hypotheses (see 2.2.1.1) emerged as a result of unification from elementary one-celled beings. Individual *intelligence* here has been fully replaced by *collective intelligence* and activities of tissues or microorganisms. Even individual displacement ability has been devoted to common displacements of whole tissues or group of beings.

At another location is a bacterial colony, in which members are not joined into one organism and have almost negligent individual *intelligence* but are powerful as a *collective intelligence* against, for example, new antibiotics or changes of environment (see 2.2.1.1).

The symptoms of individual *intelligence* are more observable at the level of social insects like ants. The vision system and "effectors" are sufficient, compared, for example, to protozoa. Thus, a being can individually displace the outside colony with a reliable probability of survival. However, its existence relies on the *collective intelligence* of the ant colony.

More highly organized animals can exist individually for a long time because their individual *intelligence* is relatively high. Only for procreative purposes do they need another representative of their own type. In some cases (e.g., wolves during a difficult winter), they may create *temporary social* structures that display *collective intelligence* (e.g., for hunting).

Finally, primates mainly exist in social structures of different sizes; however, individualism is very clear during the ranging period.

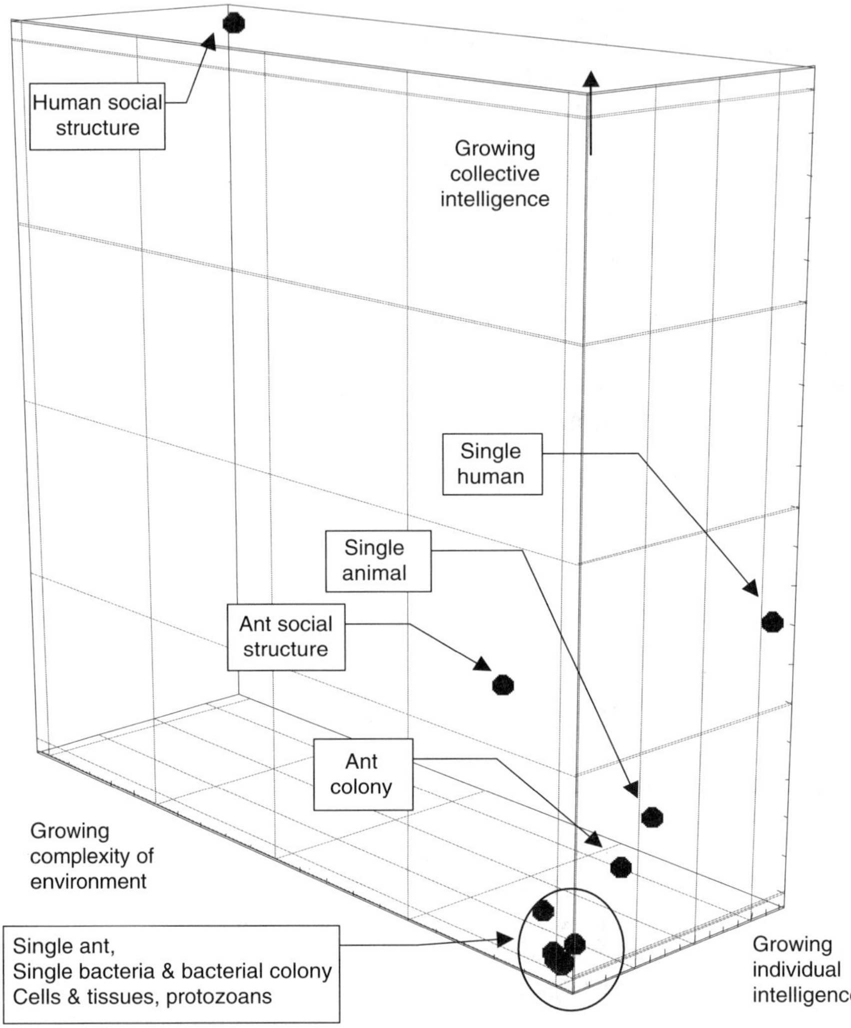

Figure 2-2. 3-D space of intelligence and environment complexity.

If a single being undergoes an IQ test (in vitro) and later achievements of this being are observed in real life (in vivo), results should differ because we see "a projection" of a part of a social structure into the IQ scale, not "a projection" of the single being's *intelligence*.

2.1.1. Problems with a General and Cohesive Evaluation of Individual Intelligence

To focus our discussion on the problem of a general and cohesive evaluation of individual *intelligence*, we must clearly state our goals:

> The *intelligence* assessment has the basic goal of evaluating a given *being* in such a way that the resulting assignment of a measure (IQ) will predict with the highest possible accuracy its future behavior, and/or the performance of the *being* in an assumed specific environment.

This approach is very well characterized by the definition given in 1975 by David Wechsler (39), who stated in his paper entitled "Intelligence Defined and Undefined . . .":

> *Intelligence* is the global capacity of the individual to act purposefully, to think rationally, and to deal effectively with the environment.

Because of this approach, it is a priori required that such a specific environment should be well characterized. Later, if possible, for example, experimentally, (even on the basis of trial-and-error identification), a proper battery of tests can be constructed, and then it can be expected that there will be a high correlation between the being's IQ and its future performance.

Herein is hidden an explanation of the early success of the Binet test, which emerged from elementary school needs and was designed for a school environment. In an elementary school there are children who are a representative sample set taken from society, a program of teaching that is highly unified, and course subjects that are adapted to the average mental abilities of children through long years of experiments and observations. Moreover, schools (even universities) have "crystallized" into a form that is not affected too much by the introduction of new teaching tools such as computers. The size of lectures, the organization of classes, even the use of blackboards, and finally the relationships between students and teachers are all still similar to those of the last century. As a result, teaching is a specific profession requiring special mental properties; the school provides a well-defined almost laboratory-like environment for children, considered during the tests as: *Beings which are perceiving, reasoning, and acting.*

Thus, we can expose the first major difficulty in creating a general and cohesive method of evaluating individual *intelligence.*

> The human being, even the individual, is able to deal with so many different environments that it is essentially difficult to select a specific one (or more, as a representative set), where individual *intelligence* should be evaluated.

The second difficulty comes from the following question:

> What would be an optimal data structure to record a measurement of individual *intelligence?*

Remember that we always have the problem of identifying the internal structure of the "*black box*" of the human brain and through the analysis of *input* and *output* relations only to define the proper data structure to describe this "*black box*."

This problem has not been dealt with either in past or present efforts of psychologists to devise a cohesive general test of individual *intelligence*.

From the history of research on *intelligence* (40), it is a well-known fact that Binet and Simon were totally against the use of the IQ scoring designed by W. Stern in 1914, in such a way that:

$$IQ = \frac{\text{mental age}}{\text{chronological age}} * 100$$

Stern used the simplest available data structure (i.e., integers), to measure the extremely complex system of a human as a thinking being. However, this approach can be defended to some extent because integers as a scalar data type are very easy to use for the following reasons:

1. For defining ordering, beings can be set along an axis, and various minimum and maximum points can be introduced. The *intelligence* coordination system is one-dimensional.
2. Processing of such integer-based data structures is easy.
3. IQ evaluation in such a system is unequivocal.

Objections to the "one single factor" that is assumed to determine the global performance in all mental tests took researchers through various trials, eventually to the use of much more complex data structures.

From a historical point of view, the first significant attempt was made by C.E. Spearman (41,42), who from 1904 started to propose a "two-factor-theory" of *intelligence* (broadly named the *g-s theory*). The concept was to use a general factor called g and many small specific factors called s that influence performance on any given test. Factor g is intended to express a general ability (general *intelligence*), whereas s factors are responsible for specific abilities. A factor s can be considered as a projection of g done on a given specific ability test. The relationship between g and s can be derived on the basis of a positive relationship among scores on the subtests of *intelligence* tests.
Here is the basic problem:

1. Precise *identification* of s components;
2. Establishing analytical relations between g and s.

It is well known from other disciplines, including control theory, pattern recognition (43), and so forth, how difficult the final identification of a given system can be, even if its internal structure is a priori defined, and it is necessary only to compute coefficients in formulas.

Another problem resulting from *g-s* theory is comparing beings with the *g-s intelligence* evaluation because of the topological[7] properties resulting from such a definition.

As an example of an attempt to refine the *g-s* approach, there is the tree designed by P.E. Vernon (44) shown in Figure 2-3.

Significant consecutive attempts to define a proper data structure recording *intelligence* measures of individuals were made in 1938 by L.L. Thurstone, who proposed the so-called "seven primary mental abilities," which can be used in this data structure (record) as *fields*:

1. Verbal comprehension
2. Numerical ability
3. Spatial relations
4. Perceptual speed
5. Word fluency
6. Memory
7. Reasoning

Thurstone believed that mapping a human being through tests into such a data structure would provide a more accurate formal picture of a person's mental ability. This is reasonable because seven independent mental abilities can more precisely cover the huge domain of human activity evaluated by tests. In his early studies, Thurstone believed that the set of seven mental abilities he proposed could obtain without the *g* factor of general *intelligence*. However, a second analysis of correlation factors pointed to a superfactor, which can be interpreted only as "general *intelligence*."

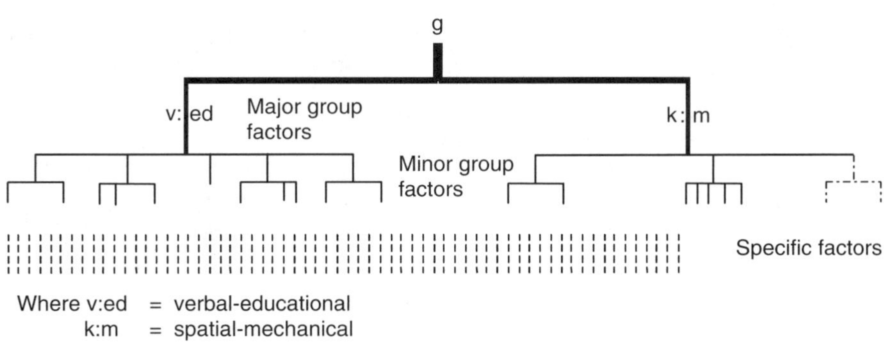

Figure 2-3. Hierarchical structure of human abilities by Vernon.

[7] The study of the properties of geometric figures or solids that are not normally affected by changes in size or shape.

For readers who are not familiar with statistics, we should mention here a formal tool, the *correlation coefficient*, which is responsible for creating all those links between "points" representing abilities.

The *correlation coefficient* was proposed by K. Pearson (1857–1936); it is usually denoted by r and is appropriate for describing the linear relationship between two quantitative variables X, Y every measured n times. It can range from $+1$ to -1. If one variable increases and the other decreases, the r will be negative; if they both head in the same general direction, the correlation coefficient will be positive. If there is no linear relationship between them, the coefficient will be zero. The easiest form for reading of a formula for r is as follows:

$$r = \frac{\dfrac{\sum_{i=1}^{n}(X_i - \overline{X})(Y_i - \overline{Y})}{n}}{\sqrt{\left[\dfrac{\sum_{i=1}^{n}(X_i - \overline{X})^2}{n}\right]\left[\dfrac{\sum_{i=1}^{n}(Y_i - \overline{Y})^2}{n}\right]}}$$

where $\overline{X}$, $\overline{Y}$ denote mean values

It should be remembered that even now the nature of "brain work" is not clear to us, so neuropsychological models must be used. Thus, formulas like the one given previously can very easily introduce *virtual elements* as considerations. A good example is the concept of *center of mass*, which is widely used for consideration of static and dynamic properties of mass objects linked together, even with soft links such as those involved with gravity. This is one of the most useful concepts in mechanics, but it can lead us, for example, to look for the global *reduced mass* of a group of objects anywhere in the empty space between them.

A further extension of this concept is the 3-D data structure to describe and evaluate individual *intelligence* proposed by J.P. Guilford (45,46) and illustrated in Figure 2-4.

Guilford has assumed that to describe the "structure of the intellect" it is necessary to use three basic "*dimensions*": the *dimension of operation*, the *dimension of product*, and the *dimension of content*. Every dimension is discrete in nature and has respectively 5, 6, 4 coordinate locations. Thus, in this approach to data structure describing intellect, the $\text{matrix}_{5,6,4}$ of 120 discrete fields is necessary. The performance at any specific task should be derived from this matrix if values there will be assigned by proper *intelligence* tests.

Guilford's approach has been criticized mainly for being too complicated (47) and lacking any predictive value (48). This approach can be viewed as at the opposite end of the single g factor approach.

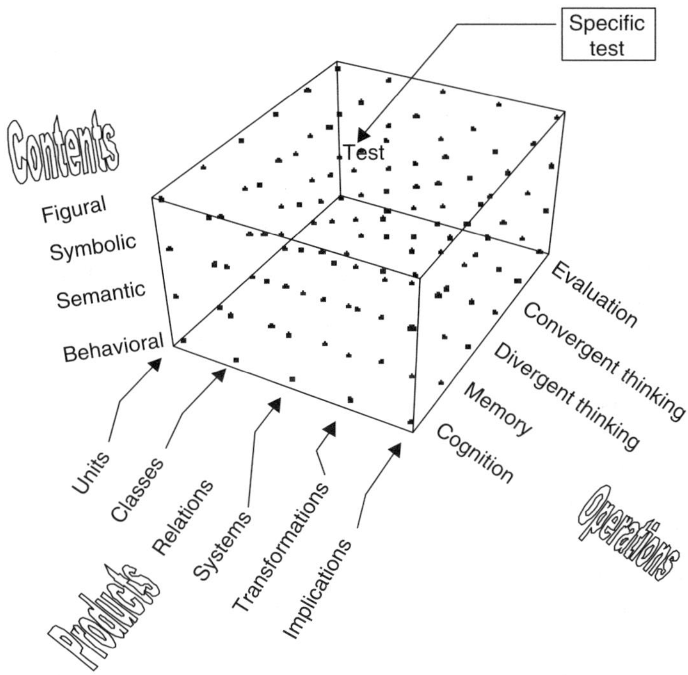

Figure 2-4. Guilford's 120-factor measure.

To finish this chapter considering problems with a general and cohesive evaluation of individual *intelligence*, the concept of "*multiple intelligences*" suggested by H. Gardner (35) should be mentioned. As we noted in the chapter devoted to difficulties with comprehension of the term *intelligence*, Gardner proposed the existence of seven independent and equally important forms of *intelligence*:

1. Linguistic
2. Logical-mathematical
3. Spatial
4. Bodily-kinesthetic
5. Musical
6. Intrapersonal
7. Interpersonal

Gardner argues that there is no single thing called *intelligence* (he denies the existence of the *g* factor) and suggests that *intelligence* cannot be measured with "paper-and-pencil" tests.

We have observed that perceiving *intelligence* through its performance measured by any even complicated data structure must finally lead to confusion, which is obvious as we learn more and more about the nature of *intelligence*. The exit from this impasse is to move into perceiving *intelligence* through its functional models. The introduction and rapid expansion of computer science and technology into all disciplines of life has provided us not only with scientific tools but also with a broader acceptance and understanding of this approach.

2.1.2. The Individual Intelligence of Humans

In their excellent book on assessment of cognitive processes (1), J.P. Das, J.A. Naglieri, and J.R. Kirby write in the chapter "Prediction versus Explanation:"

> Prediction is not the same as explanation or understanding. When measurement is not theory based, it is impossible to know why prediction has been successful. Traditional tests for intelligence are made up of items and subtests that have been selected because they correlate with other measures, not because they are derived from theoretical notions of what is being measured. Thus, it is difficult to be sure that the process is not circular. Explanation and understanding, rather than blind prediction, are the proper goals of science; they should contribute toward making selection or diagnosis more efficient as well.

Conclusively, they start the next paragraph of their book with the title, which is also the conclusion for our next chapter: *What Is Measured: Abilities or Processes*?

2.1.2.1. Review of significant models of individual human intelligence

In this chapter, we review the most significant models[8] of the individual *intelligence* of humans. The term *mathematical model* is defined to force us to reflect on how restricted our knowledge is of the brain and *intelligence*. We have problems fulfilling all the requirements imposed by the definition of mathematical *model* when applied to the term *intelligence*.

It is important for us to be able to perceive *intelligence* as a certain process resulting in specific abilities that later can be measured and assigned IQ values because we have this type of situation in the case of the *collective intelligence* of closed social structures. It is demonstrated later in the book that *collective intelligence* is also a property of the processes running inside social structures. It emerges (is amplified and sometimes vanishes) and can be observable under certain circumstances in such social structures of beings that are socially united in solving problems, even unconsciously.

Most of the present models of individual human *intelligence* are oriented to summarize present knowledge of IQ measure and to describe relations between

[8] A mathematical model represents a given *system* in terms of logical or quantitative relationships that are then manipulated and changed to see how the model reacts and thus how the system *could* react if the mathematical model were a valid one (49).

recognized *intelligence* factors. Thus, it is difficult to consider them as real models of *intelligence*; they are rather like data structures, as discussed in the previous chapter. They reflect the previous way of thinking about *intelligence*, not yet affected by the concepts of computer science, which emerged after World War II. Let us take a look at them.

We can distinguish two different structural models of individual *intelligence*:

- The hierarchical model
- The bifactor model

In the structural model of Figure 2-5, squares represent *observables* (such as specific tests, or the specific items of which a test is comprised), and circles represent *unobservables* (factors, the hypothetical entities that explain the correlations among the observables). The arrows represent the correlations of the tests with the factors; such correlations are known as factor loadings.

The hierarchical model is considered to be more efficient because it uses fewer parameters, obviously, counting the arrows (parameters) in Figure 2-5. will suggest that the hierarchical model should be more efficient.

However, the bifactor model allows one to talk about independent components or factors of *intelligence*. The factors in the bifactor model are pure, uncorrected, and non-redundant, which is not true for the hierarchical model. One would rather include independent factors in a regression equation[9] than nonindependent factors.

As an example of the hierarchical model of *intelligence*, there is a model in which the correlation between verbal abilities and spatial abilities is $r = 0.58$. In

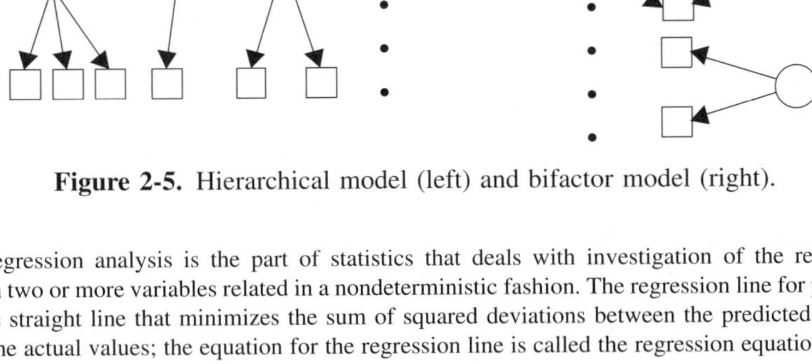

Figure 2-5. Hierarchical model (left) and bifactor model (right).

[9] The regression analysis is the part of statistics that deals with investigation of the relationship between two or more variables related in a nondeterministic fashion. The regression line for predicting Y is the straight line that minimizes the sum of squared deviations between the predicted values of Y and the actual values; the equation for the regression line is called the regression equation. (50,51)

contrast, an example of the bifactor model of *intelligence* is a model in which verbal and spatial abilities do not correlate (i.e., they are orthogonal).

It is obvious that this empirical difference between verbal and spatial abilities in the hierarchical model and the bifactor model would require that verbal and spatial abilities also differ conceptually between the two models.

Beyond the question of structure lies the deeper question of meaning in terms of understandability or theoretical utility of these two different models.

If g is brain size in an *intelligence* sense, and everything else is an independent cognitive module, the bifactor model makes sense. If g is the common variance of verbal and spatial abilities, a hierarchical model is better.

The overwhelming takeover of our world (and almost all sciences related to the problem of *intelligence*) by the digital computer has raised proposals to consider the brain to be organized and to work in a manner similar to a digital computer. On the basis of this approach, *intelligence* should be derived as the *ability*(*s*) of such a functional system, and IQ tests would be conceptually similar to computer benchmarks. Computer science and the theory of *individual intelligence* can be linked by the following concepts:

- Modularity of mind (*intelligence*)
- Computational theory of mind (*intelligence*)

Let us present them now:

THE MODULARITY CONCEPT

The modularity concept can be dated as early as the Prussian philosopher Immanuel Kant (*Critique of Pure Reason*, 1781), but the major recent contributors to this approach are Newell and Simon with their concept that the mind is a general problem solver (GPS). Their contribution to the development of *artificial intelligence*, which actually bridged psychology and AI, is well known (52). However, Piaget should also be mentioned here for his book *Biology and Knowledge* (53). Current programming of digital computers is based on creation of programs that are composed of modules of various levels, starting with a main program, which is also a module itself, to modules of procedures, down to the smallest modules of machine instruction on the assembly programming level. This modularization can even be continued down to microinstructions. Similarly, J.A. Fodor and H. Gardner (35,54,55) have claimed that the intelligent mind is made up of special-purpose modules. Such modules are independently functioning, are genetically specified, and can be considered as units characterized by input and output and defined as processing relations between them.

This concept is interesting and promising, at least for the near future because modularity seems technology-independent. Modularity, which is obvious in digital computers, has also been found valid for analog computers[10], which use totally different representations of information (i.e., are characterized by continuous, not discrete functions) and methods of information processing. Recently, modularity has also been found to be valid in molecular models of computation (5,8,56). For *collective intelligence*, modularity is also applicable (57), etc.

COMPUTATIONAL THEORY OF MIND (INTELLIGENCE)

The foundation of this approach is an assumption that there is a *language of thought* and that mental processes are causal sequences driven by the syntactic but not the semantic. However, the trick here is to build a model effectively without introduction of abstract, nonphysical concepts defining semantics and meaning. The syntactic is hidden behind the semantics in such a way that the model, facts, rules, and goals are designed very carefully to allow and license only such *language* transformations that are correct from the *thought* point of view.

H. Putman (58), J. Fodor (59), and Z.W. Pylyshin (34) can be mentioned as recent significant contributors to this approach, which can be claimed as a direct continuation of some other streams of research, such as *mental representation, intentionality*, and so forth.

The development of formal grammars (N. Chomsky (60)) has provided a theoretical base for this approach and has even introduced the term *psycholinguistics*.

This approach fits very well with our present major tool, that is, digital computers and the different shells of programming languages that run the hardware level below them.

CONNECTIONIST MODELS

One of the most important and productive approaches to the problem of modeling of human *intelligence* is called *connectionism*. In general, it can be defined as an approach to understanding the mechanisms of human cognition through the use of simulated networks of simple, neuronlike processing units. Connectionism resulted from attempts to understand and model the structure of the brain cortex, which is composed of biological structures called *neurons* (see Fig. 2-6) and bursts of action potentials traveling in one direction down a single-celled neuron by a network of simple electrical structures like those of the *perceptron* (term introduced in 1962 by F. Rosenblatt (61); see Fig. 2-8).

The question is what the structure of an *artificial neuron* should be. The basic *perceptron* concept assumed threshold function discrimination, as shown in Figure 2-7, which is very close to the digital 0/1 approach.

[10] A concise description of the analog computer can be found in the McGraw-Hill *Encyclopedia of Science and Technology*, 7th edition, 1992, pp. 535–548. Analog computers cannot be definitely considered outdated, as the reader can be tell from many available literature resources, because neural networks have once again raised interest in this technology.

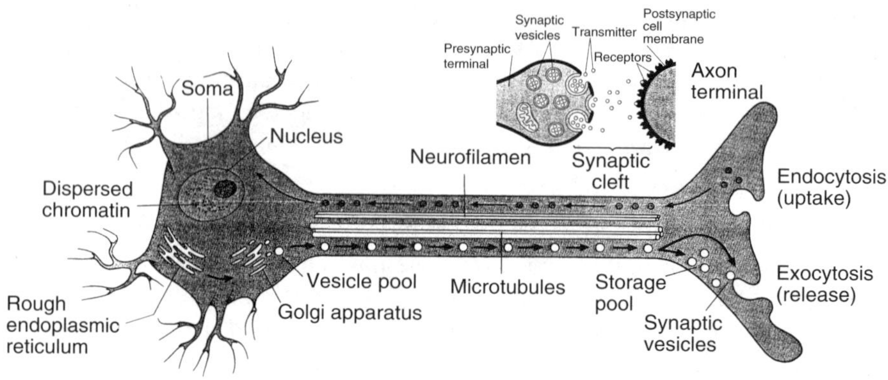

Figure 2-6. The structure of the neuron and its communication. With permission from: Rhoades R., Pflanzer R.: *Human physiology*. 2nd ed. Harcourt. 1992.

However, to overcome difficulties with learning more complicated patterns, it was necessary to use more complicated transferring functions than thresholds, that is, the sigmoid

$$o(\overline{x}) = \frac{1}{1 + e^{-\sum_1^n w_i x_i}} \quad \text{i.e.}$$

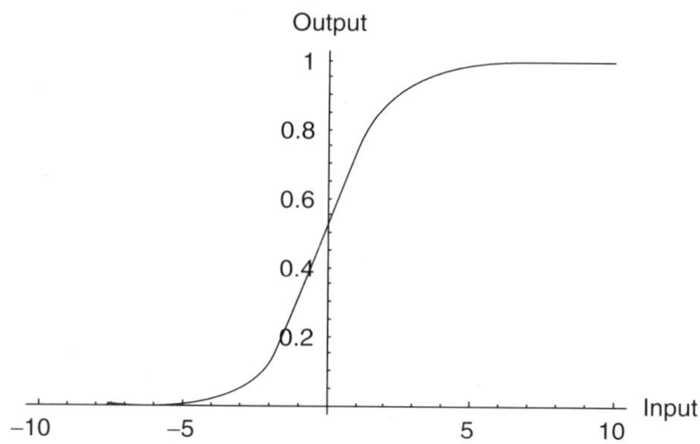

Figure 2-7. Threshold function.

In general, the *perceptron* is not a concept from the digital computer area but an element of the analog computer because the *perceptron* deals better with continuous signals. However, our present computers can easily and very efficiently simulate perceptrons, and it is widely claimed that hybrid architectures of neural networks and digital computers should be used with a digital computer as a supervisory one. A monographic description of an attempt to model the brain with artificial neuron networks (ANN) can be found in O.J. Amit (62).

Perceptron-like elements organized into ANN have demonstrated amazing properties, so similar to properties of the brain that even terminology used in

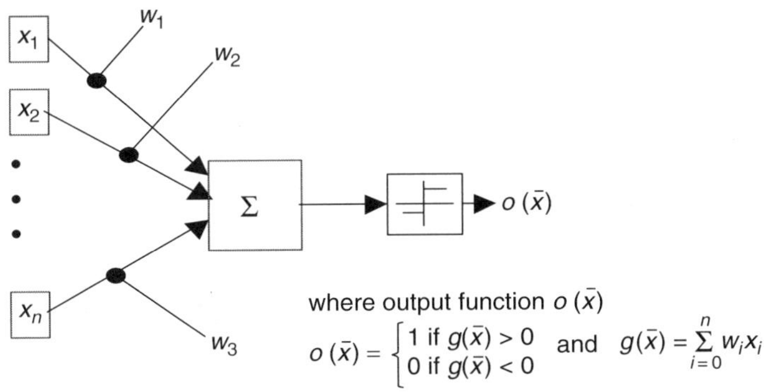

Figure 2-8. Perceptron.

neuroscience has been adopted for ANN. Probably the most amazing property is that the neural network has the structural ability to learn and that knowledge is stored as a structure setting (weights w_i), not as explicit data.

Neural networks can be used especially well for the following applications:

- Pattern recognizers and associative memory
- Pattern transformers
- Dynamic inferencers

As a result, it was soon proposed to model *intelligence* through systems of trainable perceptrons able to *perceive, reason, and act* as is presented in Figure 2-9 (63).

The difficulty with modeling the brain and *intelligence* through ANN is that simple-structured ANN can do almost nothing (this was the reason for the famous, almost total suspension of research on ANN for almost a decade in the 1970s after objections M. Minsky and S. Papert raised in 1969 (64)). To build efficient applications with ANN, it is necessary to have complicated, multilayer ANN structures and to use sophisticated algorithms translating the ANN learning process into tuning of matrices of weights w_i. The learning process is long, and the flow of information must be bidirectional in ANN.

So far, in general, ANN is the best approximation of human *intelligence* as a process of *perceiving, reasoning, and acting*. This direction is so promising that a level of "mechanical consciousness" can be reached on an ANN platform.

In 1923 the psychologist E.G. Boring (65) expressed what many scientists working on *intelligence* believe, that a definition of *intelligence* should be based on the definition of the tests measuring it. He wrote that *intelligence* is "what *intelligence* tests test." Now let us review IQ[11] tests for humans.

[11] Intelligence Quotient (IQ).

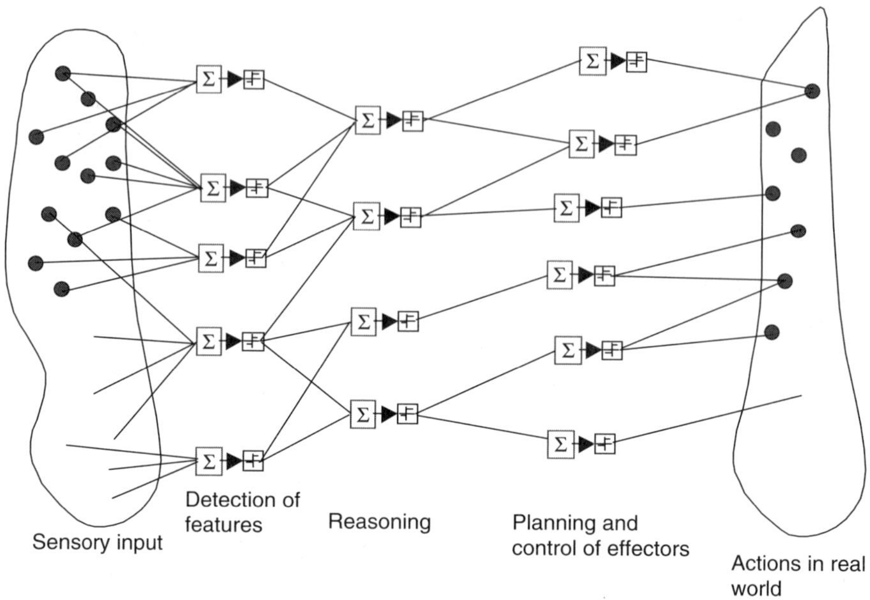

Figure 2-9. Intelligent system based on neural network.

2.1.2.2. Intelligence Tests for Humans

In our brief overview of the most significant concepts and examples of IQ tests, we should take into account several points:

- The human individual as a being *changes* during its development, rapidly progressing at first and later slowly recessing, that is, cognition changes during the life span. This is because of biologically driven differences between the mental performance of children, adolescents, adults, and elders.
- *Intelligence* (measured by IQ) is highly affected by the environment (education). Depending on the researcher, approximately 60 percent of IQ is thought to be genetically inherited and about 40 percent is considered to be a matter of environment (66).
- The IQ test should evaluate general *intelligence*, specific abilities, and future performance (aptitude).
- IQ tests are more or less based on culture. For *collective intelligence* purposes, we must be familiar with the problem of cultural difference because soon we will face the much more serious problem of type differences. Thus, we will give an example of culture-fair tests as an introduction to the problem of designing IQ tests for different types of beings and a comparison of the *collective intelligence* of social structures of different beings.

Piaget theorized that cognitive development occurs in stages, with each successive stage being qualitatively different from the preceding stage, while building on the learning achieved in that preceding stage (e.g., 67).

Piaget's Cognitive Stages of Development:

1. Sensorimotor stage (birth to 2 years)
2. Preoperational stage (2 years to 7 years)
3. Concrete operational stage (7 years to 12 years)
4. Formal operations (adolescence to adulthood).

In literature there are various graphs that show how the abilities of humans change during a life span. They differ highly; for example, the development of children up to age 16 and development and regression in adulthood are given separately. Graphs also differ in which abilities are presented across a life span or the average over which set of abilities is presented.

In general, however, a curve can be formed (see Fig. 2-10), showing how the *intelligence* of humans changes during the life span, using for example, tests like J.C. Raven's Matrices (68). A test similar to Raven's progressive Matrices is shown in Figure 2-11. This test is also interesting from the point of view of *collective intelligence*, because according to H.J. Butcher (24), "norms on the test . . . apparently do not vary greatly between developed countries, and it is possibly

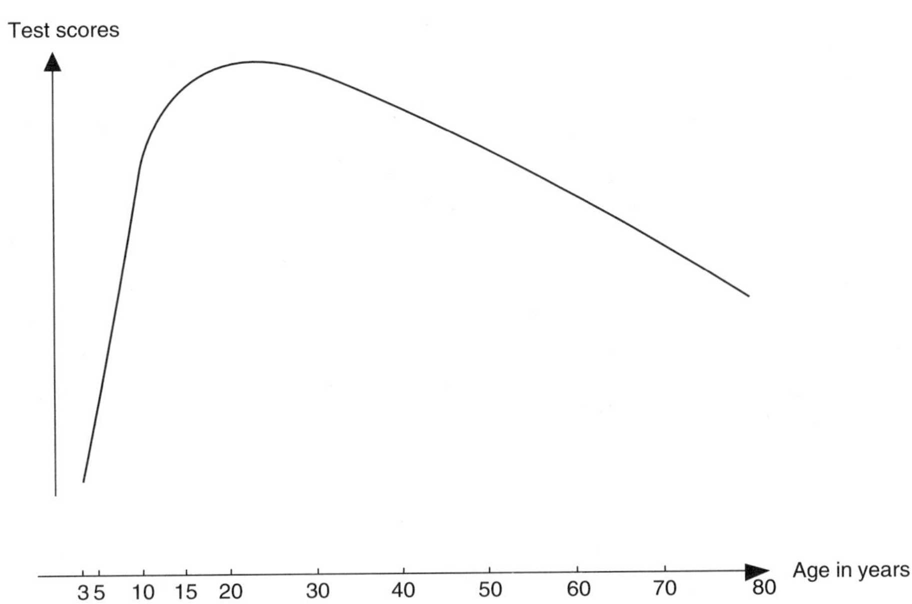

Figure 2-10. Age differences in performance.

Instructions for test:
"Each pattern has a piece missing. From the eight choices provided, select the one that completes the pattern, both going across and down."

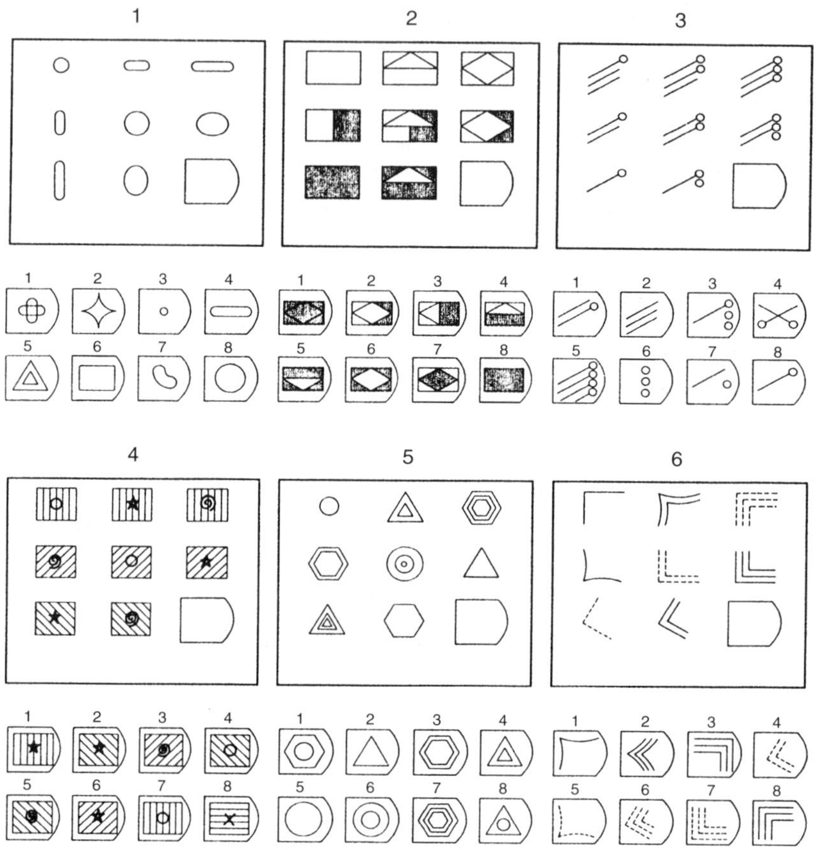

Figure 2-11. Concept of Raven's progressive matrices test. (from Introduction to psychology. 3rd ed., by J. Kalat 1993, Reprinted with permission of Wadsworth/Thomson Learning)

as little affected by cultural differences as tests that claim to be culture-fair or culture-free." This test is considered one of the best tests for "fluid *intelligence*."[12]

Also note that to some extent the "culture of children" is different from the "culture of teenagers" and the "culture of adults." Thus, Raven's Matrices point in the direction where tests universal for biologically different beings should be devised.

[12] Crystallized intelligence is defined as an aspect that includes verbal ability and accumulated knowledge that tends to increase over the life span. Fluid intelligence is defined as an aspect of intelligence involving abstract reasoning and mental flexibility, which peaks in the early twenties and declines slowly as people age.

In general, tests for human beings can be classified as follows:

- Tests administered to groups versus tests given to one human being at a time
- Tests based on "pencil and paper" (verbal or nonverbal) or performance tests
- Tests for children or adults with subdivision according to age
- Wide-range tests or tests oriented to specialized groups or people of particularly high ability
- Tests measuring general intelligence or specific abilities

As mentioned in section 2.1.1, the simplest and oldest formal definition of an IQ *intelligence* measure of individuals is given by the formula:

$$IQ = \frac{\text{mental age}}{\text{chronological age}} * 100$$

which has now been widely replaced by the "deviation IQs" or rather the "deviation score" (69):

DEFINITION 3: DEVIATION SCORE:

A test score calculated by comparing an individual's score with the scores of others of the same age."

The disadvantage of the use of *mental age* is that such an approach is not applicable to adult humans because at a certain age the maturity in *intelligence* is reached and later *intelligence* can only decline, as shown in Figure 2-10. Therefore, in the *deviation score*, *intelligence* is referred to as *norms*, that is, standards based on the scores of a large number (samples) of human beings representative of those who will be taking the test in the future. As a result, it is difficult to say much about IQ with this approach because such an *intelligence* measure is relative, not absolute.

To evaluate such a nonhomogeneous sample of beings, a so-called "bell curve" approach is used. The bell curve is created on the basis of observation, so that when a large number of test scores are compiled, they are typically distributed according to the normal (Gaussian) distribution curve. On the Wechsler *intelligence* scales, the average (mean) IQ score is set at 100.

Figure 2-12 also gives the classification of a given human population into levels of *intelligence*.

Now let us look at types of items on the two most important tests: the Stanford-Binet test (Figure 2-13) and the Wechsler test for children (WISC) (Figure 2-14) and adults (WAIS-R) (Figures 2-15, 2-16).

The Stanford-Binet test designed by Binet and Simon was modified by Terman and developed by a group of Stanford University psychologists. Test items are

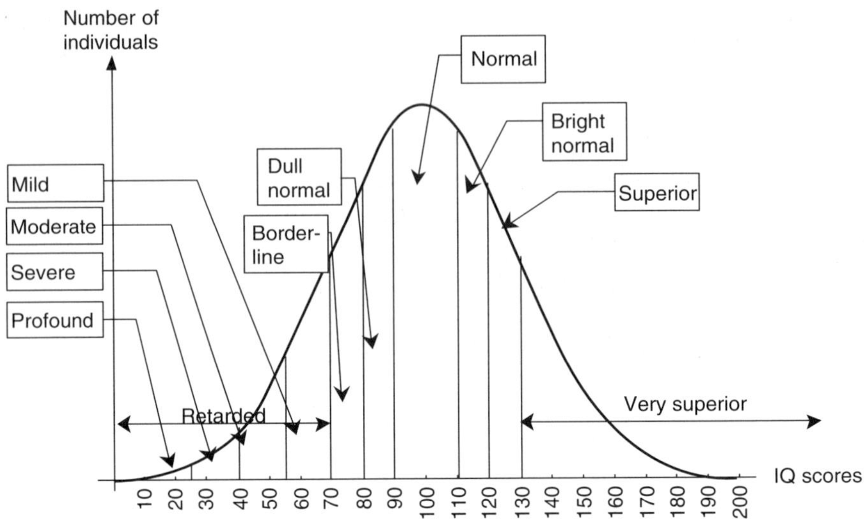

Figure 2-12. Bell curve of IQ distribution.

shown in Figure 2-13. A second major test (now more commonly used) is the Wechsler test. The main advantage of the Wechsler test is that in addition to an overall score, provides scores in two main categories (verbal and performance), each of which is divided into component abilities. At the end of this section, let us do a short summary. It is impossible to separate achievement tests from aptitude tests. All tests assess the being's current status. Both kinds of tests use the same types of questions, and these tests are highly correlated. It is very useful to think of them as falling along a continuum of some type, such as shown in Figure 2-17 and because there is a great variety of tests available designed by different researchers and research groups, even companies, under different assumptions and targeting different abilities.

2.1.3. Artificial Intelligence (AI) Considered as a Projection[13] of Human Intelligence into Digital Computers

First let us look at a dictionary definition of *artificial intelligence*:

> The branch of computer science concerned with enabling computers to simulate such aspects of human intelligence as speech recognition, deduction, inference, creative response, the ability to learn from experience, and the ability to make inferences given incomplete information. Two common areas of artificial-intelligence research are Expert Systems and natural-language processing.[14]

[13] In mathematics, the image of a geometric figure reproduced on a line, plane, or surface. In psychology, the attribution of one's own attitudes, feelings, or desires to someone or something.

[14] Microsoft® Bookshelf® *Computer and Internet Dictionary*© 1997 Microsoft Corporation. Microsoft Press® *Computer Dictionary*, Third Edition.

Age Two

1. Three-hole Form Board. Placing three geometric objects in form board.
2. Delayed Response. Identifying placement of hidden object after 10-second delay.
3. Identifying parts of the Body. Pointing out features on paper doll.
4. Block Building Tower. Building four-block
5. Picture Vocabulary. Naming common objects from pictures.
6. Word Combinations. Spontaneous combination of two words.

Age Six

1. Vocabulary. Correctly defining 6 words in 45-word list.
2. Differences. Telling difference between two objects.
3. Mutilated Pictures. Pointing out missing part of picture object.
4. Number Concepts. Counting number of blocks in a pile.
5. Opposite Analogies II. Items of form "Summer is hot; winter is ______".
6. Maze Tracing. Finding shortest path in simple maze.

Age Ten

1. Vocabulary. Correctly defining 11 words on same list.
2. Block Counting. Counting number of cubes in three-dimensional picture, some cubes hidden.
3. Abstract Words I. Definition of abstract adverbs.
4. Finding Reason I. Giving reasons for law of preference.
5. Word Naming. Naming as many words as possible in one minute.
6. Repeating Six Digits. Repeating six digits in order.

Average Adult

1. Vocabulary. Correctly defining 20 words.
2. Ingenuity. Algebraic word problems involving mental manipulation of volumes.
3. Differences between Abstract Words. Differentiating between two related abstract words.
4. Arithmetic Reasoning. Word problems involving simple computations.
5. Proverbs I. Giving meaning of proverbs.
6. Orientation: Direction II. Finding orientation after a verbal series of changes in directions.
7. Essential Differences. Giving principal difference between two related concepts.
8. Abstract Words II. Meanings of abstract adverbs.

Figure 2-13. Typical test items on Standford-Binet test according to Mayer (22).

Perhaps it could be asked why AI is called a *projection*, not just a *simulation*; there is an important difference. A simulation is an attempt to model a given process as precisely as possible, and the point of interest is the modeling process itself, not the model. Precision of simulation and knowledge about the process being simulated are fundamental here.

With projection, we create a quite new object, sometimes in another dimension, and we focus on it, not on the pattern (source). Often we have no idea of the internal structure of the pattern, just as our shadow on the wall is a projection of our body. This projection will imitate only our external behavior, which with films or television movies give pretty good results. The same thing is true with

Verbal Scale	
Information	From what animal do we get milk? Either "cow" or "goat" is an acceptable answer.
Similarities	How are a plum and a peach similar? (Correct answer: "They are both fruits." Half credit is given for "Both are food." or "Both are round.")
Arithmetic	Count these blocks: ■■■■■■■■■■
Vocabulary	Define the word *letter*.
Comprehension	What should you do if you see a train approaching a broken track? (A correct answer is "Stand safely out of the way and wave something to warn the train." Half credit is given for "Tell someone at the railroad station." *No* credit is given for "I would try to fix the track.")
Digit Span	Repeat these numbers after I say them: 3 6 2.
Performance Scale	
Picture completion	What parts are missing from this picture? 
Picture arrangement	Here are some cards with a gardener on them. Can you put them in order? 
Block design	See how I have arranged these four blocks? Here are four more blocks. Can you arrange your blocks like mine? 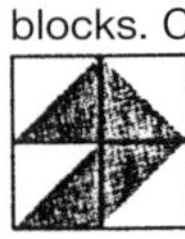
Object assembly	Can you put these five puzzle pieces together to make a dog? 
Coding	Here is a page full of shapes. Put a slash (/) through all the circles and an × through all the squares. △ ○ □ ▱ ○ △ ▱ □ ○
Mazes	Here is a maze. Start with your pencil here and trace path to the other end of the maze without crossing any lines. 

Source: Based on Wechsler, 1949.

Figure 2-14. Wechsler Intelligence Scale for Children (WISC). (From Introduction to Psychology. 3rd ed., by J. Kalat 1993, Reprinted with permission of Wadsworth/Thomson Learning).

Test	Description
	VERBAL SCALE
Information	Questions tap a general range of information; for example, "How many nickels make a dime?"
Comprehension	Tests practical information and ability to evaluate past experience; for example, "What is the advantage of keeping money in a bank?"
Arithmetic	Verbal problems testing arithmetic reasoning.
Similarities	Asks in what way certain objects or concepts (for example, egg and seed) are similar; measures abstract thinking.
Digit span	A series of digits presented auditorily (for example, 7-5-6-4-8) is repeated in a forward or backward direction; tests attention and rote memory.
Vocabulary	Test word knowledge
	PERFORMANCE SCALE
Digit symbol	A timed coding task in which numbers must be associated with marks of various shapes; tests speed of learning and writing.
Picture completion	The missing part of incomplete drawn picture must be discovered and named; tests visual alertness and visual memory.
Block design	Pictured designs must be copied with blocks; tests ability to perceive and analyze patterns.
Picture arrangement	A series of comic-strip pictures must be arranged in the right sequence to tell a story; tests understanding of social situations.
Object assembly	Puzzle pieces must be assembled to form a complete object; tests ability to deal with part-whole relationships.

Figure 2-15. Revised Wechsler Adult Intelligence Scale (WAIS-R).

AI. We have managed to project some algorithms of our instinctual or conscious behavior onto digital computers so well that a new "quality" has been generated, *artificial intelligence*. Note also that a projection process results in a reduction of information, for example, a 3-D cube projected onto a screen shows a two-dimensional (2-D) object only. Projecting our *intelligence* from the human brain into a digital computer results in a similar reduction of *intelligence*. Several authors indirectly support our opinion:

> ". . . a production system framework can account for how people transfer a general skill they learned in one domain to another domain but not for how a creative solution is invented" (70).

Now AI itself is growing independently, without looking for a human as a pattern. What is really necessary for future development is hardware progress in the area of processors for optical vision systems, for voice analyses and synthesis, and for progress in the area of effectors. The last but not least important requirement is a serious application for which AI systems are the only solution.

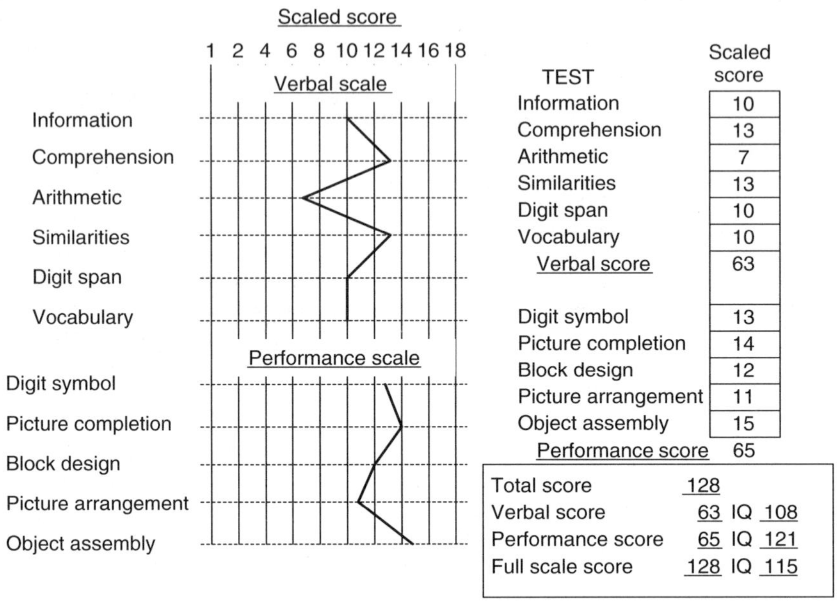

Figure 2-16. Example of profile for Wechsler Adult Intelligence Scale (WAIS-R).

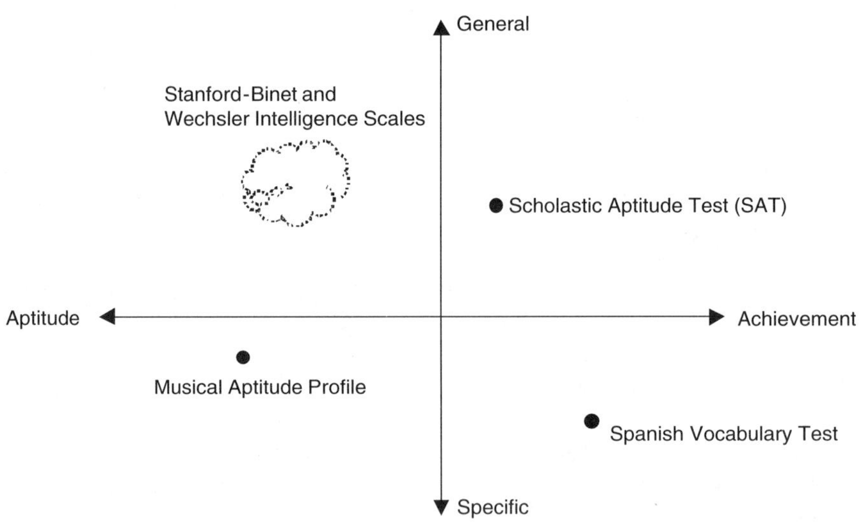

Figure 2-17. Example continuum of tests. (66)

Let us now go through the most fundamental concepts underlying mapping of human individual *intelligence* into digital computers. A conceptual model of a digital computer, the Deterministic Turing Machine, (DTM) is widely known; however, it is presented and discussed in Part 3 of this book because a comparative overview of possible models of computations is necessary there.

2.1.3.1. Mapping Human Ways of Solving Problems into Artificial Intelligence Systems

If we look at a list of successful mappings of typical human ways of thinking into digital computer systems, we find several key paradigms[15] (25). However, we should remember that even by using a specific paradigm, we can still be far from a successful implementation on the digital computer. This is because after a paradigm is discovered, it is usually presented through the *language of our thinking*, such as mathematics, flowcharts, or pseudo-code programming. Later, this form must be efficiently translated into instructions specific for the target computer or family of computers.

To write a program that will successfully solve a certain class of problems, it is usually necessary to apply a mixture of several paradigms, using the advantages of specific paradigms at a certain point in the algorithm and avoiding their weaknesses in other areas, depending on the temporal situation of the computational process. Here are two examples of the most typical "amalgamates":

- *Goal tree* and *Problem reduction*
- *State–space representation of the problem* and *Means–ends analysis*

There is still a chance that future research in psychology, neuropsychology, or AI will discover other more sophisticated paradigms used by intelligent beings that are still hidden in the back of our minds. This possibility can be overlooked because researchers may unconsciously refer and restrict themselves to present computational resources. Recent rapid progress in the area of digital computers and cameras can, however, change this situation. Many of the paradigms we use are on a very low instinctive, unconscious level, that, in general, makes identification of them very difficult[16].

Let us list and briefly discuss the most important (i.e., successful from an application point of view) paradigms:

- *State–space representation* of the problem[17]
- Goal trees
- Generate and test method
- Means-ends analysis
- Problem reduction.

STATE-SPACE REPRESENTATION OF THE PROBLEM. We are not usually able to concentrate on one problem for more than a few minutes; however, for

[15] An archetypical example or pattern that provides a model for a process or system (Microsoft Encarta'98).

[16] Teaching AI, the author has frequently observed that it is difficult even during a lecture to convince some students that they as beings really use these paradigms in everyday life.

[17] *State–space representations* and *goal trees* can be considered as special cases of semantic-net representation (25).

implementing a problem-solving process on a digital computer, it is necessary to start with coding, and later loading the complete description of the problem into the computer.

The coding problem with *State–space representation* requires the following steps:

1. Identification of an *initial state* in which the problem-solving starts.
2. Identification of a *final state* or a relationship that identifies a family of acceptable *final states*; it is said that problem-solving is successful if one or more of such final states are reached after application of allowed actions.
3. Formalization of *intermediate states* to allow defining the data structure describing every state. Sometimes this can be much more difficult (complex) than identification of initial and final states.
4. Identification of links denoting transitions between states.

As a result, we obtain a *State–space representation* of our problem that is in fact a graph (a static description of the problem) where the next step (dynamic) of problem-solving can take place. An advantage from some points of view but also a weakness from that of *State–space representation* is that it usually provides short, concise descriptions of all possible states of the problem, which implies that descriptions are too general to identify solution paths "well hidden there" (if any).

The formal definition of *State–space representation* can be shown as follows:

State–Space representation $= \{D, S_i, T, G\}$, where

D is a set of intermediate states

$S_i \in D$ is the initial state

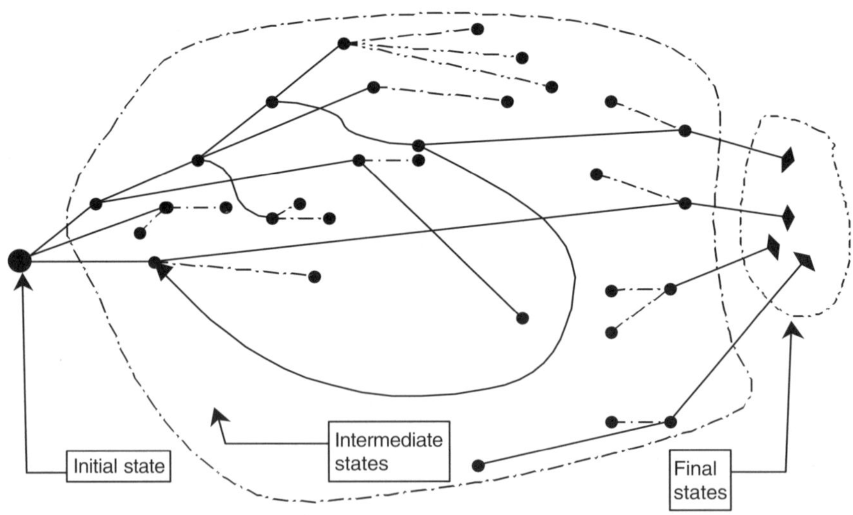

Figure 2-18. Example of a *State–space representation of a problem.*

$T = \{t_1, t_2, \ldots\}$ is a set of transformations (operators, rules) for transforming one state into another

$G \subset D$ is a set of final states

GOAL TREES. The concept of a *Goal tree* is to some extent a mirror-reflection of the *State–space representation*, where the focus is on an "objective description of a problem in terms of its states," whereas a *Goal tree* is "a subjective but formal description of goals assumed by the problem solver related to the problem." The choice of *State–space representations* versus *Goal trees* depends on which representation is more easily applied in a specific case.

Goal(s) can be anything:

- Certain points in the *State–space* can be nominated as goals (to be reached or avoided). The ultimate example of a goal is a final state.
- Properties of states can be defined as goals, such as elimination of certain formulas in the expression describing this state of the process.
- Problems can be assumed as goals, such as our goal is the transformation of our problem into another problem (e.g., of the same complexity) that has a well-known solution or procedure to provide the solution.

Links in the *Goal tree* represent methods by which goals can be achieved. A root goal is defined as the initial goal that must be reached to solve the problem. Even for the same problem, a *Goal tree* can be defined in different ways, depending on, for example, whether an applied strategy is *forward chaining* or *backward chaining* (see Fig. 2-19).

GENERATE AND TEST METHOD. This is probably the most fundamental problem-solving method, because the *Generate and test* approach has been observed as an *instinctual* behavior of animals, children, and even adults. This paradigm is applied "automatically" (or in an unconscious way) when the problem to be solved extends beyond available (educated) patterns of problem-solving and/or there is no obvious similarity to other situations for which methodology exists.

The *Generate and test* paradigm can be used on two levels:

- As a sampling technique to get basic knowledge about the process (problem). Usually the problem or process is "activated" by elementary tools or operators without any strong belief that a solution will appear this way.
- When the set of candidate problem-solving strategies is crystallized, the *Generate and test* paradigm can be used to generate the proposed solution on the basis of "ad hoc" selection of a strategy from this set. Such a solution can be tested later, for example, from the point of view of distance from the required solution.

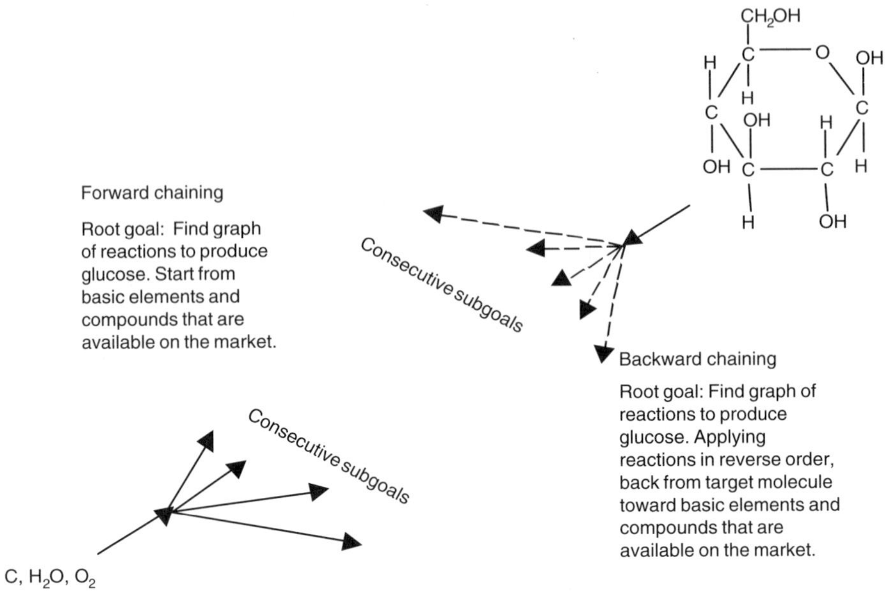

Figure 2-19. Example of a *Goal Tree.*

The *Generate and test* paradigm requires implementing the following loop of actions:

Repeat until a satisfactory solution is found or no more candidate solutions can be generated;

- generate a candidate solution
- test the candidate solution.

Test: If before the exhaustion of the given time or resource limits an acceptable solution is found by loop, **exit**: report it as a success; otherwise **exit:** report failure.

The *Generate and test* paradigm is not very suitable for digital computers with a single processor. For massive parallel computer systems and especially for quasi-chaotic models of computations, the *Generate and test* paradigm suddenly becomes the center of interest because it requires only simple synchronization (multiple copies), that reduces communication costs. If multiple copies are necessary any way, and the system is able to extract a solution in a natural way (if any such appear), the *Generate and test* method is a perfect tool.

L.M. Adleman's DNA computer can be given as an example (5).

MEANS-ENDS ANALYSIS. The key idea in *Means-ends analysis* is to reduce *differences*. For the purpose of discussion here, let us denote a difference function by D. The basic procedural idea is to select operators (from an available set) that seem to provide a means to some end, most often the goal. *Means–ends analysis* assumes that $D(S_p, S_g)$ exists for every pair of states S_p, S_g. Then, $D(S_p, S_g)$ is used at each step to choose an operator that makes the decrease in $D(S_p, S_g)$ the largest (at least from a global point of view). Alternatively, *Means–ends analysis* may be used to achieve a certain goal by driving the system to the state where it allows other "more desirable" rules or operators (or perhaps previously derived subplans) to be applied, with an expected high reduction of D.

The popular way to implement *Means–end analysis* is to define and use a *Difference-procedure table*, which provides information on how certain operators can change D.

To perform *Means–end analysis* the following procedure can be applied:

Test: until the goal is reached or no more procedures are available
Repeat:

- Describe the current state, the goal state, and the difference between the two.
- Use the difference between the current state and the goal state, possibly with the description of the current or goal state, to select a promising procedure.
- Use the promising procedure and update the current state.

Test: if the goal is reached, **exit** with success; otherwise, **exit** with failure.

The most famous example of the successful use of *Means–ends analysis* was the GPS (General problem solver) program developed by A. Newell, H.A. Simon, and J.C. Shaw in the late 1950s (29). GPS greatly influenced the direction of development of AI.

PROBLEM REDUCTION. The concept of *Problem reduction* assumes that a solution to a problem can be found through "consciously reducing the problem with the help of available actions." The basic implementation methodology is to use the so-called AND/OR tree for *Problem reduction*, which is presented in Figure 2-20. Notice the difference between a *problem* and a *goal*. A problem should be perceived as a situation that must be solved or avoided, whereas the goal is our *destination*. We cannot say that a goal must be avoided — we can only select another better goal from, for example, a newly emerging set of goals.

Problem-solving with *Problem reduction* includes two major steps for each node of the tree being investigated:

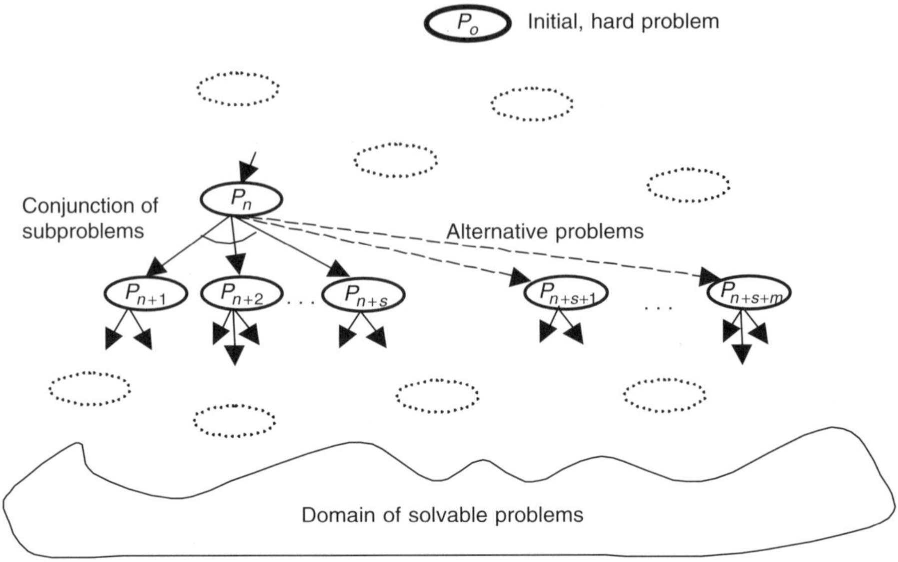

Figure 2-20. The concept of AND/OR Tree.

1. Determination of the equivalence of problems at a node (see Fig. 2-20.), in terms of its solvability, which will be the following for Figure 2-20:

$$P_n \equiv P_{n+1} \; AND \; P_{n+2} \; AND \ldots AND \; P_{n+s} \; OR \; P_{n+s+1} \; OR \ldots OR \; P_{n+s+m}$$

2. Determination of difficulty (complexity) functions for all problems and, later, evaluation of the difficulty (complexity) relation between a parent node and accumulated difficulty (complexity) of its successor nodes.

Let us denote difficulties of successor problems: $f_n, f_{n+1}, \ldots, f_{n+s}, \ldots, f_{n+s+m}$. The reduction of the problem P_n into AND/OR subtree of subproblems is significant (from the illustrated problem-solver point of view), if

$$f_n > f_{n+1} + f_{n+2} + f_{n+s-1} \; OR \; f_n > f_{n+s} \; OR, \ldots, OR \; f_n > f_{n+s+m}$$

that is the AND composition of subproblems is simpler or any successor OR subproblem becomes a simpler alternative than the parent problem.

Problem-solving with *Problem reduction* is said to be terminated if any subtree emerges such that all member-nodes are connected by AND relations and leaf nodes belong to the domain of solvable problems. This subtree when backtracked shows the exact order of how subproblems must be solved to provide a solution for the initial complex problem.

Primarily, this is a subjective method because reduction and difficulty evaluation depend on available operators (methods) of the problem solver.

2.1.3.2. Intelligence in Expert Systems The most advanced and complete creations (from an *intelligence* point of view) of humans in the area of *artificial intelligence* are Expert Systems[18].

Presently, designing and programming Expert Systems is some kind of *intelligence engineering* (the official name is *knowledge engineering*) because it has become a well-defined and profitable area of software design. There are hundreds of working Expert Systems that are constructed and tested for various areas of life; there are even *generators* to allow fast construction of Expert Systems (so-called Expert System Shells), and there are companies specializing in Expert System design and customization.

The Expert System has been assigned the following sort of definition:

> A type of computer application program that makes decisions or solves problems in a particular field, such as finance or medicine, by using knowledge and analytical rules defined by experts in the field. Human experts solve problems by using a combination of factual knowledge and reasoning ability. In an Expert System, these two essentials are contained in two separate but related components, a knowledge base and an inference engine. The knowledge base provides specific facts and rules about the subject, and the inference engine provides the reasoning ability that enables the Expert System to form conclusions. Expert systems also provide additional tools in the form of user interfaces and explanation facilities. User interfaces, as with any application, enable people to form queries, provide information, and otherwise interact with the system. Explanation facilities, an intriguing part of Expert Systems, enable the systems to explain or justify their conclusions, and they also enable developers to check on the operation of the systems themselves. Expert Systems originated in the 1960s; fields in which they are used include chemistry, geology, medicine, banking and investments, and insurance.[19]

When we look into the general structure of the Expert System (see Fig. 2-21) and then into its internal design to compare it with research results on the structure of the human brain, its memory, and its problem-solving methods, we find a striking similarity between the two.

Expert Systems seem to have all the basic and necessary mental components required for a specific *being* that is enclosed inside a computer, such as a "genie in a lamp." From the point of view of *collective intelligence*, it is important to discuss these similarities.

The User Interface is the subsystem by which user and Expert System communicate. Expert Systems are built for professionals in specific areas, for example, a specialist in blood diseases in medicine, who wants to interact

[18] A good textbook used by the author to teach Master's level students, also equipped with a simple Expert System Shell (CLIPS) on CD-ROM is *Expert Systems* by Giarratano and Riley, PWS Publishing, 3rd ed., 1998.

[19] Encarta® 98 Desk Encyclopedia © & ℗ 1996–1997 Microsoft Corporation.

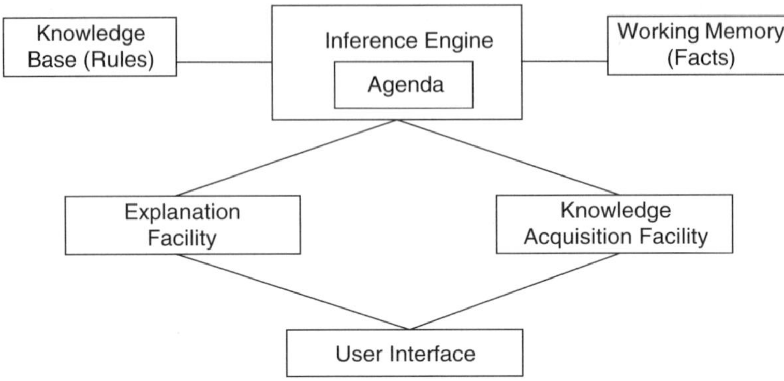

Figure 2-21. Structure of rule-based Expert System.

with a computer but is not familiar with programming languages. This requires the use of a quasi-natural language and advanced User Interface (e.g., trees, 3-D graphics), knowledge of specific terminology, and the ability to parse incomplete or imprecise statements. As a result, the User Interface subsystems are complicated and expensive. Thus, like an *intelligent being*, the Expert System has an advanced communication facility, based on natural language perception, and in some cases other advanced input–output devices.

The Explanation Facility explains the reasoning of the system to the user. It is a well-known paradox that it is usually more difficult to answer questions regarding the validity of a solution than to find the solution itself. The questions WHY? and HOW? can be relatively easily answered by tracing through the tree of the basic solution. However, the questions WHY NOT? and WHAT IF? require such a serious upgrade of the inference system (e.g., multiple runs for alternative inferences), that they are considered "expensive options" for a kernel of Expert System (e.g., TEIRESIAS) (14).

The Working Memory is a global database of facts used by the rules.

The Inference Engine makes conclusions by deciding which rules are satisfied by facts or objects, prioritizes the satisfied rules, and executes the rules according to priority.

The Agenda is a prioritized list of rules created by the Inference Engine, whose patterns are satisfied by facts or objects in Working Memory.

The Knowledge Acquisition Facility entails automatic ways for the user to enter knowledge (to teach) into the system instead of having the knowledge engineer explicitly code the knowledge.

Now, let us discuss some of the most important elements of Expert Systems that are interesting from a human *intelligence* point of view.

The necessity of "software engineering design" for the memory of an Expert System resulted in a structure that clearly reflects the memory model used

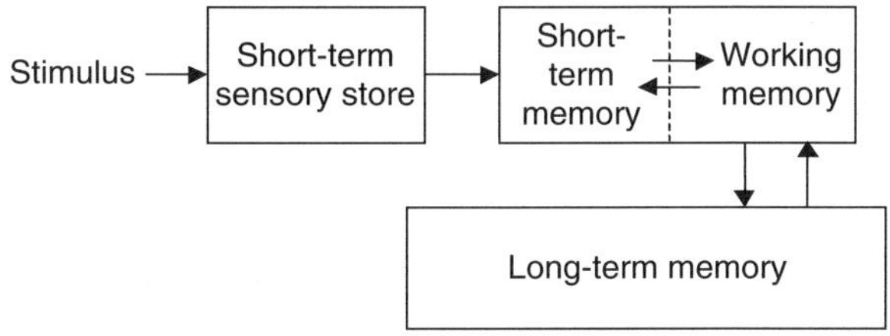

Figure 2-22. Components of memory (according to Mayer (22)).

in psychology (see Fig. 2-22). Short-term memory is implemented by the "working memory (facts)" module, and long-term memory is implemented by the "knowledge base (rules)."

Surprisingly simple in Expert Systems is the basic concept of the inference engine, which uses two standard methods, that is, either *forward-chaining* (e.g., CLIPS that is well known even to students) or *backward-chaining* (applied in MYCIN) or both (e.g., ART). The production rules have a very straightforward form (Horn clauses): "`IF...THEN...`," for example, in MYCIN:

```
IF
   The site of the culture is blood                and
   The identity of the organism is not
     known with certainty                          and
   The stain of the organism is gramneg            and
   The morphology of the organism is rod           and
   The patient has been seriously burned
THEN
   There is weakly suggestive evidence (.4) that the
     identity of the organism is pseudomonas.
```

The number of rules in an Expert System varies from hundreds to thousands, depending on the application.

The following interesting element of similarity to the brain and its method of functioning is that the request for functionality of inference forces designers of Expert Systems to introduce the mechanism of *refraction* known in neurobiology. In Expert Systems *refraction* prohibits trivial loops of inference because a rule "cannot be fired" more than once for a specific set of facts. In neurophysiology, *refraction* means that a neuron cannot be stimulated again for a certain time after receiving stimulus.

Another important similarity to the model of the brain, which emerged as a "software engineering need" around 1982 during the development of Expert Systems, is the similarity of the *Rete pattern-matching algorithm* (71) to *connectionism-based* concepts and the behavior of a neural network. Let us discuss how it happened.

One of the basic technical problems of Expert Systems was the question of how to manipulate hundreds or even thousands of rules. When an Expert System starts, it faces an entry set of facts and later faces permanent changes in this set (emergence of new facts—conclusions and retractions of some old facts from the database). The facts imply which rules can be used; thus, a temporary set of facts is a very sensitive issue for a run of an Expert System.

The basic concept of the *Rete algorithm* is that facts are looking for rules during the inference process, and not rules for facts. Typically, every inference action (*firing*) during Expert System activity will only change a few facts in the fact list, for example, new facts are added, but it is also possible that some facts could be retracted. This will change the status of some rules, perhaps those waiting for this fact to complete its list of premises (we say that a rule is activated or instantiated), or the removal of a fact will deactivate certain rule(s) previously activated but waiting for firing, because certain facts will no longer be valid. The difference between activating and firing comes from the one-processor model of execution. Activated (i.e., ready because all premises are fulfilled) rules must wait (there are often priorities) for *firing* (inference action).

To "grasp" its similarity to neural networks, let us discuss the *Rete algorithm*[20].

- The first step after the system is started with a given set of rules is to compile the set of rules into a network. An example of such a network resulting from some simple rules is shown in Figure 2-23. The basic idea here is that even if the Expert System has several thousand rules, the set of "atomic" conditions used on the *Left Hand Side* of the rule (LHS) is very limited and much shorter than the number of rules. Thus, passing the "token" representing a given fact through properly connected "atomic" conditions will deterministically point to rule(s) that should be activated (if any) by this fact. Every "atomic" condition, no matter how many rules are used, is evaluated only once.
- The *Rete algorithm* is used in Expert Systems as a *recognition system* because new facts act like stimuli at the input of the neural network. The output from *Rete algorithm* are decisions about which rules could be used presently.

To understand Figure 2-23, Let us assume that among the rules of this Expert System, there are two illustrated in PROLOG notation:

```
new_fact1 :- a(4, 5), d(X, X), d(Y, 5).
new_fact2 :- a(X, 4), d(6, X), d(X, X).
```

where X, Y are free variables and 4,5,6, are constants.

[20] Kogge (17) classifies the Rete Network from an operational point of view as similar to *data flow graphs*.

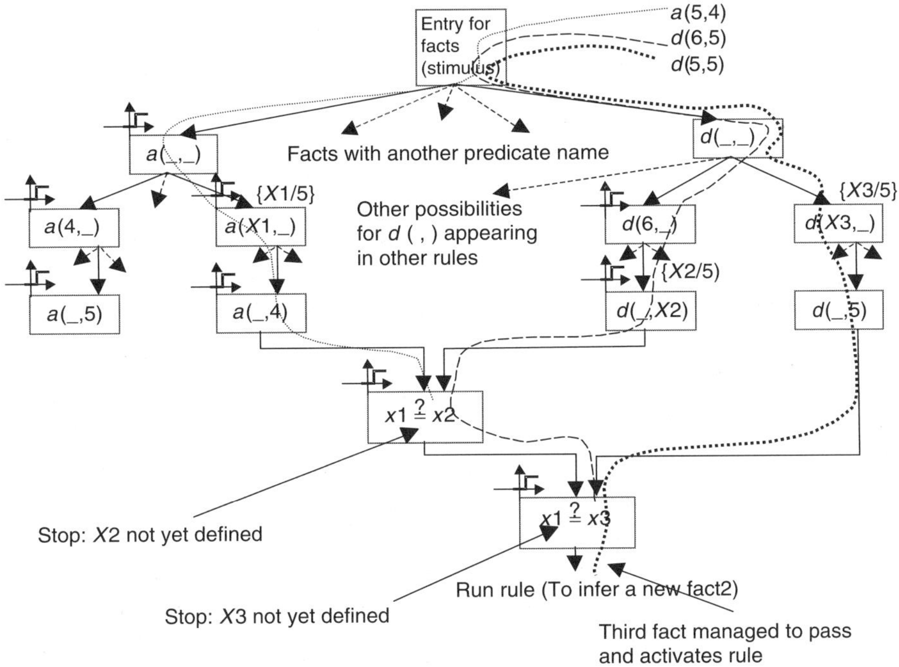

Figure 2-23. Example of so-called "Pattern and Join Networks" for *Rate algorithm.*

The preceding two rules causes the network to be constructed as in Figure 2-23. Expressions such as a(*X*, _) mean that there is a two-argument predicate a(,) where *X* is an unbound variable, and the second argument, which is denoted by_, is not essential.

Symbols 4, 5, 6 denote constants (integers).

The symbol

denotes the discriminator for a fact (stimulus): if the fact does not fulfill a given specification, it is not allowed to pass through the node.

Figure 2-23 demonstrates how three facts (stimuli) try to pass through a network generated by compiled rules. When trying to pass, they change the state of the network locally by binding free variables. Finally, only the third stimulus manages to successfully pass and start an action, that is, to make an inference.

The *professional intelligence* of a good Expert System is comparable with that of the human; however, it is closely restricted to a given domain. The importance of an Expert System lies in providing a human expert with a deterministic chance to immediately confirm or interactively verify a given difficult case through search in a *space of alternatives*. Another equivalent human expert may not be reachable within the time limits imposed by the case. Despite the high price of good Expert Systems, this solution can be cheaper and more reliable than to call for support from another human expert or committee of experts.

2.1.3.3. Determinism and Nondeterminism in Artificial Intelligence In general, *determinism* is defined as "*that every event, act, and decision is the inevitable consequence of antecedents*." Consequently, *nondeterminism* means, for AI, that despite prior inference processes or actions taken (if, e.g., a robots effectors are available), there is a certain probability that some unexpected events can happen that have not been calculated before (e.g., have been overlooked). Also, decisions taken under the threat of reality may be different than previously calculated. *Nondeterminism* can also be referred to as the *uncertainty* of the future.

Despite the fact that *nondeterminism* can be easily considered a threat to AI, it can also have some important *flavors* which should be selectively discussed. First, let us look at the possible sources of *nondeterminism*.

- A given problem may be observable and formally describable but becomes *nondeterministic* through its complexity. A good example (17) is an Expert System where let us say there are r rules, p patterns per rule, and w working memory elements; there are up to $r \times w^p$ combinations of rules and objects to try at each loop iteration. For nontrivial examples, this number easily exceeds the capacity of any current available computer.

  This means that even if we know what potentially is possible, because all data is at hand, we cannot calculate or predict every conclusion accurately. The *intelligent system* or human operator must make decisions on the basis of incomplete or approximated inferences, which cause that the future events do not completely depend upon the assumed antecedents we started with.

  On the basis of this approach, we can define the *formal border* between *determinism* and *nondeterminism*. This can be accomplished by giving specifications of problems with equivalence relations to other problems that we consider so complicated that they are *nondeterministic* for us. A "testing tool" for this border is the definition of the *Nondeterministic Turing Machine* (NDTM), which is fully described in Section 3.4.2. Its formal definition is also illustrated there.

  Precisely speaking, this formal border should be called a *nondeterministic polynomial* (NP). The border is created by a set of problems that can be solved in polynomial time on the NDTM machine. Behind this border there is an *outer space* of much more complicated (also *nondeterministic*) problems.

- There is another possible source of *nondeterminism* in the area of *artificial intelligence* problems, which is related to real life and not to abstract mathematical considerations, such as those given earlier.

Such problems are partially *observable* and partially *describable*. Our approximation of problem-solving algorithms is based on "a posterior" (i.e., experimental) probability and on regularity of behavior in the process.

The simplest example is the coin-tossing process, where we can get "heads or tails" or the coin can even land on its edge. Another example can be an autonomous, intelligent robot that is observing a big building and is trying to predict objects hidden behind it. Theoretically, such a robot can create a space of all the possibilities that could be behind the building (on the basis of its prior experience) and could try to build a plan of future actions, taking into account all of those possibilities. However, in this case, the robot would fall into the pit of complexity discussed in the previous section.

As has been noted there are also important *flavors* attracting us to *nondeterminism*.

First is that the acceptance of *nondeterminism* allows us to have extremely short and clear algorithms for class NP problems. For example, the famous "Hamiltonian cycle" problem, which is NP, can have an algorithm such as this (31):

```
    V1  ←  1                     ; starting vertex
    S  ←  (2, 3, ..., n)         ; vertices to be visited
    cost  ←  0                   ; total cost
    nv  ←  1                     ; number of vertices already
                                     visited
repeat while successor(vnv) ≠ 0 ; (successor(v)
                               denotes set of vertices that
                               can be reached from vertex v,
                               that is, there are no
                               circuits that do not pass
                               through all vertices)
    vnv-1  ←  choice(successor(vnv));
    nv  ←  nv + 1;
    cost  ←  cost + cost(arc(vnv-1, vnv));
end repeat
if nv = 1 and cost ≤ b than SUCCESS stop
                               else FAIL;
```

where *choice[S]* is a special instruction of the NDTM that creates as many copies of the current state of the machine as there are elements in the set S.

When implemented on single-processor computers, such an algorithm is difficult to execute. However, if we assume a molecular model of computations such as those of Adleman's DNA computer (5), then this algorithm starts to be feasible from the implementation point of view.

Thus, the *flavor* here is the short, clear structure of the algorithm and a powerful model of computations—if *nondeterminism* is posed as a principle and not as an obstacle.

The second source of *flavor* resulting from *nondeterminism* is applicability of *probabilistic algorithms*. *Probabilistic algorithms* can be defined in at least three ways (311). Here is one of those definitions:

> *The probabilistic algorithm is a polynomial algorithm, which for the problem of sufficiently big size, finds a solution with the probability* $c > 0$*, where* c *is a constant.*

From the point of view of an individual being (living alone) that is under any kind of pressure, *probabilistic algorithms* are dangerous. *Deterministic algorithms* are much more suitable (safe).

However, if we consider a *social structure of any type of agents*, for example, of ants, where a loss of some *agents* (*beings*) is not a threat for the whole *social structure*, even paying off if a solution can be found, *probabilistic algorithms* are suitable. Another gain is that *probabilistic algorithms* can be polynomial for NP problems. This implies that the complexity of brain and behavior of a single *being* can be significantly simplified.

This demonstrates how *social structures* as a whole can be so powerful. If we assume that an individual *agents* (*beings*) thinking is "an independent experiment," then the probability that the *social structure* will be awarded with a solution is

$$P(r, s) = \frac{r!}{s!(r-s)!} p^s (1-c)^{r-s}$$

where: r — number of *agents (beings)*
s — number of *agents (beings)* that could discover the same solution
c — probability that a single *being* will be successful while applying the *probabilistic algorithm*

Probability $P(\ldots)$ will quickly approach value 1. Thus, even a few *agents* in the *social structure* are sufficient. Moreover, if any language or other form of cooperation is introduced, experiments will get no more independent and the probability of cooperative success will rapidly grow.

2.1.4. Review of the Individual Intelligence of Animals

Charles Darwin's theory of evolution suggesting common ancestors for humans and animals implies that animals should exhibit varying degrees of human characteristics, including *intelligence* similar to human *intelligence*.

However, comparative psychologists, such as D. McFarland (74), soon realized that measuring animal *intelligence* turned out to be more difficult than it sounded. Levels of animal *intelligence* are not arranged in linear ways along our order of species. Often a given animal species displays *intelligence* low in one test and very high in another. The border between such extreme cases can be very slight; for example, zebras are generally slow to learn to approach one pattern instead of another for food, unless the patterns happen to be narrow stripes versus wide stripes, in which case *zebras reach genius levels* (75).

The difficulty with assessing animal *intelligence* has been shown in animal research:

- Animals have various perception systems that affect their cognition (76). For example, rats perform poorly when they have to find an object that looks different from the others, but do very well when they have to find an object that smells different (77). Cats see more of red colors than humans do (the spectrum is shifted). Dogs, who are commonly considered by humans as intelligent animals have relatively weak eyes (are short-sighted) but have an excellent sense of smell. Bulls can see only in black and white, but when an object is moving, it is seen more clearly. Animals lower down the evolutionary tree are often not equipped with three-dimensional vision (stereopsis), and see two-dimensional pictures separately with each eye (frogs). Additionally, some animals can see only moving objects (e.g., frogs).
- B.L. Whorf (78) proposed the "linguistic relativity hypothesis[21]" saying "*the language a person speaks largely determines the nature of that persons thoughts.*" Despite many experiments (79) that question this important and conclusive statement and claim that Whorf's hypothesis "*goes too far with the statement on direct relation between language and thought,*" we have to keep in mind that language is the least a important tool for thinking.

  From the point of view of assigning *intelligence* to animals, Whorf's hypothesis is of key importance and can be considered as a reasonable starting point for research. Without explaining the language or communication system of a given species or investigating in any way how to communicate with them, designing IQ tests for animals is almost fruitless; otherwise, the concept of testing IQ must be dramatically changed. With the traditional approach, we have to at least *communicate* with the animal being tested, informing them that a *food reward* is a solution for a given problem (of course, from the animal's point of view).

  To support these statements, it is useful to look at research with chimpanzees (80), who cannot speak a human-type language because their vocal tract is not adapted to the process of sound production. In the 1960s and 1970s, Allen and Beatrice Gardner managed to successfully teach the chimpanzee named Washoe (81), to use the sign language of deaf people. However, the most impressive achievement in this direction was with one pygmy chimpanzee, Kanzi, who learned a special language (Yerkish), designed by researchers at Emory University to communicate[22]

[21] Also referred as "Sapir-Whorf Hypothesis" or "Whorfianism".

[22] The concept of this communicative language was based on the use of icons representing words, displayed on a special board and later on a *touch-screen monitor*. Note here the successful use of the computer to provide a communication link between two different species, human and chimpanzee.

with chimpanzees, just by observing how her mother was trained!

Kanzi's performance quickly surpassed that of her mother and of every other chimp the researchers were testing; Kanzi reached a level of 13,000 "utterances" (82). Thus, with such systems, chimpanzees were even able to build language structures describing objects not named in the dictionary (e.g., orange ≡ red apple).

Remarkable experiments (83) have been reported on teaching an African gray parrot (named Alex) to make human sounds and to understand the meaning of some words. Alex was able to successfully answer questions, such as "WHAT COLOR IS THE CIRCLE?," given among some objects in front of the parrot, even without food reinforcement. Alex was also able to use numbers up to six in a striking way.

With most other species, with the exception of dolphins, researchers have not been so successful. Some successful attempts to teach bottlenose dolphins have been reported (84). The dolphins were given visual commands like "PIPE FETCH GATE" (take the piece of pipe to the pool gate). Longer sentences were also used and the grammar was designed in such a way that about 2000 sentences could be constructed, of which only a few were explicitly taught. Chance was only four percent, but the dolphins performed at about 65 percent accuracy. It was impressive that the dolphins responded correctly to suddenly introduced sentences containing major innovations, such as "PIPE TAIL-TOUCH PIPE OVER" (touch the pipe with your tail, then jump over it). Based on the complexity of such experiments and subsequent performance, dolphins can outperform chimpanzees (80).

We are stuck here with the problem of recognition, first, of what a language is for a given species, and later, how to recognize and somehow learn this language. In general, this task seems almost impossible, even assuming *computer-based translators and synthesizers*, because for millions of years different species have created totally different communication systems. Let us look at some examples of extremely different systems:

- ♦ Pheromone system used by ants
- ♦ Honeybee dance for communicating the location of food to others.

Conclusively, using language to assess *intelligence* in animals is not the best choice. This is similar with humans because vocabulary tests are only part of general individual *intelligence* assessment (see Section 2.1.2.2).

- With animals, we have to work on the fuzzy border between *instinct* and *intelligence* (85). Most animals live in narrow *niches* where their behavior must be extremely economical; simple instinct is quite sufficient there, and the neurological tool for running *higher intelligence* can be exorbitant from an energy point of view. Instinct provides, for example, *paramecium* with a negative chemotropic response to alkaline solution when it is dropped into its environment (*paramecium* will escape along the gradient of intensity). Another example of *instinct* is the "trial and error" behavior of a hen to solve the detour problem, such as when a pile of grain is visible behind a wire fence. We should also remember that *artificial intelligence* uses different forms of "trial and error" behavior as a most fundamental strategy. Even an intelligent human facing an unexpected problem automatically switches to "trial and error" behavior.

Some behavior is purely reflexive or instinctive (inherited). Any animal seeing danger responds by secreting adrenaline and undergoes Canon's Fear, Flight or Fight response, that is, stays in fear, runs away from danger, or confronts it.

It is said (85) that "*an animal has acted intelligently when, confronted with a problem situation, it*:

1. *Understands the situation*
2. *Invents the solution*
3. *Acts appropriately*"

Viaud illustrates (85) an example of a jaguar that was confronted with a large piece of meat behind some bars. On the left side there was a wall, and on the right side a square 3 × 3-yard obstacle. Access to the meat was only through backtracking from the bars and taking a detour around the obstacle on the right side. The jaguar facing this test performed very poorly, even though it was taught beforehand to detour around similar obstacles when compared to a dog that was able to solve this problem almost instantly. However, in its natural environment, hunting along curved riverbanks, the jaguar has been observed solving much more complicated detour problems. This means that a jaguar "*is mentally equipped with a proper problem-solving engine*" but is not able to apply it to any generalized problem, even if the "*basic language of hunger has been applied.*"

- Many researchers in *intelligence testing* underline the importance of tools as natural extensions of limbs, consciously designed, manufactured, and used by humans as well as by some birds and apes (80,85).

  However, we must be very careful because definition of a *tool* can be easily extended to also include language (see previous discussion), and to use as tools certain "natural processes" such as fire or water to get a desired result. Finally, instead of designing a mechanical lift, we can organize a *social structure* which will do the same thing. In other words, we can hunt a deer with a gun (tool), or like wolves do, by "chasing and surrounding it in a specific way[23]." It is also our unflattering human habit to find a subordinate person, or any type of "a workman" to do such tedious work for us instead of thinking.

  It is important to conclude here that synergy is a tool, because this book focuses on *collective intelligence*, and as is demonstrated, *collective*

[23] As the central part of the group of wolves slows down, so does the deer, instinctively trying to save energy for the end of this fatal race. In the meantime, the fastest wolves, on both sides, try (behind the cover of bush or terrain) to overtake the deer, and at the proper moment, to surround, stop, and attack it.

intelligence can emerge even without the use of language, simply on the basis of reacting to observations of another *being* and/or the environment around it.

Now, let us discuss possible IQ tests for animals.

The *intelligence* of animals seems to reach the highest level with chimpanzees and dolphins. The moment a child starts to use language, it immediately outperforms the *intelligence* of chimpanzees; thus, only selected parts of IQ tests given to small children can be used when working with animals. Let us discuss several approaches that have applied.

Researchers have used two-year-old monkeys and chimpanzees to determine *intelligence* factors. The monkeys were able to identify a physical representation, such as matching Xs. They could perceive similarities in relationships, but could not use them to solve conceptual matching problems.

For example, Thompson et al (86) trained chimpanzees and monkeys in the use of matching symbols and asked them to show relationships between identical and different pairs of symbols, namely, letters AA, BB, CC, and YZ. For instance, if the chimps and monkeys were shown an X, and later shown an X and Y, both animals were able to match the Xs. When the animals were shown XY, then shown AA and AB, they were able to match the XY with the AB because they perceived that the XY and AB were somehow similar. When each was taught that a symbol, such as a triangle, was a representative of *similarity*, chimpanzees could use this symbol to determine relationships. The monkeys could learn that the triangle "meant" similar but were unable to apply the use of this symbol in matching problems.

Perhaps the most significant approach that is suitable for testing the perception and inference abilities of animals and allowing us to compare their performance are *intelligence* tests based on the discrimination approach. These are interesting from the point of view of *intelligence* testing, because they require (usually visual) recognition of several situations, discovering and learning of general rules, and finally, application of those rules to be awarded with food. Notice that such tests are language-free, that is, the sole communication issue is to make the animal aware of the food-for-problem-solving situation. Food discovery (or not) is the solely expected response.

The concept of testing is as follows:

1. The animal is given a series of discrimination problems. This provides a learning set to discover a rule.
2. Objects change from problem to problem.
3. The animal has to discover the general rule for under which object there is a hidden food reward.

Passinham's (87) types of discrimination problems are given in Figure 2-24.

(a) Simple discrimination: the arrow indicates the correct choice.

(b) Reversal task: the animal has to reverse its originally correct choice.

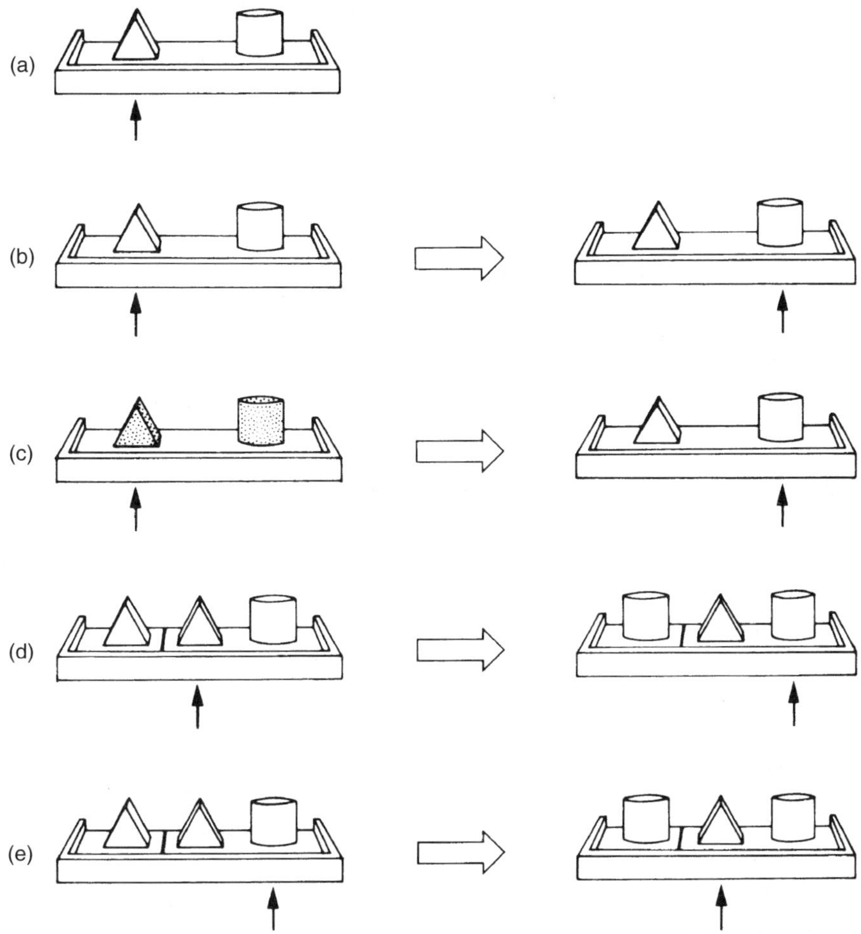

Figure 2-24. Types of discrimination tess. With permission from McFarland D. Animal behavior, 2nd ed. Longman, 1993.

(c) Conditional task: one object is correct when both are gray; the other, when both are white.

(d) Matching task: the animal has to match the sample on the left side of the tray.

(e) Oddity task: the animal has to choose the odd man out.

The importance of a test of this type is that when animals are ranked in terms of their rate of improvement over a series of problems, their rank can be predicted from an index of brain development. This index is an estimate of the number of nerve cells in the brain that are additional to those needed for the control of body functions. Such tests are similar to those used for humans.

Figure 2-25 shows a comparison of species with discrimination tests (87).

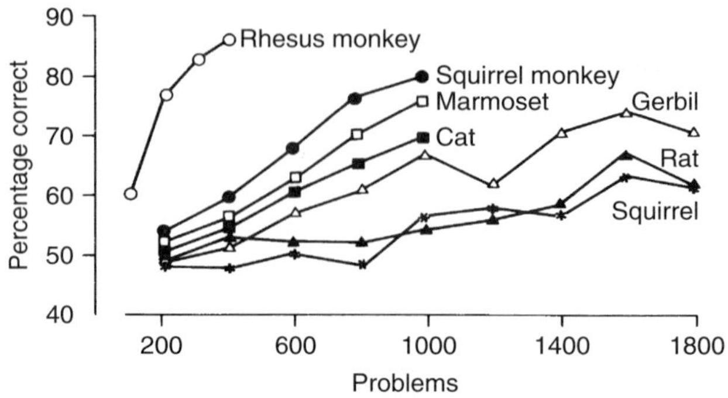

Figure 2-25. Comparison of intelligence of different mammals based on discrimination tests. With permission from D. McFarland, *Animal behavior*, 2nd ed., Longman, 1993.

Conclusively, we suggest that animal *intelligence* evaluation can be based on the same principles, which are proposed later in the book for defining and calculating an *intelligence* quotient for *social structures* (IQS) of all *beings*.

1. The IQ value should be a data structure of the function type (generalized surface), at least over time (given to solve a given problem), and the domain of problems.
2. The function mentioned here should express the probability that the given problem will be solved, for example, in a certain time.
3. The domain of the problems should be given not as a set of explicit problems directly, but as a series of complex values indirectly addressing certain problems.
4. This method can be compared with different problem-solving apparatus, for example, by pigeons the navigational ability used versus, for example, the problem-solving ability of a human playing a specific game.
5. This proposal is not contradictory to concepts of assessing *intelligence* based on the ability to generalize problem-solving methods. Defining *intelligence* through a generalized surface will give, for example, in the pigeon example, only a local maximum for pigeon, whereas another *being* able to generalize will have the significant area of his IQ-surface up on scale, above pigeon results.

2.2. THE CONCEPT OF COLLECTIVE INTELLIGENCE (CI)

It is a well-known situation that before a certain notion "crystallizes," there are other competitive terms in use that are usually trying to capture parts or specific elements of a given phenomenon. When we take a look at the following set of terms, it can be concluded that the concept of *collective intelligence* is hidden under this set of related terms, which refer to our intuition and/or observation of real life.

- Collective behavior
- Swarm intelligence
- Herd intelligence
- Bacterial communities
- Synergy
- Social cooperation
- Emerging behavior
- Collective awareness
- Collective mind
- Mind of the swarm
- Global brain
- Collective processor
- Social brain, social organism, social will . . . and so forth.

The concept of *collective intelligence* encompasses all of these terms.

First, we will try to give an entry, that is, not a very formal, but a maximally universal definition of *collective intelligence* that will be valid for all predictable types of beings and agents. The formal definition of *collective intelligence* is given in Section 3.1. The next Section (2.2.1) is devoted to analyzing many other concepts or definitions that could be related to the definition of *collective intelligence* or are trying to cover a related semantic area.

First, we will list the conditions necessary or sufficient for defining *collective intelligence*. The most important conditions will have specific labels for future reference.

"G": For *collective intelligence*, it is necessary to have at least two interacting *beings* or *agents*. This is required a priori by the first component of the term, that is, *collective*. The label **G** is mnemonic for group.

"A or B": For *collective intelligence*, it is necessary to have two or more subjects for interaction: ***Agents*** or ***Beings***. However, here we come to the first difficulty — regarding the definitions of *agent* and *being*. Russel and Norvig (88) give a very short definition of an *agent* from the AI point of view:

> *An Agent is just something that perceives and acts.*

In this book, the term *agent* is used because we suggest that the property of being *alive* is not always fulfilled or questioned. In contrast, the term *being will suggest something that perceives and acts and is alive.*

This approach is necessary because these terms are very fuzzy. Commonly, *collective intelligence* has been by default associated with *live* creatures.

Recent rapid development of research on *software intelligent agents* existing in the computer sense, and our considerations here, demonstrate undoubtedly that *collective intelligence* can be defined in the computer–network environment that is (so far) considered as *not supported by any form of life*.

Moreover, the use of the terms *agent–being* proposed here can resolve our problem of what to call prions[24] and viruses, that is, very low-level forms of biologic life on earth.

Another problem that must be mentioned is that this definition (88) specifies nothing about the cohesion of *agents*, and it says nothing about whether any well-defined border exists between an *agent* and its immediately surrounding environment.

"I": Interaction is the fundamental requirement for *collective intelligence*. The problem is that the spectrum of possible patterns of interaction ranges from simple, mutual, visual observation, through to the release of pheromones into the environment, absorption of pieces of DNA discovered in the environment, and up to sophisticated language and education systems.

"PS": Problem-**S**olving ability is necessary; however, this property is by default fulfilled by the definition of *agent* or *being* participating in the *collective intelligence* phenomenon.

The biggest problem with the preceding properties is that they are mutually overlapping; thus, at the present state of formalization we cannot tell which ones of them are necessary and which are independent from the others.

For example:

- Can "people with multiple personalities" create *collective intelligence* inside "one *being*?"
- Can we say that our body is a *social structure* of cooperating single cells displaying *collective intelligence*?
- If "transistors or VLSI circuits" are considered components of an *intelligent* computer, can they be nominated as *beings* or *agents* creating a *collective intelligence*, which we perceive as the single, individual *intelligence* of this computer?

The problems with defining *collective intelligence* are eased if we consider *collective intelligence* as a certain temporary property of a *social structure* or a group of interacting *agents–beings*. This property can emerge under certain

[24] A microscopic protein particle similar to a virus but lacking nucleic acid, thought to be the infectious agent responsible for scrapie and certain other degenerative diseases of the nervous system.

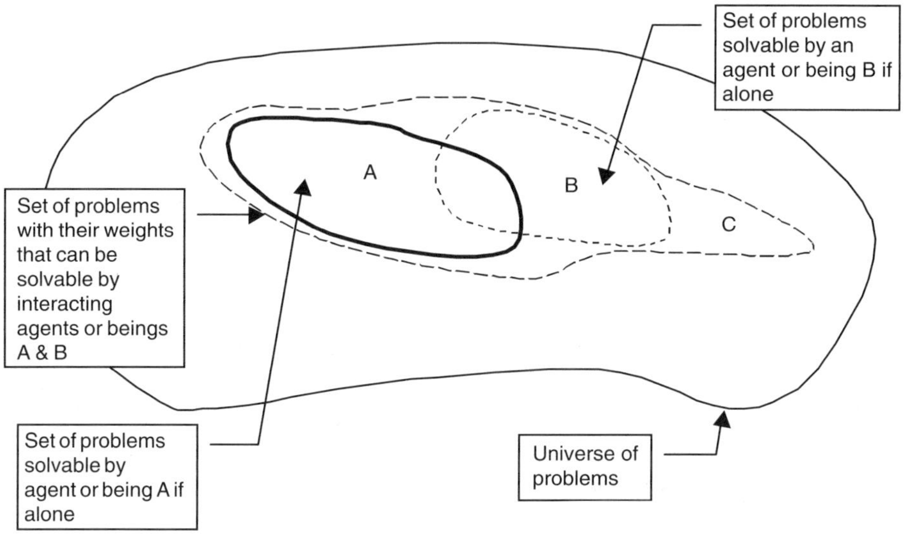

Figure 2-26. Nonformal definition of *collective intelligence*.

circumstances and can also vanish, leaving *agents* or *beings* (at least most of them) in the same state as before. A nonformal, descriptive definition of *collective intelligence* is illustrated in Figure 2-26.

We cannot simply say that *agents* or *beings*, A or B are *collectively intelligent* if and only if $A \cup B \subset C$. A counter-example is a case where an *agent* or *being*, let us say A, voluntarily (or is forced to do so!) devotes some of its abilities to amplify specific abilities of another *agent–being* B, either in an emergency, or if those abilities of B are more valuable than the abilities of A. Similar considerations lead us to the conclusion that a definition of *collective intelligence* should be written like this:

DEFINITION 4: COLLECTIVE INTELLIGENCE (NONFORMAL)

We can say that the phenomenon of *collective intelligence* has emerged in a *social structure* of interacting *agents or beings*, over a certain period, if and only if the weighted sum of problems they can solve together as a *social structure* is higher during the whole period than the sum of problems weighted in the same way that can be solved by the *agents or beings* when not interacting.

Remarks:

- This definition allows the emergence of *collective intelligence* in *social structures* based on social inequalities or under the pressure of specific situations, for example, emergencies. However, the unselfishness, altruism, or self-sacrifice of some *agents* or *beings* can significantly magnify the *collective intelligence*, especially if they are leaders.

- Observe that this definition provides (theoretically only) a primitive prototype measure of *collective intelligence* based on the simple subtraction of weighted sums of problems.

  With this approach we can have *positive*, *zero*, and *negative collective intelligence*, which seems strange initially. Real life easily provides many examples in a *social structure* when a situation deteriorates at a certain point (e.g., because of unrest, conflicts, etc.), which implies that it will become suddenly unable to solve problems that could easily be solved by some members alone, if not disturbed.
- The measured value of *collective intelligence* for a given *social structure* can be "in waves," as a function of time over certain periods of time, depending upon the development of the situation in the *social structure*.
- Problems are weighted for this definition of *collective intelligence* — this is obvious in certain cases only from a specific point of view. A good example is when a group of very weak students suddenly create a highly cooperative, temporary *social structure* to collectively cheat on a difficult exam. The *collective intelligence* of such a temporarily emerged *social structure* can peak to levels above the experience and knowledge of professors who are experienced with many methods of cheating.

Perhaps this definition looks good, but its main drawback is its unproductivity — not allowing us to provide any efficient *collective intelligence* measure for evaluation and comparison of *social structures*.

The remedy for this is a more suitable (formal, and allowing computability) definition of *collective intelligence* which is be given in Section 3.1.

2.2.1. Symptoms of Collective Intelligence in the World of Animals

This section attempts to give an overview of forms of *collective intelligence* in animals. In some cases *collective intelligence* is not clearly manifested or may take forms very different from patterns observable among human beings in their social structures. This is logical because animal biologic forms and communication systems are also very different from human ones.

On the basis of available examples, this section assures readers that the mathematical model of *collective intelligence* proposed in this book is valid for animals as well.

It is widely assumed that animals "do not think, but rather follow instinct." To successfully discuss the issue of *collective intelligence*, first we must relate it to the notion of *instinct*. Let us look at a common encyclopedia definition of instinct.

Instinct in zoology and psychology, innate programming typical of a particular animal species that organizes complex patterns of animal behavior, enabling members of a species to respond appropriately to a wide range of situations in the natural world. Such behaviors are usually complex patterns of responses to particular stimuli, often typical of feeding, mating, parenting, and expression of aggression. Instinctive behaviors are vitally important in helping an animal adapt to its particular ecological environment.

Instinctive behaviors can be extremely complex even in relatively simple animals. An example is the remarkable navigational and communication skills possessed by honeybees. A worker bee may fly a quarter of a mile or more from the hive in search of flowers that are a good source of food. When it finds a source, the bee is able to calculate a true course back to the hive, allowing for wind and for apparent movement of the sun. Upon returning to the hive, it communicates the location of the food through a so-called dance that conveys information about distance and direction. Other bees use this information to go directly to the food.[25]

Let us use a slightly modified definition to provide interface with the nonformal definition of *collective intelligence* (CI).

DEFINITION 5: INSTINCT AS AN IMPRINTED COMPUTATIONAL PROCESS

Instinct is defined as a set of computational processes, internal to a considered being and imprinted on the being by *evolution* to solve specific problems.

LEMMA: RELATION BETWEEN *COLLECTIVE INTELLIGENCE* AND *INSTINCT*

The *collective intelligence* of lower beings results from concurrent and partially coordinated actions, fired by instinct-related computational processes to solve problems in easier (more economical) ways, or ways that are too difficult for a single being.

The above lemma assumes that some components of instinct must exist to enable interfacing of problem-solving processes run by individual beings to provide cooperation or interaction. For beings gifted with consciousness, this interfacing is provided as conscious profit and loss evaluation.

The intention of these two definitions is to remove difficulties in conceptual differentiation between individual and group behavior. Now *collective intelligence* can be considered an extension of instinct for unconscious beings. At the human mental level *collective intelligence* results more from *consciousness* than from *instinctual* behavior.

[25] Encarta® 98 Encyclopedia. Microsoft Corporation.

2.2.1.1 Is a Bacterial Colony Collectively Intelligent? Here is a short description of bacteria derived from some recent encyclopedia definitions.

> Bacteria are classified as prokaryotes, that is, their cells have no internal membranes. They are subclassified into archaebacteria and eubacteria. Both developed from a common ancestor. Archaebacteria live mainly in high-temperature environments, such as hot springs, where no other life forms can grow. The eubacteria include all other bacteria. A large number of them, including the cyanobacteria, are called phototrophs (i.e., are able to capture the sun's energy through photosynthesis). Bacteria that require oxygen are called aerobic bacteria (aerobes). Those that live without oxygen are called anaerobes. Both aerobes and anaerobes can be either phototrophic or nonphototrophic.
>
> The shape is also used to classify bacteria. Spherical bacteria are called cocci; corkscrew-shaped, spirilla or spirochetes; rod-shaped, bacilli; and threadlike, filamentous. Some bacteria, called pleiomorphic, take various forms depending on conditions.
>
> Bacteria are also classified as gram-negative or gram-positive, according to the composition of their cell wall and how it holds the laboratory stain called Gram's stain.
>
> The deoxyribonucleic acid (DNA) in bacteria has a circular arrangement, not the strands that exist in most cells. Bacteria often have additional genes on smaller rings called plasmids. Bacterial DNA is not enclosed in a nucleus, as is the DNA of eukaryotic cells.
>
> Many bacteria have small protrusions from their outside surface called pili. These hairlike outgrowths assist the bacteria in attaching to surfaces. Flagella are hairlike extensions found at either end or both ends of a bacterium or on its body surface. Flagella beat in a circular motion to move the bacterium.
>
> The photosynthetic reaction in many phototrophic bacteria differs from that in plants. Anaerobic phototrophic bacteria use the gas hydrogen sulfide instead of water, releasing sulfur rather than oxygen as a waste product. Another type of bacteria, called chemolithotrophy bacteria, obtain energy from inorganic compounds such as ammonia. Chemolithotrophs live near deep-sea vents, cracks in the earth, where magma (molten rock) heats sea water that seeps into the cracks. Other bacteria use either fermentation or respiration to get energy from organic compounds such as sugars. The process of fermentation takes place in an anaerobic environment. Respiration is a more complex process that requires oxygen to yield energy.
>
> A bacterium reproduces by a process called binary fission. First the DNA is copied; then the outer membrane of the bacterium pinches inward, dividing the bacterium into two identical cells. Binary fission does not provide bacteria with a way to exchange genetic information. Bacteria transfer genetic material in a process called conjugation, in which one bacterium attaches itself to another bacterium and introduces DNA directly into it by using one of its pili.

The preceding description shows that a single bacterium is a well-defined active agent or being, that is, properties **"A or B"** and **"PS"** are firmly fulfilled.

Thus, next we must demonstrate properties **"G"** and **"I"**, that is, interactive existence in a group, which are necessary conditions for the *collective intelligence* phenomenon.

Finally, we must find some evidence showing that the property of *collective intelligence* emerges in specific situations in bacterial colonies.

Working with the problem of resistance of bacteria against drugs, it has been discovered that even if a given bacterial organism was susceptible to an antimicrobial agent when tested in isolation, the same organism appeared resistant when protected by other members of its normal community.

Moreover, it has been discovered that this is a general habit for bacteria. Probably less than 1 percent of bacteria can be artificially grown and isolated in pure cultures from the companion strains of their natural habitat. These reciprocally supporting strains need each other and behave like the specialized cells of an animal (89).

Soil bacteria associate in teams of many cooperative types of strains. Bacteria proliferate and evolve as consortia, bioaggregates, biofilms, and other biologic networks in which the synergisms between associated organisms determine the success or failure of the entire association as opposed to the success of solitary individuals (90).

This sudden change in the perception of bacteria by researchers comes because, for a long time bacteria were investigated through the study of purely "in vitro cultures" that displayed only their fundamental abilities. It was only later that successive discoveries indicated that the bacterial world is original and more complex than initial observations on parasitic strains had led bacteriologists to believe. On this basis we can confirm that bacteria possess the property "**G**."

The next question involves the type of interaction between bacteria, that is, how they communicate; which language is used—this is necessary to demonstrate property "**I**."

With a bacterial colony there are two major possible methods of communicating for cooperation (91):

- Through chemical outpourings with which one group transmits its findings to all those in its vicinity; or
- Through transfer of fragments of genetic material, from one end of the population to the other. This is a very powerful method of transferring knowledge. According to D. Freifelder (15), there are several types of such transfers, called DNA recombinations:

  Transformation: where DNA is released to the environment by the death of a donor bacterium entering a recipient cell

  Transduction: in which a phage[26] carrying cellular DNA, picked up by growth in a donor bacterium, injects this DNA into a recipient bacterium

  Conjugation: in which DNA from an Hfr[27] cell is transferred from one cell to another by cell–cell contact

[26] A virus that infects and lyses certain bacteria.

[27] Hfr (High frequency recombinant) strains transfer genes at a much higher rate.

These methods are much more than enough to provide very efficient communication and knowledge-transfer not only between members of a bacterial colony, but also between different types of bacteria.

On this basis and observation of the growth and behavior of bacterial colonies, several microbiologists have started to claim the *collective intelligence* of bacterial colonies (92–94), and so forth. Some authors, for example, Jacob and Shapiro, have even started to use terms such as *the networked bacterial brain*, *bacterial wisdom* (95) or to consider bacterial colonies[28] as "a computer to solve environmental problems."

The conclusion about the existence of *collective intelligence* on the level of bacterial colonies has been also strengthened by the so-called Proliferation Theory (e.g., 96–98) saying that

> ... biological organization arises through the association of evolving systems, as well as through the mutation and genetic recombination of these systems. Higher levels of order thus gradually emerge from lower levels ...

The Proliferation Theory assumes that the sequence of development of life on earth is as given in Figure 2-27.

The Proliferation Theory can even be considered to the one of the main arguments to support the computational model of *collective intelligence* given in section 3 of this book. The Random PROLOG model of computations, which is the kernel of this model, assumes necessity of structured computational space through use of membranes or incomplete membranes. Please observe in Figure 2-27 that the stages of evolution of life are similar to stages of increasing complexity of *computational space (CS)* used for formalization of *collective intelligence*.

2.2.1.2. The Collective Intelligence of Social Insects First let us discuss the general characteristics of insects as *beings*. Insects are the largest class in the animal world, with nearly one million known species. This class is distributed throughout the world in essentially all environments, reaching the greatest number and variety in the tropics. *Insecta* as a class is divided into two subclasses: the *Apterygota*, wingless insects and the *pterygota*, including the greater number of insects, most of which have wings in the adult form. Insects vary in size from less than 0.25 mm to about 30 cm in length when fully grown. They are the most highly developed class of invertebrates. In their living and feeding habits, insects exhibit extreme variation. Some insects are scavengers or predators, and others are parasites. Certain anatomical elements are common to the entire class. Adult insects have bodies composed of three parts — head, thorax, and abdomen, each of which is composed of a number of segments. On the head are two antennas, a pair of jaws, a pair of auxiliary jaws, and a fused second pair of accessory jaws. In some insects, the antennas carry organs of smell and touch. Insect mouths are often adapted for piercing and sucking rather than for biting. All insects have

[28] See also *http://star.tau.ac.il/~inon/wisdom1/preprint.html*

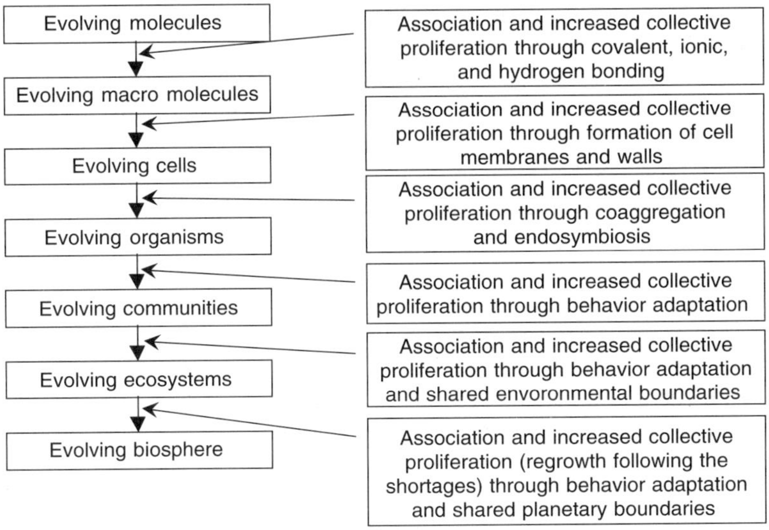

Figure 2-27. Proliferation Theory on development of life on Earth.

three pairs of legs, each pair growing from a different part of the thorax. In winged insects, the wings, usually four in number, grow from the thorax.

The insect nervous system centers around a nerve cord that runs from the head to the abdomen along the underside of the body. The brain receives stimuli from the antennas and from the eyes, which are of two types: compound and simple. Each of the two compound eyes contains from 6 to 28,000 or more light-sensitive structures.

From our point of view, what is most important is that insects such as bees, ants, and termites have elaborate, very obvious, and sophisticated social structures. Despite the fact that *collective intelligence* can even emerge with "just two" interacting *beings*, we should keep in mind the rule (which is probably true):

> The lower the individual intelligence of beings, the higher should be the number of members of a given social structure for emergence and amplification of the *collective intelligence* property.

Because of the restricted size of this book, and the available convincing research resources (e.g., 99,100) to support discussion of *collective intelligence*, we focus mainly on the symptoms of *collective intelligence* in ants and honeybees, and only remark briefly on other species.

The Social Structures of Ants

The *social structures* of ants are probably the best place to demonstrate that the *collective intelligence* property has really emerged, and has been amplified to a comparatively high level. This is due to the easy observation of ant nests and on the basis of a large library of research papers that demonstrate how powerful simulation models of ant colonies are when used to solve even hard problems, such as the "traveling salesman problem" (101).

If a single ant is observed, it is even difficult to claim that it is an intelligent being, its behavior is quasi-chaotic, and if left alone, the ant will not survive for a long period.

The single ant can be easily considered (and successfully simulated) as an automata, simply responding to stimulus coming from the environment. However, if we consider ants in a *social structure*, suddenly we find them displaying *collective intelligence* and behavior similar to that of beings in our cities. The following is an overview of the *social structure* of ants[29].

THEORETICAL ANT ORGANIZATION. Ants are social animals that tend to live in highly organized and regulated colonies. At the center of each colony is the nest. In the center of the nest there are one or more female reproductives, of the queen caste, which tend to be immobile egg-laying machines. The queen is attended by specialized workers (queen's attendants) who clean and feed her. Some of the worker ants (nursery workers) remove the newly laid eggs and take them to nursery areas where they tend them until they become adults. The young develop into a number of castes, such as replacement workers, replacement soldiers, and replacement reproductives. In many cases replacement reproductives are only produced after the death of queen(s) or king(s).

The general organization includes the fact that the nest is protected from attack by a series of guardians, or soldier ants. Food is gathered by foraging workers from outside the nest. Thus a caste system exists, whereby each ant has a specific role within the community and different morphology to meet the needs of that role. The castes, such as the soldiers, the workers, and the reproductive ants, are all morphologically different. This system of cooperation between specific castes allows for the success of a society as complex as an ant colony.

Communications between individuals is essential to maintain the colony as a stable entity. Hölldobler (73) reviewed communication in ants and other social insects and recognized twelve functional response categories:

1. Alarm response
2. Simple attraction
3. Recruitment, as to a new food source or nest site
4. Grooming, including assisting individuals to shed their skin during moulting
5. Trophallaxis (the exchange of oral and anal fluids)
6. Exchange of solid food particles
7. Group effect; either facilitating or inhibiting a given activity
8. Recognition of both nest mates and members of a particular caste

[29] This description is based on research cooperation with Prof. R.H. MEAKINS. The title of the research is "An evaluation measure of the *collective intelligence* of ants"

9. Caste determination
10. Control of competing reproductives
11. Territorial and home range signals and nest markers
12. Sexual communication

The system developed appears to be a mixture of tactile responses and the release of specific chemical substances, pheromones that initiate specific responses. O.E. Wilson (102) stated that the complex social behavior of ants was mediated mainly by chemoreceptors.

Here we introduce the term semiochemicals, which are substances used in both inter- and intra- specific communication, and which can be divided into pheromones, allomones, and kairomones, on the basis of their mode of effect. For example, social insects tend to have a queen pheromone, produced by the queen, the result of which is to prevent any female larva from becoming sexually mature. In this way the queen controls the nest, but when she dies, is rapidly replaced. Reproductive males (kings) may secrete a similar inhibitor substance in cases where only one king exists.

To maintain an ant colony, there are several types of necessary communication:

1. Between foraging workers as to the type and whereabouts of food
2. Between workers as to where food will be stored
3. Between the queen's attendants and the queen
4. Between the queen's attendants and other workers
5. Between soldiers to warn of danger and to repair damage afterwards

The following pheromones are fundamental for ant communication:

Pheromone 1. In many ant and termite colonies there is an alarm pheromone produced by the soldiers when the nest is attacked by a predator of ants eggs, such as an anteater or aardvark. The soldiers respond by crowding the area under attack and biting the aggressor or squirting it with substances such as formic acid. The extent of the pheromone used may determine whether the nest is abandoned, and the eggs and the queen moved to a safer location, that is, as in the case of fire or flood.

Pheromone 2. The pheromone secreted by the queen and used (as mentioned earlier) to suppress the development of reproductives is established in many insect groups. In many cases a king pheromone also exists to suppress the development of other reproductive males.

Pheromone 3. Many ants are believed to mark trails within the nest and outside it using pheromones (trail markers). The more recent the pheromone marking and the higher the intensity, the greater the stimuli, and so the foragers or workers know which trail to follow.

The complexity of an ant community can be understood more easily by noting that there are certain job descriptions and areas of activity allocated to the different castes in the nest.

1. The queen is the only active female reproductive and is the source of new replacement individuals. The much smaller male, the male reproductive, is often found living with her.
2. The queen's attendants stay around the queen feeding her, removing her waste products, and moving the eggs to the nursery, often by handing them over to the nursery workers.
3. The nursery workers tend and feed the developing eggs until they are adult.
4. The soldiers guard the nest at all times and remain at the periphery of the nest.
5. The foragers leave the nest to collect food and return it to workers in the nest.
6. Food distribution workers probably take the food from the foragers and deliver it to the individuals within the community.

Let us investigate what the "problem-solving ability" of a group of cooperating and communicating ants entails. Because different types of ants have different visual and communication systems, the best approach may be to analyze simulation models of cooperating ants.

The first system was introduced in 1992 by M. Dorigo, and was called the Ant System (AS). AS resulted from research on computational *intelligence* approaches to combinatorial optimization, and was conducted by M. Dorigo in collaboration with A. Colorni and V. Maniezzo (11). AS has been very successfully applied to the *Travelling salesman problem* (TSP) (101), and to the *Quadratic assignment problem* (QAP).

The generalization of AS is Ant colony optimization (ACO), which studies artificial systems that get inspiration from the behavior of real ant colonies and are used to solve discrete optimization problems. There are various extended versions of the AS paradigm depending on what is assumed about the ant's method of communicating (local or distant), remembering, and learning ability, and so forth. This is allowed on the basis of the physiologic diversity of ants. Ant-Q system is a hybridization of AS with Q-learning, a well-known reinforcement-learning algorithm. The Ant colony system (ACS) is a further extension of Ant-Q. Both have been applied to the symmetric and asymmetric TSP. There are also proposed hybrid versions of ACO with *local search.*

Other researchers such as Schoonderwoerd, O. Holland, J. Bruten, and L. Rothkrantz, have developed an Ant colony algorithm, called ABC, for routing and load balancing in circuit switched telecommunications networks (103), and G. Di Caro and M. Dorigo have done one for routing in packet-switched telecommunications networks (104). G. Bilchev has developed an ACO method for the optimization of continuous functions (105).

Summarizing, according to the ACO homepage[30] by Marco Dorigo, (IRIDIA, ULB), collective ant behavior displays computational power in the following problems:

- Symmetric and asymmetric TSP
- *Sequential ordering problem*
- *Quadratic assignment problem* (QAP)
- *Vehicle routing problem*
- *Scheduling problems*
- *Graph coloring problem*
- *Partitioning problems*
- *Telecommunication networks*
- Real functions optimization, and so forth.

There are many problems in common between ant life and human life, namely TSP, QAP, the *Scheduling problem*, and so forth. This is not surprising since ant colonies and humans both have to somehow optimally solve similar types of everyday problems, for example, farming, housekeeping, and management. The difference is in the scale only. Most of these problems are high on a complexity scale.

An interesting research problem would be a comparative study on "who is better or faster: the ant *collective intelligence* or the human individual *intelligence* (not necessarily supported by the computer), for example, at solving the TSP." A first approximation of this problem is given in the following text.

Assuming that a single human is working with only a *pen and pencil*, and has in mind that the TSP problem is an NP-problem, it can be safely assumed that a human can solve it in a reasonable amount of time with only a few cities. This is because the combinatorial complexity of the TSP problem grows too fast. However, analyzing the research of M. Dorigo and L.M. Gambardella, (101,106) on how a solution emerges when AS system is applied, we can expect that collectively working ants should outperform the human when more cities are involved because they work in parallel when working out a graph, and transfer the information through use of the pheromones. Thus, what is the power necessary for a computer to allow us to outperform ants with this or any related problem?

Ants find an approximate solution, not an exact one, but if it is a size problem, for example 43 cities (locations), it is sufficient from the "existential point of view" just to find a solution which is reasonably close to an optimal one.

It is also interesting to ask how far the use heuristics will empower humans over ants. The simulation results (106) show that ants represented in this challenge by AS algorithms also outperform heuristics such as *simulated annealing*, the *elastic net*, the *self-organizing map*, the *farthest insertion*, and perhaps others.

[30] Bibliography also provides important Internet locations.

The final supposition here is that if the test for *intelligence* were composed of problems such as those previously mentioned, the ant colony would probably do better than a single human. Thus, the *collective intelligence* of "unintelligent" ants with certain specific problems could prevail over the *individual intelligence* of a highly "intelligent" human.

The Social Structures of Honeybees

In McFarland's book (74) on animal behavior there is a sentence which clearly reflects our point of view about animal *intelligence*:

> Because the honey-bee is an insect, we tend to think of it as a mere automation. However, its behavior is surprisingly complex.

Honeybees create a social group (107), and single bees can survive only as members of the society. They nest (hive) in natural wooden hollows or manmade hives. The center of the society is the queen, surrounded by infertile young female nurses and male drones. The drones are useful only for mating, whereas the workers (numbering 80,000 or more) build the honeycomb, rear the young, clean, guard, and collect the food. The queen is the only sexually productive female in the colony, often laying more than 1500 eggs per day. Anatomically, the queen is different from the drones and workers. Her body is long, with a much larger abdomen than a worker. Her mandibles (jaws) contain teeth, whereas her offspring have toothless jaws. She can use her stinger repeatedly without endangering her own life, whereas the workers have stingers that tear off when used. In addition, the queen bee lacks the tools of a worker, such as pollen baskets, beeswax-secreting glands, and a well-developed honey sac. The average life of a queen is one to three years. The queen controls the sex of her offspring by determining whether the eggs passing from her ovary to her oviduct are fertilized. A fertilized egg develops into a female honeybee, either worker or queen, and an unfertilized egg becomes a drone. The queen lays the eggs that will develop into more queens in specially constructed downward-pointing cells filled with royal jelly, a secretion produced by workers to secure the larvae and to feed them. Workers are raised in the multipurpose, horizontally-arranged cells of the comb. Future workers receive royal jelly only during the first two days, compared to future queens, who are fed royal jelly throughout their larval life.

Bees gather nectar and pollen from insect-pollinated flowers. Nectar provides their carbohydrate. It is converted to honey by applying enzymes to convert the sugar to unmetabilizable chemicals, fanning to kill micro-organisms, and finally adding other enzymes to prevent spoiling. Pollen is a protein source used to feed young and nurture the queen.

A natural nest is constructed inside a log cavity with a small entrance. The bees construct wax combs with hexagonal cells in which they rear brood and store pollen, nectar, and honey. The nest is designed to allow the bees to proceed easily with their many tasks and activities. The honeycomb is a back-to-back array of parallel hexagonal cells. Each comb is vertical in the hive, with each cell angled at about 13 degrees to prevent the honey from running out. The combs are equally spaced in the hive. Two different sizes of cells make up a comb, smaller ones for workers and larger ones for drones. Both types can be used to store honey and pollen. During the queen-breeding season, 10–20 elongated conical cells are constructed at the combs' edge for the queen's eggs. In general, honey is placed in the upper areas of the hive, minimizing stress on the comb. Broods are reared near the bottom, with pollen stored nearby. Drone cells are grouped together, usually on the edge of the comb. Separating drone and worker cells makes the comb stronger and assists the queen in batch male and female laying. In the event of colder weather, the drone cells are the first to be left unattended as the bees cluster together. This reflects the fact that drone pupae are larger and are able to survive without attention, and also that drones are more expendable than workers. To construct a comb, workers gather in a cluster, generating a temperature of about 35 °C. Construction begins at the roof or side of the hive. It proceeds in a seemingly random fashion, with bees moving from cell to cell contributing to construction in whatever way they perceive necessary. The result of these individual actions is a seamless comb construction. The strength of the construction is remarkable, and "honeycomb"-like structures are one of the most amazing "technical structures" discovered in nature. Walls thinner than 1/10 mm, constructed at exactly 120° degree angles can support 20 times their own weight in honey.

During winter, the bees cluster tightly together around the queen over the honey and pollen stores. Shivering wing muscles are used to generate heat. As the winter ends, the bees near the queen feed her highly proteinaceous royal jelly. Vacant cells in the heated portion of the comb are filled with eggs. Larvae hatch from these eggs and are fed first on royal jelly, and then after three days, on honey and pollen. The larva fills its cell after ten days and spins a cocoon in which it metamorphoses into an adult bee. Workers cap the cell with wax until the bee can chew its way out. Most of these new bees will be workers, but a few will be drones.

When the flowering of spring begins, the bees begin foraging and rearing more and more workers. By mid-spring the colony becomes too large for the hive, and preparations are made to swarm. Special queen cells are created at the bottom of the honeycomb. The larvae in these cells are fed a diet of only royal jelly, and thus become queens. At this time the queen diets to 70 percent of her normal weight. The thin queen and half the bees now leave the hive and cluster on a nearby tree. Scouts then search for a new nest site. Once the scouts agree on a site, the swarm moves in.

The queens now hatch in the parent colony. If the hive population is still too big, further afterswarms may occur, led by new queens. When the parent colony gets a reasonable size, the next queen attempts to kill any further emerging queens. The virgin queen then flies up in the sky to mate with the newly born drones. The queen can now return to the hive and take up egg-laying duties. The emphasis of the hive then changes to collecting pollen and nectar for the winter ahead. The drones are tolerated after swarming season, as the queen may run out of sperm or possibly die. But as autumn arrives, the drones are sent out of the hive to die. All bees go through the developmental stages of egg, larva, and pupa before becoming adults. When a worker hatches, she grooms herself, and then begins cleaning cells for eggs or food storage. The queen inspects each cell thoroughly before laying eggs in them, so the cleaning is a painstaking process. As the worker matures, she begins to nurse the larvae and queen with royal jelly. When her mandibular glands atrophy, she builds a comb and caps the cells containing metamorphosizing larvae. Once she is unable to produce wax, she begins the task of unloading incoming nectar. At two weeks old the worker begins guard duties and making short excursions to the outside world. By 21 days of age the worker is ready to begin foraging. She will make maybe 400 sorties in about nine days before her wings literally wear out, and she dies. This cycle is variable, dependent on the needs of the hive. Workers may begin foraging after as little as five days or remain nursing for up to three weeks. Hives also differ in their cycle based on environmental factors. It is the hives in the northern hemisphere which require the largest amounts of winter food storage, and hence produce the largest quantities of honey.

After acquiring some basic knowledge of requirements of the life and organization of the *social structure* of honeybees, let us look into the idea of *collective intelligence* in their *social structure* (100,107).

The methodology discussed in the previous part of book, elaborated by M. Dorigo (and other researchers) to demonstrate the potential computational power of cooperating ants, can be applied only partially to the social structure of honeybees. The reason is that a honeybee as a single being is more complicated in behavior and communication, and also from a simulation point of view. The ant displacement and pheromone-based communication system can be "mapped," for example, into a graph that represents the problem (e.g., TSP, QAP) to be solved, whereas honeybees displace in the open air (up to 10 km away from the hive) and the transfer of information to partners of their *social structure* takes place inside the hive.

The most promising approach (similar to M. Dorigo's) has been proposed by P.S. Fisher and G.E. Mobus in the paper: "Foraging Search at the Edge of Chaos" (108). Despite the fact that the authors consider only the model of a single honeybee as a *being* without taking into account their cooperation, their approach can be an entry to the evaluation of the power and complexity of collective problem-solving by honeybees. Let us look at what they write in the introduction to the paper (108) to understand the difficulty with honeybees:

> Many animal species are faced with the problem of finding sparsely distributed resources that occur (and disappear) dynamically in a huge space. Furthermore, the dynamics of these resources are stochastic and probably chaotic in terms of both spatial and temporal distribution. But they are not completely random. The search strategy is called foraging. It involves two interrelated phases which dominate the behavior of the animal based on the amount of knowledge it has regarding the location and timing of the resource. In the absence of knowledge or cues, foraging animals adopt a stochastic search pattern that will have a reasonably high likelihood

of bringing them into encounters with the resource. With knowledge or cues, the animal switches to a more directed search behavior.

The honeybee as a being exists in a more complicated environment than the ant, and thus must be equipped with a more powerful perception system.

Because of the works of Karl von Frisch and his colleagues, it is known that honeybees have relative good eyes. Despite the fact that they are not able to differentiate between some colors (e.g., red from gray), and that the honeybee is insensitive to red, compensatively honeybees are sensitive to ultraviolet, and are able to recognize and remember small details of flower patterns (109).

The honeybee uses the sun for navigation, but even on cloudy days it can find the position of the sun behind clouds on the basis of the plane of polarization of sunlight in the ultraviolet region of the spectrum. The honeybee is also sensitive to the earth's magnetic field and its daily changes.

Honeybees learn landmarks (110), especially if they are linear and lead to food directly, for example, lines of plantation or solitary big trees (74). This is important because good memory abilities are also required by the fact that some flowers (with specific patterns) open only at specific times of day, and are available only in specific areas. All this data must be remembered and somehow transferred in a short time period to other workers, immediately after their arrival to the hive. S.W. Zhang, K. Bartsch, and M.V. Srinivasan (111), have confirmed the honeybee's great ability to recognize and learn or remember on the basis of their experiments with honeybees in a maze. Let us quote their results directly:

1. Bees can learn to fly through a complex maze by following a trail of colored marks.
2. Bees, initially trained to follow color marks through an initial part of the maze, are immediately able to "blaze a trail" by using the same cue to fly through the rest of the maze that is unfamiliar to them.
3. Bees trained to follow marks through a particular maze can use the same cue to negotiate a novel maze.
4. Bees trained to use a particular color to negotiate a maze can immediately use a novel color to negotiate the same maze, or even a novel maze.
5. After learning to negotiate a maze by following colored marks, bees can find their way through the maze even when the marks are removed.
6. Bees can learn to use color as a signal even when it indicates the path through the maze in a more abstract way; for example, blue indicating a turn to the right and green a turn to the left.
7. Bees can learn an unmarked maze. Performance under these conditions is poorer than when marks are provided, but is still significantly better than chance level.
8. Control experiments rule out the use of external landmarks in all of these situations.

R. Menzel, et al (112) conclude that honeybees have multiple memories that are integrated, but not in the form of a cognitive map[31].

The elements discussed earlier are important because they show that the honeybee as a single being has high-level abilities. It is oriented to perceive, preprocess, and store information for further transfer of this highly temporary, dynamic knowledge to the social structure it belongs to, where a higher level of processing (global hive knowledge) takes place.

Probably the most convincing demonstration of such collective, rapid problem-solving is the investigation process for new hive location. After the old queen departs from the previous hive with about one half of the population, those that are left swarm together and form a compact cluster on a nearby tree. They can remain there for several days, while scout honeybees fly out to investigate possible sites for a new hive. Please note that the developed bees — workers (not the queen individually) do the collective decision-making. They return one after another, and perform a dance on the vertical surface of the swarm. This dance (long and vigorous if an attractive site has been found) provides information about the direction, distance away, and quality of new hive sites. The information is given to the whole social structure, so that the other workers can fly to inspect the site. When the others return, they dance for information transfer. Usually more than one site is investigated. Differences in the quality and distance become gradually apparent from the number and vigor of the dancing honeybees advertising their discoveries. Gradually the honeybees that have discovered hive locations of lower quality stop pushing their discoveries. When universal agreement is reached, the swarm move to the new hive.

It is probably an analogous decision-making mechanism that allows ants, using a pheromone communication system, to find the optimal path between the nest and the food. The problem takes a higher optimization level with honeybees, because the complex problem of quality of the hive site has to be solved, not just the simple problem of the shortest path (or the most economical in general). In the case of ants, gradually more and more decide to turn to those sides of the obstacles where there is a higher intensity of pheromone deposits. In the case of honeybees, more and more scouts (perhaps even those who were proposing an alternative site) fly to the better location for verification and "personal" comparison. After their return they "vote" in favor or against a site, but finally this "bee democracy" provides an optimal decision.

To complete our investigation of *collective intelligence* in the social structure of honeybees let us briefly discuss their communication system.
The language of honeybees has the following components:

1. Transfer of food and olfactory elements (to provide olfactory cues while looking for food or a specific place)
2. Antennae contact

[31] A cognitive map is an abstract representation of the locations of important sites stored in memory.

3. Acoustics (wing vibrations)
4. The dance

Elements 1 and 4 are considered as key, whereas antennae contact and wing vibrations are considered as supplementary. However, A. Michelsen et al. (113) demonstrate that "a robot simulating a dancing bee" trying to force them to fly to a specific location will not work without the acoustic element.

The honeybee dance is considered the major element of information transfer, and can be described as follows:

1. Foraging honeybees return to the hive and communicate the location of a food source by making a set of rhythmic movements. These movements communicate the direction and distance of the food source with respect to the hive.
2. There are 2 types of bee dances:
   - The *round dance* means that food is near the hive (within 50 meters but indicates no direction).
   - The *Waggle Dance* means that food is 50–100 meters away; this dance encodes both direction and distance.

   The distance is indicated by the number of times the honeybee runs forward while waggling, whereas the direction (related to sun) is shown by the angle of the dance to the hive. If the food source is located in the same direction as the sun is in the sky, the bees dance vertically; if the food source is 60 degrees to the left of the sun, the dance is angled at 60 degrees with respect to vertical.

Honeybees continue to dance till the food source becomes scarce and then stop dancing.

The honeybee dance for information transfer is considered very important evidence in support of our proposal in this book, a computational model of *collective intelligence*. Most information among honeybees is transferred through the observation of others inside the hive. Such transfers can also take place with other, perhaps antagonistic beings inside a social structure they belong to (e.g., rival shoemakers in competition on the same street).

Experiments with an "artificial bee robot" done by A. Michelsen et al. (113) demonstrate the possibility of and provide some technical advice about how to implement a human–animal interface, for example, to run the "Turing test" to verify the *intelligence* of insects. "Individual insect *intelligence*" seems to be too low to be fruitful; however, the chance to study *collective intelligence* is more interesting.

Remarks on Other Types of Social Insects[32] and Summary

The scope of this book does not allow us to analyze all insects who seem to demonstrate *collective intelligence*. Only the obvious *social insects*, that is, bees,

[32] There is, in fact, a journal on this subject published by Birkhäuser Verlag AG: Insectes Sociaux (IS). International Journal for the Study of Social Arthropods. This is the official journal of the

ants, wasps, and some social spiders have been considered in this book. Many other insects display social cooperation sufficient to suspect the emergence of *collective intelligence*. However, if *collective intelligence* can be triggered with as few as two human beings, the number of members of a social structure of insects would have to be much higher unless their *collective intelligence* was very specific, that is, problem-oriented. Ants and honeybees have been discussed because they appear almost worldwide, and create manifest social structures with a high number of members, which obviates the emergence of *collective intelligence*. For this reason, other insects are not discussed, for example, termites, which live mostly in warm regions.

Social structure and *collective intelligence*, however, have their "price" (74,114). For societies to persist, they must survive and reproduce more successfully than solitary individuals. Let us briefly summarize advantages and disadvantages of sociality:

ADVANTAGES

Solitary Insects	Social Insects
Hide from predators	Colony productivity increased
No direct competition with others of same species	Group defense and alarm system
Live in small spaces	Food gathering
Exploit small food resources	Nest building
	Care of young

DISADVANTAGES

Solitary Insects	Social Insects
Lack of social benefits	Intense predation, parasitism, disease

Emergence of *social structures* among insects has profited them with the "discovery" of elements surprisingly similar to those discovered by human *social structures*:

- Slavery (ants)
- Warfare (fire ants)
- Farming (some ants keep other insects as livestock). Other ants and some termites do gardening, that is, they collect plant material, bring it into the nest, compost it, and finally use it for farming fungus which they feed on).
- Homeostasis (steady state temperature and humidity) is maintained in the nests.

In the *social structures* of insects there is a phenomenon significant to future *collective intelligence* considerations. Social structures can be organized among

International Union for the Study of Social Insects (IUSSI). There is also online Internet edition: at *http://link.springer.de/link/service/journals/00040/index.htm*

insects in several ways: on the basis of polymorphism, cooperation between different species, or even slavery. The importance of this statement lies in the fact that the nonformal definition of *collective intelligence* given at the beginning of Chapter 2.2 does not restrict the emergence of *collective intelligence* to specific species or their bindings in a *social structure*. One level up, some birds and dogs readily accept humans as social partners, especially when imprinted by the presence of humans in their early life (74).

2.2.1.3. Can Different Types of Intelligence be Compared? The Collective Intelligence in the Relationship between Predator and Prey

So far *collective intelligence* has been considered a tool necessary to optimally solve foraging-by-collecting problems around the hive or nest. These uses of *collective intelligence* deal with the environment only, not with other *beings* representing their *intelligence* for survival, but we should also remember that *collective intelligence* can be used for catching a prey, or in reverse, for collective defense against predator(s).
While dealing with other *beings*, there are some fundamental differences:

- The time limit for solving a problem is reduced from hours to single seconds, or even fractions of seconds.
- The behavior of natural processes is easier to predict in short time periods than the behavior of live beings, barring some exceptions.
- The solution must be "generated or sketched" in advance on the basis of prediction of situation development, and immediately implemented in the form of action (e.g., stealing followed by an attack against prey, or defense itself), which will be successful or not. Thus, much higher requirements are imposed on computational processes that are responsible for implementation of a given kind of *intelligence*.

Predative situations (115) include the following:

1. A single, strong predator versus a group, flock, or shoal of smaller prey. For example, a goshawk versus red-billed weaver birds. A large predator can easily chase and catch a single prey if alone (114).
2. A group of cooperative hunting predators versus a bigger prey, for example, African wild dogs hunting for wild beast. A single predator cannot chase or defeat a single prey (115).
3. A group of cooperative predators against a group of prey, for example, arctic wolves against a defense formation[33] of musk oxen, or chimpanzee predation on red colobus monkeys. In this case the force ratio between the single predator or prey can vary.

Cases of type 1 prevail over cases of type 2 and 3, and cases of type 3 are relatively rare.

[33] J. Alcock (116) gives an example of almost the same ring defense formation with insects (sawflies).

First, let us discuss what "*collective and intelligent* behavior" can offer in a situation where a single, strong predator creates a threat to groups, flocks, or shoals of smaller *beings*. Collective defense has the following advantages:

INCREASED GROUP VIGILANCE. It is widely confirmed by observation and experiment with artificial goshawks that solitary, for example, birds often fail to respond to an approaching goshawk, whereas even a few birds while foraging together, are able to immediately detect such a predator (114). The same thing has been confirmed with individual lions and wild dogs, who are almost never able to steal toward a group of potential prey to fully surprise them.

Some animals even create *social structures* with professional vigilantes, for example, meerkat. The important secondary advantage of group vigilance is that more time can be spent for foraging.

DILUTION EFFECTS. This is also known as the "selfish herd" effect, that is, *beings* are protected by jumping into a group—because the chance of being taken is lowered when a *being* is in a large group. Predators rarely attack an individual in a crowd; their most common strategy is to make swoops toward the group, which may cause them to scatter, allowing the predator to single out an isolated animal. This "flickering" and overlapping multiple pictures of "potential prey" also provides, in many cases, the significant decision and perception problem for the predator.

PREDATOR DETERRENCE THROUGH MOBBING. A lot of animals apply this active collective defense. A good example is songbirds, mobbing owls, or crows. They move toward the predator harassing and screaming until they drive it off. Another example is baboons, which will mob any small carnivore, even cheetahs and jackals. When an animal lives in large groups, it can mob large predators, which it cannot do if it was alone. Chimps have been seen to mob leopards and lions. Rhesus monkeys have been seen to mob tigers (116).

Another case where *collective intelligence* is confronted with *individual intelligence* is a group of cooperative hunting predators versus a bigger prey. Probably the best examples are lions, wolves, and wild African dogs.

In general it is difficult to claim that collective hunting is always better. While analyzing the case of cooperatively hunting female lions, according to R. Heinsohn, C. Packer (117), R. Plomin, R. Rende (38) and so forth, it has been found that groups of hunting lions do not feed any better than solitary females. In fact, large groups end up at a disadvantage when the members refuse to cooperate in capturing prey. Once one female has started to hunt, her companions may or may not join her. If the prey is large enough to feed the entire group, as is the usual case, the companions face a dilemma: although a joint hunt may be more likely to succeed, the additional hunters must exert themselves and risk injury. But if a lone hunter can succeed on her own, the members of her group might profit with a free meal. Thus, the advantages of cooperative hunting depend on the extent to which a second hunter(s) can improve her companion's chances for success, and this in turn depends on the companion's hunting ability. If a lone animal is certain to succeed, the benefits of helping could never exceed the cost. But if she is incompetent, the advantages of a latecomer's assistance may well exceed the costs. Examples taken from other species (birds, insects) also suggest that, as expected, cooperation is mostly supported when lone hunters need help. The flip side of this trend is that species are least cooperative when hunters can most easily succeed on their own. It has been found that the (Serengeti Park) lions most often work together when tackling such difficult prey as buffalo or zebra. But in taking down easy prey, such as wildebeest or warthog, a lioness often hunts alone; her companions watch from the sidelines. The same dilemma can be observed with solitary or group hunting by humans.

Hunting techniques may vary. Sometimes, for example, wolves will slowly herd larger prey onto frozen lakes, water, or loose snow. The purpose is to make footing and balance treacherous. In this vulnerable state the animal can be attacked from different directions and is made helpless to protect itself. Wolves can literally run all night long. They can wear down their resistant prey by following at a constant distance adjusting to the animal's speed till exhaustion sets in. Even strong animals (that are not without defense against the wolf) eventually succumb to this relentless pressure. Some animals unwittingly set themselves up to be killed because they feed or travel alone. Musk oxen, practically invulnerable to attack while standing in a defensive formation together, are easy prey for wolves once they stray from the herd. Working in unison, the wolves surround a large animal such as this, making it impossible for it to face all the intruders. The wolves strike from the sides and rear, slashing at the hams, ripping at the flanks and abdomen. The animal weakens from the continuous harassment and loss of blood, and then the wolves move in for the kill.

The last example is a "group of cooperative predators against a group of prey". The basic problem is to break the defense lines of the prey. For example, Arctic wolves may try to provoke a stampede of musk oxen by staring at them, making false-charges at them or by nipping at them. A stampede exposes the weak, vulnerable calves, which are attacked by the entire pack. Sometimes one or two wolves chase their prey right into another group of wolves. Wolves also try to run their prey into exhaustion, or they may surround a herd and drive it into the open to expose the weakest animal.

2.2.2. The Collective Intelligence of Humans

After having discussed symptoms of the phenomenon of *collective intelligence* in the world of animals, even down to the lower domain of bacteria, we now start to analyze the phenomenon of *collective intelligence* among humans.

As has been mentioned earlier, people have been aware of the phenomenon of *collective intelligence* for a long time, but it has never been examined closely enough to be scientifically considered. It has even been wondered about as some kind of mirage or a figment of the imagination, but rarely considered seriously as a real, external process.

In the case of some animals, for example ants, or honeybees, the situation seems relatively simple because it is easy to conclude that such beings are "not very intelligent" singly, but their nest or hive behaves to some extent in an intelligent way because it is *collectively intelligent.*

Before switching (in Section 3) to the formal approach to the phenomenon of *collective intelligence*, let us discuss the various situations in which *collective intelligence* arises with human beings.

2.2.2.1. Difficulties with the Concept of Human Collective Intelligence — Simon Newell's Objections It is difficult to perceive and evaluate human *collective intelligence* for several reasons:

1. It is a probabilistic process (this will be clear in the formal definition to be given later on); thus it is difficult to duplicate any experiment on group intelligence and get the same results.

Even when evaluating the same, single human with repeated IQ tests, we could get different results biased by different factors, external or internal (related to the condition of the human) from experiment to experiment. As mentioned in Section 2.1.2.2, the IQ tests for individuals currently available are not designed to include the probability factor.

2. Social structures are constantly changing.

Changes resulting from the rhythm of days or weeks or seasons and from characteristics of displacements of those humans in the area occupied by this social structure, affect the distribution of people in a social structure.

A variety of emotional, political, economic situations and emergencies, and so forth, affect the level of cooperation in any social structure. Thus, the same structure can in a certain time period display a very high ability to solve difficult problems, whereas after a short time the same group cannot solve problems considered routine.

3. Occasionally a single human can display intelligence higher than the group.

Perhaps the best way to express why this affects the perception of *collective intelligence* is to quote the question occasionally discussed: "How much do scientific genius(es) like Einstein speed-up research progress in a certain area — how much progress would be made in this area if all the researchers had the same scientific level of ability?"

4. Achievements of collective intelligence are frequently attributed to a single person.

This often happens, for example, when ad hoc some individual members of the social structure, or more frequently leaders (because of their position), credit to themselves successes of the social structure they rule or belong to, whereas they were in fact void from the *collective intelligence* point of view in solving this specific problem. Another possibility is that a given person may profit from being the last link of the chain to make an inference, and on this basis the ability to solve the whole problem is attributed to him alone, whereas he is not capable of solving the problem alone at all.

5. Collective intelligence "gets fuzzy" behind technical terms related to the difficulties of a given problem.

Because of this approach, sometimes the results of *collective intelligence* problem solving are renamed according to terms related to the technical problem itself, for example, collective foraging, collective defense, collective decision-making, collective responsibility, and so forth.

6. Collective intelligence is believed to be more complex than individual intelligence.

The existing situation regarding the research on *collective intelligence* can probably be explained by a widespread, unconscious fear of scientists that *collective intelligence* must surely be something much more complex and complicated than *individual intelligence*. Many believe that *collective intelligence* a priori is at a higher level than that of the individual.

The next difficulty with comprehension and perception of *collective intelligence* has been the lack of a set of appropriate formal tools that can be used to work with the phenomenon of *collective intelligence*.

It is natural to consider *collective intelligence* as a certain computational process running somehow unconsciously in the background of the social structure behavior to solve its problems. However, immediately we are trapped by the question "what computational processes do we have in our scientific library" to tackle this "call for the problem to be solved?"

Predominant and very successful at the present time is the computational process based on the Deterministic Turing Machine and von Neumann architecture of digital computers. It is tied to the 0/1 data coding system, but a more crucial problem from a *collective intelligence* point of view is that all data must have an address, because computations done by the processor requires access twice along the address path: to fetch data and to store results. This implies that data should take a specific location (windows with *characters* in Fig. 2-28) and should not have multiple occurrences; otherwise, there would be trouble with addresses (or labeling of multiple data).

Fixed locations for data implies the greatest bottleneck — the communication problem between agents in the system.

Thus, assuming certain a priori models of computations, for example, those of the digital computer, we arrive at the same conclusion as one of the "founders of *artificial intelligence*" A. Newell. Let us quote again (see preface) what he said:

> A social system, whether a small group or a large formal organization, ceases to act, even approximately, as a single rational agent.
> Both the knowledge and the goals are distributed and cannot be fully brought to bear in any substantial way on any particular decision.
> This failure is guaranteed by the very small communication bandwidth between humans compared with the large amount of knowledge available in each human's head.

> Modeling groups as if they had a group mind is too far from the truth to be useful scientific approximation very often.

Moreover, A. Newell assumed (118) that *collective intelligence* would require that all members of the group share the complete body of knowledge and goals relevant to the task but held separately by its individual members. This objection is not very serious, but the difficulty with communication in a social structure is more serious.

However, the difficulty with the communication problem between agents can be bypassed if we remember that interaction or cooperation between agents is relatively rare when looking at their day- and night-time axis. This is because they are almost always displacing around a certain domain for daily needs. Thus, the acts of communication take place not between fixed, remote locations, but on a rendezvous basis, with very short distances between agents, which allows a high speed of data transfer between them. In the case of humans, this is an aggregate of acoustic, mimicking, and other data transfers. Additionally, such rendezvous-based communication does not affect communication of other agents if they are not nearby.

Thus a system (e.g., social) shown in the lower part of Figure 2-28 can be much bigger than one such as the upper part. Even in such a system, communication difficulties still emerge. For example, when it happens in far corners of the social structure, at least the size of a nation, discoveries have been done twice (duplicated) because of scientists' lack of contact and research synchronization.

This is the *collective intelligence* point of view, but such a technical possibility has also been discovered in the theory of *mobile agents*, where the Remote Procedure Calling (RPC) approach designed in the 1970s was replaced by Remote Programming (RP) with agents.

W.T. Cockayne and M. Zyda (119) give an example that for the remote deletion of n files, sending and receiving of $2(n + 1)$ messages is required. Instead, an agent can be delegated to resolve problems and delete all files in situ, without excessive communication between client and server[34].

In contrast to the nondeterministic situation in *collective intelligence*, the agent is a deterministic solution because agents are created, delegated, and applied in a deterministic way. This concept is illustrated in Figure 2-29, where the Remote Programming approach is expected to reduce bandwidth problem.

Let us review some existing approaches to the *collective intelligence phenomenon*.

2.2.2.2. Review of Existing, Nonformal Computer-Related Approaches to Human Collective Intelligence

The intangibility of the *collective intelligence* phenomenon has led researchers working with humans to analyze *collective intelligence* through the direct analysis of certain domains that can be affected by *collective intelligence* activity, or

[34] The "governor" sent by the king to a remote province is the same concept.

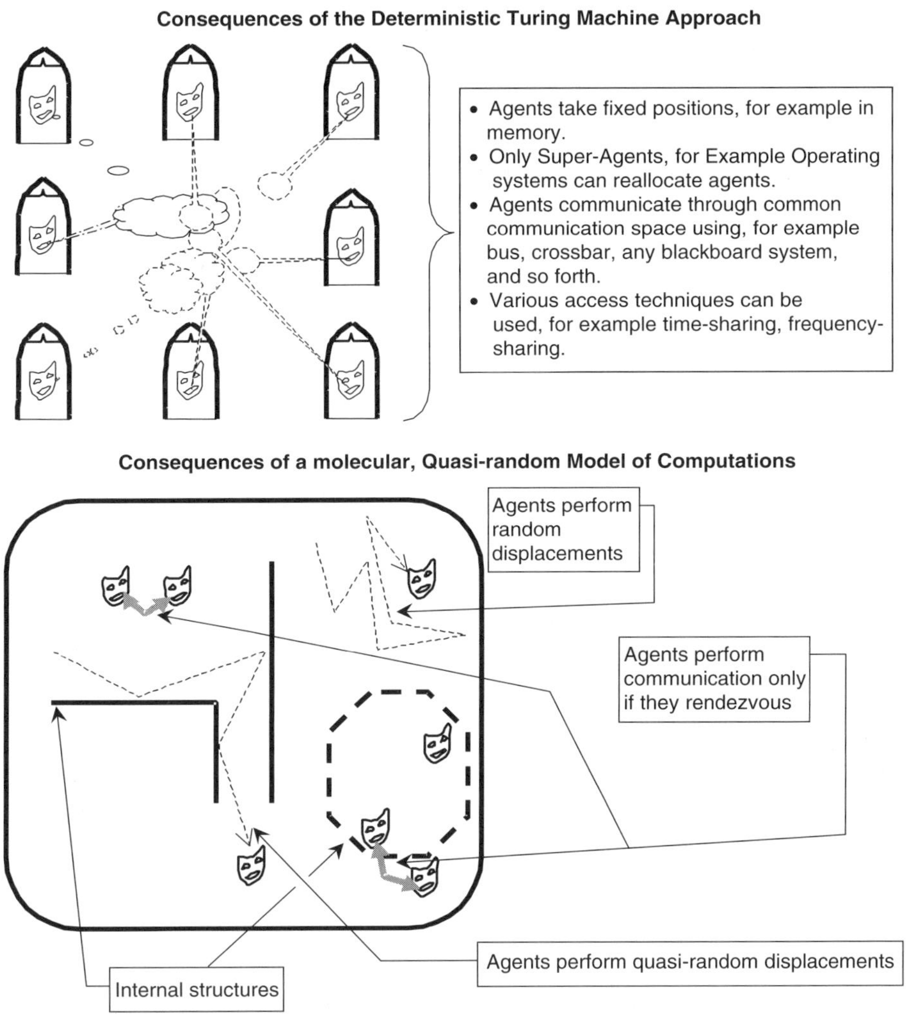

Figure 2-28. Implications of different models of computation to the communication problem.

alternatively to analyze how a group modifies its behavior for the needs of *collective intelligence*. Both elements can be observable, and can provide entry points for *collective intelligence* analysis. There are at least two possibilities:

- Analysis of the structure of the data and how it is processed by a group of humans when it is obvious that the group manifests *collective intelligence* entails the *collective memory* approach.
- The second possibility is to analyze the activity of a group of humans, that is, *collective strategies* for problem solving.

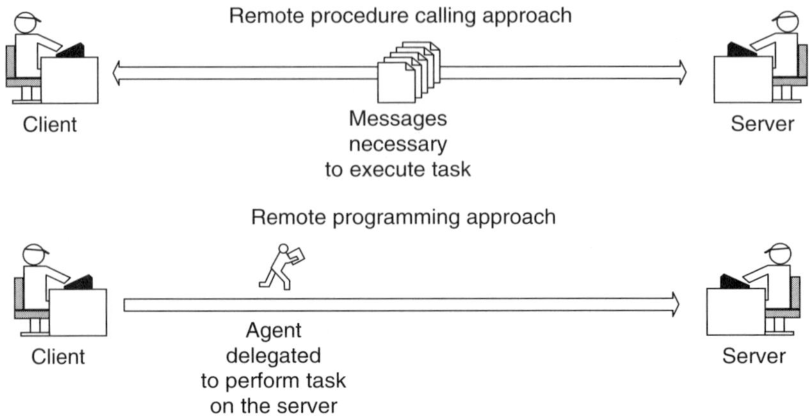

Figure 2-29. Bypassing bandwith problems by using remote agents.

In both cases we have tangible artifacts[35] of *collective intelligence*. We can approach this problem with the distinctive methodology of two different scientific areas: computer science and the social sciences.

The theory of *collective intelligence* presented in this book, examining it through the analysis of possible "models of computations" that are run by social structures, can be considered as one more approach.

In this part only results related to computers are summarized; results from the domain of psychology and sociology are be given in the next section (2.2.2.2).

The most complete analysis of computer-based approaches has been done by J.B. Smith (120), who explains the relationship between computers and *collective intelligence* in the following manner:

> The view of collective intelligence as a form of behavior made possible by some form of mediating computer system places it within the general tradition of intelligence amplification[36] (IA). This perspective takes the position that computer systems can be developed that partially mirror human mental functions; thus, by increasing the capacity or speed of operation of those functions, these systems can thereby increase or amplify the mental capacity of the human user working with them. As a result, quantitative increases in specific functions may produce qualitative differences in intellectual behavior, making the computer a necessary but not sufficient tool for enabling this mode of thinking[37].

[35] A structure not normally present but produced by an external agent or action.

[36] Please note that the term *intelligence amplification* fits well with our definition of *collective intelligence* as a property that emerges in certain situations. However, the term *intelligence amplification* intuitively requires the existence of some "basic, reference intelligence", which may (or may not) be *amplified*. The formal theory proposed in this book allows the emergence of *collective intelligence* even if there is no prior intelligence at all (e.g., bacterial colonies).

[37] Smith at *http://www.cs.unc.edu/~jbs/research/ci/c1-2.html*

Thus, this approach does not focus on the problem of "what *collective intelligence* is, and how it works", but on the construction of one more future *collective intelligence system*, which includes agents that are alive (humans) and not alive (computers).

In general the research here is quite broad in its scope, encompassing work in many different disciplines and on many different topics. The *Computer Supported Cooperative Work* (CSCW) term includes research on (computer) systems development, software engineering, and studies on human–computer interaction, social sciences, and management. Contributions range from development of CSCW systems (termed *Groupware*) to analysis of user interaction with such systems and the effects of these technologic systems on user–user communication (Computer-Mediated Communication), on coordination of this communication, on group dynamics, and on organizations and organizational change. In each of these areas, there is both empirical analysis of actual Groupware systems and their effects (as studied in practice in the field or by testing in the laboratory) and theoretic investigations. An overview of the literature done by K.J. Merck can be found online: *http://www.cs.wpi.edu/~kmerck/research/cscw/annotatedbib.html* or from a range of CSCW conference proceedings, for example, CSCW'90, '92, '96, '98, '2000. Let us review collective memory and collective strategy approaches.

Collective Memory for Collaborating Groups

The approach to *collective intelligence* through the concept of collective memory is presented in general in Figure 2-30. Naturally, it is a simplified presentation that does not take into account how complicated collective memory really is, for example, if we look at it through our present experience with the internet.

Analyzing recent literature (121,122), it is apparent that the collective memory approach is more an attempt to build *collective intelligence* systems based on human–computer interaction than an analysis of how collective memory works in pre-computer human systems, which were based on printed or oral data transfer.

We should mention here one precomputer attempt to build such a collective memory system, that is, *memex* based on microfilm technology proposed by V. Bush (123) in 1945, but at that time, without computers, this task was impossible. The concept was to permit a human user to store large amounts of data, to add new information, and what is most important, to add cross-references at the bottom of any microfilm page that could be instantly continued on some other page. Thus, the human user could construct large networks of semantic relationships within the *memex*.

The next step after *memex* was the emergence of hypertext[38] systems that were conceptually initialized by D.C. Engelbart, R.W. Watson, and J.C. Norton (124).

[38] Text linked together in a complex, nonsequential web of associations in which the user can browse through related topics.

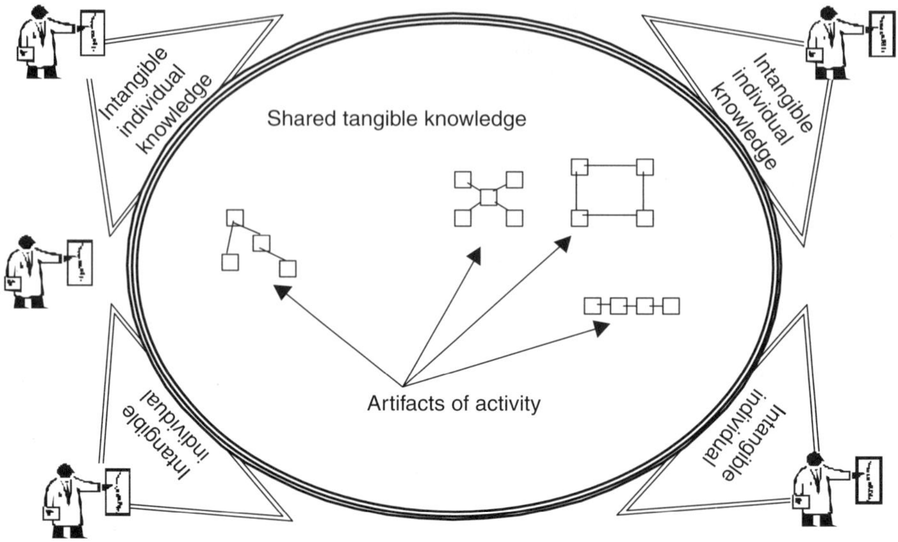

Figure 2-30. Collective memory approach to *collective intelligence.*

From the moment that computers emerged, we can quote J.B. Smith (120) about the existence of "*collective intelligence in computer-based collaboration*".

In general, when analyzing *collective intelligence* through the concept of collective memory, there are two possible situations:

- Asynchronous work, when collaborating members of a group work independently on the same tangible product, such as a document, a set of architectural drawings, or the source code for a computer system. E-mail systems and distributed file systems are examples of this category (see Section 2.2.3.1).
- Synchronous work, when collaborating members of a group work with *shared editors* (125) or through *video conferencing* (see Section 2.2.3.1).

Collective Processing

In the literature, (120) there are a number of attempts to analyze *collective intelligence* through analysis of collective strategies of processing information. However, despite technologic progress that has extended, in fact has multiplied our ability to communicate (126), to store, and exchange data, collaborative groups still use the same organizational schemes for processing as were known in precomputer, and even prebook times. This can be easily observed when computer processing with agents is considered, for example Y. Shoham and M. Tennenholtz (127), Wagner et al. (128), and so forth. Thus, let us summarize (from K.D. Blakeley (129)) the following basic used modes of activity:

- Discussion
  - *Discussion in its basic form*

    The goal is to externalize information owned by individuals and evaluate it. The process is based on real-time dialog. The product of the discussion is a group-level awareness of information.
  - *Conflict resolution*

    The purpose is to evaluate information in case of source-driven inconsistency.
  - *Brainstorming*

    The aim is shared problem solving in which all members of a group spontaneously contribute ideas. The difference from the *discussion in basic form* is that structures imposed on the discussion are almost all removed, to get more solutions that could be filtered out by structuralization.
- Presentation
  - *Presentation in its basic form*

    The goal is to introduce information owned by an individual to the group. There is a well-defined leader for this method of information processing.
  - *Summary*

    The task here is to introduce reduced or compressed information to the group. There is a well-defined leader.
  - *Demonstration*

    The purpose is to introduce information mainly through presentation of artifacts, for example, devices, software, and so forth.
- Delegation

  The aim is to assign the task, and to explain and evaluate work responsibilities. The process is based on assigning priority to individuals or groups of individuals officially elected or appointed to represent another or other individual(s).

Thus, it is necessary to discuss the concept of *social structures* because they are fundamental to collective processing as a consequence of *collective intelligence*.

First we concentrate on social structures of live *beings*. The problem of agents is discussed in Section 3.4.5.4.

2.2.3. Real (Conscious) and Virtual (Unconscious) Social Structures

In our work on *collective intelligence* we deal with a variety of *beings*, ranging from software agents through bacterial colonies, from social insects up to human social structures. This makes some existing definitions inadequate or imprecise. In some cases, these definitions must be modified or reinterpreted to fit our requirements.

The term *sociology* originates from a combination of Latin: *socius* = *friend* and Greek: *ology* = *study of*. The French philosopher Auguste Comte created the term in 1838 to refer to the science that studies relationships between people. Sociologists investigate how people become social actors and how forms of social reality are constructed.

Now sociology extends into the world of animals also, where the subclassification "social animals or insects" is used. Thus, for our purposes, let us replace the term *human* with the term *individual*, which will extend its meaning. This is the first departure from the principles in the minds of the founders of sociology. However, there are more, for example, how to answer the question: is it a social structure? for cases of structures of nonhomogenous types like "a hunter and his dog working together to get rabbits"; "a cowboy and his horse cooperating to move cattle."

A second departure from a simple definition of the term *sociology* can be demonstrated easily if we take a look at the example of the shoemakers spying on each other. They create a social structure and their interaction increases *collective intelligence*, but they are not friends (*socius*). This direction is confirmed by growing interest in virtual structures, which are impersonal in nature and lack face-to-face interaction.

All such doubts must be addressed when using the tools and research results of sociology because they will affect our work with *collective intelligence*.

Thus first let us look into some sociological terms and definitions in use today.

DEFINITION 6: SOCIAL ACT

According to Max Weber[39] (130), a social act is any action oriented to or influenced by another or others. Social action means that the behavior or anticipated behavior of others is taken into account by the acting individual. Weber pointed out that social action may occur even when only one individual is present and also that an absence of action or acquiescence to the actions of others is included as a part of social action.

DEFINITION 7: SOCIAL STRUCTURE

In societies, we can generally distinguish two components — social structures and social processes — that interpenetrate each other, that is, are dialectically interrelated. The key to understanding social structure in a society is understanding its social institutions and their intertwining combinations. Social structure is the institutional framework that makes for order in an assumed time span of interaction between individuals. It is social institutions that promote the necessary order to make social structure possible.

[39] Max Weber, 1864–1920, German sociologist and pioneer of the modern analytical method of sociology.

DEFINITION 8: SOCIAL SYSTEM

This is a term characteristic of functional analysis (and specifically of Parson's[40] structural functionalism (131)). The social system consists of both a social structure of interrelated institutions, statuses, and roles, and the functioning of that structure in terms of social actions and interactions of individuals. The social system thus is said to include both social change ("dynamics" according to Comte) — the processes and patterns of action and interaction — and social stability ("statics" according to Comte) — stable social structural forms. Furthermore, the social system constitutes a unitary social whole reflecting a real value consensus — the sharing of common values, social norms, and objectives.

Now, let us try to differentiate between real (conscious) social structures and virtual (unconscious) social structures. The basic difference lies in the *personality* of contact between *beings*, not directly in the distance between *beings* at the moment of interaction. A good example of the *personality* problem is a letter from one scientist to another with a research critique or report of a discovery; these are very personal interactions (especially if the author is somehow known). The distance between them does not matter. *Time* is not a major issue here (the letter can even arrive after several months); the researcher (receiver) can even be inspired by a letter written by a person who is no longer alive. However, a letter is a more anonymous interaction than a face-to-face presentation. The same critique can be fully anonymous, suchas in a journal review.

M.K. Ahuja and K.M. Carley (132) define a virtual organization (133,134):

> as a geographically distributed organization whose members are bound by a long-term common interest or goal, and who communicate and coordinate their work through information technology.

In real social structures, *beings* usually interact face to face; they are conscious of interaction with another *being*. Other elements not related to the merit of cooperation can also affect social structure, for example, personal human relations. On the other hand, in a virtual structure, the interaction based on artifacts produced and perceived by *beings* can be unconscious because the receiver may not directly realize that it is an artifact and not an element of the environment.

A key feature of virtual organizations is a high degree of informal communication. A virtual social structure is characterized by reduction or lack of formal rules, procedures, clear reporting relationships, and norms. Formal communication is noninteractive, impersonal, and involves use of media, such as reports and structured meetings.

[40] Talcott Parsons, 1902–1979, American sociologist noted for developing the structural-functional approach to studying social systems.

Recently, there has been a growing research interest in virtual social structures, teams, and organizations because of the rapid growth of Internet use and emergence of social structures not observable before.

J. Lipnack and J. Stamps (134) have defined a "virtual team" as "a group of people who interact through interdependent tasks guided by a common purpose" that "works across space, time, and organizational boundaries with links strengthened by webs of communication technologies."

Some researchers talk about virtual teams, (e.g., S.L. Jarvenpaa and B. Ives (135) and others), as evolutionary forms of network organizations enabled by advances in information and communication technology. Theoretically, the concept of virtual teams implies permeable interfaces and boundaries; project teams that rapidly form, reorganize, and dissolve when the needs of a dynamic marketplace change; and dispersal of individuals with differing competencies who are located across time, space, and cultures.

However, this concept also brings some dangers for social structures, such as low individual commitment, role overload, role ambiguity, absenteeism, and social loafing. It is not yet clear how it will affect the stability of social structures.

The importance of virtual social structures for *collective intelligence* lies in two basic facts:

- Lack of the requirement for conscious cooperation fits well into social structures of low-level organisms, such as bacterial colonies.
- The assumed model of *collective intelligence* as a quasi-chaotic process in social structures fits very well with the concept of virtual organizations when considering higher organisms, such as human social structures.

2.2.3.1. What is a Social Structure? There is a serious perceptual problem with what a *social structure* really is because the definitions mentioned earlier are formal ones, and when interpreting them, difficulties arise. An example is a virtual *social structure* or organization.

We have mentioned before that there is doubt as to whether a group of nonhomogenous *beings* can be considered as one social group. This leads to a more general issue; the problem is that we cannot differentiate between an *organism* and a *social system*.

Before we get to a more precise discussion of this problem, let us just state that this difficulty "fits in" and provides one more piece of evidence for the computational concept of *collective intelligence* presented in this book. As we try to demonstrate throughout the book, *collective intelligence* can emerge as easily in a bacterial colony, which creates the beginning of primitive tissue in the form of *biofilm* (according to the proliferation theory, see Section 2.2.1.1.), as in a human *social structure*. In both cases, the formal definition is the same.

Let us summarize what J.P. Scott writes in his excellent book on social systems (136), where he makes the following general conclusion:

no single general theory of systems organization is possible.

The main reason is that the nature of interaction varies from level to level with regard to *beings*. Thus, for unification of considerations, it is very convenient to consider society as a *superorganism* or *superorganization* as A.E. Emerson proposed in 1952 (137).

Pertinent to this discussion is Scott's comparison of physiological and social systems, in a form similar to Table 2-2 presented below.

This table should be considered as a generalization only because communication in some species (e.g., ant pheromones) and even in humans (e.g., certain odors) can be considered as chemical signals that may produce direct effects on the nervous system and so stimulate behavior.

R.L. Daft (138) provides (from K. Boulding) an interesting hierarchy of complexity that orders all open systems[41], as shown in Figure 2-31.

With social systems, the dynamics of spatial relationships start to play a significant role and are used as concepts of proximity, social distance, home range, and so forth. This fits easily into the computational model of *collective intelligence* based formally on rendezvous and logical interaction of individuals.

Interaction between individuals can be analyzed and measured in a number of different ways. For example, by using the frequency of association or interactions between individuals, we can adopt association hierarchy patterns, for example, like the ones proposed for baboons by R.I. Dunbar (139) in Figure 2-32.

The prevailing proportion of our knowledge about *social structures* comes from research on human *social structures* —which is obvious.

We will restrict our considerations here to topics essentially related to the computational concept of *collective intelligence*. We will limit the typology of the presented *social structures* only to *groups* (as representatives of small *social structures*) and to *organizations* (as large ones). This approach fits well with the hierarchical concept of *computational spaces* of level 0, that is, CS^0 to represent individuals, and CS^1, CS^2 for groups and organizations.

Higher levels and specific *social structures* (e.g., the family) are not discussed.

TABLE 2-2. Comparison of Physiological and Social Systems (136)

Characteristic	Social System	Physiological System
Spatial relationship	Movable	Fixed (in a short time period)
Unit of organization	Organism	Cell
Interactions	Behavioral	Chemical Electrical (neurons)
Organization	Relationship Group Institutions	Tissue Organ Organ systems

[41] An open system is defined as a self-sustaining system that transforms input from the external environment into output, which the system then returns to the environment.

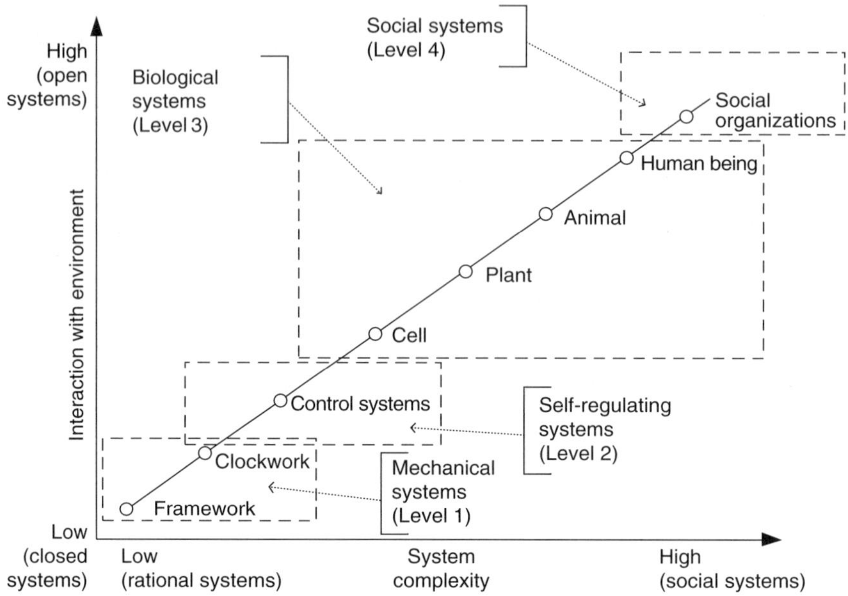

Figure 2-31. Hierarchy of system complexity according to R.L. Daft from K. Boulding (138).

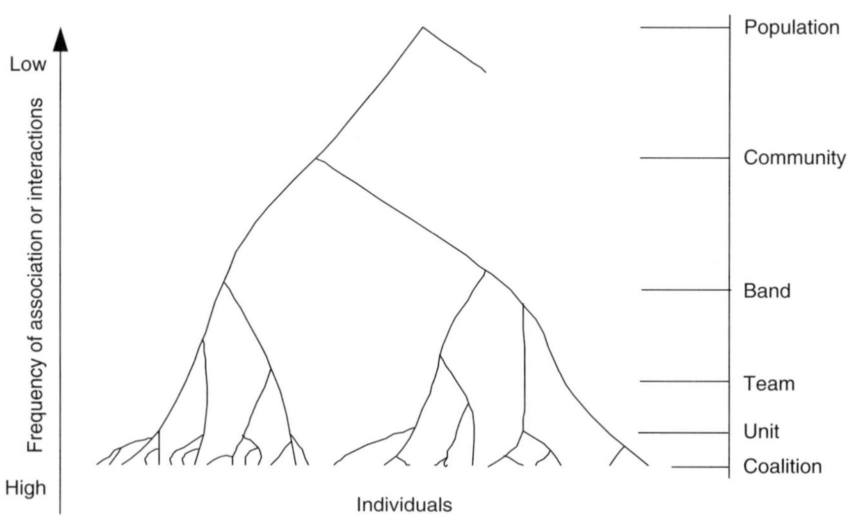

Figure 2-32. Association patterns based on frequency of interactions (139).

In general, in this book we tend to present *social structures* in a certain "minimalist way" that will allow their mapping into specific "black boxes" of *information molecules*.

The intention of the author is to suggest as wide as possible a spectrum of applications of the computational model of *collective intelligence* presented in this book to *fuel* wide interest in *CI* theory. This theory should provide an opportunity for analysis and conclusions both for the needs of private organizations and companies as well as for the use of government institutions. Therefore, the coming part on human social structures takes up a significant percentage of the book.

Small Social Structures – Groups

As we can effectively analyze *beings*, it is useful to have a clear concept of a group, as in the following definition (140):

> Group: collection of two or more interacting individuals who maintain stable patterns of relationships, share common goals, and perceive themselves as being a group.

Including the concept, we should also be able to assume certain criteria:

1. Two or more individuals (people) in social interaction
2. A stable structure at least temporarily
3. Common goals among members
4. A common perception of being a group

In general, beings join groups for several possible reasons:

- to meet the need to belong
- to fulfill needs for attention
- to achieve goals that cannot be achieved alone
- to pool knowledge and information
- to meet the need for security
- to help in establishing a social identity

Most groups created by human beings pass through several phases or stages as the groups emerge, develop, and disband. B. Tuckman's model (141) distinguishes five stages of group development:

1. *Forming*: This is the orientation stage — a period of uncertainty. Members try to determine their place in the group and the procedures and rules of the group.
2. *Storming*: Conflicts begin to arise as members sometimes resist the influence of the group and even act against accomplished tasks.
3. *Norming*: During this third stage, cohesiveness and commitment replace inter-member conflicts. A feeling of group unity arises. New ways to work together are discovered, and norms of appropriate behavior inside the group are settled.

4. *Performing*: The group develops proficiency in achieving its goals and improves its patterns of cooperation.
5. *Adjourning*: Finally, the dissolution stage occurs.

Some authors, such as D.W. Johnson & F.P. Johnson (142) define even more stages and provide charts with group efficiency and time for each stage, as shown in Figure 2-33.

S.P. Robbins (143) gives another simple but essential and suggestive graphic interpretation of group formation stages, characterized by developing relationships and cohesiveness (see Fig. 2-34). This system of group development has six stages.

While observing groups in general, we can characterize several possible types of groups from a certain perspective. According to J. Greenberg and R. Baron (140), the following types can be derived at the highest human level (see Fig. 2-35).

Let us explain the terms illustrated in Figure 2-35.

Formal Groups are created by the superordinate organization. They are intentionally designed to direct members toward some organizational goal. Good examples of the two types of formal groups are regular military units and special task forces in the military.

Command Groups as a subtype, are group structures defined by the connections between individuals. Some members can legitimately give orders to others because of their position. The hierarchy is clearly discernible.

Task Groups are formed around a specific task to be done, usually by experts in specific disciplines. Their position in the general hierarchy is not as important from the *task group* point of view as their knowledge or abilities are.

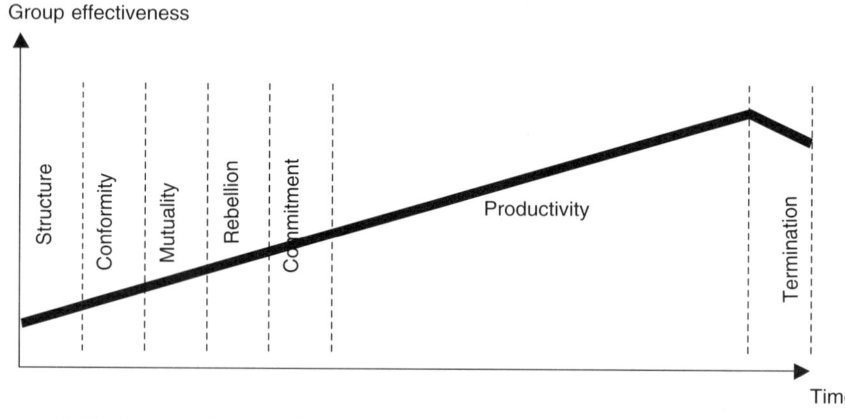

Figure 2-33. Stages of group development according to D.W. Johnson and E.P. Johnson (142).

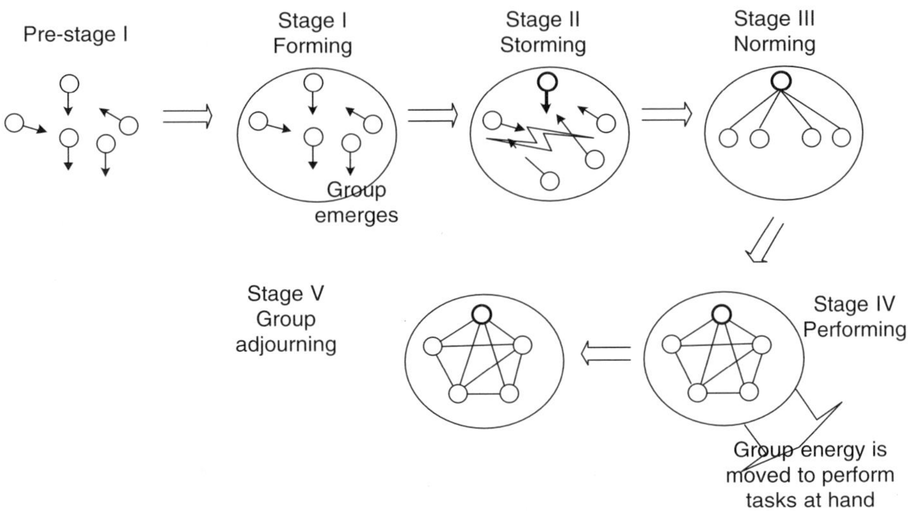

Figure 2-34. Stages of group development in terms of relationships (143)

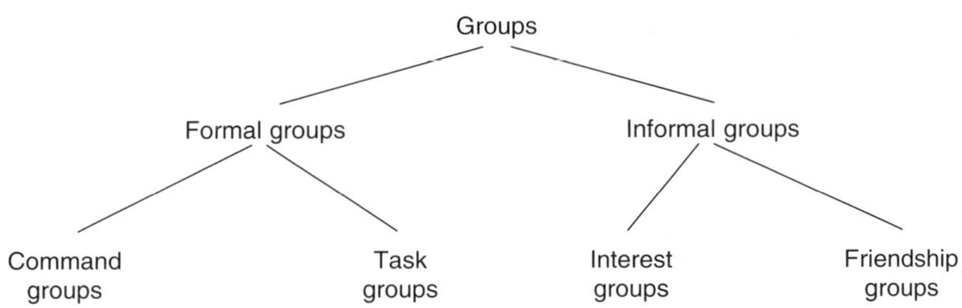

Figure 2-35. Types of groups (140).

Informal Groups are defined as those that develop naturally among people without any direction from the organization within which they operate. The key factor for formatting an informal group is a common interest shared by members, which emerges spontaneously. Here we differentiate between *interest groups* and *friendship groups* based on their different types of personal interaction. *Informal groups* can emerge inside any other bigger structure, such as a company.

Now, let us look inside the group at how it works and behaves. S.P. Robbins (143) provides a simple diagram to serve as a model of group behavior (Fig. 2-36.).

This diagram provides a reasonable starting point for a discussion of small *social structures* (groups) and on this basis allows us to expand some functional blocks, important from the *collective intelligence* point of view, into separate

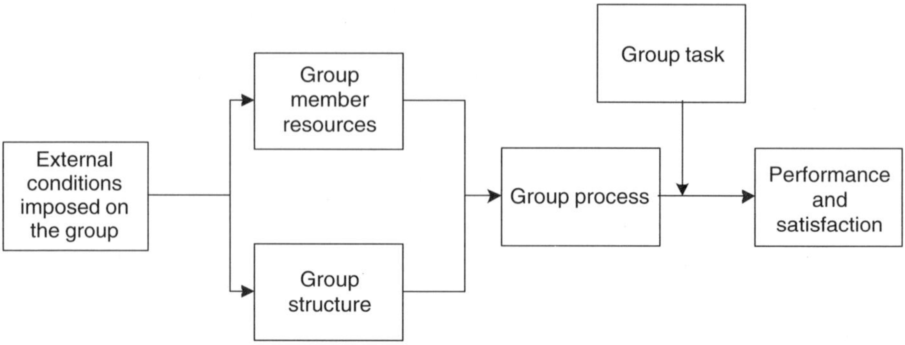

Figure 2-36. Group Behavior Model (143).

sections. Let us discuss components of the *Group behavior model* illustrated in Figure 2-36.

However, before any high-level discussion, we should note that *groups are almost always subsets of larger organization systems*, either companies or external *social structures* (e.g., cites, states, etc.), which impose, among other things, regulations, goals, and resources, that is, impose external conditions on the group. Let us briefly discuss these.

EXTERNAL CONDITIONS IMPOSED ON THE GROUP. Robbins suggests that to create these external conditions, the following components must be there:

- **Organizational Strategy**

  An example might be a company where a group exists such that it is either downsizing after some losses or expanding as a result of successful development. Thus, the group is affected by organizational strategy.

- **Authority Structures**

  External conditions also affect the structure of the group, for example, when a formally designated leader exists in the group, and another leader emerges from the group informally, for example, on the basis of knowledge or expertise.

- **Formal Regulations**

  Organizations of all levels existing above the group always have standards, rules, procedures, laws, policies, and so forth, which affect group structure and behavior.

- **Organizational Resources**

  Groups and even individuals usually profit from (or suffer from the lack of) resources available in the superordinate structure.

- **Human Resource Selection Process**

  Groups are considered secondary substructures of an *organization* or *social structure*, emerging on the basis of the human resources available in the *organization*. Thus, better human resources will affect its structure and behavior as building blocks for the group.

  An example is *a state* with a high-level educational system, which is generating a spectrum of high-quality "building blocks for companies," that is, qualified young people looking for jobs. Another such example is high salaries widely attracting *good* candidates to a given company from a superordinate structure (a country or even from abroad).

- **Performance Evaluation and Reward System**

  Beyond the group benefits (if any), a secondary evaluation and reward system created by the upper structure can exist. This can be even more valuable than advantages from the group itself from an individual point of view.

- **Organizational Culture**

  Every organization or *social structure* has an unwritten culture that defines standards of acceptable or unacceptable behavior of individuals in the group.

- **Physical Work Settings**

  Finally, the group exists in a certain "physical" environment that will affect group activity, for example, the combination of the available communication system + distance + configuration of the site, and so forth.

In Section 2.2.3.2. and 2.2.3.3., this problem is specifically addressed because the internal structure of *computational space* has a decisive impact on the speed of inferences in formal models of *collective intelligence* in most cases. Thus, we should have an idea of how it works in human *social structures*.

GROUP MEMBER RESOURCES. The next component (in Fig. 2-36.) to be discussed is *Group member resources*. S.P. Robbins (143) gives the following definitions:

- **Abilities**

  Abilities set the parameters for what members can do and how effectively they will perform in a group.

- **Personality Characteristics**

  It has been observed that attributes that have a positive connotation in our culture tend to be positively related to group behavior (143). Attributes most important in many cultures include sociability, self-reliance, and independence.

In contrast, authoritarianism, dominance, and unconventionality may affect the group negatively.

GROUP STRUCTURE. The next functional block from Figure 2-36. is the *Group structure*. The most important structural variables are formal leadership, roles, norms, group status, group size, composition of the group, and degree of group cohesiveness. Using Robbin's concepts (143), we give the following explanations:

- **Formal Leadership**

  Groups almost always have formal leaders, typically identified by distinctive titles of different natures. In almost all cases, the role of the formal leader is decisive to the situation and performance of the group.

- **Roles**

  Human beings are so complex and so capable of varied behavior that we are able to play different roles in the *social structure*, even simultaneously.

  > By the term "role" we understand a set of expected behavior patterns attributed to someone occupying a given position in a social unit.

  This statement, however, is not always feasible for simpler social *beings*, such as ants, bees, and so forth because of their restricted mental abilities. The various roles in their case require "reconstruction" of the organism, influenced by the presence or lack of specific pheromones, suppressing development in a specific direction (e.g., bees).

  Different groups impose different requirements on roles to be played by individuals, and different individuals are more or less prepared, talented, and willing to play certain roles in the group.

  With humans, equipped with powerful brains and universal hands, it is possible (and widely observed) that the same person plays different roles whenever they take part in the activities of several groups at the same time. The same person can even play different roles at the same time. For example, it is often said, "When you are self-employed, you wear many hats." (140).

  When speaking about roles, we can identify the following terms:

  (a) *Role Identity*: certain attributes and behaviors consistent with a role.

  (b) *Role Perception*: an individual's view of how he or she is supposed to act in a given situation.

  (c) *Role Expectations*: how others believe a person should act in a given situation.

  (d) *Psychological Contract*: an unwritten agreement that sets out what management expects from the employee and what the employee expects from the management.

(e) *Role Conflict*: a situation in which an individual is confronted by divergent role expectations.

- **Norms**

Norms are defined as acceptable standards of behavior within a group and are shared by the group's members. Norms tell members what they ought to do and ought not to do under certain circumstances. The majority of norms in *social structures* are informal. They are even considered as characteristics of the group because they are so unique. However, some classes of norms are quite common and are listed at the end of this discussion.

Norms typically develop gradually as group members learn what behavior is necessary for the group to function effectively. Emerging norms have several possible sources:

(a) Norms can be imposed in explicit ways by powerful or ruling members.

(b) Critical events can impose precedents of norms.

(c) Early patterns of behavior can create norms.

(d) Norms can be imported by group members from their past activities in other groups.

When norms are defined, the group directly or indirectly "presses" its members for *conformity*, that is to adjust one's behavior to align with the norms of the group. As a result, some individual behavior can be seriously affected by, for example, judgments because of the conformity effect.

Common norms include the following classes:

(a) *Performance Norms*: every group requires certain results, usually to be in between certain upper and lower limits. Individuals can even be punished in some nonformal way if they exceed performance norms imposed by the group.

(b) *Appearance Norms*: usually groups tend to create formal dress codes, for example, to be distinguished from other groups or environments or to emphasize loyalty to the group.

(c) *Social Arrangement Norms*: these norms primarily regulate social interaction within the group.

(d) *Allocation of Resource Norms*: regulate pay, assignment of easy and difficult tasks, equipment, and so forth.

- **Status**

Status is the socially defined relative position or rank given to the group or group members by others. It is in fact ordering of groups or group members and will affect their prestige, privileges, and influence, for example, on decision-making and for various benefits. Typically, there are obvious direct status symbols, for example, titles or indirect privileges that result from position such as quality of the office. It is a well-confirmed fact in *group dynamics* that high-status members of the group tend to be more influential than low-status members.

Status and norms are related within the group. It is observed that high status members of the group have more freedom in departure from group norms and are less affected by the pressure of conformity.

- **Size**

  The size of the group seriously affects its behavior. Most researchers define a small group as having at least three and no more than 12 to 15 members. A group needs to have at least three members; otherwise it would simply be a dyad. With three members, coalitions can be formed, and some kind of organization is present. Too large a group (more than 12 to 15 members) inhibits the group members' ability to communicate with everyone else in the group. This problem is discussed more extensively later because "the size of *computational space*" while modeling and evaluating the *collective intelligence* of a given *social structure* is one of the key parameters. It also affects the level of nondeterminism, and as a result, the computational methods used for analysis and evaluation of *collective intelligence*.

  > In general, it can be stated on the basis of observation that large groups are good for gaining diverse input, but small groups are better at doing something productive with that input (143).

  Large groups have greater abilities than individuals but not proportionally to the number of group members, as would be expected. This is an important problem[42] from the *collective intelligence* point of view and should now be briefly discussed.

  For specific problems, we are able to measure individual performance of a member's participation in group-solving of a problem. With problems like, for example, *rope pulling*, the individual and group performance can be precisely measured. Here, the summing up of an individual group member's input is required to maximize the group product; such tasks are called *additive tasks*. However, it has been observed that group performance is normally lower than the sum of individual abilities, which is called the *Ringelmann effect*.

  The easiest explanation for this phenomenon is to refer to the *so-called social loafing* effect. This term defines the tendency of individuals to expend less effort while working collectively than while working individually. The increase in size of the group is inversely related (143) to individual performance; however, this depends on many factors, such as culture, how the group is organized (management), and so forth.

[42] Surprisingly, the same phenomenon has been observed while analyzing the speed-up of computations when the number of processors in a multi-processor configuration is increases. See Amdahl's law in the Introduction.

Surprisingly, it also happens with mental cooperation (142), in tasks such as the following:

- Intellectual puzzles
- Creative tasks
- Perceptual judgments
- Complex reasoning

B.W. Johnson and F.P. Johnson (142) provided summarized results (Fig. 2-37.) from an unpublished review and theoretical analysis of the *social loafing* effect on the basis of 49 studies involving more than 4000 participants.

In general, the *social loafing* effect will not occur under the following conditions:

1. When individual contributions are clearly identified by fellow group members
2. When subjects are personally involved in the task
3. When there is high group cohesion
4. When the task is challenging and unique
5. When the task is salient or prominent

Speaking of "*cases of group inefficiency*," we should also keep in mind that groups can also perform tasks that are beyond the abilities of individuals, where it makes no sense to speak about the ability of the individual with such a problem; so the term *social loafing* is no longer appropriate. This problem is discussed more when speaking about *Group processes*, such as *synergy*.

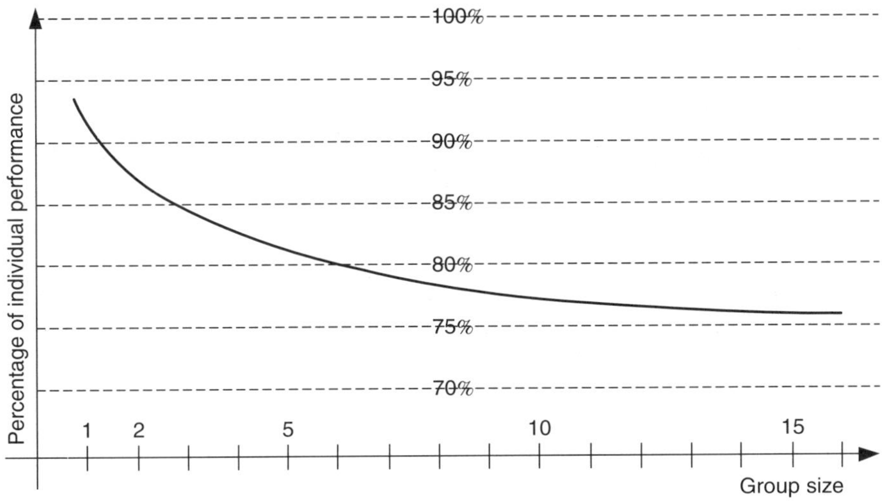

Figure 2-37. Social loafing dependency for additive tasks according to B.W. Johnson and F.P. Johnson (142).

The size of the group affects group structure and behavior on at least two levels:

(a) The number of possible relationships increases rapidly when the size of the group is growing. According to R.W. Napier and M.K. Gershenfeld (144), an increase in potential relationships is related to an increase of group size, as shown in Table 2-3.

(b) Every human requires a certain living space (or *personal space* according to M.E. Shaw (145)); thus an increase in group size will affect the distance between them and as a consequence, the general communication abilities. Increasing distance makes interpersonal communication more difficult and as negative *feedback*, reduces the number of relationships. As a result, communication technology used in a *social structure* must be altered and/or individual and group behavior must be changed.

Therefore, if a group grows larger, the individuals tend to travel more, and larger groups tend to break into subgroups (144), which can lead to creation of *organizations*.

Communication then takes on another dimension as subgroups relate to each other. Besides individual interactions, interaction emerges in between subgroups.

When groups are larger, there are greater available member resources for accomplishment of problem-solving, the average contribution of each member declines, and it becomes more difficult to reach agreement on a group solution.

The optimal size of groups according to Robbins (143) is five to seven members, because this size has the best properties of both small and large groups and is of the preferred odd number of members, which eliminates the possibility of ties while making group decisions.

- **Composition**

Except for specific tasks, where amplification (sum) of a specific ability is required, most of the active groups require a variety of skills and knowledge.

For this reason, heterogeneous groups (composed of dissimilar individuals) are, in general, more effective. However, heterogeneity can also act against the group, for example, cultural heterogeneity, because it makes contacts between members of the group (at least at the beginning) more difficult and thus, delays emergence of efficient internal structure. As a result, such a group begins to be very efficient after some time.

J. Greenberg and R. Baron (140) provide a very illustrative comparison of culturally homogeneous and heterogeneous groups over a span of four months from the performance point of view (see Fig. 2-38.). For the first month, the homogeneous group has a much higher performance, which later vanishes as the heterogeneous group takes advantage of its diversity.

TABLE 2-3. Correlation of Increases in Potential Relationships with Increase in Group Size

Size of Group	Number of Potential Relationships
2	1
3	6
4	25
5	90
6	301
7	966

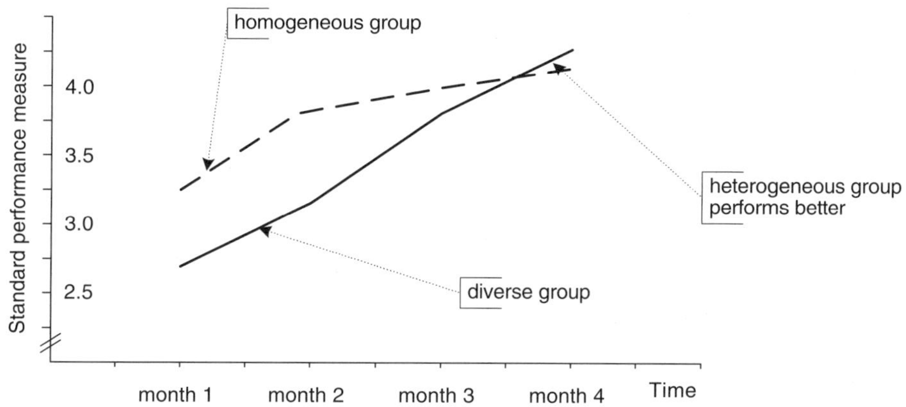

Figure 2-38. Comparison of performance for culturally homogoeneous and diverse groups (140).

In general, the problem of group composition can be viewed from a different perspective: as static (for example, sex, race, demography, educational level) or as dynamic, when the problem of new members entering and "stirring" the composition of the group is considered.

- **Cohesiveness**

This term defines the degree to which group members are attracted to each other and are motivated to stay in the group. *Cohesiveness* is considered an important factor for providing greater productivity of the group. The interdependence between *cohesiveness*, imposed *performance norms*, and resultant *group productivity* can be simply assembled as illustrated in Figure 2-39.

An increase in group cohesiveness can be accomplished with the use of the following methods:

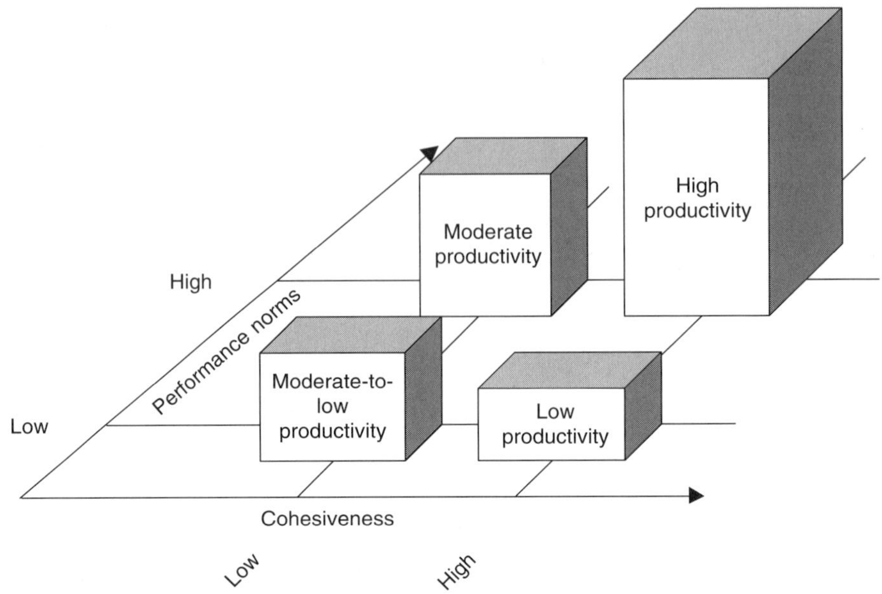

Figure 2-39. Impact of cohesiveness and performance norms on productivity (143).

- □ Reduction of the size of the group
- □ Group organization encouraging agreement with group goals
- □ Behavior of the group that causes members to spend more time together
- □ High status of the group and high barriers for membership
- □ Competition with other groups
- □ A reward system that focuses on "group, not on individual awards"
- □ Isolation of the group.

GROUP PROCESS. The next component (shown before in Fig. 2-36.) is identified as *Group process*. Here, we discuss only the basic concepts and properties of *Group process* to build our understanding of groups (for readers not familiar with *group dynamics*).

For the understanding and evaluation of the *Group process* from an organizational behavior point of view, there are several important elements:

1. The communication system applied by the group or used there by default
2. The decision-making process
3. The nature of the leaders and their behavior
4. Power dynamics
5. Conflict interaction

These elements are responsible for creating the group as an entity observed from the outside.

There are two important terms used in sociology and related to *Group processes*:

Synergy: A similar definition was given in Part 2 of the book to introduce the concept of *collective intelligence*. Now, let us look at this term in a slightly different form:

> Synergy: An action of two or more substances that results in an effect that is different from the individual summation of the substances.

Sociology allows negative synergy, giving as an example the effect of *social loafing*. This is fully consistent with our formalization of *collective intelligence* given in Part 3.1, where positive and negative *collective intelligence* are also defined and can be computed giving positive or negative values when properly interpreted.

Social facilitation effect: a tendency to improve or reduce individual performance in response to the presence of others (members of the group).

Taking into consideration the following:

- Performance of a simple, routine, well-learned task is better, that is faster with greater accuracy in the presence of others.
- More complex tasks require more concentration,
- Tasks are negatively affected by the presence of others

J.F. Nunamaker et al. (146) have distinguished five positive factors that lead to *group process gains* and 15 negative reasons for *group process losses*.

GROUP PROCESS GAINS (+)

(1+) More Information

A group as a whole has more information than any one member.

(2+) Synergy

A group member uses information in a different way than others might because that member has different information and/or skills.

(3+) More Objective Evaluation

Groups are better at catching errors than are the individuals who propose ideas.

(4+) Stimulation

Working in a group may stimulate and encourage individuals to perform better.

(5+) Learning

Group members may learn from and imitate more skilled members to improve performance.

GROUP PROCESS LOSSES (–)

(1–) Air-time Fragmentation (Time-sharing)

The group must partition available speaking time among members.

(2–) Attenuation Blocking

This occurs when group members, who are prevented from contributing comments as they occur, forget or suppress their comments later in the meeting because they seem less original, relevant, or important.

(3–) Concentration Blocking

Fewer comments are made because group members concentrate on remembering comments (rather than thinking of new ones) until they can contribute them.

(4–) Attention Blocking

New comments are not generated because group members must constantly listen to what others speak and cannot pause to think.

(5–) Failure to Remember

Group members lack focus on communication, missing or forgetting the contributions of others.

(6–) Conformance Pressure

Group members are reluctant to criticize the comments of others due to politeness or fear of reprisals.

(7–) Evaluation Apprehension

Fear of negative evaluation causes group members to withhold ideas and comments.

(8–) Free Riding (see Social Loafing)

A group member notices that his colleagues contribute more than enough and therefore decides not to participate.

(9–) Cognitive Inertia

Discussion moves along one train of thought without deviating because group members refrain from contributing comments that are not directly related to the current discussion.

(10−) Socializing

Nontask discussion reduces task performance, although some socializing is usually necessary for effective functioning.

(11−) Domination

Some group members exercise undue influence or monopolize the group's time in an unproductive manner.

(12−) Information Overload

Information is presented faster than it can be processed.

(13−) Coordination Problems

There is difficulty in integrating members' contributions because the group does not have an appropriate strategy, which can lead to dysfunctional cycling or incomplete discussions, resulting in premature decisions.

(14−) Incomplete Use of Information

Complete access to and use of information is necessary for successful task completion.

(15−) Incomplete Task Analysis

Incomplete analysis and understanding of the task can result in superficial discussions.

GROUP TASKS. Now let us discuss how to understand the *Group tasks* in Figure 2-36. Many scholars of group behavior have argued that the nature of the task plays an important role in a group's interaction process and performance. Thus, relatively high attention is paid to this problem in our discussion. Extensive discussion on *group tasks* can be found in a paper by I. Zigurs and A.B. Buckland (147). Later, we will refer several times to this paper.

According to M.E. Shaw (145), we can relate *group task* and *group goals* as follows:

> A group forms[43] and continues its existence for some purpose; when this purpose no longer exists, the group disintegrates unless a new purpose can be established. There may be, of course, more than one group purpose. The purpose is usually labeled "group goal," but sometimes it is referred to as "group task."

It is obvious that Shaw does not consider *group goals* and *group tasks* as logically equivalent, although they are considered as interrelated and in some cases as identical.

[43] According to the author this should be: forms or is formed.

He considers a *task* as something superior that generates *goals*. For example, the *task* could be to assemble a machine as a group, which implies the *goals* "to finish the production process as soon as possible, with the least possible effort for the highest quality of final product."

This sociological approach is compatible with the general dictionary[44] definition of the terms *task* and *goal*:

Task: A piece of work assigned or done as part of one's duties or a difficult or tedious undertaking or a function to be performed; an objective.

Goal: The purpose toward which an endeavor is directed; an objective; closely related to the term *intention*.

Shaw (145) provides (as do D. Cartwright and A. Zander (148)) the sociological definition of *group goal*, which fits very well with the "engineering" theory of control. He utilizes the concept of the *space of states* of an object or system, and the transition of the object or system from an *initial* (start) *state* to the one or more alternatives, which is the desired (target state).

This shows an important link between group dynamics and *artificial intelligence* because the concepts of *space of states* and *initial/goal state(s)* are also widely used in AI, as discussed in Section 2.1.3.1

Let us quote Shaw's definition of the *group goal*:

> Group goal is a preferred location of the group in its environment. That is, a group occupies some location in its environment, which can be changed by certain activities of group members. When the group engages in such activities, it is assumed that another location is preferred by all or some of the group members. The location of the group when these activities terminate is regarded as the preferred one and therefore the group's goal.

Such a definition is "formally elegant" and also very convenient (and supportive) for our proposed model of computational *collective intelligence*, but from a *group dynamics* and sociological point of view, it is not very useful and has been criticized.

Group goals must be considered *compositions* of individual goals, despite difficulties at the level of definition, to allow insights into the role of an individual in the group and to control and manipulate participation of the individual efficiently. The previous definition takes the group to the position of an *atomic*, abstract object.

However, the question here is what the *composition* of such complex objects as goals entails and how they should be "*computed*" eventually.

The group members may be trying to achieve only individual goals, only *group goals*, or both individual and *group goals*. Some individual goals may be contradictory, such as maximizing their own profit in the case of two partners

[44] The American Heritage Dictionary of the English language, 3rd ed., Houghton Mifflin, 1992.

in a business. Some people are in fact forced[45] (enslaved) to be members of a group and thus committed to specific goals imposed by more prominent or master members.

Thus, the fundamental difficulty while speaking about groups here is that we have to consider *group* versus *individual tasks (goals).*

The group may have one main goal but may have at the same time multiple lower level goals. Moreover, goals can be considered as immediate or long-range.

The difficulties discussed here with the problem of *group tasks and goals* resulted in the emergence of *task analysis*, where we can discuss three general approaches:

1. **The Development of Standard Group Tasks**

   A standard task is defined as a task with known characteristics that is adaptable to the study of a variety of problems relative to group behavior.

   From our computational *collective intelligence* point of view, the importance of research results here lies in the fact that *standard group tasks* are potential candidates for tests to estimate the *collective intelligence quotient (IQS).*

2. **Typology of Tasks**

   In practice, this means division of tasks into specific categories.

   There are several possible approaches to this problem, starting, for example, from complexity of tasks, if they are conjunctive or disjunctive, and so forth. Several methods to present typology are also used. This variety is "self explanatory", if we remember the variety of IQ tests and even applied, multidimensional presentation methodologies, as given in Section 2.1.2. Zigurs and Buckland's (147) classification of the basic task categories is given in Table 2-4.

   There is also a widely used typology suggested by McGrath (149) who has combined the main ideas of a number of scientists into a conceptually related set of distinctions about tasks.

   McGrath has constructed a typology diagram (see Fig. 2-40) that he called a *task circumplex*. His attempt represents a reasonable way to classify *group tasks*; virtually all tasks used in group research can be accommodated.

   Let us now explain the elements of McGrath circumplex.

   McGrath has proposed four basic processes, represented by the four quadrants that are distinguished within this model. They are labeled for the particular performance processes that are engaged by the task. The quadrants indicate types of tasks:

   - Generation
   - Choosing answers

[45] For example, slaves on galley ships.

TABLE 2-4. Classification of Basic Task Categories (147)

Classification	Basic Task Categories
Group activities	Clerical, discussion, intellectual construction, mechanical assembly, motor coordination, reasoning
Complexity	Simple vs. complex
Difficulty	Easy vs. difficult
Behavior requirements of intellective tasks that yield written products	Production, discussion, problem-solving
Behavior requirements of intellective tasks	Discussion, decision, performance
Unitary tasks ultimately classified into one of four types on the basis of how member contributions are permitted to be combined to produce a single final product	Unitary vs. divisible, maximizing vs. optimizing, prescribed process vs. permitted process (disjunctive, conjunctive, additive, discretionary)
Six nonexclusive continua	Difficulty, solution multiplicity, intrinsic interest, cooperation requirements, population familiarity, intellectual–manipulative requirements
Group member relationships and task performance processes	Among cooperative groups: intellective vs. decision-making; among competitive or mixed-motive groups: two-person, two-choice tasks vs. bargaining & negotiation vs. coalition formation
Dimensions of tasks at the work unit level	Difficulty, variability, interdependence
What the group or individual is to do, presented as a "circumplex," a circle divided into four quadrants with two categories in each quadrant	Generate (planning vs. creativity); choose (intellective vs. decision-making); negotiate (cognitive conflict vs. mixed motive); execute (contests/battles vs. performances/psychomotor)
Various combinations of four basic complexity attributes	Simple, decision, judgment, problem, fuzzy

- Negotiation
- Execution

These quadrants can be subdivided into two types of tasks each:

Quadrant I: Generate

Type 1: Planning tasks. Generating plans for actions. The basic concept is the *action-oriented plan.*

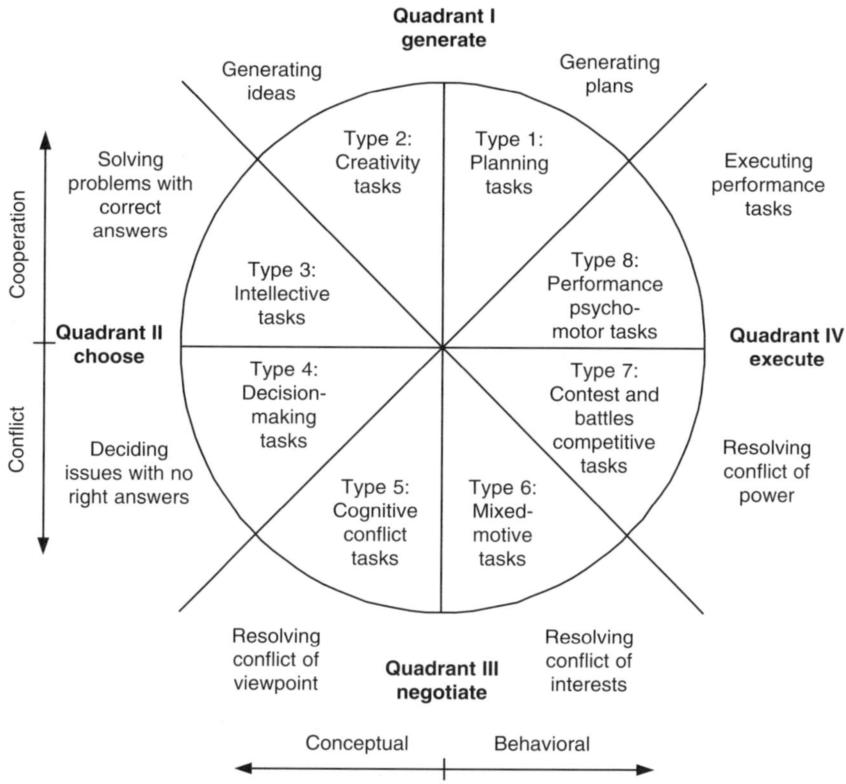

Figure 2-40. McGrath task typology with *circumplex.*

Type 2: Creativity tasks. Generating ideas or images. The basic concept is *creativity.*

This category is related to the adjacent intellective problem category in having an emphasis on cognitive matters.

Quadrant II: Choose

Type 3: Intellective tasks. The basic concept is *the correct answer.*

Performing intellective tasks means to find a correct answer for a given problem. Examples of intellective tasks are logic problems and other problem-solving tasks with correct but not compelling answers — tasks for which expert consensus defines answers.

Type 4: Decision-making tasks. The basic concept is the *preferred answer.*

Typically, for such tasks there is no correct answer provided. The *group's task* is to select by some consensus (based on what is morally right or what is to be preferred), an appropriate alternative. Examples include tasks used in risky shift, choice shift, and group polarization studies.

Quadrant III: Negotiate

According to McGrath, this quadrant is more or less an extension of quadrant II, Choose, under conditions where there is intraunit conflict. The basic concept here is not solving but *resolving*.

Type 5: Cognitive conflict tasks. The basic concept is *resolving policy conflicts*.

In this case, members not only have different preferences but also have systematically different preference structures.

Type 6: Mixed-motive tasks. The basic concept is *resolving pay-off conflicts*.

In this category, a number of subtypes may be distinguished. They range from those with an emphasis on resolution (compromise or agreement) to ones with an emphasis on power. Examples include negotiations and bargaining tasks as well as coalition-formation tasks.

Quadrant IV: Execute

This quadrant deals with physical behavior. Though such tasks are very heavily represented in the workaday world, they are quite under represented in research on groups, according to McGrath.

Type 7: Contests and battles. The basic concept is *winning*. Contests are tasks for which the group is in competition with an opponent or in the worst cases, an enemy. Performance results are interpreted in terms of a winner and a loser. The pay-offs are interpreted in those terms as well. Examples are competitive sports, all winner-take-all conflicts, and wars.

Type 8: Performances. That include tasks that do not involve competition against an opponent but rather involve striving to meet standards of excellence with the pay-offs tied to such standards. These tasks involve complex sets of activities requiring coordination between members over time. Examples include many physical tasks (lifting, digging, pushing, etc.) and some sports events.

The McGrath's task *circumplex* is a two-dimensional representation.

- The horizontal dimension shows a contrast between behavioral or action tasks to the right and conceptual or intellectual tasks to the left.
- The vertical dimension reflects a contrast between cooperation and facilitative compliance at the top and conflict or cooperative interdependence at the bottom.

3. Dimensional Analysis of Group Tasks

In his book on *group dynamics* Shaw (145) provides us with an important and interesting presentation of his work on dimensional analysis of group tasks. He followed the methodology of identifying dimensions and constructing the attitude scales proposed by Thurstone (in 150) to describe individual *intelligence*.

Thus, Shaw provides one more bridge between the abilities of an individual and a group of individuals, which is one of the key elements for the general computational model of *collective intelligence*. We should keep in mind that an individual is also a one-member group, and all ability tests designed for groups should also work when scaled down to one individual.

Shaw's methodology was to first identify ten potential task dimensions on the basis of a literature review and discussion with other prominent researchers. Next, a sample of 104 tasks was sorted by 49 specialists along the 10 previously selected potential task dimensions, using eight categories.

Later to remove redundant dimensions, Shaw computed intercorrelations among task dimensions, and the factor analysis was carried out.

As a result of that analysis and additional theoretical considerations, six task dimensions were identified as relatively independent. They are given below with some basic comments:

1. **Difficulty**

   This can be defined as the amount of effort required for completing the task.

2. **Solution Multiplicity**

   Solution multiplicity may be defined as the degree to which there is more than one correct solution to the task. This dimension is itself complex because several parameters are involved here, such as the number of alternatives and the number of methods needed to arrive at a given solution.

3. **Intrinsic Interest**

   This dimension for the *group task* is defined as the degree to which the task, in and of itself, is interesting, motivating, or attractive to the group members.

4. **Cooperative requirements**

   This may be defined as the degree to which integrated action of group members is required to complete the task.

5. **Intellectual–Manipulative Requirements**

   This dimension is given by the ratio of mental requirements to motor requirements of the *group task*. It has been assumed that tasks at the upper extreme of this dimension require only mental activities for task completion, whereas those at the low end of the continuum require only motor activities for completion.

6. **Population Familiarity.**

   This is defined by the degree to which members of the larger society encounter the task. It means that there is a higher probability that certain members of the group are more familiar with certain tasks because during their normal activities, they practice solving similar tasks.

PERFORMANCE AND SATISFACTION. The last functional block in Figure 2-36 is *Performance and Satisfaction*. Here we briefly discuss the problem of *satisfaction* because *performance* of the group requires a special, longer presentation. This is discussed in Section 2.2.3.4, where there is a list of findings and observations on the *performance* of *beings* and *social structures*.

Greenberg and Baron (140) define *job satisfaction* as people's cognitive, affective, and evaluative reactions toward their jobs.

In general, larger groups are associated with lower satisfaction; however, this situation is not clear. The mean correlation between *job satisfaction* and *performance* is considerably small; there are two main explanations (140):

1. Performance of many jobs is highly restricted by "definition of position and task" occupied by individuals. This is due to both technological and interpersonal factors.
2. *Satisfaction* and *performance* can not be directly related, but they are related indirectly by the fact that they stem from the same factor: "receipt of various rewards."

For a more formal summary of the *satisfaction* problem, we should refer to one of the available theories of *job satisfaction*. For example, V.P. Richmond and J.C. McCroskey (151) discuss three approaches to the problem of *job satisfaction*, illustrating the gradual development of current research on it. These approaches provide some explanations regarding the nature and origins of *job satisfaction*. We can present them as follows:

1. **A Global or One Factor Approach to *Job Satisfaction***

   This approach presents the global reaction in which an employee's single response is put on a continuum from very satisfied to very dissatisfied. While this approach does not deny that an employee may like some things in the work environment while disliking others, it views the interface of these competing reactions to represent a general, single-dimensional *satisfaction* response. Such a response does not allow an employee to express reactions to various facets of his or her work environment.

2. **Herzberg's Two Factor Theory of *Job Satisfaction***

   A second approach, which grew out of the limitations inherent in the one-factor approach, was Herzberg's two-factor theory of *job satisfaction* (152). This two-factor theory suggested dual continua, one for *satisfaction* and one for *dissatisfaction*, rather than a single *satisfaction–dissatisfaction* continuum. It posits that an employee can be potentially very satisfied and very dissatisfied at the same time in response to different elements in the employment environment. The *satisfaction* factors are known as *motivators*, and include [according to (140)] the following:

- Promotion opportunities
- Opportunities for personal growth
- Recognition
- Responsibility
- Achievements

The *dissatisfaction* criteria are known as *hygiene* factors and they include the following:

- Pay,
- Security
- Physical working conditions

3. Multiple Factor Approach to Job Satisfaction

The third approach discussed by Richmond and McCroskey (151) presents *job satisfaction* as being comprised of multiple factors, where each factor represents a separate *satisfaction–dissatisfaction* continuum. This approach has been the most commonly used in recent years. The dimensions of the multiple factors vary from one another. For example, the popular Job description index (JDI) isolates five dimensions of satisfaction:

- Supervision
- Work
- Pay
- Promotion
- Co-workers

At the end of our discussion about *groups* as forms of *social structures*, teams should be mentioned as special kinds of groups. According to Greenberg and Baron (140), the team can be given the following definition:

> a group whose members have complementary skills and are committed to a common purpose or set of performance goals for which they hold themselves mutually accountable.

The team is considered a group with a higher level of integration of members, as is clear in the comparison [based on (143)] given in Figure 2-41.

Now, let us advance in size and complexity of human *social structures*, that is, to consider groups and teams as components of *organizations*.

Large Social Structures — Organizations

We would like to consider the following definition (140) of *organization*:

> a structured social system consisting of groups and individuals working together to meet some agreed-upon objectives.

Property	Work Group	Work Team
Structure	Loosely coupled	Highly integrated
Goal	Share information	Collective performance
Synergy	Neutral, sometimes positive	Positive
Accountability	Individual	Individual or mutual
Skills	Random or varied	Complementary

Figure 2-41. Work groups vs. work team (143).

Groups and organizations can be considered both from a static (structural) and a dynamic (how the organization evolves or changes in a given span of time) point of view.

However, from the computational *collective intelligence* point of view, the essential thing is the dynamic process of logical inference (problem-solving) performed by the group or organization (inside) and not how the group or organization evolves in space or time.

In the next section, there will be some basic considerations on phases starting from creation (emergence) through evolution to disintegration of the group or organization, but in general, the problem of evolution of the group or organization is left for later, with more advanced considerations on computational *collective intelligence*. Regarding organizations, only some basic terms and concepts will be considered here.

Organizations are often looked at from the external point of view using the concept of the so-called *open system* (definition given earlier), as presented in Figure 2-42.

Figure 2-42 presents *organizational behavior* (OB) concept from the external point of view. In terms of computational *collective intelligence*, we will express this in the following way:

> this is the information molecule of a certain level CS^i, with a specific, surrounding degenerated membrane, allowing input and output of specific types of CS^j of lower levels.

First, we ask how the organization behaves from the external point of view and then we have the question "what could or should be inside the functional block representing such organizations?," that is, what does the theory of *organizational behavior* say about the practice of internal ordering of organizations as *social structures*. This is an important question for us because it points to some possible configurations of *computational spaces*, optimal at least from a human point of view. In other words, we are interested in the problem of mapping given organization into a proper *computational space* of a certain order and then making use of computational *collective intelligence* by optimizing the organization's IQS.

In recent literature on *organizational behavior*, there are two distinctive structural models:

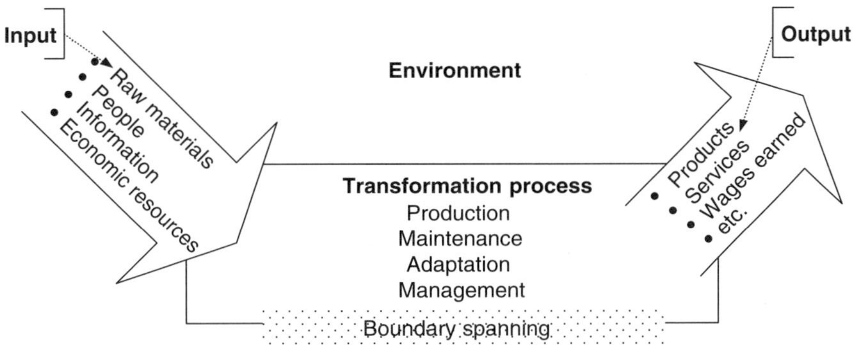

Figure 2-42. Organization as an open system.

- **Mechanistic Model**

  Such a model can be defined as a structure with extensive departmentalization, high formalization, a limited information network, and centralization.

  Moreover, Robbins (143) also attributes the mechanistic model with high specialization, a clear chain of command, and a narrow span of control.

  J.R. Gordon (153) attributes the mechanistic structure of organization as bureaucratic and inflexible, with jobs and tasks clearly defined. As an example, he gives the structure of a hospital.

  Figure 2-43 presents a graphic interpretation of the mechanistic and organic models of organization, illustrated here for better perception of the structural differences between them.

- **Organic Model**

  This type of model is defined as a flat, decentralized structure that uses cross-hierarchical and cross-functional arrangement of groups or teams, with low-level formalization and a comprehensive information network, where the flow of information is free and the structure relies on participative decision-making.

Organizations emerge, develop to some extent, and gradually disintegrate, similar to smaller groups, or are absorbed by other organizations as a whole or in part.

It is interesting to see diagrams of the development of organizations similar to those in Figures 2-33 and 2-34 for smaller *social structures*, that is, groups.

D.J. Cherrington (154) provides us (from (155)) with a diagram of an organizational life cycle, as presented in Figure 2-44.

Let us comment briefly about this table for clarification because some concepts here are new as compared with the life cycle of a small group.

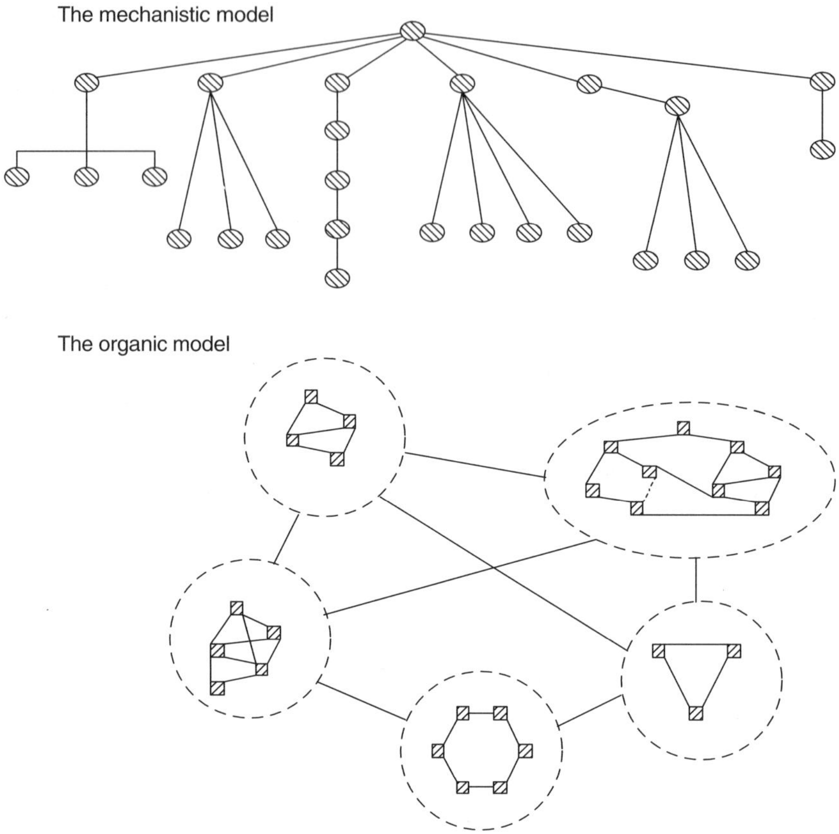

Figure 2-43. The mechanistic and organic models of organization.

Stage 1: Entrepreneurial Stage

If it is a business/production organization, the emphasis in this cycle is on creation of products or services or any kind of activity that will survive in the marketplace (survive the destructive impact of environment). There must be entrepreneur(s) or *beings* who start (initialize) the organization. When the organization is small, it adopts an organic structure. Strong leadership is required at this stage of the life cycle.

Stage 2: Collectivity Stage

Substructures emerge in this stage, based on division of labor along with hierarchy of authority. At this stage, the structure is still organic. A strong, charismatic leader should provide the goals and direction for the organization in this phase. Inside the organization, there must be found mechanisms to coordinate and control substructures. This stage is also characterized by high involvement and productivity of individuals.

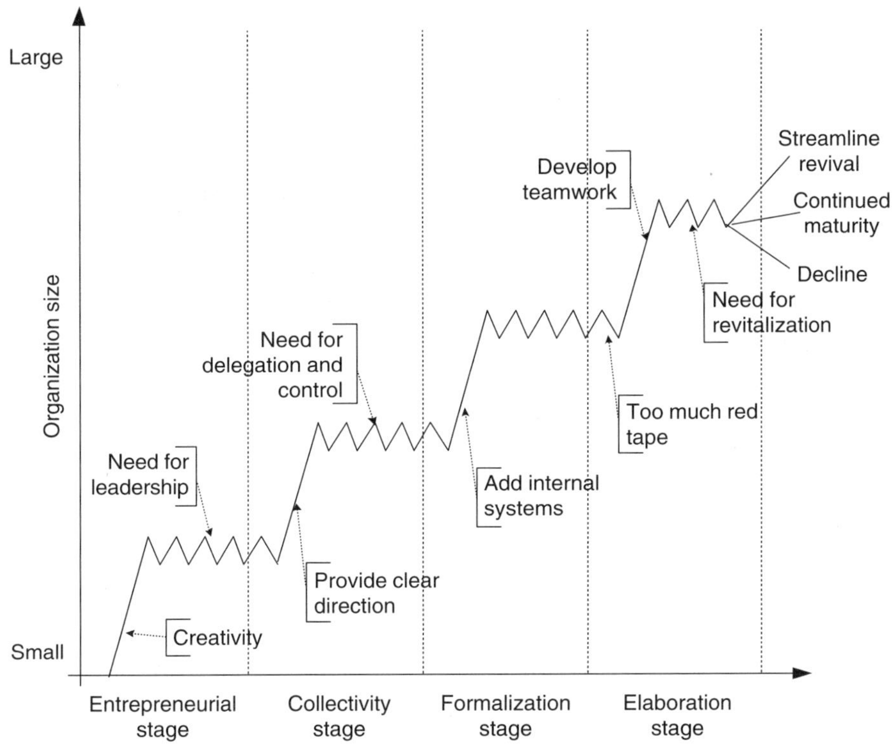

Figure 2-44. Organizational life cycles.

Stage 3: Formalization Stage

At this stage, the bureaucratic characteristics of the organization emerge and start to affect its activity. The style of work changes both for management and for lower level staff since support groups emerge and the division of labor is clarified. Problems with coordination and control of organization also appear.

Stage 4: Elaboration Stage

The organization must overcome the unnecessary ballast of bureaucratic procedures to continue its growth, development, and existence. It is characteristic that the highest percentage of individual energy is spent on maintaining the organization and not on activities like production and innovation.

The organization can decline after a certain period of time either because it is no longer able to compete in the market place or because the environment has changed in a critical way. Fundamental for survival of the organization is the ability to enter the *renewal process*, either through change of management or restructuralization, recentralization, reallocation, and so forth.

We will not go deeper into considerations on organizations here, but at the end of this discussion, let us give some conclusions prevalent in the literature on *organizational behavior*. Here is the basic conclusion:

IN GENERAL, THERE IS NO SINGLE, BEST ORGANIZATIONAL DESIGN

There are several reasons:

- Successful organizations in relatively stable and in secure environments tend to be mechanistic.
- Relatively organic organizations tend to be the successful ones when the environment is unstable and unreliable.
- The organic structure works best when technological complexity is either very low or high.
- When technological complexity is moderate, a mechanistic structure is more effective.

2.2.3.2. Information-Related Behavior of Beings in a Social Structure

The basis for all interaction between beings, especially between humans, fundamental to all group and organizational functioning is *communication*.

Every being or group must take in and use information. The existence of *beings*, groups, and organizations depends on *communication*: on exchange of information and on transmitting meaning.

When analyzing social structures through the concept of *communication*, the difficulty of "how to start" arises because there are many alternative definitions of communication — approximately one hundred according to the analysis of F. Dance (156).

The fundamental difficulty in our comprehension of *communication* is shown in the example, often used in this book, of the "two rival and thus hostile shoemakers," who do not speak to each other when they meet on the street because they are business competitors in the shoe market. However, they both very carefully watch the products of the other, as well as own position and share in the shoe market, through constant observation of the shoes worn by passers-by on the street. In this case of communication, the artifacts, the frequency of appearance, and so forth of the other shoemaker's products are transferring *bits*, *bytes*, and *words* of complex and general information. They speak "in the name" of other shoemaker.

> Generalizing communication between beings, exchange of messages can be generated consciously or unconsciously and can take the form of any change in a common (for beings) environment or outlook of the beings (sender).

The communication process can be expressed according to Gordon (153), very generally with the terms of *sender, receiver, channel, noise*, and *feedback*, as given in Figure 2-45.

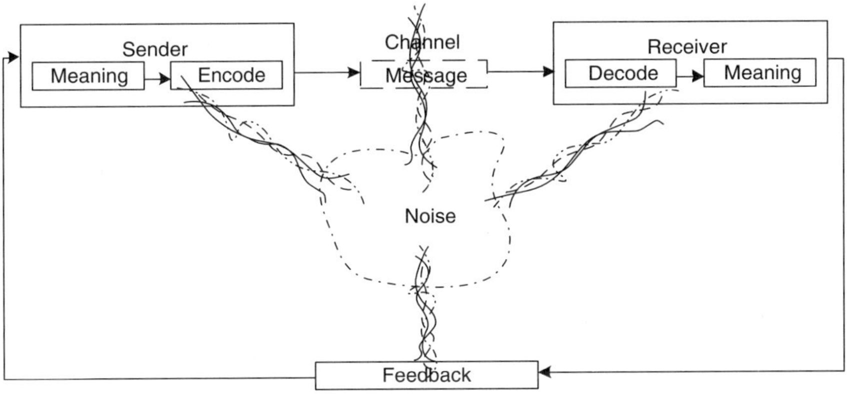

Figure 2-45. The communication process.

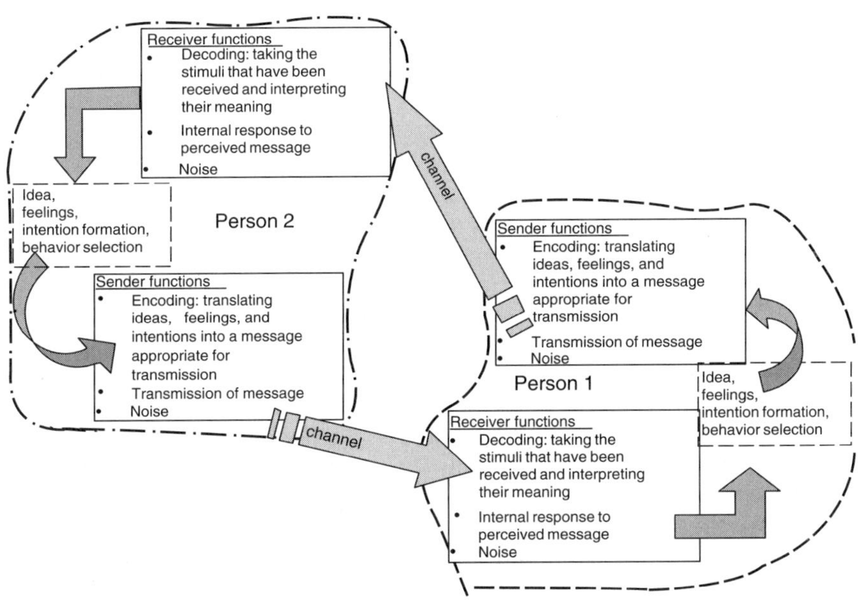

Figure 2-46. Model of the interpersonal communication process (142).

However, if we restrict ourselves here to interpersonal communication between two people, we can assume the model of a communication process presented by Johnson and Johnson (142) in Figure 2-46. The terminology used by them (142) (sender, receiver, message, and channel) corresponds well to that of computer technology and computations with agents, which are discussed later on in Section 3.4.5.4.

From the organizational behavior of groups and organizations the following (see Table 2-5) communication methods can be distinguished with their advantages and disadvantages (153).

TABLE 2-5. Communication Methods with their Advantages and Disadvantages

Method	Advantages	Disadvantages
Face-to-face	Visual Personal contact Show and explain possible Can set the mood Immediate feedback	Timing may be inconvenient Requires spontaneous thinking May not be easy to terminate Power or status of one person can cause pressure
Meetings	Can use visuals Involve several minds at once Two-way flow	Time-consuming Time may be inconvenient One person may dominate the group
Telephone	Verbal Permits questions and answers Convenient Two-way flow Immediate feedback	Less personal No record of conversation Message may be misunderstood Timing may be inconvenient May be impossible to terminate
Teleconferencing	Saves time for travel Visual Lessens impact of power/status Makes users be better prepared	Miss interpersonal contact Not good for initial brainstorming session Expensive
Memorandum	Brief Provides a record Can prethink the message Can disseminate widely	No control over receiver Less personal One-way flow Delayed feedback
Formal report	Complete; comprehensive Can organize material at writer's leisure Can disseminate widely	Less personal May require considerable time in reading Language may not be understandable Expensive One-way flow Delayed feedback

From a social structure point of view, communication can go in three directions:

1. *Downward Communication*

   This kind takes place when communication flows from a higher level of organization or group to a lower level. It is the standard means of communication between managers and subordinates when assigning goals, job instructions, policies, procedures, and so forth.
2. *Upward Communication*

   In the group or organization, upward communication provides the flow of information to a higher level, in general to provide feedback for management, for example, about current problems, progress toward goals, and so forth.

3. *Lateral Communication*

   This type of communication takes place between members of the same, for example, work group at the same level. They can be workers or managers, but it is required for them to transfer messages between horizontally equivalent personnel in a given structure of the group or organization.

Lateral communication is necessary for optimal synchronization and is the base for informal channels.

The quality of communication, according to J.R. Gordon (153), is affected by the following factors:

- **Structure of Organization**

  This issue is so important that the next Section of the book will be an attempts to discuss this problem more extensively.

- **Interpersonal Relationships between the Sender and Receiver**

  There are four subfactors:

  1. The sender's and receiver's trust of each other
  2. The sender's and receiver's influence over each other
  3. The sender's mobility aspirations
  4. The norms and sanctions of the group or organization to which the sender and receiver belong

- **Nature of Feedback**

  In general, in organizational behavior we define feedback as *knowledge about the impact of the message on the receiver*. The basic function of feedback in a social structure is that it is a means of reducing distortion in the communication process.

- **Noise**

  The noise is the factor capable of distorting the clarity of a message at any point during the communication process. There are many possible sources of noise in communication between group members, for example, poorly encoded messages (written in unclear ways), poorly decoded (not comprehended). The receiver's attention can be diverted from the message; time pressure can result in distortion of transferal of information. Furthermore, organizational policy, physical properties of the environment, or accidental or random changes in the message can act as noise.

- **The Use of Language**

  The choice of words or language in which a message is encoded influences the quality of communication. We should remember that language is a symbolic representation of real objects and processes; thus emerge problems with the perception of language and later on in interpretation. From a social structure point of view, problem-oriented language (e.g., technical jargon) is also important in communication.

- **Listening Skills**

  Listening is not just a *passive* process of perceiving messages, as it is widely considered. In a social structure working for performance, *active listening* is required, that is, the receiver should actively try to grasp the facts and feelings, for example, through modeling and predicting the mental activity of the sender during the communication process.

- **Attitudes of the Parties**

  Here we differentiate between the *collaboration* and the *competition* mode of the sender and the receiver during the communication process.

- **Nonverbal Communication**

  The use of gestures, material things, time, space, and so forth can either clarify or confuse the meaning of, for example, verbal communication, which is basic for human beings. Nonverbal cues serve five basic functions:

  1. To repeat the message
  2. To contradict the message
  3. To substitute for a verbal message
  4. To complement the message
  5. To accent (underline) the message or its elements.

- **The Extent of Cross-cultural Sensitivity**

  Effective communication requires decoding of basic values, motives, aspirations, assumptions, and methods, and can vary significantly from one culture to another. It can be the result of different cultures and religious heritages, or different educational systems resulting from the cultural approach or environment, and so forth.

In conclusion, we present one more element, that is, how *the carrier* of the message affects the quality of communication.

In general, research has shown (157), that:

> The communication is most effective when it uses multiple channels, such as both oral and written messages.

This is not a surprising conclusion because, for example, an oral message can be used to get immediate attention, followed-up by the written part of the message, which is to some extent permanent. Moreover, the oral message profits the sender with an immediate response, even if it is partial. The written message, even

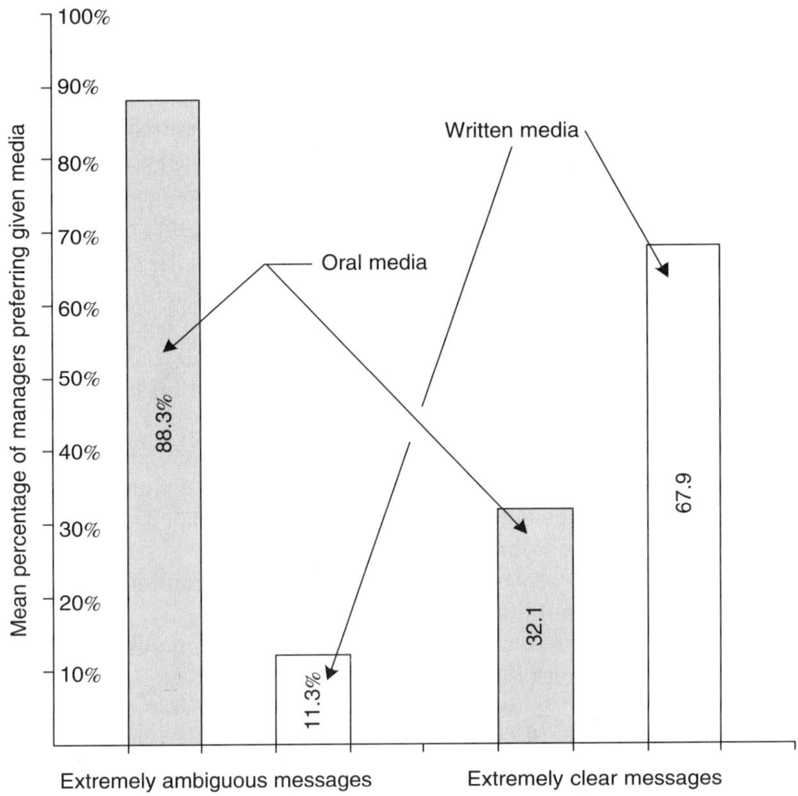

Figure 2-47. Preference between oral and written media.

characterized by a long delay in response, is more formal, and it is more difficult for the receiver to abandon, that is not respond to.

In Figure 2-47, an example comparison (140) shows which type of media managers prefer, depending on the nature of the message. Figure 2-47 can be summarized as follows:

- Oral media are preferred for sending ambiguous messages
- Written media are preferred for sending clear messages.

2.2.3.3. Structuralization and Communication Problems when a Social Structure Grows The *theme* of this book is that *collective intelligence* can be successfully formalized and measured as a quasi-chaotic computational process, performed by a social structure of any nature or size, for solving existing problems in parallel.

It has been observed that the dominant approach presented in books on collective or organizational behavior is to consider groups or organizations in the prevailing static way, as networks of beings organized into structures, with certain dominant networks of information exchange for underlying problem solving. Perhaps this research bias has its roots in the structure of today's digital computers and computer networks, which also create fixed networks of elements.

Communication networks can be also considered in a dynamic way, that is as a process of emergence and reduction (dissolution) of links between dependent elements, for example, in interfirm alliances. This research is labeled as "network dynamics" or "network evolution", such as by N. Contractor (158).

In contrast, the computational model of *collective intelligence* presented in this book assumes that real and abstract *information molecules* representing beings, messages, and so forth, displace quasi-chaotically, and the inferences take place because of rendezvous. Thus no fixed communication network exists, only some *information molecules* representing beings that rendezvous and infer more frequently (compared to others) because of the configuration of *computational space* and their mutual logical compatibility.

To complete our summary of the current understanding of social structures, we should, however, take a look at how the literature on group and organizational behavior describes the exchange of information between members of a group or organization when its size is increasing.

A complex review of recent efforts and tendencies on communication networks has been done by F.M. Jablin and L.L. Putman (159).

For small groups there is an accepted concept of communication networks (e.g., Greenberg and Baron (140,143)):

> Communication structures or networks define how communication within a small group is arranged, who can communicate with whom, and if the communication is direct or through another group member.

Monge and Contractor in (159) provide a more general definition of a communication network:

> Communication networks are the patterns of contact between communication partners that are created by transmitting and exchanging messages through time and space. These networks take many forms in contemporary organizations, including personal contact networks, flows of information within and between groups, strategic alliances between firms, and global network organizations.

Depending on the number of members, we can define and analyze different basic topological structures, reflecting how humans in the real world are communicating. Some examples with their traditional names are given in Figure 2-48. Arrows indicate that only one direction of communication is allowed.

Such networks have been widely analyzed from different points of view, for example for problem-solving efficiency (see Table 2-6), for leadership problems, and so forth (142,145).

There are several possible quality measures; thus, to enter the discussion given in the next section, let us look at one example of an evaluation (see Table 2-8, (142)) for the communication networks given in Figure 2-48.

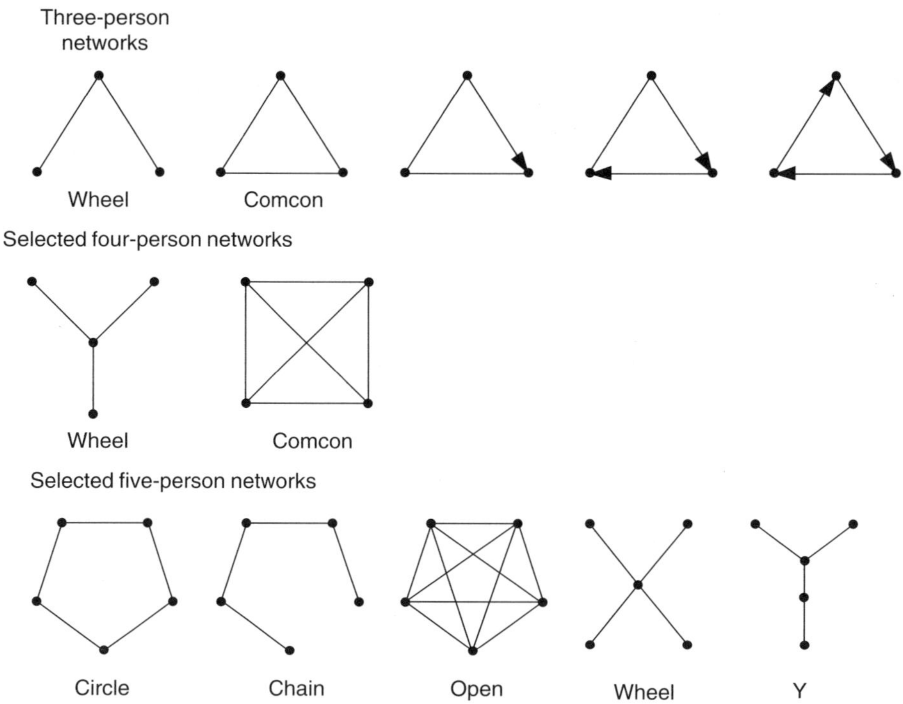

Figure 2-48. Examples of communication networks.

TABLE 2-6. Efficiency Comparison of Centralized (Wheel, Chain, Y) and Decentralized (Circle, Comcon) Networks. Reprinted with permission from McGraw-Hill Companies from M.E. Show, Group Dynamics, 4th ed. 1971.

Aspect	Simple Problems[a]	Complex Problems[b]	Total
Time			
Centralized faster	14	0	14
Decentralized faster	4	18	22
Messages			
Centralized sent more	0	1	1
Decentralized sent more	18	17	35
Errors			
Centralized made more	0	6	6
Decentralized made more	9	1	10
No difference	1	3	4
Satisfaction			
Centralized higher	1	1	2
Decentralized higher	7	10	17

[a]Simple problems: symbol, letter, number, and color identification tasks.
[b]Complex problems: arithmetic, word arrangement, sentence construction, and discussion problems.

TABLE 2-7. Typical Social Network Measures of Ties

Measure	Definition	Example
Indirect links	Path between two actors is mediated by one or more others	A is linked to B; B is linked to C; thus A is indirectly linked to C through B
Frequency	How often the link occurs	A talks to B 10 times per week
Stability	Existence of links over time	A has been friends with B for 5 years
Multiplexity	Extent to which two actors are linked together by more than one relationship	A and B are friends; they seek each other out for advice and work together
Strength	Amount of time, emotional intensity, intimacy, or reciprocal services (frequency and multiplexity often used as measures of strength of tie)	A and B are close friends, or spend much time together
Direction	Extent to which link is from one actor to another	Work flows from A to B, but not from B to A
Symmetry (Reciprocity)	Extent to which relationship is bi-directional	A asks B for advice, and B asks A for advice

In Tables 2-7, 2-8, and 2-9 there are summaries given of major network concepts according to Brass (160).

Studies on communication networks in social structures have been criticized, according to D.J. Cherrington (154), because they are done in vitro in a laboratory, and thus do not reflect real life situations.

To study communication networks in real life situations (life organizations), the following methodology has been proposed, which uses the concept of "communication matrices" (161):

Step 1. A matrix is created for who speaks to whom, that is, the members of the organization are listed down the side of the matrix and across the top, and the communication patterns of who speaks to whom are recorded.

Step 2. When interpersonal communication patterns begin to emerge, the names of individuals are rearranged so that those who interact more frequently are placed closer together on the matrix.

Step 3. Analyzing the emerging communication patterns over time, there are identified cliques.

TABLE 2-8. Typical Social Network Measures Assigned to Individuals

Measure	Definition
Degree	Number of direct links with other actors
In-degree	Number of directional links to an actor from other actors (in-coming links)
Out-degree	Number of directional links from the actor to other actors (out-coming links)
Range (Diversity)	Number of links to different actors (defined as different to the extent that they are not themselves linked to each other, or else represent different groups or status)
Closeness	Extent to which an actor is close to or can easily reach all the other actors in the network, usually measured by averaging the path distances (direct and indirect links) to all others; a direct link is counted as 1; indirect links receive proportionately less weight
Betweenness	Extent to which an actor mediates, or falls between any two other actors on the shortest path between those actors, usually averaged across all possible pairs in the network
Centrality	Extent to which an actor is central to a network. Various measures (including degree, closeness, and betweenness) have been used as indicators of centrality. Some measures of centrality weight an actor's links to others by centrality of those others.
Prestige	On the basis of asymmetric relationships, prestigious actors are the object rather than the source of relations. Measures similar to centrality are calculated by accounting for the direction of the relationship (i.e., in- degree).
Roles	Importance of role and quality of performance
Star	An actor who is highly central to the network
Liaison	An actor who has links to two or more groups that would otherwise not be linked, but is not a member of either group
Bridge	An actor who mediates or controls the flow (is the single link) between one part of the network and another
Isolate	An actor who has no links, or relatively few links to others

An analysis of interaction within communication matrices has suggested the existence of four different basic types of communication roles that occur in group communication networks. According to Cherrington (154) they are as in Figure 2-49. Let us give a brief explanation of basic communication roles:

TABLE 2-9. Typical Social Network Measures Used to Describe Networks

Measure	Definition
Size	Number of actors in the network
Inclusiveness	Total number of actors in a network minus the number of isolated actors (not connected to any other actors). Also measured as the ratio of connected actors to the total number of actors
Component	Largest connected subset of network nodes and links. All nodes in the component are connected (either direct or indirect links) and no nodes have links to nodes outside the component.
Connectivity (Reachability)	Extent to which actors in the network are linked to one another by direct or indirect ties, sometimes measured by the maximum or average path distance between any two actors in the network
Connectedness	Ratio of pairs of nodes that are mutually reachable to the total number of pairs of nodes
Density	Ratio of the number of actual links to the number of possible links in the network
Centralization	Difference between the centrality scores of the most central actor and those of all other actors in a network is calculated and used to form a ratio of the actual sum of the differences to the maximum sum of the differences
Symmetry	Ratio of number of symmetric to asymmetric links (or to total number of links) in a network
Transitivity	Three actors (A, B, C) are transitive if whenever A is linked to B, and B is linked to C, then C is linked to A. Transitivity is the number of transitive triples divided by the number of potential transitive triples (number of paths of length 2)

- **Gatekeepers**

  Individuals who control the flow of communication through a communication channel

- **Liaisons**

  Individuals who connect two or more groups within an organization without belonging to either group

- **Opinion Leaders**

  Individuals who informally influence the attitudes and behaviors of other group members

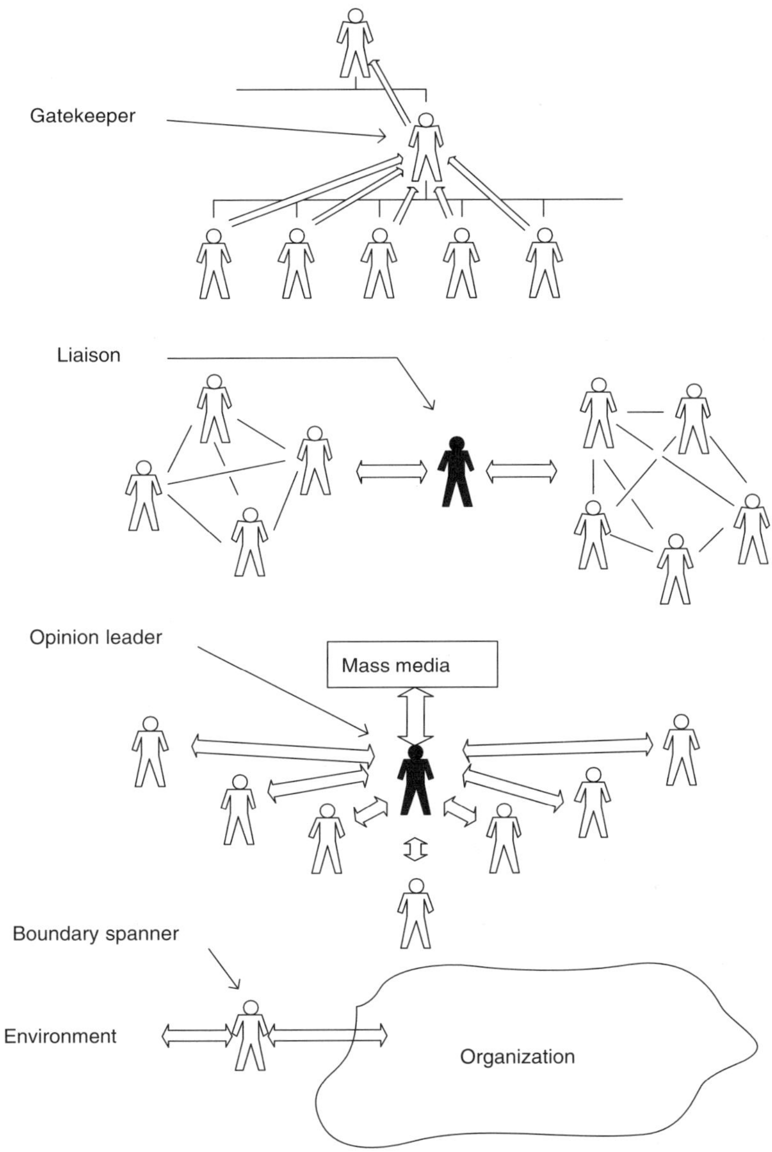

Figure 2-49. Communication Roles.

- **Boundary Spanner**
  Individuals who communicate with the organization's environment

Methodology using communication matrices is considered successful in studying real, large organizations, in vivo. However, it has also been criticized for its inability to manipulate the independent variables such as size, task complexity, and network structure.

Let us now look into prevailing ways of structuring organizations. Greenberg and Baron (140) present and discuss three dominant models:

- Hierarchical organizations
- Matrix organizations
- Boundaryless organizations

HIERARCHICAL ORGANIZATIONS

This type of structure is typical for so-called *product organizations*, where separate units are established to handle different products or product lines. Each of these divisions contains all of the departments necessary for operating as an independent unit.

The general structure can be *tall* or *flat*. In a tall organization, the hierarchy has many layers, and managers have a narrow span of control (i.e., they are responsible for few subordinates). In a flat organization the hierarchy has few layers, and managers have a wide span of control, that is, they are responsible for many subordinates. Figure 2-50 shows the concept of a functional organization in a typical manufacturing firm (140). The so-called *departmentalization* can be done in several ways, for example, by task (as in Fig. 2-50) or by type of output. In general, *departmentalization* is the basis for grouping jobs together to coordinate common tasks. It is possible to *departmentalize* in various ways:

1. *By function*: while grouping people of the same background together, for example, in marketing, engineering, finance, and so forth. It profits by placing shared skills and knowledge into work-groups.
2. *By product*: used to increase accountability by placing all activities related to a product under one manager. Some functions might be duplicated, such

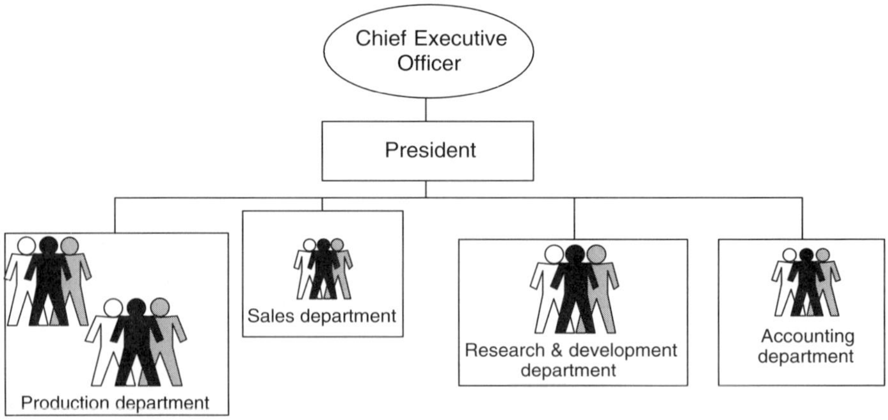

Figure 2-50. Functional Organization of a Typical Manufacturing Firm.

as marketing and engineering for product A, and marketing and engineering for product B.

3. *By geography*: similar to product structure, but the goal is to serve territories better, not specific product users.
4. *By process*: when grouping by work activities; for example, banks have a loan department, teller activities, investment services, and internal investment management. Each area requires different activities.
5. *By customer*: when grouping by customers that have a common set of problems that need specific specialists, for example, law firms, universities with a graduate school and an undergraduate school.

The general observed trend is to apply customer departmentalization and cross-functional teams (teams with members from each function).

In the past, the dominant structures were hierarchical organizations oriented for mass production efficiency, with standardized rules and regulations, and rigid bureaucratic controls. The current tendency is oriented toward flattened hierarchies, decentralized decision-making, blurring structural boundaries, and multiorganizational strategic alliances. Since 1990, more than 75 percent of large U.S. companies have significantly altered their structures to make them more flexible (162).

MATRIX ORGANIZATION

The matrix organization is defined as the type of departmentalization in which a product or project form is superimposed on the functional form of an organization. This organization is especially suitable when it is necessary to assign

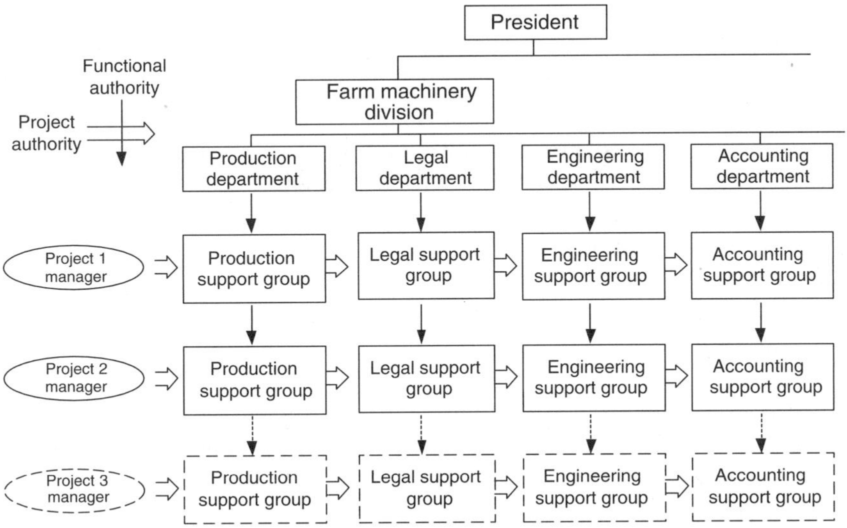

Figure 2-51. A Typical Matrix Organization.

personal responsibility for specific, key products as illustrated in Figure 2-51. This results in a dual system of authority in which some managers report to two bosses, that is, to a project (or product) manager and a functional (departmental) manager.

The weakness of this structuralization is that it creates confusion, fosters power struggles, and increases employee stress. The strengths are that it allows coordinates multiple projects that are complex and interdependent, efficiently allocating available specialists.

BOUNDARYLESS ORGANIZATION

Recently there has been a growing popularity of and a number of attempts to organize a real company on the pattern of *boundaryless organization*. This is supported by globalization of certain companies which must work efficiently beyond national borders, cultures, and habits of local employees, or local rules and regulations (e.g., KLM Airlines, (163)). Greenberg and Baron (140) give the boundaryless organization the following definition:

> An organization in which chains of command are eliminated, spans of control are unlimited, and rigid departments give way to empowered teams.

The *true* boundaryless organization is free of both internal and external barriers. On the basis of the method of elimination of the external boundaries, there are known variations of boundaryless organizations, such as modular and virtual organizations. They are presented together in Figure 2-52a, 2-52b for better comparison.

In general, the *boundaryless organization* can be characterized in the following ways:

- Departments replaced with empowered teams
- Chains of command minimized, spans of control limited
- Vertical barriers broken down through creation of cross-hierarchical teams, participative decision-making, "360 degree" performance appraisals
- Horizontal barriers broken down, introducing cross-functional teams, project-driven activities, lateral transfers and job rotation
- External barriers broken down through globalization, strategic alliances, customer-organizational linkages, and telecommuting
- Business boosted by possibility of building company–owned computer networks that expedite communication across intra-organizational and inter-organizational barriers.

Now let us give some basic definitions of the variations:

Modular Organization: an organization that surrounds itself by a network of other organizations to which it regularly outsources noncore functions.

Virtual Organization: a highly flexible, temporary organization formed by a group of companies that join forces to exploit a specific opportunity.

In general, a virtual organization is flexible but is characterized by very limited control over many parts of the organization.
Finally our presentation and analysis here has taken us to some general questions:

1. Which group or organizational structure is better?
2. What are the benefits of the different structures?

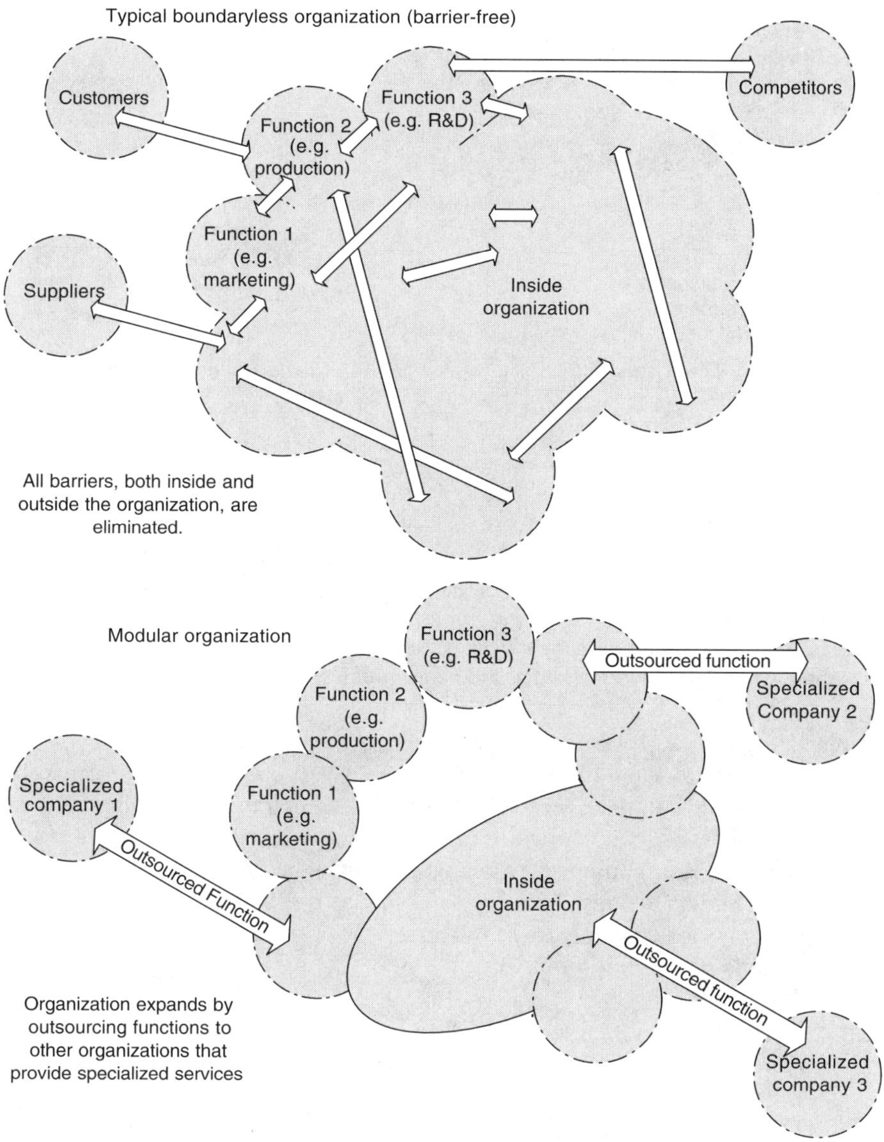

Figure 2-52a. Boundaryless Organization in various Forms

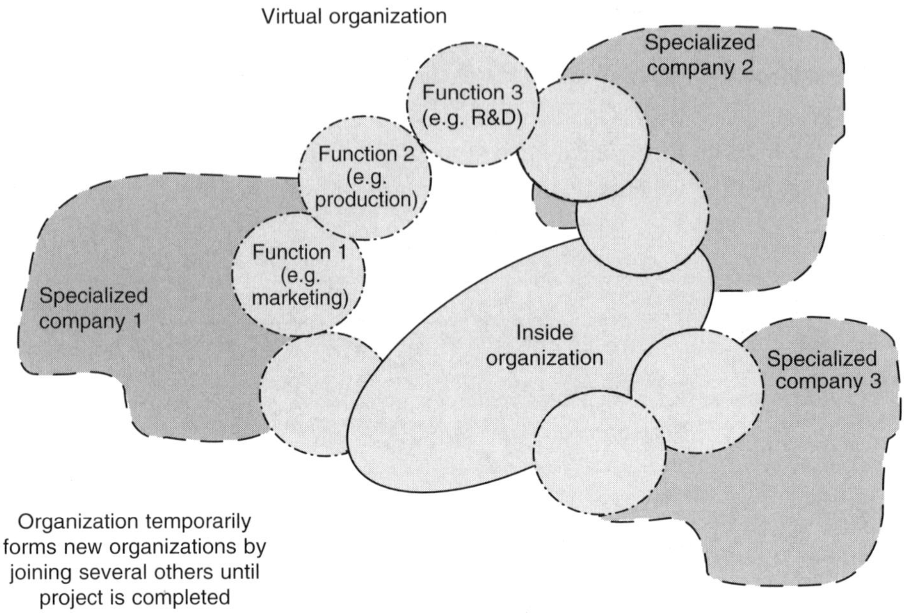

Figure 2-52b. The Virtual Organization: A Variation of the Boundaryless Structure.

Some partial answers have been given to these questions, for example in Figure 2-38. on the influence of cultural homogeny and in Figure 2-39 on the influence of cohesiveness on performance of social structures.

> Moreover, the entire discussion of the structure of groups and organizations and their methods of information exchange was in fact a "veiled" response to these questions. Human beings are improving their social structures with underlying communication technology in order to attain better and better problem solving ability.

The better organized group or organization is more powerful from the *collective intelligence* point of view because there is a higher probability that it can solve more problems and can most probably do it faster, which fulfills the requirements for a higher value of social structure intelligence quotient (IQS).

Now that we are equipped with such knowledge about social structures organized by human beings, let's try to compare the ability of a single being against the ability of a social structure, since it is not always true that the group is more capable of solving problems.

2.2.3.4. Differences Between Abilities of Single Beings and Social Structures (Groups) When the surrounding world is observed, that is, the whole spectrum of beings, we realize that certain types of beings exist as individuals; others live permanently inside social structures, and others temporarily create social structures after a period of existing in an individual way,—that is, all possible combinations of collectivism and individualism are applied over the spectrum of living beings.

Neither does the complexity of organisms nor the level of individual intelligence seem to be a deciding factors here, at least at first glance.

Human beings depend heavily on the products and the support of all hierarchies of human social structures where a given human is nested. This starts with family support and school (group learning), and later on to groups or teams in companies, till existence and activity rely on general products (artifacts, e.g., medicine, media) of worldwide human civilization.

Despite this, individualism is highly praised by our educational system, local public opinion, and even global media.

Therefore, after having briefly presented the concepts and structures of groups and organizations (with some glimpses of their properties) we will give a final quick comparison of the *individual versus the group*, that is, a comparison of *individualism versus collectivism.*

This problem has been widely discussed both in textbooks on group dynamics (e.g., Shaw (145)), organizational behavior (e.g., Cherrington (154)), human cooperation (e.g., Johnson and Johnson (142)), and in a multitude of related research papers (164–166).

A basic approach of to Shaw's (145) is to analyze *individual versus group* performance in three categories:

1. Individual versus group judgment
2. Individual versus group problem solving
3. Individual versus group learning.

According to D.J. Cherrington (154), there are both advantages and disadvantages to group decision making as given in Table 2-10.

In the literature there are descriptions of different experiments and resultant hypotheses analyzing the problem of how groups versus individuals perform. Let us review some of them from the points of view of judgment, problem solving, and finally learning.

INDIVIDUAL VERSUS GROUP JUDGMENT

Without any doubt, group judgments are superior to individual judgments on tasks that involve random error (145). While evaluating, for example, weight, temperature, and so forth, over a short period when an individual is not able to repeat the experiment, a group performs much better, that is provides answers closer to correct value (see Fig. 2-53).

However, when an individual is allowed to repeat a test as many times as the number of group members, the individual gets almost the same results as a proper group (145), but it takes more time.

The function given in Figure 2-53 is important in general because it gives us a clear indication of the size of group sufficient for specific tasks.

TABLE 2-10. Assets and Liabilities of Groups in Making Decisions

Assets	Liabilities
Greater knowledge and information	Social pressure to conform
Greater variety of approaches to a problem	Loss of valuable time of group members
Increased acceptance of the decision	Hasty convergence on a solution
Reduced communication problems	Possibility of control by a dominant individual Distraction by hidden agenda and secondary goals Insufficient time to reach a decision Problem with disagreement and interpersonal conflicts Possibility of final decision being an irrational compromise

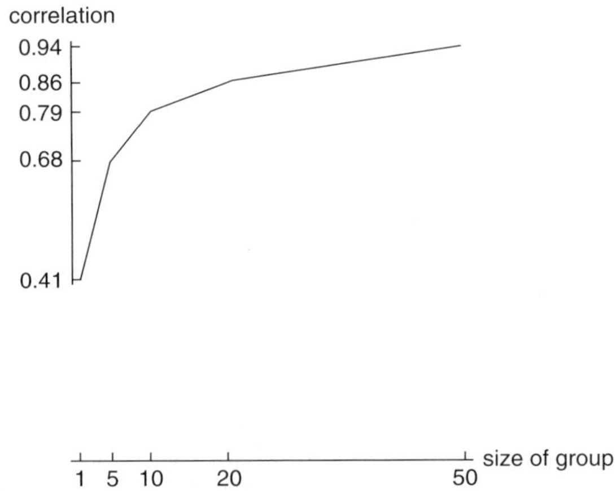

Figure 2-53. Individual versus Group Judgment of Weight.

Group judgment is also more accurate than individual judgment on estimation problems, for example, forecasting the demand for the next year's sales (154).

In the case of the "witness problem" (154), when members of the group provide group versus individual testimony on a "classroom incident," it has been found that a "single, trained judge" provided better judgment than group. It should be noted that during experiments it has been observed that some members change their decisions after a group discussion.

INDIVIDUAL VERSUS GROUP PROBLEM SOLVING

Shaw (145) provides an interesting review of experiments done by different researchers on *individual versus group* problem solving. When solving problems, results and performance can be evaluated from several points of view:

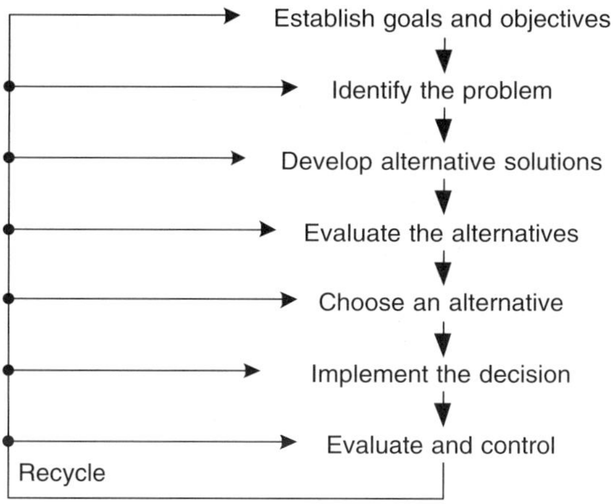

Figure 2-54. The Decision-Making Process.

- Number of problems solved in an assumed time
- Time required, either taking into account the number of individuals or not
- Number of trials
- Number of interactions
- Quality of solution

To understand conclusions of experiments better, let us look at a diagram of the decision-making process (see Fig. 2-54) for groups (154). This diagram is fully compatible with problem-solving strategies known in artificial intelligence, discussed before in section 2.1.3.1.

With the simple problem of constructing as many new words as possible in ten minutes from the letters available in a specific word, the best individual averaged 49 words, whereas groups averaged 75 words (145). Please keep in mind that in this problem labor can be divided, and solutions overlap.
For more sophisticated problems such as:

- □ Missionaries–cannibals
- □ The Hanoi Towers problem
- □ Optimizing location of a school and school bus route planning
- □ Rearrangement of letters for the end of specific prose and sonnet lines

Shaw's (145) experiments show the following:

1. Groups usually produce more and better solutions to problems than individuals working alone.

Specifically, individuals found 7.9 percent of all correct solutions, whereas groups 53 percent, in other cases it was 5.7 percent versus 27 percent, which is a serious difference.

2. Groups usually require more time to complete a task than do individuals working alone.

> For the earlier mentioned problems, groups were slower compared to individuals. Group solutions took 6.5, 16.9, and 18.3 minutes as compared to individuals, who took 4.5, 9.9, and 15.5 minutes for the same task.

When problems were related to arithmetic or mathematical logic, there were no significant differences between individuals and groups (145).

INDIVIDUAL VERSUS GROUP LEARNING

D.A. Kolb et al. (167) define the "experimental learning cycle" as shown in Figure 2-55.

This model of learning assumes that it is possible to start anywhere in the cycle

> In general, groups learned faster than individuals (145); moreover, individuals who had had previous experience in a group learned faster after that!

This is clear in the diagram given in Figure 2-56, where groups are compared to *"individuals who were experienced in group learning"* versus *"individuals who were not"*.

Shaw (145) agrees with Yuker's conclusions that groups learn more than individuals on certain tasks:

1. When several persons can work without interference
2. When individual contributions can be added
3. When parts of the solution are independent.

Summarizing this section on collectivism versus individualism, according to Cherrington (154), the group decisions tend to be more accurate than individual decisions for situations with certain problems:

1. Problems with multiple parts, allowing for division of labor among the group members

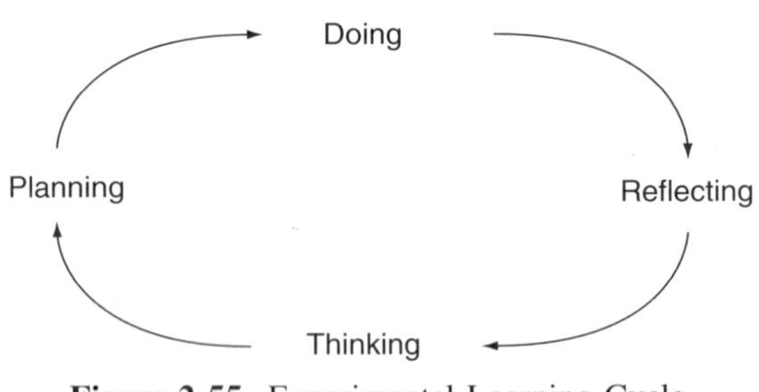

Figure 2-55. Experimental Learning Cycle.

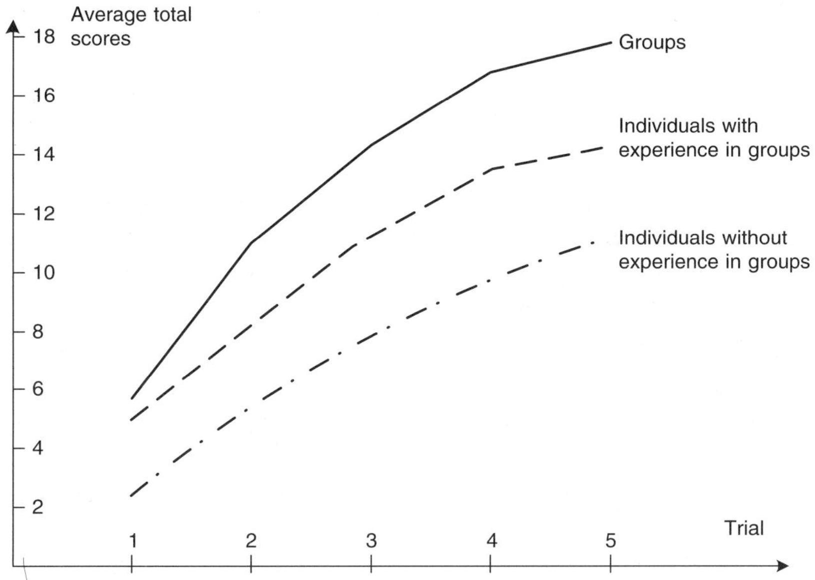

Figure 2-56. Individuals versus Group Learning. Reprinted with permission from McGraw-Hill companies from M.E. Shaw, Group Dynamics, 4th ed. 1971.

2. Group members with complementary skills and information
3. Problems involving estimation rather than creativity
4. Problems involving remembering information

Individual decisions tend to be superior for situations with other problems:

1. A sequence of multiple stages is required.
2. The problem is not easily divided into separate parts.
3. The correctness of the solution cannot be easily demonstrated.

Shaw (145) has made some important conclusions:

Hypothesis:
The presence of others increases the motivation level of a performing individual.
We should keep in mind, however, our previous considerations on the problem of *social loafing*, discussed in section 2.2.3.1.1.

Hypothesis:
Decisions made after group discussion are more risky than decisions made by the average individual prior to group discussion.

Johnson and Johnson (142) make an important statement that

> ". . . the interaction among group members results in ideas, insights, and strategies that no one member had previously thought of."

This is very consistent with and supportive of our concept of *collective intelligence*.

2.3.3.5. Use of Quasi- Brownian Motions as a Tool for the Description of Social Structure Dynamics At the end of the part of our book where the *collective intelligence* of humans is discussed from a sociologic point of view, we must address the problem of how to ***efficiently*** describe, analyze, and model and compute the general *spatial behavior* (168) of a set of beings creating a given social structure. This will be one of the key components for our computational model of *collective intelligence*.

It has been observed that despite our personal will, individual intelligence, imposed organizational (e.g., company) duties, and attempts at scheduling activity, human beings are more or less permanently and quasi-randomly displacing (personally) during their daily, weekly or yearly activities. Moreover, recently equipped with high-tech communication tools, human beings also perform a large number of quasi-random "virtual travels through communication channels" to rendezvous with other beings or information.

It is a paradoxical statement that the increase of individual intelligence in connection with certain jobs such as advanced scientific research, trade, and so forth, can lead to characteristics of spatial behavior which, observed from the outside, have more and more of the properties of random processes, especially Brownian movements.

In a monograph on spatial behavior (168) R.G. Golledge and R.J. Stimson mentioned the problem of the random behavior of human beings from the following points of view:

- *Weakly motivated and random behaviors* associated with an exploratory phase of the learning process
- Quasi-random behavior, for example, related to consumer decision-making analyzed through so-called *random utility models*.

In general, the activities of an individual being in a social structure are affected by three main contradictory factors:

1. Temporary and long-term goals of beings
2. Chaotic, unpredictable events in the environment "interrupting[46], and therefore affecting our daily, weekly or yearly agenda." They can be of different natures, for example, gossip on a "special sale," unexpected customers, and so forth.

[46] In Brownian movements this could be a bombardment of pollen by molecules of surrounding gas.

3. Restrictions (constraints in (169)) formal or real *walls* of different natures, for example, traffic jams when going to the airport for departure.

Golledge and Stimson (168) proposed a simplified model for scheduling the activities of human beings as given in Figure 2-57. However, nondeterminism of the environment plus complexity of human behavior makes the *spatial behavior* of individuals, and thus the behavior of a set of human beings even more similar to quasi-Brownian behavior. Thus a model like that given in Figure 2-57 provides only a modification of the characteristics of assumed Brownian behavior of an individual, to transform it into quasi-Brownian. Obviously, models such as the one given in Figure 2-57 are not able to specify details of spatial behavior.

Later on in this chapter there will be an example of methodologies used in research of spatial behavior to bypass the inefficiency of such models, even for social groups such as those of students, which have the well-defined duties of lectures and tutorials on a university campus.

In the computational model of *collective intelligence* proposed in this book, we are not interested in the spatial behavior of a single representative of an analyzed social structure, but in the global probability of a specific sequence of inferences resulting from the spatial behavior of all (at least active) members of this social structure. A specific being can be void from a certain logical point of view, in general or at a given moment, and the property of being void can be unpredictable when initializing such a system. Because we cannot predict even the number of copies of specific information nor the abilities in a social structure, and which offset of the process will be successful later on, we must consider the global behavior of an analyzed social structure.

To get a basic understanding of why we propose to use quasi-Brownian motion for analysis of *spatial behavior* in social structures, let us look at the sequence of pictures providing some data on the behavior of selected individuals and (if available) resultant global behavior of a group of such beings.

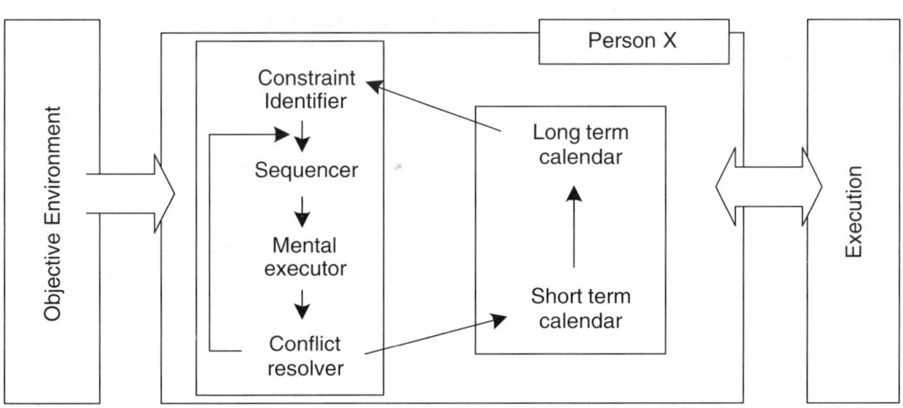

Figure 2-57. Household scheduling model (168).

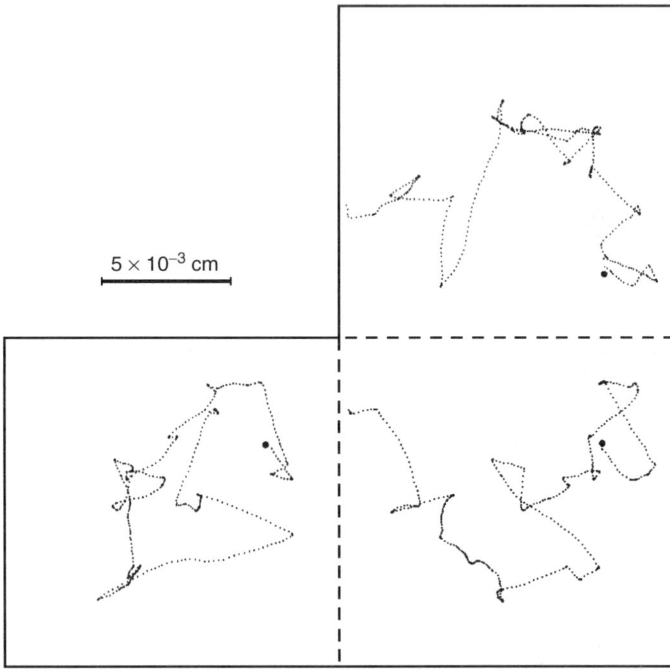

Figure 2-58. A digital plot of the displacement of a wild-type bacterium, E. coli strain AW405, executing a random walk in a homogeneous, isotopic medium. The plots are planar projections of a three-dimensional path. Observation began at the end of the path denoted by a large dot and continued for about 30 sec. The cell swam at a speed of about 2×10^{-3} cm/sec. Run intervals were relatively long, about 1 sec on average, and tumble intervals were relatively short, about 0.1 sec on the average. From H.C. Berg: *Random Walks in Biology*. 1993. Reprinted by permission of Princeton Univ. Press.

Simple *information molecules* of viruses and bacteria perform "pure" Brownian motion in a natural way because they are not able to control their displacements, but some types of bacteria possess the ability to move using different mechanisms, for example, Escherichia coli uses six flagellar filaments (170).

H.C. Berg (170) provides an interesting plot of the behavior of such a bacterial being performing random walk in a homogeneous isotropic medium, as shown in Figure 2-58.

Let us also compare the spatial behavior of humans and ants (our smaller *brothers* in *collective intelligence*) with respect to random (Brownian) motion.

An example of the foraging trips of three ants is given in Figure 2-59, without specifying the nature of the environment or the constraints that are present there. Goals for ants are obvious: effective foraging and successful return to the nest. This picture can suggest some determinism resulting from searching strategies applied at the level of individual ant intelligence.

However, if we take into account that ants are *collectively intelligent* and search for food in a coordinated way, as is shown in Figure 2-59, and then we

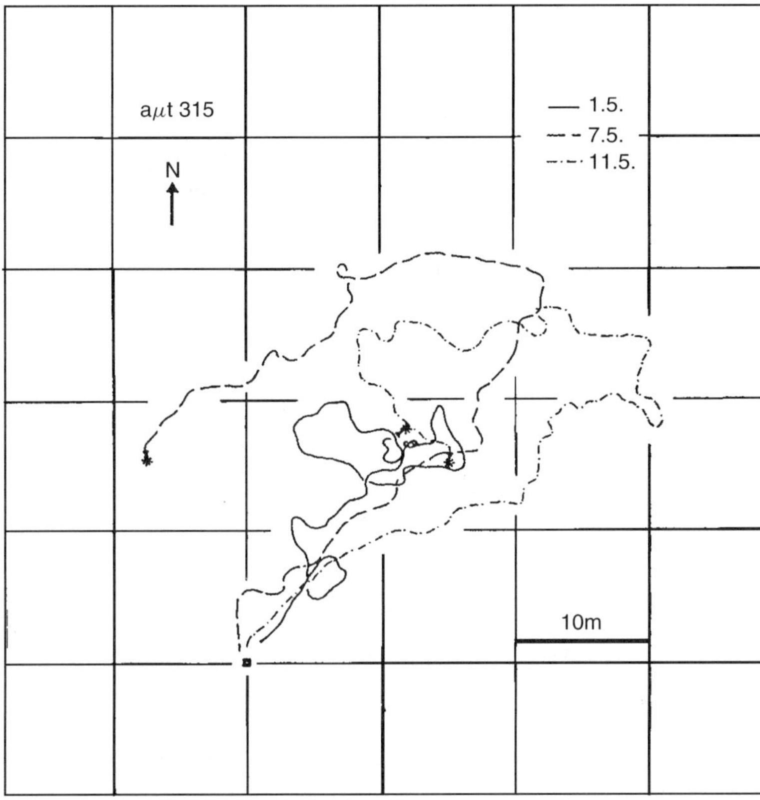

Figure 2-59. An example of a spatial layout of three foraging trips of an ant during May. The individual always keeps to the same foraging sector with respect to the nest denoted with a square. Symbol * indicates sites of food findings. Trip durations are 15 and 83 min, respectively. Reprinted with permission from Birkhäuser Publishing from a paper by P. Schmid-Hempel (171).

analyze ants in a group, the picture of displacements look like a simulation of chaotic behavior.

In Figure 2-60 we have a graph showing ants foraging from every position in a social structure. Please observe that the resultant (as given in Fig. 2-61) distribution now looks the same as provided by random, for example, Brownian displacements of ants in the area.

Now, let us look at the spatial behavior of a human. Figures 2-62 and 2-63 (172,173) provide two graphs of different complexity of spatial behavior.

Difficulties in analyzing and computing such complex processes as a person's behavior entail on the one hand a necessity to generate solutions, for example, for occupation and traffic analyses; on the other hand, they have resulted in several approximation concepts for description and analysis of spatial behavior (169):

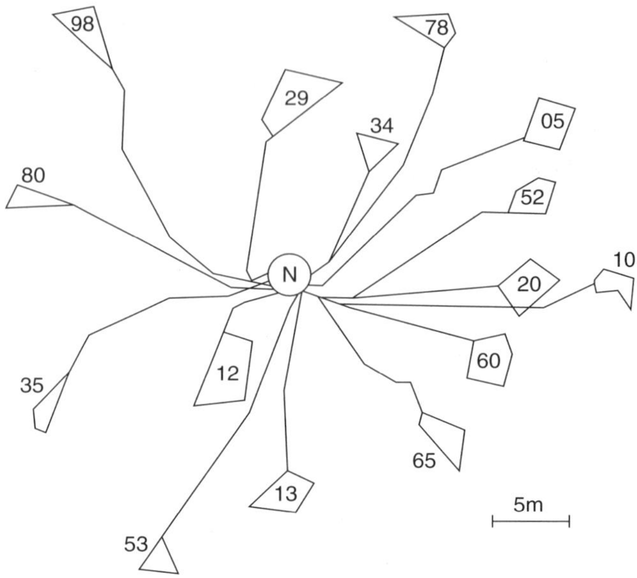

Figure 2-60. Individual foraging zones of some ants (labeled by a number), which exhibit high spatial fidelity. Nonspecialized foragers are found much closer to the nest. Reprinted with permission from Birkhäuser Publishing from a paper by P. Schmid-Hempel (171).

- **Analysis of Spatial Behavior with use of Time-Space Prism**

  This concept was initialized by T. Hägerstrand (174). In terms of time and geography, the individual, family, or other groups can be grounded in the notion that time space coordinates can always define the location. This has been illustrated by mapping the area of interest and the period of time concerned onto a three-dimensional *time-space prism*. The individuals who stay in one place may be successively represented by vertical lines (as a process in the time dimension alone), and changes of place can be represented by horizontal lines (as a process in the space dimension). An example is Figure 2-64 (169), which illustrates potential interaction of two humans (students), by constructing intersecting prisms, to find areas of their common spacetime during their university campus activities.

- **Use of Probable Presence**

  Example of such an analysis is given in Figure 2-65.

The fundamental problem with approximation of *spatial behavior* of members of a given social structure (in our case with quasi-Brownian motion) is to find the proper type of Brownian motion, modify it, and later on to correctly *identify* the necessary parameters of the approximating process.

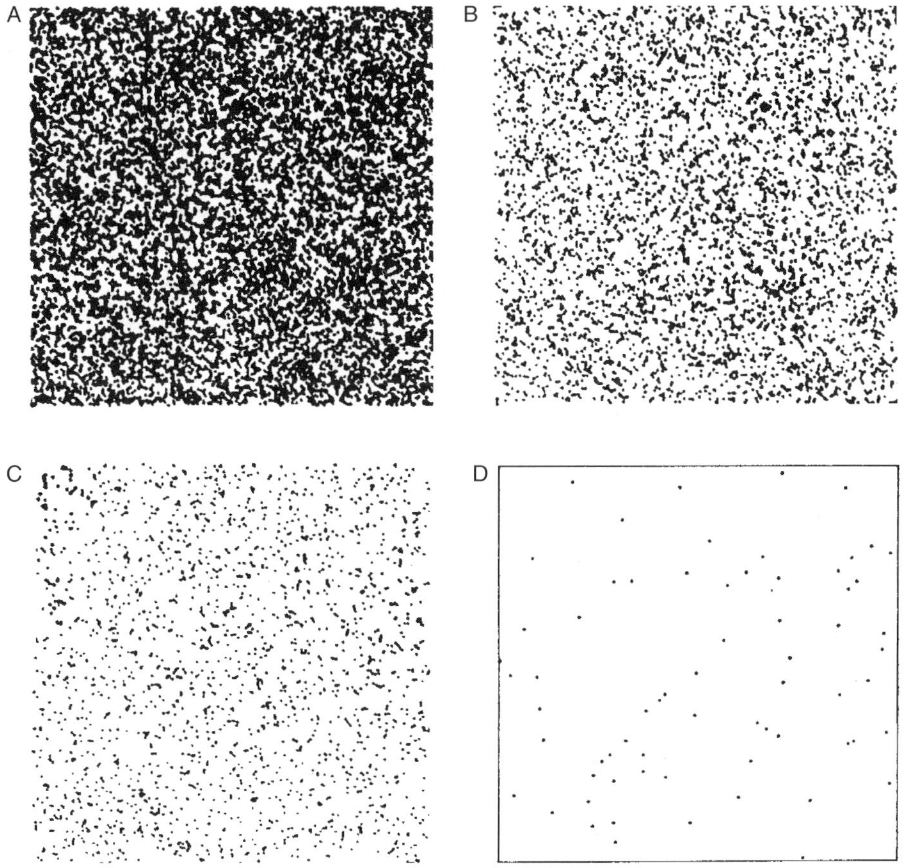

Figure 2-61. Absolute search densities of four Caaglyphis and Ocymyrmex ant populations. Each plot represents an area of 25 × 25m^2. The position of each foraging ant was given every 10 min over a one-day period. Reprinted with permission from Birkhäuser Publishing from a paper by P. Schmid-Hempel (171).

Thus, let us look into the theory of random walk and Brownian motions[47] in a few environments, for example, (13).

In general, Brownian motion is a random walk, and this process on the higher level of abstraction is a random process. According to A. Leon-Garcia (175), the definition of a random process can be given as follows.

[47] It is surprising how Brownian motion fascinates researchers, and how wide the area is where Brownian motion as a concept is applicable. Einstein used kinetic theory to derive the diffusion constant for such motion in terms of fundamental parameters of the particles in a liquid, and this equation was subsequently used by Perrin to determine Avogadro's Number (Encarta'98 Encyclopedia).

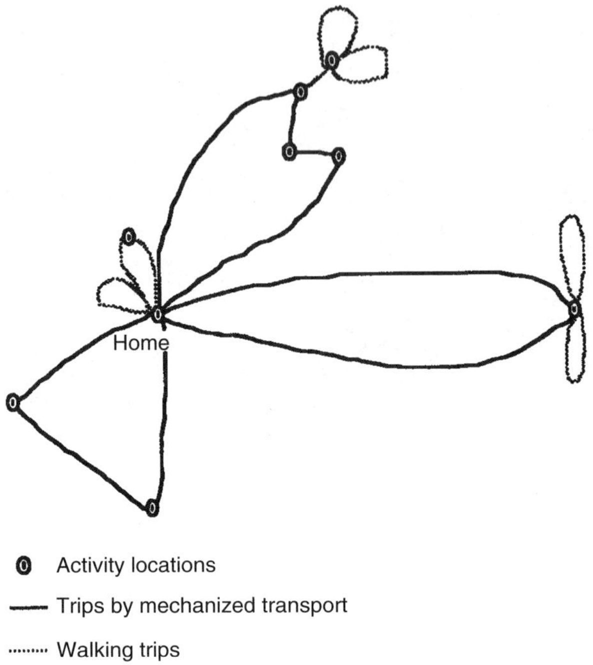

Figure 2-62. Individual activity space. From Jakle in Golledge and Stimson (168).

DEFINITION 9: RANDOM PROCESS

Consider a random experiment specified by outcomes ξ from some sample space S, by the events defined in S, and by the probabilities of these events. Suppose that to every outcome $\xi \in S$, we assign a function of time according to some rule:

$$X(t, \xi)t \in I$$

The graph of the function $X(t, \xi)$ versus t, for ξ fixed, is called a realization sample path, or a sample function of the random process. For each fixed t_k from the index set I, $X(t, \xi)$ is a random variable.

Random processes are also referred to as stochastic processes. A random process is said to be discrete-time if the index set I is a countable set (i.e., a set of integers or a set of nonnegative integers). A continuous-time random process is one in which I is continuous.

With problems of spatial behavior we are interested in outcomes ξ, which are places in a space of mainly geometrical nature, for example, in one, two, or three-dimensional space, that is, in *random walk*. According to the Encyclopaedia of Mathematics (177), there is no precise generally accepted definition of *random walk*. We can give a rough definition:

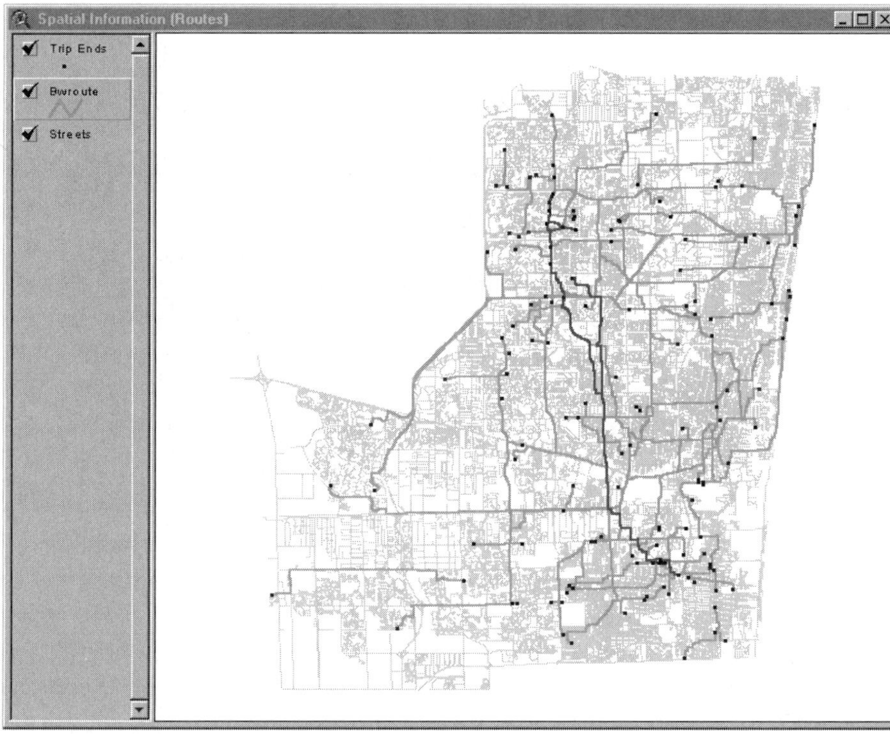

Figure 2-63. Routes and trip ends for one person (ten trips in one day). Thanks to the courtesy of Shih-Lung Shaw, Dept. of Geography, The University of Tennessee, Knoxville, TN.

Random walk:

A stochastic process of a special form that can be interpreted as a model describing the movement of a real or abstract object in a certain state space under the action of some random mechanism.

The *state space* is usually any *d*-dimensional Euclidean space or the integral lattice in it. The *lattice* can be formally defined (178) as given later; however, for *collective intelligence* purposes it is not necessary to have such a "tough" definition.

DEFINITION 10: LATTICE

A partially ordered set in which every pair of elements has a unique *greatest lower bound* (*glb*) and a unique *least lower bound* (*lub*).

There is an infinite number of possible examples of *random walk* on lattice, e.g., when playing games, atom impurities wandering in a crystalline or metallic

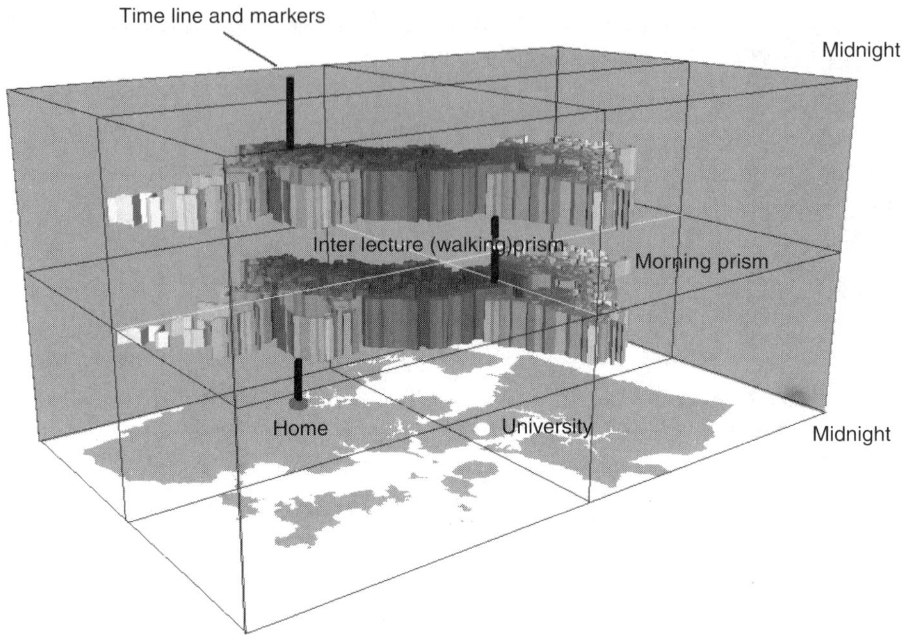

Figure 2-64. Potential interaction—intersecting prisms to find areas of common space-time (169). Thanks to the courtesy of Otto Huisman and Pip Forer, Department of Geography, University of Auckland, New Zealand.

lattice, or even *collective random walks* of spin clusters in spin glasses (179), and finally a random walk of human beings performing more or less *random walk* in a lattice of streets and corridors.

The trajectories of the simplest *random walk* in the case $d = 1$ are described by the initial position $S_0 = 0$ and the sequence of sums

$$S_n = X_1 + \cdots + X_n, \quad n = 1, 2, \ldots, \quad X_n \text{ are independent and}$$
$$\text{have a Bernoulli distribution:}$$
$$P(X_i = 1) = p, \quad P(X_i = -1) = 1 - p$$

Among other surprising properties of *random walk*, it has been proven (Pólya, 1921, for example, (180)) that on a one-dimensional and two-dimensional lattice, a random walk has a unity probability of reaching any point (including the starting point) as the number of steps approaches infinity, but probability P(...) < 1 for lattices more than two-Dimensional.

A very convenient form of describing and simulating *random walk* is to use vectors (13), that is, to consider walks in which the vector displacement $\mathbf{x}_{t+1}$ at time t can be derived from the displacement at the single preceding time, t, by

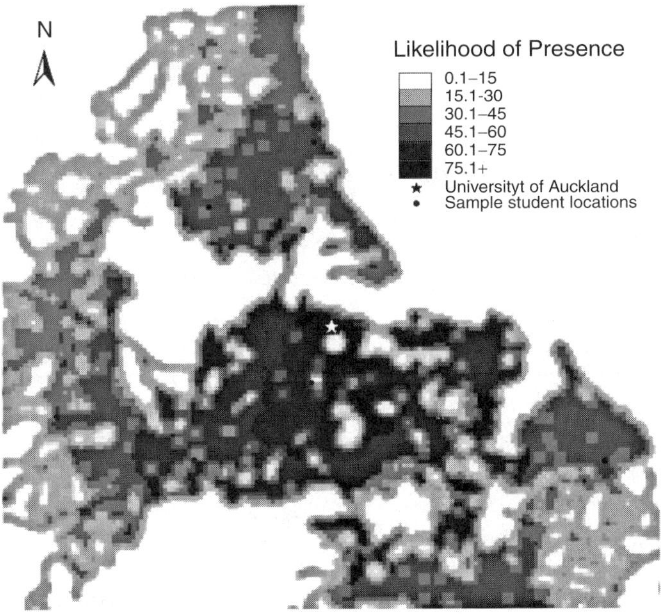

Figure 2-65. Probable presence of students with discretionary time (176). Thanks to the courtesy of Otto Huismanand Pip Forer. Department of Geography, University of Auckland, New Zealand.

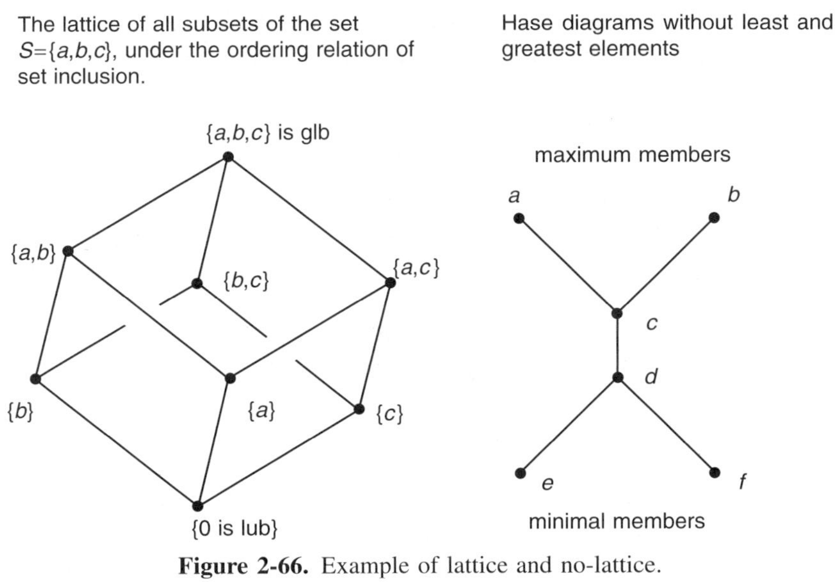

Figure 2-66. Example of lattice and no-lattice.

the equation of the form

$$\mathbf{x}_{t+1} = \mathbf{x}_t + \mathbf{e}_t, \text{ where } \mathbf{e}_t \text{ is a randomly selected vector}$$

From our point of view very useful for the *collective intelligence* problem, is the so-called *random walk with memory*, which is defined according to C.A. Whitney (13) as:

$$\mathbf{x}_{t+1} = \mathbf{a}\mathbf{x}_t + \mathbf{b}\mathbf{x}_{t-1} + \mathbf{c}\mathbf{x}_{t-2} + \cdots + \mathbf{e}_i$$

where a, b, c, ... are adjustable parameters. The behavior of such a walk critically depends on the parameters.

While speaking about *random walk* behavior in time there must be a specified method of averaging, that is, a mode of averaging. According to Whitney (13), among all possibilities we can distinguish two major modes:

- **Synchronous Mode:**

all the exit paths from the node (present position) have the same probability — the same as the probability to stay in the node.

- **Asynchronous Mode:**

the exit paths of all nodes have the same probability. Thus nodes with more exit paths are exited more quickly, and the probability to stay in the node will be consecutively less. In general, various forms of *random walks* are everywhere around us (170).

Brownian motion is considered as *random walk*, where time is continuous, and x_t evolves over time according to a stochastic differential equation:

$$\mathrm{dx} = \mu \mathrm{dt} + \sigma \mathrm{dw}$$

where dt represents an increment in time, and dw denotes a random component. The expected value of x_t given an initial condition x_0 becomes

$$x_0 + \mu t \text{ with a variance } \sigma^2 t$$

Brownian motion can be perceived mathematically, not as an object jumping from one location to another, but rather as an object that has a velocity of displacement jumping from one value to another (13).

The random mechanism in the background of Brownian motion can be of various kinds; the most common *random walks* are those generated by a summation of independent random variables or by Markov chains.

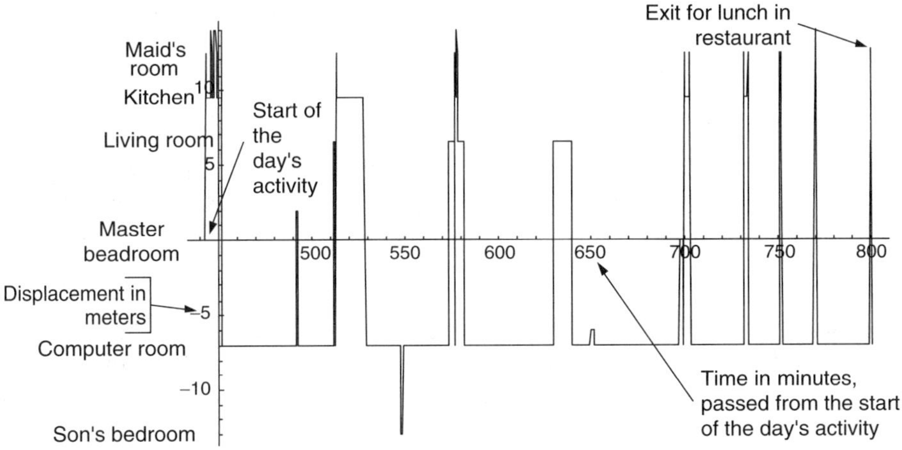

Figure 2-67. Displacements of the author around his apartment during morning hours of a weekend day.

Discrete Brownian motion can be defined as follows.

Let Z_n be a sequence of *i.i.d.*[48] Gaussian random variables with a mean equal to 0 (i.e. $\mu = 0$) and variance σ^2. The random process

$$X_n = \sum_{i=0}^{n} Z_i \quad for\ n = 1, 2, \ldots$$

is sometimes called discrete Brownian motion.

While speaking about objects such as ants, humans, or even bacteria equipped with the ability to move in certain directions, we cannot consider ants or humans as "inert particles of pollen" displacing under random bombardments of molecules of the surrounding gas. Even such *motionless* particles can steadily undergo displacements resulting from any attractor or vector field. Ants implementing a foraging strategy in-between obstacles, or humans trying to follow a presumed daily schedule are even more complicated examples of such a process. To deal with such objects, let us define quasi-Brownian displacements more formally.

DEFINITION 11: QUASI-BROWNIAN MOTION

Let there be given any object O with the deterministic characteristic of displacement f in any real or abstract space S. It is assumed that f includes the ideal behavior of object O, and the deterministic influence of the environment E (any attractors and repulsors). Now, assume that in E there exists any stochastic process P, which affects the behavior of O in such a way that

[48] Independent, identically distributed (random variable).

displacements of O are purely Brownian if $f \equiv 0$. Such displacements f of O, perturbed by P, we define as quasi-Brownian motion.

Example:

A particle of desert dust in the environment without gravity will perform (pure) Brownian motion; however, gravity as an attractor changes this behavior into quasi-Brownian, as the deterministic sedimentation process of heavy mineral particles of dust prevail. Another example could be a ferry jerked by currents while passing, for example, across a bay.

Finally, let us take a look into a bit of Brownian-like behavior of the author in the area of his apartment on a university campus during the early morning hours of the 14th of January, 2000, just after waking up, when the he intended to spend as much time as possible on this weekend day working with the manuscript of this book.

The intention was to stay in the "computer room" as long as possible to work with the manuscript. However, even during the "silent early morning hours" interruptions of various kinds plus various necessities occurred, that is, "bombarded him", and as a result, displaced the author to other locations and back around the apartment.

The apartment has an almost linear structure, imposed by a long, straight central corridor with offsets of rooms to one side only. Thus, the displacements can be presented in the same way as one-dimensional Brownian motion are on the chart of *position x time as* given in Figure 2-67.

CHAPTER 3

Toward the Formalization, Modeling, and Measuring of *Collective Intelligence*

It is surprising that more research has not been done on the evaluation of the *collective intelligence* of social structures as it is obviously easier than the evaluation of the *intelligence* of a single being.

Individual *intelligence*, even if we temporarily ignore the problem of what *intelligence* really is, can be evaluated only on the basis of external results of the behavior of a given being during its perceptual, reasoning, and acting processes. Thus, we can only observe a single being as "a black box" in a given environment, because it is usually difficult to separate a being from its environment.

Additionally, the starting point for our research in this area is made more complicated because we are using computers based on digital, binary electronics to model and evaluate intelligent systems that are implemented with the totally different technology of biological systems.

Our current science, that is, knowledge, is oriented to digital computer technology, which has been justified by exponential progress in all disciplines — fired and amplified by the use of digital computers.

Meanwhile, the neuropsychological processes in the brain that are necessary for problem-solving are still very far from being observable in a satisfactory way. Consequently, it is necessary to create abstract models of brain activity (1) based on neuropsychological hypotheses (e.g., Luria (181)) or on computer-oriented models like those in *artificial intelligence*.

On the contrary, we can observe, measure, and evaluate many more elements of collectively intelligent activity in a social structure:

- The beings creating a social structure can be (in most cases) identified as its functional elements, which is still difficult and far from a satisfactory stage with the brain. Thus we start investigation of *collective intelligence* on the much more comfortable level of an information network between "black boxes" of beings, as opposed to the level of one global, unknown "black box" representing a single brain.

- We can easily observe the displacements and actions of those beings and the exchange of information between them, such as in human language; the ant's pheromone communication system; or bacterial, chemical, or DNA-generated interaction.
- If we consider a small social structure, we can identify the exchange of information and interaction between beings in almost a deterministic way. Here, we are supported by recent research results in sociology. For large social structures, individual *intelligence* and behavior is scaled down as a factor to accidental, local, and probabilistic processes; thus, statistical approximation can be used, and again, sociology provides us with a strong database of research results. Thus, the situation here is much more promising from a research point of view than it is in the case of analyzing individual intelligence.

The research hypothesis of this book is that:

> *collective intelligence* can be evaluated with the help of specific, abstract, and chaotic models of computations and statistical evaluation of the behavior of beings in structured environments.

The Random PROLOG Processor (RPP) seems to be an appropriate choice as a chaotic model of computations here.

For a better understanding of *collective intelligence* with which we can move to formalization of the phenomenon in the next Section (3.1), let us restate some of the underlying premises:

- In a socially cooperating structure, it is difficult to differentiate thinking and nonthinking beings (abstract beings must be introduced).
- The individuals inside a social structure usually cooperate in chaotic, often noncontinuous ways. In a social structure, beings move randomly because needs and opportunities of real life force them to do so. Inference processes are made randomly, starting when there is a need, when higher level needs are temporarily not disturbing a given being, or when there is a chance to rendezvous and make inference(s). Most inferences are never finished. This makes the similarity to Brownian movements almost striking (13) and suggests the use of quasi-Brownian movements for modeling behavior in a social structure.
- Individual inferences are also accidental and chaotic. We can easily observe how frequently a given line of inference is suddenly abandoned and another is started. It is also a common situation that an old, abandoned inference suddenly emerges from our subconscious and is (successfully) concluded.
- Resources for inferences are distributed in space, time, and among beings.
- The performance of a given social structure is highly dependent on its organization.

- Facts and rules can create inconsistent systems. Multiple copies of facts, rules, and goals are allowed. This is very clear in any scientific environment and often during committee meetings.
- Probability over the domain of problems must be used as an IQ measure for a social structure. The basic reason is nondeterminism of processes there.
- The property of *collective intelligence* is temporary, changing over time, and can even have negative values, that is, a group can behave less intelligently than some of its members will behave if alone. To support this conclusion, remember B. Tuckman's model (141) saying that every group undergoes *forming, storming, norming, performing*, and finally *adjourning*. Dependency on time is even more complicated with *collective intelligence*.

At this point the formal definition of *collective intelligence* should be presented.

3.1 A FORMAL DEFINITION OF *COLLECTIVE INTELLIGENCE* AS A SPECIFIC PROPERTY OF A SOCIAL STRUCTURE

The entry assumption for the forthcoming definition is that *collective intelligence* itself is a certain property of a group of beings, which is expressed or is observable and measurable. If we do not want to fall under the crossfire of counterexamples[1], we cannot assume too much, for example, that the beings are cooperating (although interaction is required) or that they are conscious beings. Nothing is assumed about the communication system; we do not even assume that these beings are alive (subsequently, a definition of *being alive* is not necessary).

To better understand the above issues, let us look at some selected examples.

Suppose that we observe a group of ants that has discovered a heavy prey that must be transported to the nest and we also observe a group of human workers who gather to transport a long metal beam through a building site.

Ants are simple beings, but when we observe what they do, it looks like quasi-chaotic jerking and pulling that results in mean displacement toward the nest. For this method of problem-solving, the necessary *intelligence* can be very low, and a simple perception–communication system can be used; however, it is clear that ants display *collective intelligence* here.

On the other hand, humans, perhaps under supervision of a foreman, will gather, discuss, and analyze the future transportation path: they will find a way to grip the beam, create a safe and economic procedure for raising the beam, find a method of transportation, and finally find a method of lowering it. This will

[1] we intend to give a universal definition of *collective intelligence* valid for a wide spectrum of beings; thus, it would be easy to find counterexamples, for example, what is true for a bacterial colony can be false for human social structures and vice versa.

take a lot of time, thought, and discussion (perhaps even too much); however, this is also *collective intelligence*.

Because of such situations, the definition of *collective intelligence* must be abstracted from possible methods of thinking and communication between individuals. The definition must be based on observable results of group behavior.

Let us look again at the example of medieval shoemakers, introduced in part one of the book. This example combines "in a magical way" most of the fundamental issues necessary for understanding the concept of *collective intelligence* presented in this book.

Their social structures, that is, streets with shoemaker shops only, could have emerged in many different ways. It could have been a king's direct order or the creation of something like a "free trade zone" by a local mayor or governor. It could have also been the result of observation of a street of shoemaker shops in another city. Later, such a process can self-propagate, that is, shoemakers could have gravitated to such an area because they realized that the benefits overwhelmed the disadvantages such as competition of other shoemakers having shops perhaps next door. The benefits can be small (even difficult to define), underhanded, for example, to have the possibility of spying on methods used by other shoemakers. Some shoemakers could have even been enemies.

The interaction in this social structure can be implemented on various levels, for example, in the case of enemy shoemakers, through just observation of shoes worn by people in the city, not necessarily through personal communication.

Another interesting issue is that the environment can also "amplify" such a social structure. The concentration of shoemakers would have immediately "attracted" dealers of raw materials, tools, or other "necessities" for shoemakers, which would have made their life and work much easier.

In a social structure like that of the shoemakers, *collective intelligence* emerges without any doubt but perhaps only from a business point of view. This is an important remark because if the definition of *collective intelligence* pretends to be a general one, over the entire spectrum of beings, we must evaluate the *collective intelligence* of a social structure through artifacts or abilities, not through, for example, communication or structural issues. Only artifacts or abilities are universal.

In general, it is a well-known paradox that technical progress is fastest during wars, such as during World Wars I and II:

- *collective intelligence* can then be more specific and less general. In this case, we observed *collective intelligence*, especially for weapon production, and a catastrophic lack of *collective intelligence* in other areas.
- Enemies do not cooperate; they interact, but even such an interaction is more than enough to boost this specific kind of *collective intelligence*.
- The *collective intelligence* we are discussing now is a very temporal ability and will usually be extinguished after the peace treaty.

Bacteria also cooperate (182); they do this through exchange of genetic information[2] over generations; they are using *collective intelligence* to survive in a given environment, such as against antibiotics. However, if we consider the "edges of life," the question is whether some forms are alive or not, for example, the most primitive forms such as prions[3]. Thus, the assumption about the necessity for live agents should also be dropped.

Now, after a handful of examples and related discussions, we are ready to present our formalized concept and resulting definition of *collective intelligence*.

The definition we give now is constructed on the basis of the above assumptions and should provide formal cover for any type of being, any communication system, and any form of synergy, virtual or real. Let us now look at the notation necessary for the definition.

First, we should define "beings" in a concise and general way.

Let there be given a set S of individuals labeled $indiv_1, \ldots, indiv_n$ existing in any environment Env. No specific nature is assumed either for the individuals or for their environment. It is necessary to assume the existence of any method to distinguish (and analyze) $indiv_i$ $i = 1, \ldots, n$ from the Env.

We are fully aware that this is a very strong assumption, and perhaps in the future, we will be able to drop it or weaken it after progress in the theory of *collective intelligence*. The problem is that in some cases, we may not be able to find an efficient method to distinguish beings from their environment. Viruses and prions are good examples.

Let there also be given a testing period $t_{start} - t_{end}$ to judge or evaluate the property of the *collective intelligence* of $S\{\ldots\}$ in Env.

Let there now be given (or assumed by definition) any universe U of possible problems $Probl_i$ proper for the environment Env, and a complexity evaluation for every problem $Probl_i$ denoted by $f_O^{Probl_i}(n)$. Since *collective intelligence* must deal with both *logical–computational (i.e., formal) and physical* problems, we have to write a dual definition:

$$f_O^{Probl_i}(n) \stackrel{def}{=} \begin{cases} \textit{if } Probl_i \textit{ is a computational problem, apply a} \\ \textit{standard complexity definition with n defining} \\ \textit{the size of the problem;} \\ \textit{if } Probl_i \textit{ is a physical problem, use as a complexity} \\ \textit{measure any proper physical units namely, weight,} \\ \textit{size, time, and so forth to express n.} \end{cases} \quad (0.1)$$

We must have this form of definition because a *being* can face a problem of a computational nature where the complexity is well defined as the function

[2] A good example is the transfer (copying) of plasmid DNA after 15–20 generations from a single E. coli cell to a large fraction of cells previously without that plasmid (15).

[3] A microscopic protein particle similar to a virus but without nucleic acid, suspected to be the infectious agent responsible for scrapie and certain other degenerative diseases of the nervous system.

TABLE 3-1. Example of the Set Abl_U of Maximum Abilities Over U for Individuals Belonging to Social Structure S

$Probl_i \in U$	$\max_S$	**n**
Polynomial equation	$indiv_{a1}$	3
Solving TSP	$indiv_{a11}$	15 nodes
Solving crossword 30 × 30 letters	$indiv_{a21}$	3 hours
Finding hidden object...	$indiv_{a32}$	1 hour
...		
Moving steel cube $n \times n \times n$	$indiv_{a8}$	30 cm
Assembling device ...	$indiv_{a3}$	10 hours
Fixing faulty device, e.g., car ...	$indiv_{a41}$	3 days
Preparing meal for five people	$indiv_{a7}$	2 hours
...		

of size n of the problem (as in the "Traveling salesman problem" for ants), or beings can face a problem of a physical nature, such as a problem of transporting a cargo of size $n \times n \times n$.

Real physical problems are no less complicated than abstract ones, such as the problem of how to safely grip and move a steel cube of size $n \times n \times n$ cm for different values of n.

Let us denote the ability (Abl) to solve problems by our set of individuals S over U while working or thinking without any mutual interaction (absolutely alone, far from each other, without exchange of information) by the formula:

$$Abl_U^{all\ indiv} \stackrel{def}{=} \bigcup_{Probl_i \in U} \max_S \left(\max_n f_O^{Probl_i}(n) \right) \tag{0.2}$$

Let us comment on this formula. This is a definition of a set that presents the maximum abilities (like a list of all human Olympic sports records) of S, if the individuals are, for example, asked one by one to display their abilities throughout all the problems. If any problem is beyond the abilities of any individual from S, this problem will not be listed there. The example of constructing such a set is given in Table 3-1.

Now we are ready to give a basic definition:

DEFINITION 12. WEAK DEFINITION OF *COLLECTIVE INTELLIGENCE* AS A PROPERTY OF *S*

Now assume that individuals coexist and interact in some way. We say that a weak *collective intelligence* emerges because of cooperation, interaction, or coexistence in S, iff at least one problem $Probl'$ can be pointed to, such that it can be solved by a lone individual with the support of the group or by some individuals working together, such that

$$f_O^{Probl_i}(n') \overset{significantly}{>} f_O^{Probl_i}(n) \in Abl_U^{all\ indiv}$$

$$\text{or} \tag{0.3}$$

$$\exists Probl' \text{ such that } \left(\forall n\ Probl' \notin Abl_U^{all\ indiv}\right) \wedge (Probl' \in U)$$

The basic concept of the above definition is that the property of *collective intelligence* emerges for a set of individuals S in an environment U iff the complexity of the problem that somebody from the social structure is able to solve alone can now go to a higher level or there emerges (as a result of interaction) a quite new problem $\in U$ that was before beyond the range of the ability of a single being, but which can be solved from that point.

An example of the first scenario is when a second person helps someone to solve a crossword puzzle, and together, they are able to solve more difficult puzzles.

To illustrate the second part of the definition, we can point to, for example, the case of small group of Neanderthals consisting of an older, experienced but "disabled" hunter and a young, strong, and fast "greenhorn." The problem of hunting some fast or dangerous animals can be solved only if the young hunter can get and apply the knowledge of the older one. By acting alone, either of them may not be able to kill the prey (e.g., bear).

Even a small modification in the structure of a social group, or in its communication system, or even in, for example, the education of some individuals can result in *collective intelligence* emergence or increase. The old and young hunter pair is a good example.

Another example is when the medieval shoemakers suddenly moved their shops from remote villages into the city to "Shoemaker Street." The important thing is that the distance between them was reduced so much that it triggered new communication channels of various types (e.g., spying).

Defining *collective intelligence* and measuring it are quite different problems. The definition of *collective intelligence* seems to be simpler; however, the formulation of the definition given earlier was accomplished after several years of work on the problem of a *collective intelligence measure* (IQS) (8,57,183).

The difficulty with the practical and reasonable (from an "engineering" point of view) problem of measuring *collective intelligence* through, for example, its quotient, lies in the necessity to use a specific model of computations that is not based on the Deterministic Turing Machine.

To demonstrate how this problem will be solved must be reserved for another part of the book. Now we assume that such a measure somehow exists and is computable for any configuration of a given social structure S. Moreover, let us assume that the ordering with $\{<, =, >\}$ is possible for any two tests for S. This will allow making some interesting considerations on the basis of definition (0.3). Before reading Part 4, let us denote this measure $IQS(\ldots)$ as any unspecified function of some arguments. In Section 4, it is demonstrated that this assumption is fully justified.

Additionally, let us assume that the test for IQS can be applied even to a single person—one being is also *a social structure*, isn't it?

POSITIVE AND NEGATIVE COLLECTIVE INTELLIGENCE

With the hypothetical IQS (...) let us measure the *collective intelligence* of a given social structure *S* as it is configured for definition (0.2). This means that individuals do IQS tests without any interaction. This will provide us several results of problems from the test, from which we can take the maximum for every item of the test.

DEFINITION 13. Ø-COLLECTIVE INTELLIGENCE

Ø-collective intelligence is defined as a result provided by an IQS test, if applied to all individuals from social structure *S* when tested alone, without any form of interaction. This will be called $Ø^S_{\mathrm{IQS}}$.

DEFINITION 14. POSITIVE COLLECTIVE INTELLIGENCE

We say that a social structure *S* has a positive collective intelligence for a given configuration and testing time period iff $IQS(\ldots) > Ø^S_{\mathrm{IQS}}$.

DEFINITION 15. NEGATIVE COLLECTIVE INTELLIGENCE

We say, that a social structure *S* has a negative *collective intelligence* for a given configuration and testing time period iff $IQS(\ldots) < Ø^S_{\mathrm{IQS}}$.

Now we can ask if these definitions are reasonable and worthy of consideration. Let us look at some examples.

If we consider a boat about to be shipwrecked, with people on board who can cooperate or can go into panic, some of them can overpower others, using force to try to get the life resources for themselves. There are many other possibilities: to behave egocentrically, to hide resources, and so forth.

In both cases it is obvious that *collective intelligence* should be measured through behavior that increases the chances of survival of the social structure. When the group cooperates, their abilities will exceed the maximum individual abilities, that is, the *collective intelligence* will be positive. However, in case of panic, extreme egoism, or any form of conflict in the boat, in most cases the group will have less chance of survival, even compared with the chances of some strong or intelligent or vigorous individual members, if not disturbed by the group. In this case, the *collective intelligence* will be negative.

Another example is an ill-suited married couple. Together, they can make worser decisions than they would make if acting alone. In fact, this is a very similar example to two shipwrecked persons in a boat.

It is interesting that humans instinctively try to escape from a group during conflict or panic, aware that acting alone will increase personal chance of survival. Conversely, individuals try to join groups displaying high efficiency or cooperation. Perhaps instinctively, we evaluate "signs" of *collective intelligence.*

PROBLEMS OF ALTRUISM AND SLAVERY IN THE DEFINITION OF *COLLECTIVE INTELLIGENCE*

Perhaps a careful reader of the definition of *collective intelligence* will ask why it is simply said that *collective intelligence* emerges in a social structure even if only one problem (not necessarily more) can be solved better or quite a new problem can now be solved by the group.

What if, at the same time, for some reason the group loses some abilities? Perhaps this single improvement or discovery will be paid for by extensive losses in other domains of group activity.

The answer is that the definition of *collective intelligence* must take into account the phenomenon of altruism.

Let us look again at the example of the nearly shipwrecked people in a boat or at a wife and husband in a contentious marriage. In certain situations, it can be profitable from a long-time perspective to abandon (devote) one's own abilities to support or boost specific abilities of another person, such as the navigator.

It is widely observed that sometimes a wife voluntarily drops/abandons her professional career to boost the abilities of her husband, taking the position of housewife to allow her husband to have a high position in a company or business.

The use of *weights* and $\sum$ to compare the trade-off in such a case is not a good solution; it would take us into difficulties of defining such weights properly in each situation.

Another interesting case from a *collective intelligence* point of view is slavery. It is well known that some ancient slavery-based civilizations reached very high levels in the areas of art, technology, and so forth. In this case, the individual abilities of slaves were "by force" devoted to support aristocrats, which boosted the abilities of a small group of free people. In this case, *collective intelligence* can also emerge, but under the condition that the suffering of slaves is not wasted but invested into art or technological progress or at least used to increase the military ability of the civilization (e.g., Spartans, Roman Empire, etc[4].).

The dilemma discussed here can be resolved by the introduction of a strong definition of *collective intelligence*, such that nobody in the social structure will have his individual abilities reduced.

DEFINITION 16. STRONG DEFINITION OF *COLLECTIVE INTELLIGENCE*

We say that a strong *collective intelligence* emerges because of cooperation, interaction, or coexistence in S, iff at least one problem $Probl'$ can be pointed

[4] Also true with bees, that is, workers are biologically restricted.

out, such that it can be solved by a lone individual with the support of the group or by some individuals working together, such that

$$f_O^{Probl_i}(n') \overset{significantly}{>} f_O^{Probl_i}(n) \in Abl_U^{all\ indiv}$$

or

$$\exists Probl' \text{ such that } \left(\forall n\ Probl' \notin Abl_U^{all\ indiv}\right) \wedge (Probl' \in U) \tag{0.4}$$

and

$$\neg\exists indiv \in S \quad \text{such that his individual abilities are reduced}$$

HYPOTHESIS 1. FEASIBILITY OF A STRONG DEFINITION OF *COLLECTIVE INTELLIGENCE*

It is impossible to implement a case of a social structure that will fulfill the requirements of the strong definition of *collective intelligence*.

(Without proof)

Comment:–Joining or building a social structure will always require the individual to sacrifice some of his individual abilities (or freedom at least). Thus, probably the strong definition of *collective intelligence* is not feasible in practice.

3.2 DIFFICULTIES WITH MODELING AND MEASURING *COLLECTIVE INTELLIGENCE* DUE TO THE LACK OF A PROPER MODEL OF COMPUTATIONS

Before we start to discuss a model of computations, which is necessary for *collective intelligence* modeling and measuring, let us explore the underlying difficulties.

Several of them have been indirectly mentioned before; thus, we will start the discussion with these. However, we can initialize our discussion by pointing out that the basic source of these difficulties is that *CI* should be characterized as a global inference–computational process that is implemented by difficult-to-observe interactions made up of loosely coupled individual computational processes. Individual computational processes (for *intelligence*) as a "quantum of computations" are nonhomogeneous, and more difficult to observe and analyze than the macroscopic process of "*collective intelligence*." Let us look at a list of those difficulties.

- **The Black-Box Difficulty**

  Our knowledge of the internal functioning of beings is only partial. *Collective intelligence* is observed over a rich spectrum of beings that are all very different. Thus, we have to use different approximation concepts such as *black boxes* or *actors*. However, if we consider beings as, for example, black boxes, for the needs of *collective intelligence*, we cannot (in most cases) efficiently define relations between stimuli and response. Usually the variety of possible stimuli and reactions is so high that we cannot define a sufficient transition function from stimuli to response. We have been able to successfully represent simple beings as approximating automata for the needs of collective behavior in a few cases only. The best examples are ants (9).

In recent years, there has been a growing belief in the concept of agents (184,185), which will provide a new and robust research base, but the problem of how to get complete data about all relations between stimuli and response, even for simple beings, still remains.

As a result of this difficulty in our approach to the *collective intelligence* problem, beings are either labeled as a single clause of fact, rule, or goal, or approximated by local computational spaces, moving as beings do. The second approach allows us to approximate beings with an analog of a problem-oriented Expert System and thus to simulate the "logical behavior of beings." The drawback of this approach is that *collective intelligence* must be evaluated as a specific process, oriented to specific problems to allow use of simple logical expressions.

- **Nondeterminism of Individual Behavior Driven by Interaction With the Environment**

Even if a given being could be modeled efficiently in vitro by any deterministic system, this being would not behave (respond) in the same way in vivo because interaction with the environment would be added to the expected stimulus (e.g., interaction with another being). Thus, a given subset of beings, even if they are the same type, will behave in different ways. As a result, beings must be described with the use of probability or concepts such as agents with fuzzy sets, (46,186) or beings must be described "en mass" to allow use of approximation methods.

In this book, we go even further; we assume that the influence of the environment prevails over logic or the willful activity of beings, and as a result, beings behave in quasi-chaotic ways.

This approach is supported by several authors (187,188). D.L. Kiel and E. Elliot (188), in their book about chaos in social science, conclude that "no single technique can be used to diagnose and describe all chaotic processes or to identify the strengths and limitations of a variety of approaches."

- **Beings Participating in a Social Structure are in Permanent Movement**

The majority of beings that create recognized social structures belong to the world of animals and are in permanent movement around the environment, which makes their interactions and communication accidental and based on rendezvous. Rendezvous may be direct or with artifacts of another being. Clear communication networks such as those discussed in a previous section are created only for short periods, like small group meetings, which are usually restricted to only a few members of the social structure.

Our present knowledge about social structures created by *stationary* beings that could display the phenomenon of *collective intelligence* is restricted; in our book we discuss only bacterial biofilms.

- **Wealth of Communication Methods Used by Beings**

  Our computer systems are based on digital technology; thus, we rely on only one available, computer-type communication system for modeling of *collective intelligence*. Meanwhile, live beings use a variety of communication systems based on different physical properties of their environment (189,190). Acoustic, chemical, visual, and touching systems are used, and probably, more have to be discovered. Thus, we face problems of translating information carried by a specific human or animal communication system into the language of our computer communication technology. Good examples of such problems are the information dance of honeybees discussed in Section 2.2.1.2.2. and even the problem of how to code information we read from the face and body behavior of our interlocutor.

- **Incompleteness of Mathematical Knowledge**

  The example of the discovery of fuzzy sets by Lofti Zadeh in the 1960s (191) and the immediate demonstration of how this new mathematics is useful for modeling real live systems (192) demonstrates that mathematical and involved computational systems not yet known to humans can and probably do exit already.

Although digital computers are now widely used very successfully for almost all disciplines, there are also alternative models of computations, for example, analog computers are still demonstrating their usefulness in the neural network area (193) and L.M. Adleman (5) recently proposed molecular DNA computers.

As a result, we are in a situation in which the digital computer with its underlying model of computations is not suitable for the problem of *collective intelligence*, as has been noted before, and the question is "Which other model would really work?."

3.3 ARE THE CONCEPTS OF MESSAGE PASSING, AGENTS, AND ACTORS SUFFICIENT FOR *COLLECTIVE INTELLIGENCE*?

Rapid progress in computer science has occurred in recent decades, especially in the area of computer-based communications, which has created several potential tools that could be useful for the problem of defining, measuring, and modeling *collective intelligence*.

Assuming that this book is really the first that tries to present a complete formalization of the *collective intelligence* problem, one can ask what is wrong or missing in those tools that nobody[5] has successfully completed describing and formalizing *collective intelligence* through concepts of computer communication-like agents (185), multiagent systems, actors (194), message-passing (195), and other related terms.

Several reasons can be listed for this. Some of them are of a general nature, but the one given below is probably the fundamental one.

> In computer-based communication, the focus is on the development of specific, underlying tools to make communication faster, safer, smarter, and so forth, but communication as a complete process between individual humans and human social structures (organizations or companies) is left to self-develop spontaneously without any global plan or "master" design. The result and an example is the Internet, which emerged unexpectedly even to the biggest "computer gurus." It occurred as a side effect of work on a decentralized network called ARPAnet created by the US Department of Defense in 1969 to facilitate communications in the event of a nuclear attack. The situation in this area resembled a bottom-up synthesis, where lower level elements were consciously created; later they self-assembled like LEGO blocks (with the partial conscious control of humans), and finally on a higher level, an even bigger object emerged spontaneously.
> With *collective intelligence*, we face an inverted situation: this general phenomenon emerged in the past, perhaps some billion years ago, in a world of quasi-live beings, and is perhaps occurring over and over even now in some environments. Now, we are trying to match or create tools that are proper for describing it. This resembles a top-down analysis.

Thus, trying to use the concepts of agents, actors, and message-passing for *collective intelligence*, we can face the problem of nonmatching tools — notion of *information molecules* should be used. To be more specific, we must give some details.

First, let us look at some definitions of agency from M. Wooldridge and N.R. Jennings (185):

DEFINITION 17. A WEAK NOTION OF AGENCY

The term *agent* is used to denote a piece of hardware or (more usually) a software-based computer system equipped with the following properties:

- Autonomy
- Social ability

[5] It is remarkable that the methodology elaborated by W. Sulis (CIlab) and D. Wolpert in NASA Ames, tackling the problem of *collective intelligence*, directed them in general to the same basic assumptions on how the problem should be considered.

- Reactivity
- Pro-activeness

Other attributes sometimes discussed in the context of *Agency* are as follows:

- Mobility
- Veracity
- Benevolence
- Rationality

DEFINITION 18. A STRONGER NOTION OF AGENCY (ANTHROPOMORPHISM) (185)

An agent, in addition to having the properties identified earlier, is either conceptualized or implemented using concepts that are more often applied to humans. For example, to characterize an agent, *mentalistic* notions are used, such as *knowledge, belief, intention, and obligation*, or even going further and considering *emotional* agents.

To start the discussion as to why agents might not be proper tools for *collective intelligence*, let us quote objections to the notion of agency, summarized by H. Nwana (196), that it is so difficult to define precisely what agents are for at least two reasons:

1. The term *agent* is prevalent everywhere, namely, travel agents, estate agents, and so forth.
2. In software engineering, the word agent is an umbrella term for a different type of research and development. The response of some researchers to the lack of strict definition is to invent more synonyms and derived terms. Nwana asks if these solve anything or just add to the confusion. We now have synonyms including knowbots (i.e. knowledge-based robots), softbots (software robots), taskbots (task-based robots), userbots, robots, personal agents, autonomous agents, and personal assistants.

   These synonyms are used for the following reasons:

   - Agents come in many physical guises: for example, those that inhabit the physical world are called robots; those that inhabit vast computer networks are sometimes referred to as softbots; those that perform specific tasks are sometimes called taskbots; and autonomous agents refer typically to mobile agents or robots that operate in dynamic and uncertain environments.
   - Agents can play many roles; consequently we have personal assistants or knowbots, which have expert knowledge in specific domains.
   - Due to the multiplicity of roles that agents can play, there is a rich number of adjectives that can precede the word agent: search agents, report agents, presentation agents, navigation agents, role-playing agents,

management agents, search and retrieval agents, domain-specific agents, development agents, analysis and design agents, testing agents, packaging agents, and help agents, and so forth.

Nwana concludes that Expert Systems, for example, do not meet the preconditions of agenthood, as do most knowledge-based system applications. Modules in distributed computing applications also do not constitute agents because such modules are rarely smart and hence are much less robust than agents (or should be); they also do not degrade gracefully. Moreover, generally, in agent-based systems the communication involves high-level messages in contrast to the low-level message-passing in distributed computing. The use of high-level message-passing leads to lower communication costs, easy reimplementability, and concurrency. Perhaps, most important is that agent-based applications operate typically at the knowledge level and not at the symbol level, as is the case in distributed computing applications. In any case, modules in distributed computing applications are not autonomous in the same sense as described earlier for agent applications. The majority of software applications may be ruled out from the set of agent-based applications on the same grounds as Expert Systems or distributed computing applications are. Those objections are raised again by H. Nwana and D. Ndumu (197), with the additional observation that after 1994, progress in theories with agents has been rare.

For the needs of the *collective intelligence* theory, such an understanding and use of agency is not required. Except for the problem of ambiguity, the concept of agency is adequate for very high-level, individual beings, and it is because of this that in *collective intelligence* problems appear with proper definitions of agents when used for low-level beings such as bacteria or when we consider metabeings, such as social structures.

It is interesting that support for our criticism and unusual approach also comes from M. Minsky (198), who in 1985 defined "agent" as something like "mindless stuff" (elements, particles) that creates mind. Take note of his statement "... *simpler particles be — the agents that compose our minds?* ..." that is, that agents are necessary for defining mind but are themselves mindless.

The notion of *information molecules* and *membranes*, which are introduced in 3.4.4.2 will allow us to bypass the formal difficulties that emerge when, for example, two agents communicate through the exchange of messages. Are messages themselves agents? — what must the complexity of a message be for it to become an agent? In *collective intelligence*, a message is just an *information molecule* on another level. Social structures provide more sophisticated counter examples. For example, are a wife and husband cooperating easily (with the difficulties of daily life) one agent (a family) or two agents from *his* or *her* individual point of view? Their friends can consider them as either a family or as individuals. Another example is a bomber plane, for example, a B-52 on its mission over enemy territory with a crew on board — can it be considered as a single agent?

This question is important because in real *collective intelligence*, alive and not alive, thinking and nonthinking agents can interleave in inseparable ways, social and biological systems also overlap, creating one *collectively intelligent* system.

At the end of this part, let us also take a brief look into the concept of actors (194,199) and the expectation that it could be useful for some kind of computer-supported *collective intelligence* (200,201). However, if we look at actor-based metalevel architectures created to implement grouping and multiactor synchronization concepts, such as ActorSpaces (202) and Synchronizers (203), it is found that this tool is an extension of the concept of agency. Thus, the same objections can be raised, that it will not be sufficient for very low-level beings, and that the tool is not mature enough to work well with large social structures.

3.4 REVIEW OF THE MAJOR MODELS OF COMPUTATION

To measure *collective intelligence*, we need a special model of computations, which will be appropriate for chaotic, heterogeneous interaction and behavior of beings in a social structure.

To some extent, a social structure can itself be considered as some kind of biological computer that runs computations required by the *collective intelligence* of this structure. This means that the input entails problems faced by individuals or subgroups and the output involves solutions to those problems.

Here we come to the question "what is a computer?—what process could be a computer?"

In every introductory textbook in *computer science*, in the first chapters, there can be found a more-or-less brief history of human effort to find a good physical process, to get it under control, and to be awarded with having a tool "computer," which will solve or answer formal problems that are too difficult or laborious for a specific human brain. Humans have tried almost everything: water, air, mechanical structures, electrical processes, and even now, these efforts continue by trying to get the biological (DNA) processes under control, that is, to make them function as a computer.

Let us propose the following commonsense, partially formal definition of the relationship between a physical process, a computer, and a formal problem to be solved:

DEFINITION 19. PHYSICAL PROCESS AS A COMPUTER

We say that a given physical process is a computer for a given formal problem if this process provides a satisfactory answer for a satisfactory subset of such formal problems in an assumed time. It can be expressed as a 4-tuple:

$$\langle \mathit{Process},\ \mathit{Model},\ \mathit{Mapping},\ \mathit{Problem} \rangle \qquad (0.5)$$

Process describes a physical process used for computations.

Model describes our comprehension of this process, that is, our level of controlling it.

Mapping describes how behavior of the physical process corresponds to the formal problem to be solved. Here we also mean the technology of adjusting the physical process (programming) to make it solve a given specific, formal subproblem, and the method of reading (translating) the physical problem into a formal answer of the desired form.

Problem describes a formal problem that can be solved by a physical process.

Although almost anything can be claimed to be a computer[6], only a few processes appear to be efficient, and only one has exploded into the present huge digital computer industry. Before we present a model of computations efficient for *collective intelligence*, let us make a comparable review of the major models of computations.

3.4.1 The Deterministic Turing Machine (DTM)

A simple Turing Machine (TM) is neither a real device nor a draft intended to be implemented as hardware but an abstract model of a hypothetical computing system that Turing devised as a mental experiment to answer a famous mathematical question in the negative (204). The first efficient computers emerged after World War II.

In 1928, David Hilbert posed the following problems[7] (205,206):

- **Is Mathematics Complete?**, that is can every mathematical statement be either proved or disproved?
- **Is Mathematics Consistent?**, that is, is it true that contradictory statements such as $1 = 2$ cannot be proved by apparently correct methods?
- **Is Mathematics Decidable?**, that is, is it possible to find a completely mechanical method whereby, given any expression s in the logico-mathematical system S, we can determine whether or not s is provable in S? The last question is known as the Entscheidungsproblem.

In 1931, Kurt Gödel proved that every formal system sufficiently powerful to express arithmetic is either incomplete or inconsistent and that if an axiom system is consistent, its consistency cannot be proved within itself (207). In 1936, Turing offered a solution to the Entscheidungs problem (208). He showed that given the rigorous representation of a mechanical process by means of the Turing machine (TM), there are decision problems (problems that admit yes/no answers) that are demonstrably unsolvable by the TM.

The formal description of a Nondeterministic Turing Machine (NDTM) is given later, but here, we present the formal definition of the DTM:

[6] Even movements of stars can be claimed by astrologists as computers to calculate the future.

[7] In general, 23 problems were posed by Hilbert.

DEFINITION 20. DETERMINISTIC TURING MACHINE (DTM)

$$
\begin{aligned}
\text{DTM} &\stackrel{def}{=} (\text{Q}, \Sigma, \Gamma, q_0, \delta)\\
&\quad \text{Q}- \text{ finite set of states assumed not to contain } h, \text{ the halt state}\\
&\quad \Sigma- \text{ input alphabet, finite set of symbols}\\
&\quad \Gamma- \text{ the tape alphabet, is a finite set with } \Sigma \subseteq \Gamma, \Gamma \text{ is assumed}\\
&\qquad \text{not to contain } \Delta \text{ the blank symbol}\\
&\quad q_0 \in \text{Q}- \text{ initial state}\\
&\quad \delta- \text{ is a partial function Q } \times (\Gamma \cup (\Delta)) \to (Q \cup \{h\}) \times (\Gamma \cup \{\Delta\}) \times\\
&\qquad \{R, L, S\}
\end{aligned} \tag{0.6}
$$

The transition function δ is considered the program for the DTM. The problem of determining whether a Turing Machine will halt (reach halt state) for a given input and a given δ is called the Halting Problem. In general, the Turing Machine can be used as a theoretical tool in various capacities:

- As a language recognizer
- As a language generator
- As a function evaluator
- As a problem decider

Turing's work provided us with the last two elements of the 4-tuple, (0.5), $\langle Process, Model, Mapping, Problem\rangle$. The formula (0.6) can be interpreted as a device with the *Model* given in Figure 3-1.

Turing's fundamental results are summarized (204) in the following form:

- TM can compute anything a computer can compute
- TM can be physically implemented on many different types of hardware

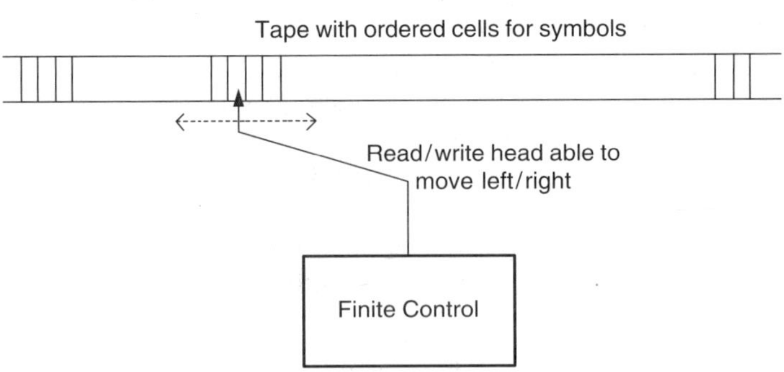

Figure 3-1. Turing Machine (Deterministic Turing Machine).

- Every conventional computer is logically (not physically) equivalent to a TM

There is also a stronger formulation of what is given above in the so-called Church-Turing thesis. The physical version of the Church-Turing thesis can be presented according to D. Deutsch (366) as follows[8]:

> Every finitely realizable physical system can be perfectly simulated by a universal model computing machine operating by finite means.

The importance and greatness of Turing's work lies in the fact that several physical processes can be used to implement the Turing machine while coding symbols with binary logic.

Early computers were built by means of electromechanical technology (MARK I) followed by vacuum tubes (ENIAC), replaced later by single transistor technology, and now by Very Large Scale Integration (VLSI) chips with millions of transistors on a chip. This is now the predominant technology; however, the digital computer can also be built with the help of the flow of liquid (as was tried in the 1960s and 1970s), and probably with light (209) in the future (210), or with biological (molecular computer) systems. There are also reasonable prospects for building a quantum computer (211). In Section 3.4.5.2 the DNA computer is discussed.

Thus, with the Turing Machine, we have a very convenient, dual continuation of scientific (complexity) and technological progress, building faster and faster computers without changing the superstructure or underlying theory.

Now let us take a look into some important problems (from the *collective intelligence* point of view), related to the Turing Machine.

3.4.1.1 Today's Implementation Approach to the DTM Von Neumann presented the basic implementation concept of the Turing Machine in 1945, when he was working with the EDVAC computer (212). Now this concept has been named after him, and has the form given in Figure 3-2. If we look into the general scheme of today's computers, the functional difference is the integration of Arithmetic and the Logic unit with the Control unit, which has resulted in the Central processing unit (CPU). This integration has created the microprocessor on the basis of VLSI technology.

G.J. Myers (213) defined four properties that characterize von Neumann architecture:

1. Instructions and data are distinguished only implicitly through usage.
2. There is a single memory, sequentially addressed.
3. The memory is one-dimensional.

[8] There have been serious discussions as to how this thesis should be correctly presented.

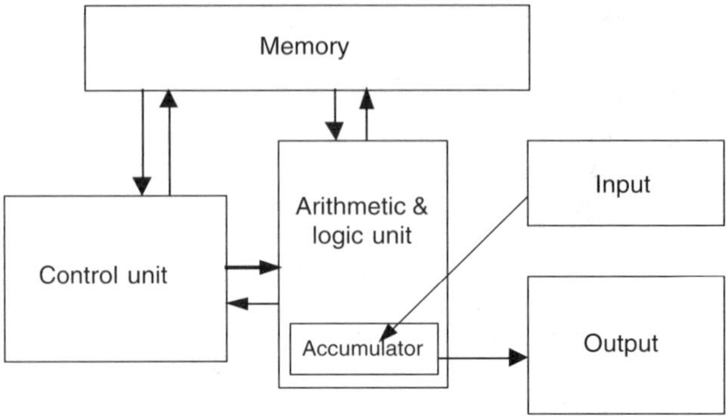

Figure 3-2. Von Neumann concept of computer architecture.

4. The meaning of the data is not stored with it. It is not possible to tell by looking at a sequence of bits whether that sequence represents, for example, an integer, a floating-point number, or a character string. In a higher level language, we associate such a meaning with the data and expect a generic operation to take on a meaning determined by the meaning of its operands.

Despite the predictive genius of von Neumann's design of computer architecture, which is still valid for today's computer (because it is so efficient), there is a serious drawback with this design. It has been called by Backus (214) the "von Neumann bottleneck":

> All of the data, the addresses (locations) of the data, and the operations to be performed on the data, must travel between the memory and the CPU in a sequential way.

As a result, the clock speed of the CPU often outpaces the ability of the memory to deliver data over the data bus. Computer designers have overcome this bottleneck to varying degrees by the use of faster memory, cache systems, wider data buses, reduced wait states, and pipelining, but no computer system can claim to be free of this bottleneck.

Throughout the development of the computer, there have been significant improvements in design:

- The structure of registers has been extended and improved, for example, index registers and general-purpose registers were introduced. The size of registers and their diversity is growing, as parts of RAM memory move closer to the "kernel" of the CPU.
- The floating-point data representation and robust FPUs were designed and later integrated into the structure of advanced processors, for example, Intel 80486 can be considered as an integration of Intel 80386 and 80387.

- Addressing techniques have been developed, for example, indirect addressing, mainly under pressure of rapidly growing availability of addressing space.
- Hardware interrupts were introduced to redirect program execution upon detection of certain events.
- Input and output were parallelized with CPU execution.
- Virtual memory was introduced.
- Multiprocessor systems and consecutive networks were efficiently introduced into the market, and now their use is widespread.

It is astonishing that although each of these were improvements over the original von Neumann design, some of which were quite significant, none have fundamentally changed the architectural concept of von Neumann. Thus, the four properties given by Myers (213) are still valid, and the von Neumann bottleneck still exists with or without these improvements. All of these improvements were designed and implemented in mainframes before 1960.

Now we should pay some attention to current selected attempts to build a "non-von Neumann" computer, because this will later allow us to characterize the model of computations to be applied to the problem of *collective intelligence*—the Random PROLOG Processor.

Selected concepts of a "non-von Neumann" machine:

- **A Computer Based on "Self-Identifying Data" (213).**

  In the von Neumann computer, the instructions themselves must determine whether a sequence of bits taken as an argument is integer, real, character, or other data-type. With typed storage, each operand carries with it in the memory some bits to identify its type. Then the computer needs, for example, only one general ADD operation (which is all we see in higher level language), and the hardware determines whether to perform an integer add, floating point add, double precision, complex, or whatever it might be. This requires more expensive hardware, but it greatly simplifies and makes shorter programs. Some computers have taken steps in this direction with high-level language architecture, becoming "slightly" non-von Neumann.

  It will be clear in Section (3.4.4.2) that the idea of successful inference when *information molecules* rendezvous and are able to unify is one more possible implementation of "self-identifying data."

- **The Use of Programs that Operate on Structures or Conceptual Units Rather Than on "Words."**

  In this approach, functions are defined without naming any data, and then these functions are combined to produce a program. Such a functional approach began with the famous concept of LISP programming, but the fate of this idea is that it has been *forced into* a conventional (available on the market) hardware and software environment.

- **Replacement of "Control Flow" Approach by a "Data Flow" Model.**

  This concept assumes that operations are executed in an order resulting only from the interdependencies of the data. To some extent this is also an idea of PROLOG-style programming, but PROLOG is (at present), like LISP, *forced into* a conventional, hardware–software environment, which destroys specific properties of this language.

  The present model of computations[9], deeply rooted in the von Neumann tradition, considers a program in terms of an orderly execution of instructions as set forth by the program. The programmer defines the order in which operations will take place, and the program counter follows this order as the control executes the instructions.

The idea of the Turing Machine has provided us not only with the foundations of today's digital computers, which has changed our lives, but also with a mathematical concept and tool to evaluate the computational complexity of the processes we are solving — under the assumption that the problem be solved with a Turing Machine-based computer.

3.4.1.2 The Complexity of Computations with the Deterministic Turing Machine The complexity theory (215–217) classifies a problem according to the minimum time and space needed to solve the hardest instances of the problem with a Turing Machine (or with some other abstract model of computations). A Turing Machine is a finite state machine with an infinite read–write tape (Fig. 3-1) and is considered a "realistic" model of computations for today's computers. This means that problems that are polynomial-solvable on a Turing Machine are also polynomial-solvable on real systems and vice versa.

Problems that are solvable in polynomial time are called tractable because they can usually be solved for inputs of reasonable size. Problems that cannot be systematically solved in polynomial time are called intractable or simply "hard", because as the size of the input increases, their solution becomes infeasible on even the fastest computers.

Turing proved that some problems are so hard that they are undecidable, that is, it is impossible to find an algorithm to solve them. In particular, he showed the problem of determining whether an arbitrary Turing Machine (or program) halts or not is not decidable.

Many other problems have been shown to be undecidable by proving that if they could be solved, the "halting problem" could be solved. Figure 3-3 shows several important complexity classes and their possible relationships (their exact relationships are not known).

[9] For an in-depth review: Savage J.E.: *Models of Computation — Exploring the Power of Computing, Addison Wesley, 1998.*

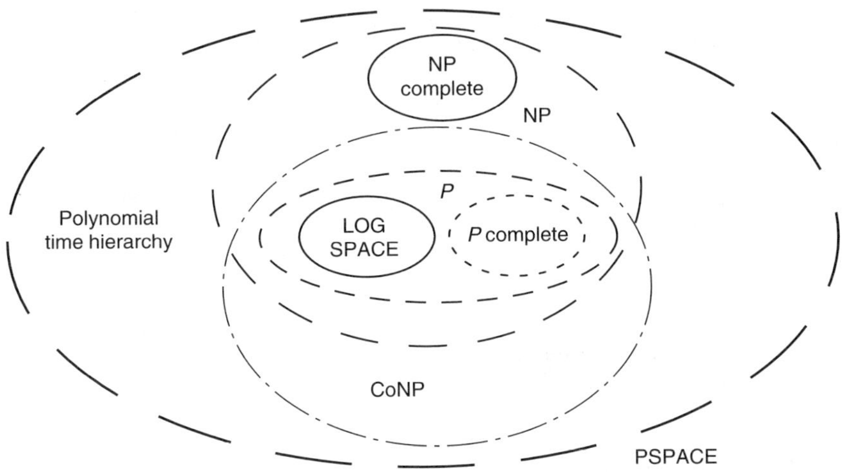

Figure 3-3. Important complexity classes and their possible relationships.

Let us list them:

- The class P consists of all problems solvable in polynomial time.
- The class NP (Nondeterministic Polynomial) consists of all problems solvable in polynomial time on a Nondeterministic TM. This means that if the machine somehow gets or guesses the solution, polynomial time is necessary for checking its corrections. However, if the solution is not known, it may require exponential time to solve certain problems in NP systematically (deterministically) .

An example of such a problem is the "knapsack problem" that can be formulated as follows:

> Given a set of n integers and an integer S, determine whether there exists a subset of A that sums to S.

This problem is clearly in NP, because for any given subset, it is easy to check whether it sums to S. Finding a subset that sums to S is however, much harder, because there are 2^n possible subsets and trying all of them has time complexity[10] $O(2^n)$.
Another example of a problem that seems to have exponential time complexity is the "satisfiability problem," which can be formulated as follows:

> Determine whether there exists an assignment of values to a set of n Boolean variables such that a given set of clauses over the variables is true.

[10] The big O notation $f(n) = O(g(n))$ is used in complexity theory for specifying that there exists a constant $c > 0$ and n_0 such that $f(n) \leq c \cdot g(n)$ *for all* $n \geq n_0$. In such a case, $f(n)$ will be said to be of the order $g(n)$.

A fraction of the large set of problems that are known to be in NP but for which no efficient algorithm has been found (despite, in some cases, persistent work on them) includes the following:

- √ Hamiltonian cycle
- √ Satisfiability
- √ Three-Coloring
- √ Clique
- √ Traveling salesman problem
- √ Integer knapsack problem
- √ Longest path in a graph
- √ Edge coloring
- √ Optimal scheduling
- √ Minimizing Boolean expressions
- √ Minimum graph partition
- √ Composite number
- √ Primality

The class NP includes the class P, because any problem that is polynomial-solvable on a deterministic TM is polynomial-solvable on a Nondeterministic one. If all NP problems were polynomial-solvable on a deterministic TM, we would have $P = NP$. Although many problems in NP seem much "harder" than the problems in P (e.g., the Knapsack problem and Satisfiability), no one has yet proved that $\mathrm{P} \neq \mathrm{NP}$.

In 1971, S. Cook (218) managed to prove that the satisfiability problem has the property that every other problem in NP can be reduced to it in polynomial time. This means that if the satisfiability problem is polynomial-solvable, every problem in NP is polynomial-solvable, and if some problem in NP is intractable, satisfiability must also be intractable. Since then, other problems (including the Knapsack problem) have been shown to be equivalent to satisfiability in the preceding sense. This set of equivalent problems is called NP-complete and has the property that if any one of the problems is in P, then all the NP problems are in P, and $\mathrm{P} = \mathrm{NP}$. Thus, the NP-complete problems are the "hardest"' problems in NP. The fastest known algorithms for systematically solving these problems have worst-case time complexities exponential in the size n of the problem. Finding a polynomial-time solution to one of them would be a major breakthrough in computer science. A problem is shown to be NP-complete by proving that it is NP-hard and in NP. A problem is NP-hard if it cannot be solved in polynomial time unless $\mathrm{P} = \mathrm{NP}$. To show a problem A is NP-hard, it is necessary to show that some NP-complete problem B is polynomial-time reducible to an instance of A, whence a polynomial time algorithm for solving A would also solve B. To show A is in NP, it is necessary to prove that a correct solution can be proved correct in polynomial time.

- The class CoNP consists of all problems that are the complement of some problem in NP. Intuitively, problems in NP are of the form "*determine whether a solution exists*," whereas the complementary problems in CoNP are of the form "*show there are no solutions*." It is not known whether NP = CoNP, but there are problems that fall in the intersection NP ∩ CoNP. An example of such a problem is the "composite numbers problem" that can be formulated as follows:

  Given an integer n, determine whether n is composite, that is, there exist factors p and q such that $n = pq$ or prime, (that is, there are no such factors).

  The problem of finding factors, however, may be harder than showing their existence.
- The class PSPACE consists of those problems that are solvable in polynomial space but not necessarily polynomial time. It includes NP and CoNP, but there are problems in PSPACE that are thought by some to be harder than problems in NP and CoNP. The PSPACE-complete problems have the property that if any one of them is in NP, PSPACE = NP, or if any one is in P, PSPACE = P. The class EXPTIME consists of those problems that are solvable in exponential time and includes PSPACE.

3.4.1.3 Parallelism in DTM Implementations As has been mentioned in Section 3.4.1.1, one of the main streams of progress in development of a computational model based on the Deterministic Turing Machine is parallelism. Parallelism has various alternatives:

1. To increase complexity of the processors, it can be implemented either by enrichment of the set of hardware-implemented instructions or by conversion of the processor into a closed, internal, multiprocessor system (e.g., Pentium). Such a processor composed of subprocessors cannot be programmed by the end-user.
2. Another possibility is to increase the speed of physical processes underlying the computations, for example, by using smaller, faster elements of the processor (transistors) or somehow by a change in technology, such as use of GaAs (gallium arsenide), superconductivity, and so forth instead of silicon-based technology.

The fundamental difficulty with *parallelism* is that parallel hardware requires parallel-oriented software, whereas most existing algorithms are specialized (made to be optimized) for a single processor. This means that the logic of programs and the programming tools are oriented toward a single processor.

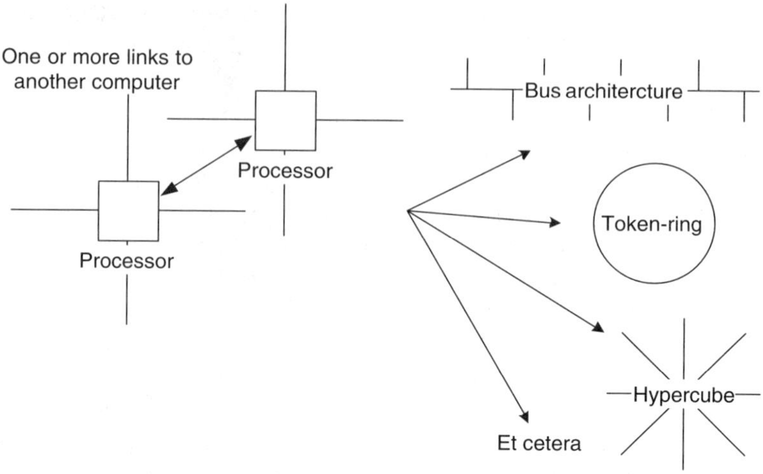

Figure 3-4. Multicomputer concepts.

The demand for *parallelism* implies a need for new algorithms and program structures that are able to perform many operations at once (219). *Concurrency* then becomes a fundamental requirement for algorithms and programs, but in practice, it is difficult to implement. This difficulty is the main "culprit" of the phenomenon that today's personal computers (PCs) outperform the "dinosaur mainframes" of the 1970s but still have only one multifunctional but fast central processing unit (CPU).

In fact, only one implementation pattern of *parallelism* is possible, that is, through connected multiple implementations of Turing Machines. In general, it is called a *multicomputer* and functions as is presented in Figure 3-4. The theoretical difficulties lie in the fact that a single processor "cannot change its position," that is, *is like a brick in a wall (of processors), so its neighbors are defined "forever."* It does not matter what the relationships between them are, for example master–slave relationship—any message-passing, that is, contact of any nature with any remote processor must go through immediate neighbors.

All multiprocessor architectures are more or less derivatives of this "through *neighbors only*" fate. Interaction of processors is implemented through interaction with a specified memory of a partner—not through direct interaction into the mode of the neighbors, that is, the control layer of the processor. This provides very convenient buffering, such as for queuing of input–output, but also imposes determinism of behavior of the processor.

Once again, it should be stressed that in the traditional multicomputer approach, only data and software (see agents) can migrate through the configuration but never the processor itself. Molecular models of computations, such as Adleman's DNA model of computations, break this barrier and assume that a processor (active molecule) can also migrate. This is also true (and necessary) for the *collective intelligence* model of computations.

Parallelism can be applied at several distinct levels, from parallelizing the simplest operations up to complicated tasks (220). The situation here can be classified as follows:

1. ***Arithmetic and bit level:***
   - Within arithmetic logic circuits
   - Between elements of a vector and matrix operation.

   In arithmetic logic itself, the arithmetic can be performed in a bit-serial fashion or on all bits of a number in parallel. Sometimes intermediate possibilities also exist, for example, in *carry look-ahead addition*, the logic can be performed in parallel on all bits of a byte; however, the bytes of the number are taken sequentially.

2. ***Instruction level:***
   - Between phases of instruction execution

   The processing of any instruction may be divided into several suboperations and pipelined (221). This provides overlap of different suboperations on different instructions. For instance, in the Pentium processor (222), the arithmetic of an instruction is divided into basic suboperations:
   a) Prefetch or fetch
   b) Instruction decode
   c) Address generate
   d) Execute — ALU and cache access
   e) Writeback

   It is pipelined during execution.

3. ***Program level:***
   - Within DO loops
   - Between parts of a program

   The program can usually be decomposed into multiple tasks on the basis of the fact that within a program, there are independent sections of code, and thus, it could be executed in parallel on different processors[11] in a multiprocessor environment. Some sections of the independent code can be recognized by a direct logical analysis of the source code, but others will be data-dependent, and therefore, the code must be redefined or execution of the program must be analyzed with the use of special software like an SGI CaseVision analyzer or debugger. In most cases, the program can be efficiently redefined (by the program's designer) to allow parallelization by the separation of variables and actions to create their independence in

[11] From 1993 to 1997, T. Szuba, R. Stras, and A. Stras wrote two consecutive versions of the Random Prolog Processor for the *collective intelligence* problem, using an eighth-processor computer (Silicon Graphics), and parallel Power C language.

an artificial way (223,224). However, it is a difficult task for automatic code-parallelizing tools.

In the case of loops, different executions of a loop may be run independently of each other, even though different routes are taken through the conditional statements contained in the loop. In this case, each microprocessor can be given the full code, and as many passes through the loop can be performed in parallel as there are microprocessors.

4. ***Job level:***
   - Between jobs
   - Between phases and jobs

   The highest level of parallel processing can be conducted among multiple jobs or programs through multiprogramming, time-sharing, and multiprocessing. At this level, the goal of a *multicomputer* installation is to maximize its performance. In the simplest case, each job may be considered dividable into several sequential phases, each of which requires a different system program and system resources. Most installations have a single processor for program execution but some contain two (dual) or more processors. It is the responsibility of the operating system to organize the sharing of the system resources between different jobs. Several programs usually reside in the fast memory of the computer, and in the case of a single processor, only one will be in execution. As soon as this program requires a slow I/O (Input/Output) facility, for example, a read from disk, this operation is initiated in the channel, and another program is put into execution. The first program waits until the data is available and control passes back to it when the other programs are similarly obliged to wait. In this way, the I/O of one job is overlapped with the execution of another in a dynamic manner, according to the needs of the jobs that happen to be sharing the computer at a particular time.

Let us now take another (not functional but hardware) point of view, and summarize some fundamental architectures of a multicomputer.

The most widely accepted is Flynn's proposed method of categorizing parallel computers (220,225). Flynn counted the number of parallel instruction and data streams and then labeled the computer with this count. As a result, he proposed the taxonomy of different parallel architectures, which can be presented as follows:

1. ***Single instruction stream, single data stream (SISD, the uniprocessor)***

   This is the conventional serial implementation of a von Neumann computer in which there is a single stream of instructions, and each arithmetic instruction initiates one arithmetic operation, leading to a single data stream of logically related arguments and results. This implies a single processor.

2. ***Single instruction stream, multiple data streams (SIMD)***

   This configuration is sometimes called *data parallel architecture*. In such a configuration, there are multiple arithmetic-logic processors and a single control processor. Each of the processors performs operations on the data in *lock-step*, which implies that functional units are synchronized at the instruction level. Each processor performs the same operation but each on its own piece of data. A single control processor synchronizes the processors.

3. ***Multiple instruction streams, single data stream (MISD)***

   There are few machines in this category; none that have been commercially successful or had any impact on computational science. One type of system that fits the description of an MISD computer is a systolic array, which is a network of small computing elements connected in a regular grid. A global clock controls all the elements. On each cycle, an element will read a piece of data from one of its neighbors, perform a simple operation (e.g., add the incoming element to a stored value), and prepare a value to be written to a neighbor on the next step. One could make a case for pipelined vector processors fitting in this category as well, since each step of the pipeline corresponds to a different operation being performed on the data as it flows past that stage in the pipe. There have been pipelined processors with programmable stages, that is, the function that is applied at each location in the pipeline could vary, although the pipeline stage did not fetch its operation from a local control memory, so it would be difficult to classify it as a processor (220).

4. ***Multiple instruction streams, multiple data streams (MIMD)***

   These machines contain multiple processors, each executing its own instruction stream to process a data stream allocated to it. Multiple instruction streams imply the existence of several instruction-processing units and therefore, necessarily, several data streams. This class therefore includes all forms of multiprocessor configurations, from linked mainframe computers to large arrays of microcomputers.

There are also other, rival taxonomies, which have been widely discussed (226).

The discussion presented here analyzed the situation where the size of the problem to be solved is arbitrary (without upper limit), but the size of an available computer (i.e., number of processors) and the architecture is fixed. Thus, solving the major problem includes, additionally, the solving of the related problem of *how to manipulate with restricted computational resources*.

However, if we assume that computational resources are unlimited, there could be a very interesting version of the Turing Machine, a so-called Nondeterministic Turing Machine (NDTM). Speaking more precisely, NDTM assumes that a *computational process* can "*give birth*" to any number of consecutive, successor computational processes, which continue computations in a parallel way. The theoretical importance of this model is obvious for taxonomy purposes while analyzing the complexity of problems.

However, let us analyze this model of computations, because it displays a striking similarity to the behavior of life processes.

3.4.2 The Nondeterministic Turing Machine (NDTM)

A formal definition of the Nondeterministic turing machine (NDTM) can be given as follows:

DEFINITION 21. NONDETERMINISTIC TURING MACHINE (NDTM)

$$\text{NDTM} \stackrel{def}{=} (Q, \Sigma, \Gamma, q_0, \delta)$$

Q– a finite set of states, assumed not to contain h, the halt state

Σ– an input alphabet, a finite set of symbols

Γ– the tape alphabet, which is a finite set with $\Sigma \subseteq \Gamma$, and

Γ is assumed not to contain Δ the blank symbol

$q_0 \in Q$ – initial state

δ– a function $Q \times (\Gamma \cup (\Delta)) \rightarrow$ subset of $(Q \cup \{h\}) \times (\Gamma \cup \{\Delta\}) \times \{R, L, S\}$

The above formalism entails the following characteristics:

- For a given state and tape symbol scanned by the tape head, the machine has a finite number of choices for the next move.
- Each choice consists of a new state, a tape symbol to print, and a direction of head motion.
- The machine can simultaneously perform an *arbitrary* number of different moves.
- There are a number of analogies that can be used to understand NDTM, and later, they are discussed more precisely. For example, a Nondeterministic Turing Machine can be perceived as a deterministic machine with an *oracle* that can guess the correct sequence of moves (227).

Now the given strict formal relation between a DTM and an NDTM is presented.

THEOREM 1. DTM VERSUS NDTM

If language L is accepted by a Nondeterministic Turing Machine M_1, then L is accepted by some Deterministic Turing Machine M_2 defined as follows:

1. For any state and tape symbol of M_1 there is a finite number of choices for the next move — let r be the maximum over all state-tape symbol pairs.
2. M_2 has three tapes:
   - Tape 1 will hold the input.
   - Tape 2 will hold a systematically generated sequence of the digits 1 through r (there are $r!$ such sequences).
   - For each sequence generated on tape 2, M_2 copies the input to tape 3 and simulates M_1 on tape 3, using the sequence on tape 2 to dictate the moves.
3. If M_1 enters an accepting state, M_2 accepts; if no sequence of moves leads M_1 to accept, M_2 will not accept.

Let us comment on the preceding definition and point out where the nondeterminism is hidden. The Deterministic Turing Machine, as it is interpreted in Figure 3-1, is changing its configuration in a deterministic way, that is, there is always only one possible next configuration.

Inversely, the Nondeterministic Turing Machine allows one configuration to imply (transit into) more than one consecutive configuration, for example, as it

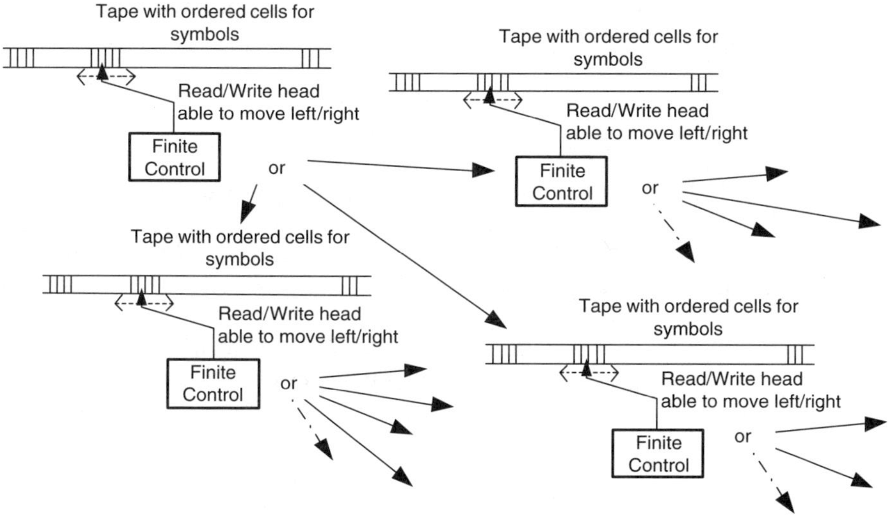

Figure 3-5. General concept of the Nondeterministic Turing Machine.

is presented in Figure 3-5. The problem is that alternative interpretations of this fact can be proposed, for example:

- It can be assumed that "one coherent" Turing Machine exists that stores all newly generated configurations in any data structure (memory) for future transitions. It can be, for example, as in Theorem 1 given earlier, or as in implementations of *breadth- or depth-search* in AI, which we discussed in Section 2.1.3.1.
- Another possible interpretation is that we can observe one Turing Machine and some kind of "nondeterministic guess" (oracle) that takes place regarding which alternative configuration should be used next for a transition.
- It is also possible to assume that the Turing Machine is itself constantly "reproducing" in a biological-like way. This means that if alternative configurations are possible at a certain point, one new Turing Machine will be "born" for each alternative, which will also continue with transitions of its own independently later.
- Another possible interpretation is that the Nondeterministic Turing Machine should be perceived in a different (mathematical) way, for example, using the concept of *Multisets* of Banatre and Metayer (228,229).
- Other interpretations are possible, for example, through the use of new physical phenomena like those in quantum physics (230).

To make more interesting conclusions about the NDTM, we have to make some additional assumptions, such as that such a Nondeterministic Turing Machine will be used as a model of computations, and not just as a mathematical abstraction for complexity considerations. Thus, we also have to consider other elements of (0.5) 4-tuple, that is,

$$\langle \textit{Process, Model, Mapping, Problem} \rangle.$$

The concept of a NDTM only provides us with the *Mapping* element of this puzzle, whereas we still do not have any idea which physical process could be used to implement the computer denoted here as (*Process, Model*), what this computer will be able to calculate, or what represents an element (*Problem*). The upcoming Section presents some possibilities.

3.4.2.1. Theoretical Advantages of the NDTM To demonstrate why the NDTM is so exciting as a theory of computations, let us look at one example.

3-CNF[11] FEASIBILITY

It is well known that a feasibility problem of logical expressions is one of the key issues in the complexity of algorithms. This is a difficult problem for

[12] A logical expression is in 3-CNF form if it is written as a logical product ($\wedge$) of logical sums ($\vee$) with at most three literals in every sum, e.g., $E(q1, q2, q3, q4) = (q1 \vee \neg q2 \vee \neg q3) \wedge (q1 \vee q2 \vee q4) \wedge (q3 \vee \neg q4) \wedge (\neg q1)$.

computations (from a time and memory-consumption point of view), because in every logical expression tested for feasibility, any variable can exist as *still free variable, or* **1** *(True), or* **0** *(False)*. This implies that for the expression with n variables, the 3^n possible nodes in the search tree should be produced (and later remembered in the memory or pruned).

Let us examine two algorithms given for the NDTM by J.L. Lauriere (31) to solve feasibility problems. Underlying both algorithms is this basic idea:

> "... The NDTM has the same set of instructions as the DTM and in addition, a special instruction ***choice[S]*** which creates as many copies of the current state of the machine as there are elements in S. By convention, the machine stops when one of these copies arrives at the instruction ***stop*** ... ".

1. *The general algorithm designed for the NDTM to investigate the feasibility of any logical expression $E(q_1, q_2, \ldots, q_n)$ with n variables will have the form*:

```
repeat for i ← [1 : n]
      q_i ← choice[T, F]
end repeat
  if E(q_1, q_2, ..., q_n) then
                    SUCCESS;
                      else
                    FAIL;
```

2. *Algorithm for 3-CNF designed for NDTM will have the form*:

```
repeat while there is still a clause C_i = f(x, y, z) that
                                          is not satisfied
     x ← choice[T, F]
     y ← choice[T, F]
     z ← choice[T, F]
  if C_i = F then FAIL
end repeat
if all clauses are satisfied then SUCCESS stop;
```

Observe how short these algorithms are for the NDTM, compared with the usual length of algorithms for deterministic computers. This is a general property of the NDTM model of computations.

Now let us try to design the *Model* of the *Process* for the preceding algorithms in the 4-tuple ⟨*Process, Model, Mapping, Problem*⟩. The property of ***choice[S]*** instruction allows us to destroy the *parent* record of the state of a machine immediately after records of all possible new states are created. Thus, we get something like an evolutionary system of computations. Additionally, every record of a new state can be retracted (or expire automatically) if it corresponds to a logical F value. The greatest problem here is the combinatorial explosion of processes, and such an approach has no implementation value in standard computers today.

In such a process, if a formula is feasible, sooner or later some record with a satisfying substitution will emerge. If there are more such possibilities, all of them will emerge and all other records representing unfeasible *streams* will decay. However, there is one more encouraging "flavor" here with such an approach to computations.

It is obvious that it is much easier to find a satisfying substitution if a logical formula is *satisfiable* than to prove that it is *unsatisfiable*. With a *satisfiable* formula, we can stop the computational process when the first satisfying substitution emerges. For a DTM, if a formula is unsatisfiable, all possibilities must be checked, for example, sequentially. However, for the NDTM, a symptom of this will be that all records will, in the end evolutionarily `FAIL`, and will simply vanish, e.g. from memory or *computational space*.

Thus, an NDTM computational process can deal with quite hard problems, but the output will be the state of the computational process itself and not just an answer, as in the case of looking for a satisfiable substitution. It is interesting to observe such an evolutionary process.

If a number of records are analyzed as a function of time during simulations (56), the dynamics of the process will look like they do in Figure 3-6 (see Section 3.4.4.2 for simulations).

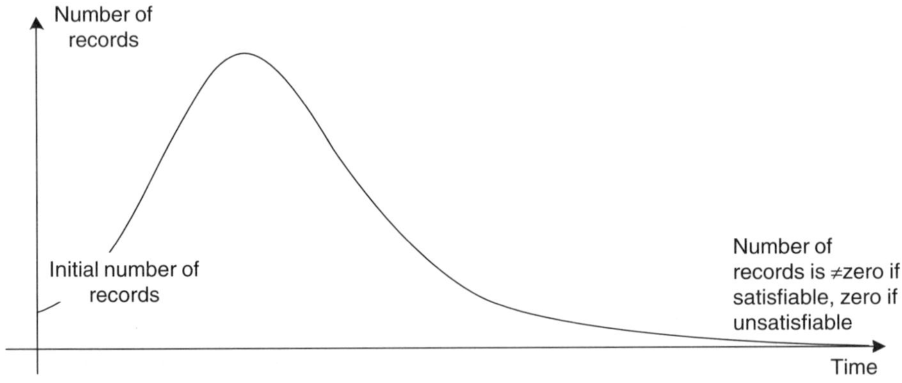

Figure 3-6. The number of variants of states of a Turing Machine available in computational space.

Moreover, it is interesting that the simulations given here demonstrate that this time-dependency is weakly bound to the size of the problem. This is similar to conclusions on properties of molecular models of computations those of Adleman (5,6) and so forth.

The basic problem is how to implement this concept of computations, what could be the physical *Process* for it, and what *Problem*(s) could be efficiently solved when such an NDTM computer is built.

3.4.2.2 Difficulties With NDTM Implementation Difficulties with NDTM implementation is also referred to as "realizability of the Turing Machine" (231,232).

As mentioned before, nondeterminism in the Turing Machine originated because of the multiple choices allowed for transition to the next state of the machine. Underlying this statement is a state of confusion.

If we assume that the set of possible states is enumerable, one way to implement nondeterminism is to use backtracking, for example, the way PROLOG systems are implemented, or to explore (all) possible solutions in parallel. This is not a very bad kind of "nondeterminism" because the present state and the set of alternative transitions can always be defined.

For the Nondeterministic Turing Machine, a more complicated scenario occurs when we make the following assumptions:

- The NDTM has a structure of fuzzy automata (233,234).
- Quantum-superposition in a quantum model of computations, for example (235,236) is used for NDTM.
- The space of states for NDTM will be assumed continuous, as in analog computers.

Theoretically, there is one more possibility. In Section 3.4.2, we mentioned that a Nondeterministic Turing Machine can be interpreted (among other possibilities) through some kind of "nondeterministic guess" regarding which next alternative configuration should be used for transition.

In this way, Turing tried to extend the concept of his Turing Machine with abstract constructions he called "oracles" or *o*-machines, which were intended to produce uncomputable numbers (227). Unlike Turing machines, which became the basis for the present computer and programming systems and have a firm physical interpretation, the oracle-machines were intended to be purely mathematical (black box)—Turing explicitly wrote,

> *We shall not go any further into the nature of this oracle apart from saying that it cannot be a machine.*

Several attempts were made to define the *oracle*, even using concepts taken from quantum mechanics, that is, Berthiaume and Brassard "Oracle Quantum Computing" (235).

If we try another approach, that is to implement the NDTM through parallelism, the *engineering question* appears to have found a physical process that is intrinsically parallel or will be able "to efficiently implement a self-replicating Turing Machine."

In the bibliography, many attempts can be found in this direction; some of them try to very strictly follow the idea of the Turing Machine while others veer away. Here, we should mention the concept of Hemmerling's *Movable Finite Automata* (237) that involves systems with entities moving about a fixed lattice. He called this model a "system of Turing automata." The idea is that there is a d-dimensional tape on which finite automata can move around to read and write the tape squares. This approach connects the two concepts to some extent.

The property of inborn parallelism was discovered with the idea of quantum computing and DNA computers. On the level of quantum physics, it is possible to consider objects storing information (qubits[13]) on the basis of quantum superposition[14], which as a result permits quantum parallelism (230,235,236,238). In general, n qubits can store 2^n numbers at once. Once the register of such a quantum computer is prepared in a superposition of different numbers, it can perform operations on all of them. For example, if qubits are implemented by atoms, then any action, let us say suitably tuned laser pulses, can affect atomic electronic states and make initial superpositions of encoded numbers evolve into different superpositions. During such evolutions, each number in the superposition is affected, and as a result, we observe massive parallel computations, even though there is only one piece of quantum hardware. This means that a quantum computer can perform the same mathematical operation in only one computational step on 2^n different input numbers encoded in coherent superpositions of n qubits.

In contrast, to accomplish the same task with any standard computer available now, it is necessary to repeat the same computation 2^n times or to use 2^n different processors working in parallel. Thus, the concept of a quantum computer offers an enormous gain in the use of computational resources such as time and memory.

DNA computers are also inborn parallel, but in a different way. We will not discuss this model of computations now because it is very close to the computational model of *collective intelligence* and a special chapter is devoted to that later.

Both systems are also intrinsically nondeterministic because the probability of any form[15] must be used to evaluate the output (results) of such computers.

[13] Qubit = quantum + bit, should be considered as a bit of information represented by any quantum object, such as a single atom, ion, or photon. Similar to a bit in the classical information system, a qubit is the basic unit of information of a quantum information system. The significance of a qubit is that it is not limited to a value of 0 or 1, but can be in a superposition state of any combination of 0 or 1.

[14] Quantum particles can exist in two or more states at the same time. This is called a superposed condition, for example, electrons at different spin levels and photons in two orientations of polarization.

[15] In quantum computations, the amplitude is associated with a state to determine the probability that the qubit will be found in that state. More precisely, the probability is equal to the square of the absolute value of the corresponding amplitude.

In such systems, it is difficult to find an analogy for the main control layer to what Operating Systems are in digital computers today.

3.4.3 A Model of Computations with a Continuous Space of States – The Analog Computer

The analog computer can be briefly defined as an electronic system that can be used to simulate the real, continuous world. The basic characteristic of analog computation that differentiates it from the classical, digital computers is the use of real constants.

Differential equations or maps in a continuous phase space easily describe physical systems that exist in the real world. Thus, analog computers are theoretically more suitable for modeling the real world than digital computers, which use discrete state space.

Despite many devices in human history that have claimed to be analog computers, reasonable analog computers emerged after World War II when progress in electronics allowed the building of amplifiers and integrators in an efficient way. During the 1940s, 1950s, and 1960s, electronic analog computers were very efficiently used to simulate the characteristics of various devices and processes, and they were widely taught as major courses in technical university curriculums.

Because of their true parallel computing nature, speed, small size, and ease of programming, analog computers were more efficient than digital computers of that epoch.

However, later progress in digital technology and eventually the emergence of very reliable VLSI processors has moved analog computers gradually into the shadows and later into museums.

Surprisingly, there has recently been a resurrection of interest in analog computers due to research sparks of hope related to neural networks (193) and a resultant increasing belief that the computational power of analog computers can go beyond the limits of the Turing machine (231).

Before we present the basic concepts of analog computer technology, let us try to find "*a common denominator*" for digital and analog computers. This is important because the approach presented below will also provide "*a common denominator*" for models of computations realized by *collective intelligence*.

According to Siegelmann (232), both analog and digital computers can be considered *dynamical systems*. A *dynamical system* can be briefly defined as composed of an abstract *phase space* or *state space*, whose coordinates describe the dynamical state at any instant, with a dynamical rule that specifies the immediate future trend of all state variables, given only the present values of those same state variables. Mathematically, a *dynamical system* is described by an initial value problem.

Dynamical systems (239–241) are *deterministic* if there is a unique consequent to every state and *stochastic* or *random* if there is more than one consequent chosen from some probability distribution, for example, a coin toss with two consequents with equal probability for each initial state.

A *dynamical system* can have discrete or continuous time. The discrete case is defined by a so-called *map* $z_1 = f(z_0)$ that gives the state z_1 resulting from the initial state z_0 at the next time value. The continuous case is defined by a *flow*, $z(t) = f(z_0)$ that gives the state at time t, given that the state was z_0 at time 0. A smooth flow can be differentiated with respect to time needed to give a differential equation, $dz/dt = F(z)$. In this case, we call $F(z)$ a *vector field* because it gives a vector pointing in the direction of the velocity at every point in the phase space.

Considering the given configuration of a Turing Machine as a state in some space, the rules describing the transition of the machine also constitute a *dynamical system*. The input for the machine is the initial condition for the *dynamical system*. The series of consecutive configurations during the computation process define a trajectory in the space of Turing Machine configurations.

This trajectory may converge or not to a halting configuration from which the output can be read. This halting configuration can be viewed as a so-called *discrete attractor*. Thus, through the concept of *dynamical systems* and *attractors*, we can have a *common denominator* for the two models of computations.

Many physical systems converge to attractors. Informally, an *attractor* is simply a state into which a *dissipative dynamical system* settles in a given (or infinite) time.

There is some controversy in mathematics regarding an appropriate definition of the *attractor*; however, we can propose the following definition:

Attractor

A set in the phase space that has a neighborhood in which every point stays nearby and approaches the attractor as time goes to infinity.

The *attractor* may be a simple fixed point, a limit cycle, or it may be chaotic with a fractal dimension. Some *attractors* (directly or indirectly) create fascinating visual forms, such as the Mandelbrot set, and are therefore widely used in computer graphics, [e.g., (242)].

The neighborhood of points that eventually approach the *attractor* is the *basin* of attraction for the *attractor*. The boundary of a *basin* of attraction is often a very interesting object since it differentiates between different types of motion. Typically, a *basin* boundary is a saddle orbit or such an orbit and its stable *manifold*. A crisis is the change in an *attractor* when its *basin* boundary is destroyed.

The correspondence between computers and physical systems presented here, with a common description as *dynamical systems*, creates one more way for us to consider evolving physical systems as possible candidate processes of computation (see discussion related to Definition 19 on a physical process as a computer).

Analyzing such processes and their complexity can contribute to the understanding of the nature of computation. In the theory of computations based on the Turing Machine, problems are classified by the growth of the computation time as a function of the size of the input. As discussed before, if the time is polynomial in the size of the input, the problem is said to belong to class *P*; if it is exponential, it belongs to the class *EXP*; moreover, if the answer is somehow guessed and it can be verified in polynomial time, it belongs to class *NP* (nondeterministic polynomial problems), and so on.

The complexity of the motion of dissipative dynamical systems can be characterized by the properties of their *attractors*. The convergence to the *attractors* is usually exponential. The complexity of an *attractor* can be quantified by its Kolmogorov-Sinai (KS) entropy and its Laypunov exponents (243). These essentially measure the sensitivity to changes in initial conditions and therefore, can be viewed as a measure of the degree of chaos (239,244). For stable fixed points and limit cycles, the largest Laypunov exponent and the KS entropy are not positive, whereas they are positive for chaotic attractors. This is a manifestation of the fact that chaotic attractors exhibit a much higher degree of complexity.

In analogy to the standard computational complexity classes (*P*, *NP*, *EXP*, etc.), there are computational complexity classes (P_d, NP_d, EXP_d, etc.) (232) that are relevant for physical *dynamical systems*. In computer science, it is an open question if $P = NP$. For the corresponding classes P_d and NP_d, it is conjectured that $P_d \neq NP_d$.

As will be clear later, the phenomenon of *collective intelligence* can also be considered a case of a chaotic *dynamical system* with some kind of emerging attractor(s). The sole difference is that with the emergence of *collective intelligence*, we observe a *map* of inferences (expressions of mathematical logic) in a certain space, and the attractor here has a more mathematical logic meaning, that is, we ask if some given N-element inferences converge to assumed final conclusions (logical *attractors*).

We observe a very similar situation with molecular computations, such as those of Adleman's DNA computer (5).

Now let us briefly describe the technology of analog computers. A more precise description of hardware and programming methodology is given by A.E. Rogers and T.W. Connolly (245).

The basic concept is that the real (physical) system under consideration must be first described in terms of equation(s), for example,

$$\frac{dy(x)}{dx} + 0.2y(x) = 0 \quad 0 < x < 10 \quad \text{for initial condition } y(0) = 5 \qquad (0.7)$$

Now the functional elements such as those given in Figure 3-7 must be properly wired into an electronic system, which will behave as the equation (0.7) describes. In an analog computer, the programming process is not a formal assembling of functional elements of a programming language to build a flowchart of execution but manual or automatic wiring of hardware elements from a finite set of available elements in a given analog computer. The output (results of computations) is in the form of plotted or recorded runs of voltage at specified points of circuitry.

Executive Device	Name of Operation	Symbol	Equation
Amplifier	Amplification	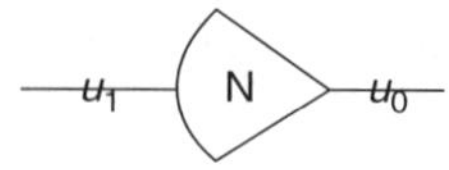	$u = -K \cdot u_1$ for $K >> 1$
Inverter	Change sign	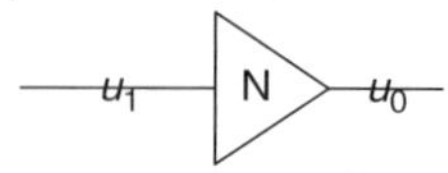	$u_0 = -u_1$
Adder	Addition with change of sign	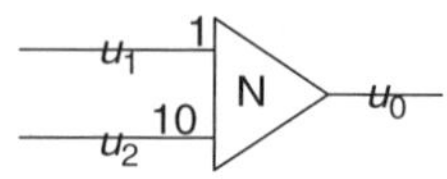	$u_0 = -(u_1 + 10u_2)$
Integrator	Integration of variable (sum of variables) w.r.t. time	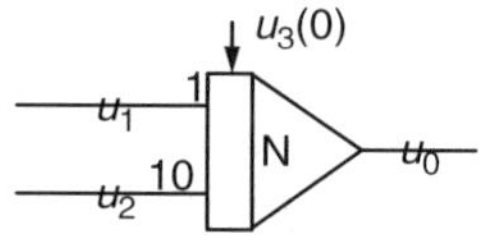	$u_o = -\left[\int_0^t (u_1 + 10u_2)dt + u_3(0)\right]$
Potentiometer	Variable is multiplied by a constant	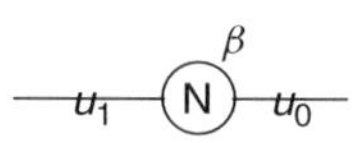	$u_0 = \beta u_1 \quad 0 \le \beta \le 1$
Multiplying unit	Two Variables are multiplied	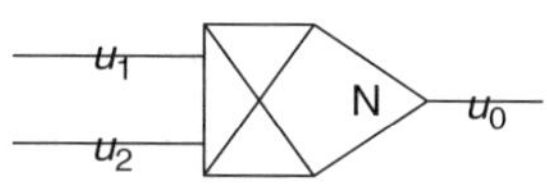	$u_0 = \alpha \cdot u_1 \cdot u_2$, $\alpha = \frac{1}{JM}$
Function generator (examples)	Function sin(x) is generated	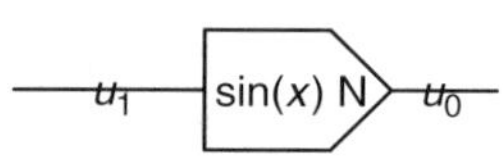	$u_0 = \sin(u_1)$
	Sign is evaluated	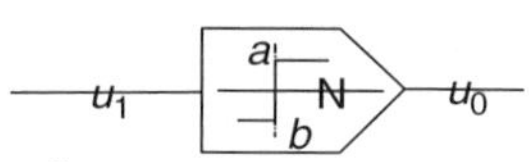	$u_0 = \begin{cases} a & \text{if } u_1 > 0 \\ b & \text{if } u_1 < 0 \end{cases}$

Remark: N is used for numbering units in diagram

Figure 3-7. Example of functional units of the analog computer.

For the preceding equation (0.7), the circuitry and result of simulations are given in Figure 3-8. This is a simple example, but for real systems when equations are more complicated or a set of equations must be solved, the chart of functional elements is much more complex (see lower part of Figure 3-8).

There is growing support for the belief that the subgroup of computational processes represented by analog computers and neural networks has theoretically higher computational abilities than digital computers. Such theoretically possible computers go beyond the Turing Machine limits to create a super-Turing Machine as a model of computations. H.T. Siegelmann (246) uses the term super-Turing to denote any system of computing that incorporates, but is more powerful than the standard Turing model.

Let us quote what Siegelmann says in a series of her papers, which can be best characterized by one of her titles, "Computation beyond the Turing Limit" (231):

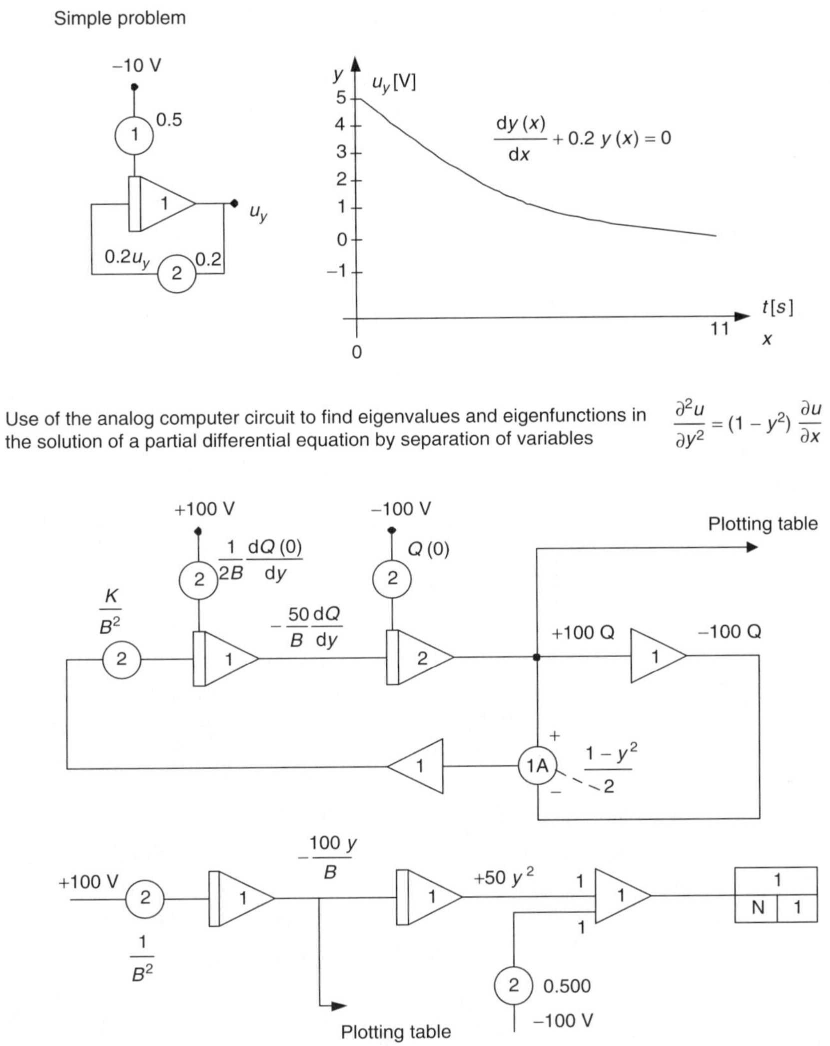

Figure 3-8. An example of analog computer circuits for finding a solution to a given equation.

> Turing machines are indeed able to simulate a large class of systems, but seem not to capture the whole picture of computation in nature, like the evolvement of many chaotic systems. We propose an alternative model of computation, whose computational power can surpass that of the Turing model. The proposed model builds on a particular analog chaotic system; by applying the system to computer science, a super-Turing model is developed (246).

Siegelmann also analyzes (246) the chaotic dynamical system, which she calls an *analog shift map*, which when viewed as a specific computational model, has super-Turing power and is equivalent to neural networks and the class of analog machines.

Results provided by Siegelmann's papers are key for us because computational *collective intelligence* assumes quasi-chaotic displacements of *information molecules* in *computational space*, and thus, any *collective intelligence* system can also be considered as a chaotic dynamical system possessing all the properties derived by Siegelmann.

Closing the chapter on analog computers, we should again summarize why one whole part of this book has been devoted to discussing analog computers (and related models of computations), which are in fact widely considered "museum" pieces.

- Analog computers help us to define a global *common denominator* for all known models of computations through the use of the concept of *dynamical systems*. Analog computers can be claimed as "nearer cousins" to the basic idea of dynamical systems than digital computers.
- Neural networks viewed as computational processes are considered analog computers, and neural networks are summoning a lot of a research interest right now, both in the area of pure computer science and in the neurosciences.
- A computational model of *collective intelligence* can be viewed as an analog chaotic dynamical system, if positioning of *information molecules* in *computational space* is with real values. Only the "upper level," that is, the inference process between *information molecules*, should be characterized by string processing, for which the Turing Machine-based model of computations is very suitable.
- From a computational power point of view, it is claimed that analog computers go beyond the limits of the Turing model and thus can be considered as very interesting from a theory-of-computations point of view. This is also true regarding considerations on the computational power of the *collective intelligence* phenomenon.

3.4.4 Nondeterministic, Molecular Models of Computations with Predicate Calculus as the Basic Tool for Collective Intelligence Modeling and Evaluation

Now we will present a model of computations that has been constructed for the needs of computational *collective intelligence*. We will also try to advocate this model as the most suitable one for the time being.

The greatest difficulty in designing a model of computations lies in the seemingly contradictory requirements for such a model. Past ways of thinking imposed by the Deterministic Turing Machine have focused our attention on computational models unfeasible for *collective intelligence*.

The *premises* for the model of computations presented below can be summarized in the following way:

- Mathematical logic is used at the highest level of the model. We propose first-order predicate calculus (16,18) to be implemented according to general PROLOG syntax. However, the model of execution of PROLOG will be totally different here than the widely used Warren Abstract Machine (WAM) (see 3.4.4.1) model of execution.
- *Information Molecules* are assumed as "symbolic" carriers of logic formulas and structures.
- Rendezvous and a unification-based model of single inferences are assumed.
- The inference process is assumed to have the form of a quasi-chaotic, noncontinuous process performed in a structured *computational space* of any nature (constructed according to the form of environment and characteristics of the social structure).
- From the beginning, it is assumed that the inference process evolves with no supervision (metaprocess) of any nature (such as an Operating System). The control and stabilization processes must be built into the inference process.

3.4.4.1. A Brief Description of the Concept of PROLOG and its Models of Execution PROLOG as a programming concept goes far beyond the concepts, style, and methods of programming of any other computer language. Despite the failure of Japanese attempts to build a Fifth Generation of computers with the use of PROLOG, the concept has demonstrated once again its potency for the computational *collective intelligence* theory.

It is not the intention of the author to present here a comprehensive textbook of PROLOG like those of I. Bratko (247), D. Crookes (248), and so forth, but it is necessary to take into account that this book is also addressed to scientists from different areas interested in the proposed theory of *collective intelligence*, such as from sociology, who could be unfamiliar with PROLOG. For this purpose, some form of PROLOG description with a bias toward its contribution to the theory of *collective intelligence* is necessary here.

History of PROLOG

PROLOG stands for "PROgramming in LOGic" and came out of research in the early 1970s of Kowalski (249), who provided the first procedural interpretation of first-order Horn clause logic (i.e., he explained how it could be executed on a computer). A. Colmerauer with his group (250) (also in collaboration with Kowalski) actually originated PROLOG and used PROLOG (among other things) for speech recognition (251).

Kowalski's research provided the theoretical framework, while Colmerauer's group gave rise to the actual programming language, building the first PROLOG interpreter[16].

[16] Colmerauer's PROLOG interpreter was written in Fortran!

However, for the real origins of PROLOG we should look back to 1965, when A.J. Robinson published a paper on the *resolution principle* for a mechanical theorem that proved and defined the *unification principle*, which is considered the root element for the PROLOG inference engine (252).

In 1975, Warren implemented PROLOG in a more efficient way, based on the Warren Abstract Machine model (WAM) of computations for PROLOG, by using some shortcuts in recursion (253). Since then, implementation of the PROLOG language has proliferated throughout the world.

In 1980, the Japanese initialized the project: "Fifth Generation Computing Systems" to capture the first truly intelligent computer and decided to base its program on PROLOG.

As a result, PROLOG began to be fairly widely used in industry for Expert Systems, *artificial intelligence*, and linguistics. It has also found some use as a relational database, prototyping language, and so fourth.

The decline of PROLOG began in 1992, when the Japanese Fifth-Generation project fizzled; however, even now PROLOG is relatively widely used. PROLOG is often used for educational purposes at universities because of its unusual style of programming, the importance its plays in the theory of programming languages, and in AI systems.

Because the PROLOG language has been used in various areas, efforts toward ISO standardization have begun, and the PROLOG Management Group (PMG) has been formatted. The PMG is an international consortium of leading PROLOG vendors and users, including Cosytec, LPA, PrologIA, SICS, IF Computers, Siemens Nixdorf, and so forth. The ISO Prolog standard: ISO/IEC 13211-1 was published in 1995.

As is obvious from our description of PROLOG, on the level of program description, it is an intrinsically parallel language (sometimes also called a declarative language). It is also intrinsically nondeterministic.

There are several possibilities for parallelized execution of PROLOG, usually on the basis of possible AND, OR, and *unification* parallelisms, which resulted in the bulk of commercial and "free" implementations of parallel PROLOGs. A special Section will be included on the parallel execution of PROLOG.

Syntax and Semantics of Programs in PROLOG

In our description of PROLOG syntax, we try to follow the popular textbook of W.F. Clocksin and C.S. Mellish (254) and ISO specifications (255).

BASIC ELEMENTS OF THE LANGUAGE

The alphabet of the PROLOG language has the following forms:

- Upper-case letters: A...Z
- Lower-case letters: a...z
- Digits 0,1...9
- Special characters: # $ & * + − . / : < = > ? @ ^ ~ \

COMMENTS

Comments can be given either delimited by `/* */`, or if a given comment does not extend beyond the end of a line, it can be started with % symbol, for example,

```
/* this is comment */
% this is also comment
```

ATOMS

So-called *atoms* are constructed on the basis of the PROLOG alphabet to represent objects from the real world and are coded in the following alternative ways:

- Atoms can be constructed as strings of letters, digits, and underscore character "_" but must start with a lower-case letter, such as

  ```
  atom_2
  nil
  my_Father
  route_from_A_to_B
  ```

- Atoms can also be constructed as strings of special characters, but care must be taken because some such strings are reserved, for example, :- to define rules (to be interpreted as a logical implication ← or constructor for a procedure).

  Also, `/*` cannot be used because this *token*[17] is reserved for creating comments.
- Strings enclosed in single quotes are also Atoms, such as

  ```
  'device No'
  ```

  The main use of *quoted strings* is to create an Atom whose identifiers violate other syntax rules of how to build Atoms. The backslash symbol \ is allowed to continue such a string on the next line.
- Special Atoms [ ] and { } are allowed.

[17] Token is used in computer science in two areas: networking, programming languages and compilers. In networking, it is defined as a special structured data object or message that circulates continuously among the nodes of a token ring and describes the current state of the network. Before any node can send a message, it must first wait to control the token. In the area of programming languages and compilers, tokens are defined as any nonreducible elements in the text that are parsed for use in a program as a variable name, a reserved word, or an operator. The concept of tokens shortens the program and speeds-up execution.

NUMBERS

Numbers are usually represented by integers and real numbers, such as

```
2222
2.0
0.3
```

We should remember that numbers are "artificial and, not natural objects" in logic programming, but the needs of efficient programming in PROLOG has forced almost all PROLOGs to be equipped with libraries of procedures (built-in predicates) to efficiently interpret and service numbers in a common-sense way.

Usually, there are also binary, octal, and hexadecimal numbers available in PROLOG implementations.

Atoms and numbers are equivalents of constants in the PROLOG language.

VARIABLES

Variables are used to denote objects that are known in run-time, sometimes only temporarily.

It is important that there are no declarations of types of variables in PROLOG; however, there are usually built-in predicates available to check the type of object which instantiates a tested variable (if any).

The syntax of variables in PROLOG assumes that a variable must start with an upper-case letter or an underscored character, for example,

`X`	uppercase letter first to express that it is a variable
`Mary`	
`_mary`	underscore first
`mary`	since it starts with a lowercase letter, this is an atom and, not a variable!

In PROLOG, we are allowed to denote a given variable by an underscored character only (in this case, it is a so-called anonymous variable) if this variable is not essential for computations in a specific PROLOG expression, in which it must be mentioned because of a need to correctly identify this PROLOG expression. For example, several clauses[18] may have the same name but a different number of arguments; thus, variables must be "mentioned", even if they are not named there, for example,

```
vehicle(X, 1992, _)
vehicle(X, mercedes, _, _, Owner)
```

Atoms and numbers and variables are the simplest language structures in PROLOG and are the so-called *terms*. More complicated *terms* can be constructed as *structures*.

[18] Clauses are facts and rules and are defined later.

STRUCTURES

Structures (or structured objects) in PROLOG are built by writing the *functor* name followed by an opening parenthesis with a sequence of terms next separated with commas and finally terminated with a closing parenthesis, for example,

```
date(Day, Month, Year)
```

In some cases, for the programmer's convenience and compatibility with another programming or mathematical systems, this *functor* notation can be rewritten with *operators* (operators are discussed later), for example,

```
2 + 2 = Sum
+(2, 2, Sum)
```

With more complicated structures, it is convenient to represent or analyze PROLOG structures as trees.

PROLOG structures can also be nested to represent more complicated objects from the real world, for example,

```
triangle(point(2,2), point(3,3), point(4,4), fill_in_color)
cos(2 * Angle / 3)
```

Looking more formally into the concept of *term*, we can define it in a recursive way. A term is a variable, a constant, or a term structure of the form:

$$f(t_1, \ldots, t_n)$$

where $t_1, \ldots, t_n$ are terms, and f is interpreted as an n-ary function.

The important (by their wide use) structures in PROLOG are lists, which are constructed with [ ] brackets. Lists can also be nested, for example,

```
[ ]   %      empty list
[a, b, c]   % a simple one level list
[father, mother, son, stepmother,[dog, cat, crocodile]]
```

PROGRAMS IN PROLOG

The fundamental element used to build PROLOG programs is the string of characters ":-" because of the similarity to the symbol of implication $\leftarrow$ in mathematical logic. We should remember that PROLOG's roots are in mathematical logic.

The structure of Horn clauses[19] is assumed as a basic restriction imposed on the syntax of PROLOG; thus, PROLOG programs should have the form:

```
<clause of head> :- <one or more clauses of body,
                               separated by commas>.
```

A simple example:

```
a  :- b, c, d.
```

Note use of :- and the dot **.** terminating the structure of the PROLOG program.

There is no direct differentiation for constructing the main program, subroutines, and so forth. Thus, for example, the main program with a subroutine can have the form:

```
main :- subr1, subr2, subr3.
subr2 :- a, b, c.
```

In PROLOG expressions, terms are usually interpreted through the concepts of mathematical function, but at the level of a program, clauses are interpreted through the concept of a relation (predicate).

For the elements of a PROLOG program, we can given a more formal summary: a *literal* is either a *0-ary* predicate symbol or a predicate structure of the form:

$$p(t_1, \ldots, t_n)$$

where $t_1, \ldots, t_n$ are terms, and p is an n-ary predicate. A clause is either a unit clause, which has the form:

$$h :-.$$

or else has the form:

$$h : -b_1, \ldots, b_k.$$

where h, $b_1, \ldots, b_k$ are literals.

h is referred to as the head literal; $b_1, \ldots, b_k$ the body literals.

Usually structures

<clause of head> **:-** <one or more clauses of body, separated by commas>.

are labeled as (inference) rules, but if there are no clauses of body, that is *h*:-**.** such a structure is abbreviated as *h***.** and is labeled as a fact (in a PROLOG program database—a conclusion without any premises).

[19] In general, a *Horn clause* is a predicate logic clause with exactly one positive (i.e., non-negated) literal. The main function of *Horn clauses* in PROLOG is to restrict its inborn nondeterminism. It is quite obvious in the second example in which two possibilities of inference emerge.

Examples:

$(A \wedge B \rightarrow C)$ is a Horn clause because it is logically equivalent ($\equiv$) to $(\neg A \vee \neg B \vee C)$

$A \wedge B \rightarrow C \wedge D$ is not a Horn clause because

$\equiv (A \wedge B \rightarrow C) \vee (A \wedge B \rightarrow D) \equiv (\neg A \vee \neg B \vee C) \wedge (\neg A \vee \neg B \vee D)$

In general, the PROLOG program can be understood in two ways depending on our way of defining the problem and the solution method:

- as declarative
- as procedural

Let us now analyze the consequences of this "interpretive nondeterminism" on the basis of the following example (this rule is not necessarily true in real life).

```
siblings(Name_of_child1, Name_of_child2) :-
               child(Name_of_child1, Name_of_parents),
               child(Name_of_child2, Name_of_parents).
```

The preceding structure can be read in two-declarative, and also in two-procedural ways:

Declarative Interpretation:

- `child1` and `child2` are true siblings if it is true that they have the same parents.
- Having the same parents implies being siblings.

This results from two possible ways to read logic expressions:

1. From a set of facts to a resultant conclusion
2. From an assumed hypothesis to the necessary facts for confirming the hypothesis

This dualism is the basis for forward and backward inferences.

Procedural Interpreting:

- To solve the problem, "if two given children are siblings", first, the name of the parents of the first child should be checked; later, the parents' name of the second child should be checked, and finally, a comparison of the two should be done to see if they are the same. This is the standard way of working with procedures: there is a procedure name with arguments and a body. First, we call this procedure by its name, and later, sequential elements of this body are activated for execution.
- When two computational processes (executed in sequential or parallel ways) activated to find the names of the parents of `child1` and `child2` "inform", for example, the operating system that they are finished, and another procedure informs that the parents' names are the same, then, the database-managing procedure will write the "statement or record" to the database that they are siblings.

GOALS IN PROLOG

Even if the program is given, it is necessary to define some "direction" of computations, that is, what should be really done before the computer will halt this program. In PROLOG, this is implemented through the definition(s) of *goals*.

This is the essential difference when comparing PROLOG to procedural languages (Fortran, Pascal, C, etc.), in which the "direction" of computations is given by the flowchart of related actions in the main program. In PROLOG, only goal(s) are specified, but the questions "how" and "when (order)" are increasing nondeterminisms in PROLOG. This question is left mainly to be decided by the assumed model of execution in the implementation of PROLOG.

A goal for a logic program P is defined to be a sequence of literals of the form:

$$?\text{-}g_1,\ g_2,\ \ldots,\ g_n.$$

separated by commas and terminated with a dot, where the g_i are referred to as subgoals.

Before we discuss general concepts (and difficulties) with the PROLOG model of execution, let us give an example of a very simple PROLOG program and present what this program implies.

Example: Inferring Grandparent Relations

```
                              rules

grandparent(Var1,Var2):- parent(Var1,Var3),                (rule1)
                         parent(Var3,Var2).
parent(Var1,Var3):- father(Var1,Var3).                     (rule2)
parent(Var1,Var3):- mother(Var1,Var3).                     (rule3)

                              facts

father(john,hans).                                         (fact1)
father(anna,ted).                                          (fact2)
mother(john,anna).                                         (fact3)
< more facts >                                               ...
```

Arguments in literals should be interpreted as follows:

```
grandparent(Var1,Var2) ≡
     grandparent(Name_of_grandparent, Name_of_grandson)
parent(Var1,Var3)      ≡
     parent(Name_of_parent,Name_of_child)
father(Var1,Var3)      ≡
     father(Name_of_father,Name_of_child)
mother(Var1,Var3)      ≡
     mother(Name_of_mother,Name_of_child)
```

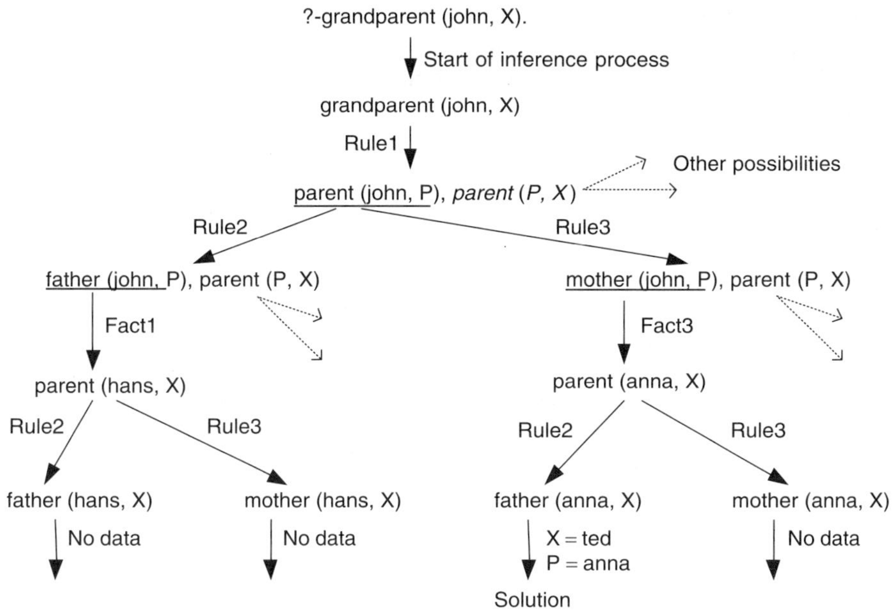

Figure 3-9. Tree of inference for simple grandparent problem.

It is noted in the preceding example that PROLOG allows multiple variants of rules and facts. Unlike procedural languages, in which the call to procedure will result in execution of only one procedure, in PROLOG, the "call" will result in first recording all possibilities of different procedure calls, and execution will start later. This means that the PROLOG execution model is completely different. Thus, the question "whose grandparent is `john`" will result in a tree of logical inferences allowed by the preceding given set of facts and rules (see Figure 3-9). The underlined literals are used for inference. Dotted arrows indicate that more variants to run this inference exist and can be exploited.

The tree as it is given in Figure 3-9 is not complete (is too big), because after a solution $\{X \leftarrow \text{ted}, P \leftarrow \text{anna}\}$ is found, a check should be done if it is not contradictory to a literal *`parent(P,X)`* marked with italics. This solution is correct. This tree can be constructed in an alternative way starting with the second literal *`parent(P,X)`*. However, in the end, we will get the same solution.

This example demonstrates clearly that even such a simple-looking inference can create a maze of possibilities, such as which rule or fact should be taken now, which literal in the clause (after selection) should be taken for inference, or how to instantiate variables, and so forth. The program itself does not specify a method of computations, which is the fundamental difference between imperative[20] and declarative programming.

[20] Imperative programming is characterized by programming with state and with commands which modify the state. When imperative programming is combined with subprograms, it is called

While the imperative programming paradigm is oriented to a model of computations based on the von Neumann machine, logic programming is based on an abstract model that has no direct relationship to any characteristic machine model or architecture. PROLOG programs as logic programs specify knowledge about a problem domain by describing attributes of and relationships between the objects of interest in that problem domain. A PROLOG programmer's efforts are directed toward creating a specification of what a given problem is in terms of the fundamental relationships and attributes that exist in the problem domain. Because of the descriptive nature of logic programs and because logic programs do not explicitly specify how a computation is to be accomplished, a variety of nondeterminisms immediately appears.

To explain how these problems are solved in the majority of current implementations of PROLOG, we have to explain first the concept of *matching* expressions in a PROLOG program, which is based on so-called *unification* and later (in the following part) to explain the general execution concepts.

In general, *unification* is *generalized matching*. It can be presented as the process of finding (computing) unifying substitutions or so called *unifiers* for two or more expressions (terms), which is usually denoted as $\{X_1 \leftarrow term_1, \ldots, X_n \leftarrow term_n\}$ where X_i are variables.

Unifiers can be applied to those terms resulting in objects that differ only in that each variable appearing to the left of an arrow is replaced by the corresponding term to the right of the arrow. A *unifier* for two terms is a set of substitutions whose application to either of them produces the same result.

Unification is used in a large number of applications: databases, knowledge acquisition, computer graphics, natural language processing, Expert Systems, algebra, deduction and rewrite systems, logic programming, and so forth.

According to V. Weber (256), automatic theorem provers like PROLOGs often spend more than 50% of the time on unification duties. Moreover, the *unification* presented later is defined for "string rewriting," that is anchored to a Deterministic Turing Machine way of thinking. Other models of computations do not have to necessarily follow this method. It is sufficient to say that Adleman's DNA computer uses the different approach of matching the "sticky ends" of DNA. This is why special attention is paid in this book to the unification problem. The present model of computational *collective intelligence* is based on "standard" PROLOG unification; however, some extensions to the model of unification may be required in the future during the development of this theory.

UNIFICATION

The basic problem with a set of facts, rules, and goal(s) like those presented in the example mentioned earlier is that we need some "mechanical" method

procedural programming. Programs are directions or orders for performing an action.

In general, programming languages can be categorized through paradigms underlying the concept of a language: imperative, for example, C; procedural, functional, for example, LISP; object-oriented, for example, C++, and declarative (logical), for example, PROLOG.

(257), applicable to a computer, to find candidate logical items for the next step of inference and to check if they "match" for inference.

The basic concept applied in PROLOG can be explained by looking at the Modus Ponens (258) inferring rule:

$$\frac{a, a \rightarrow b}{b} \quad \text{or using logical equivalence } a \rightarrow b \equiv \neg a \vee b \text{ (Modus Ponens)}$$

$$\frac{a, \neg a \vee b}{b}$$

This inference method says that if we find fact "a" and a rule with a premise as well "a", a concluding fact can be produced. In terms of "string rewriting," this means to find a, $\neg a \vee b$ and rewrite $a, \neg a \vee b \Rightarrow a \vee \neg a \vee b \Rightarrow b$ using the emergence of tautology inside.

However, the situation is more complicated for first-order predicate calculus in which variables are allowed. This is because we need a method to unify $a(n)$ and $a(X)$ to create instantiation of the rule, that is $a(n) \rightarrow b(n)$ and to conclude the inference given here.

$$\frac{a(n), \forall_X (a(X) \rightarrow b(X))}{b(n)}$$

The generalization that will also allow rule–rule inferences, i.e.,

$$\frac{a \rightarrow b, b \rightarrow c}{a \rightarrow c}$$

is the so-called Resolution inference rule (252), which can be presented as follows.

RESOLUTION INFERENCE RULE

For literals p_i and q_i, where $Unify(p_j, \neg q_k) = \theta$

$$\frac{p_1 \vee p_2 \vee \cdots \vee p_j \vee \cdots \vee p_m, \quad q_1 \vee q_2 \vee \cdots \vee q_k \vee \cdots \vee q_n}{Subst(\theta, p_1 \vee \cdots \vee p_{j-1} \vee p_{j+1} \vee p_m \vee q_1 \vee \cdots \vee q_{k-1} \vee q_{k+1} \vee \cdots \vee q_n)}$$

The preceding inference rule can be read as follows:

Step 1: Take two clauses and convert into the form:

$$p_1 \vee p_2 \vee \cdots \vee p_j \vee \cdots \vee p_m, \quad q_1 \vee q_2 \vee \cdots \vee q_k \vee \cdots \vee q_n$$

Step 2: Check if there are two literals p_j and q_k such that the unifier θ can be computed with the property $Unify(p_j, \neg q_k) = \theta$

Step 3: The conclusion (result of inference) can be built by concatenation of both premises, after p_j and q_k have been removed, and θ is applied to all resultant expressions.

Some remarks and explanations on θ (259,260) might be useful here.

A substitution θ is a unifier of two terms if the instances of these terms generated by this substitution are identical. Formally, θ is a unifier of t_1 and t_2 iff θt_1 and θt_2 are identical. We can say that this is also a solution of the equation $t_1 = t_2$, which by analogy is called the unifier of the equation. The notion of unifier can be straightforwardly extended to several terms or equations. Terms or equations are called unifiable if a unifier exists for them. They are not unifiable otherwise.

A unifier is said to be a Most General Unifier (MGU) of terms if any unifier of these terms is an instance of it. A MGU always exists for terms if they are unifiable. There are infinitely many equivalent unifiers through renaming. A substitution is idempotent[21] if successive applications to itself yield to the same substitution (it is equivalent to saying that no variable of its domain occurs in the resulting terms). There is only one most general idempotent unifier for terms whose domain is limited to the variables of the terms, up to a renaming. This is sometimes called the unique Most General Unifier.

There is algorithm called the Herbrand algorithm (261), which computes the unique MGU of given terms. The algorithm has the form given below.

HERBRAND ALGORITHM

For a given set of equations of the form $t_1 = t_2$, apply in any order one of the following nonexclusive steps:

Step 1: Exit with failure (no unification possible) if there is an equation in any of the forms given here:

- $a = b$ where a and b are different constants, or
- $f = g$ where f is a constant and $g(\ldots)$ is a compound term, or $f(\ldots)$ is a compound term and g is a constant, or
- $f(\ldots) = g(\ldots)$ where f and g are different functors, or
- $f(a_1, a_2, \ldots, a_n) = f(b_1, b_2, \ldots, b_m)$ where n and m are different.

Step 2: If there is an equation of the form $X = X$, where X is a variable, then remove it.

Step 3: If there is an equation of the form $c = c$, where c is a constant, then remove it.

Step 4: If there is an equation of the form $f(a_1, a_2, \ldots, a_s) = f(b_1, b_2, \ldots, b_s)$, then replace it by the set of equations $a_i = b_i$ for $i = 1 \ldots s$.

Step 5: If there is an equation of the form $t = X$, where X is a variable and t a nonvariable term, then replace it by the equation $X = t$,

Step 6: If there is an equation of the form $X = t$ where (1) X is a variable and t a term in which the variable X does not occur, and (2) the variable X occurs in some other equation, then substitute in all other equations every occurrence of the variable X by the term t.

[21] Acting as if used only once, even if used multiple times.

Step 7: If there is an equation of the form $X = t$ such that X is a variable and t is a nonvariable term that contains this variable, then exit with failure (not unifiable, positive occurs-check).

Step 8: If no more transformations can be applied, then exit with success (unifiable).

This algorithm always terminates. If it terminates with success (unification is possible), the remaining set of equations $(\mathrm{v}_1 = t_1, \mathrm{v}_2 = t_2, \ldots, \mathrm{v}_n = t_n)$ defines an MGU $\{\mathrm{v}_1 \rightarrow t_1, \mathrm{v}_2 \rightarrow t_2, \ldots, \mathrm{v}_n \rightarrow t_n\}$.

Example of Unification

Unify $e_1 = f(X, g(Y), h(Z, a))$ and $e_2 = f(Y, Z, h(g(X), W))$

Step 1: $f(X, g(Y), h(Z, a))$
$f(Y, Z, h(g(X), W)) \quad \sigma_1 = \{X \leftarrow Y\}$
↑

Step 2: $f(Y, g(Y), h(Z, a))$
$f(Y, Z, h(g(Y), W)) \quad \sigma_2 = \{Z \leftarrow g(Y)\}$
↑

Step 3: $f(Y, g(Y), h(g(Y), a))$
$f(Y, g(Y), h(g(Y), W)) \quad \sigma_3 = \{W \leftarrow a\}$
↑

Unification is possible in this case, and the MGU for e_1 and e_2 is the composition of unifications denoted here by • giving: $\sigma_1 \bullet \sigma_2 \bullet \sigma_3 = \{X \leftarrow Y, Z \leftarrow g(Y), W \leftarrow a\}$

Unify $e_1 = f(X, g(X))$ with $e_2 = f(g(Y), Y)$

Step 1: $f(X, g(X))$
$f(g(Y), Y) \quad \sigma 1 = \{X \leftarrow g(Y)\}$
↑

Step 2: $f(g(Y), g(g(Y)))$
$f(g(Y), Y)$
↑
Unification not possible (see step 7)

According to the summary of unification algorithms by Weber (256), the widest known algorithm is that of J.A. Robinson (262). This algorithm has an exponential time complexity. Boyer and Moore (258) have reduced the space complexity in their "structure-sharing" algorithm, but their time complexity was still as bad as Robinson's. In 1975, M. Venturini-Zilli (263) introduced a "marker strategy" that reduces the time complexity to $O(n^2)$. Later, G. Huet (264) gave an almost linear algorithm for an infinite unification strategy (a strategy that does not need to check occurrence). M.S. Paterson and M.N. Wegman (265) introduced the first linear strategy. The disadvantage of their method is a relatively complex data structure that leads to time-consuming computations in the average case.

There are also some parallel algorithms (266,267), but the unification has a very sequential nature, as has been shown (268). There have also been several attempts to base unification strategies on special hardware: transputers (269), unification coprocessors (270), and PROLOG machines (271).

Execution Concepts of Prolog — Backtrack and Cut

As discussed before, a goal (query) for logic program P is defined in PROLOG as a sequence of clauses of the form:

$$:-\ g_1(t_1),\ldots,g_m(t_n). \qquad (*)$$

The symbol `:-` is replaced by `?-` that gives the final PROLOG form of the goal (query)

$$?-\ g_1(t_1),\ldots,g_m(t_n).$$

Such a goal of computations (query) may be interpreted as "Does any binding of variables exist such that the terms t_1 are in relation g_1 and ...t_m are in relation g_n?"

If the given PROLOG system manages to prove this query, the solution (answer) to the problem, which is hidden behind (*), should be recorded by an output device during the problem-solving process or should be given in instantiations of variables.

This process results in special clauses, for example, ..., `answer(X,...,Y,Z)`, ... used as shells for variables containing solutions to a problem.

We should keep in mind that a PROLOG program may not be able to find a solution; it can fail because of time–memory limits, or the program can simply somehow go on a loop.

Our query can also be of the form to "disprove" a given problem through proving that no settings of variables are possible in this program.

The fundamental problem, however, (after the PROLOG program is ready) is how to run the execution of a program that is defined in a declarative way.

If we assume that our computer is one-processor only, the basic methodology of ordering PROLOG computations is the concept of so-called backtracking. In backtracking, the processor periodically (for various reasons) returns to the tree of possibilities to investigate other possible matches until success or failure, or the processor reaches the limits of the computational resources.

There are several basic types of backtracks:

- *Backtrack after fail*, for example, when a necessary fact or rule is not available in PROLOG program P at the moment when it is necessary, or execution of a built-in clause generates the *fail* message.
- *Backtrack after success*, that is, when a single solution to the problem is found, but the PROLOG program seeks more alternative solutions, for example, when requested by the operator of an Expert System implemented in PROLOG or in cases of optimization.
- *Backtrack forced by the programmer* (so-called *cut*—denoted by an exclamation mark "!"). Cut is allowed to be inserted into a clause of rules. An example is when something has happened that implies a need to backtrack to another possibility.

Possible backtracks can be *near* or *far*. In case of a *near* backtrack, the PROLOG system goes back to the tree of possibilities just for another variant of a recently analyzed fact or rule. In *far* backtrack, it is necessary to go back to the tree of possibilities to another available predecessor of the present node.

We should remember that every backtrack requires us to undo settings of variables. Thus, in the case of a *far* backtrack, a sequence of variable settings must be undone to try another possibility left far behind the present state of computations.

To understand the preceding issues better, let us look at Figure 3-10, which presents the basic concepts of the backtrack.

Let us define more precisely how the *cut* works and how it affects backtracking during execution of a PROLOG program.

Assume that there is a given PROLOG program P with a query or clause that contains clause h that matches the head h′ of another clause of the form:

$$\text{h}':\text{-}\ \text{g}_1,\ \cdots,\ \text{g}_n. \qquad (*)$$

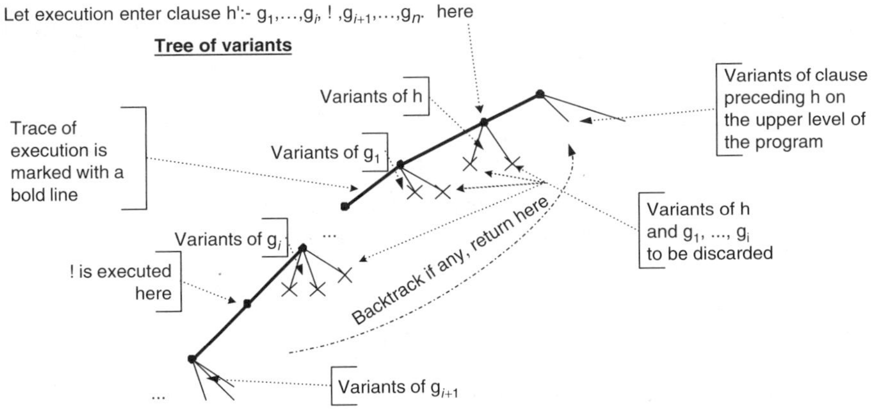

Figure 3-10. Basic concept of *cut* in PROLOG.

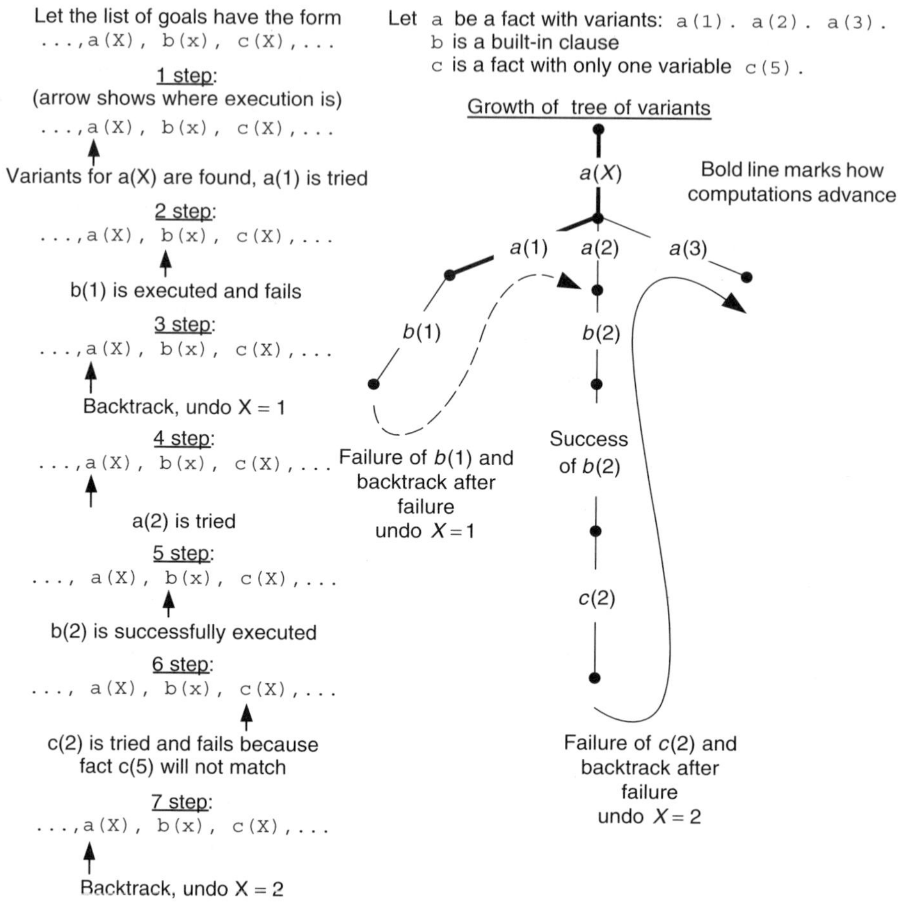

Figure 3-11. Some examples of backtrack methodology.

The (sub)goal defined by h is called the "parent goal" for clause (*). Suppose next that a *cut* is located in, for example,

$$h' :- \ g_1, \ \cdots, \ g_i, \ !, \ g_{i+1}, \ \cdots, \ g_n.$$

Cut **!** causes all remaining variants of h and $g_1, \ldots, g_i$ to be discarded. Thus, after **!** is executed, the PROLOG computations are forced to backtrack far back to still available variants of goals that are behind h. Figure 3-11 presents in graphic form the concept of cut.

Now after the preceding discussions, we are ready to look at the "straightforward" model of execution of a PROLOG program (under the assumption that only one processor is available), which is given in Figure 3-12. It is a modification of a flowchart presented by Bratko (247).

Let us have a PROLOG program P composed of clauses of facts, rules, and a query $?{-}g_1, \ldots, g_2$. The query defines a sequence of goals $L = \{g_1, \ldots g_2\}$.
There are three assumed global data objects that will be used as input and will be modified during the execution process: PROLOG program P itself, list L, and tree of variants T.
Assuming a one-processor method of execution with a backtrack, the recursive procedure of two arguments describing execution of the PROLOG program P is defined as follows (it is assumed that every backtrack will undo related substitutions for variables):

```
achieve_goal(variables: Goals, Result)
begin
  if list of goals L becomes empty
    then Result := success and return.
    else
    if goal is a built-in clause
      then execute this built-in clause, and depending on its result either L := θ•L,
        Result := success and return, or Result := fail and return.
      else
        h := head(L);
        L := tail(L);
        find all clauses {c1, ..., cs} of facts in P that match h, and/or rules with heads
                                                                        matching h;
        if none available
          then Result := fail and return
          else
            expand tree of variants T with offsets representing all just found clauses;
            take first clause ci : -b1, ..., bn. that is marked as not tried yet and mark it as
            tried on the tree of variants T. Assume that the substituion unifying this case of
                                                                        h and ci is θ
            L := append(b1, ..., bn, L);
            L := θ•L;               that is, apply substitution to L
            achieve_goal(L, Result);
            if Result = fail        that is, above recursive call failed
              then backtrack to nearest available offset in tree of variants T and
                                                              resume computations
              else Result := success and return
end of achieve_goal( )
```

Computations for PROLOG program P should be initialized by call:
achieve_goal($L = \{g_1, \ldots, g_2\}$, < undefined >);

Figure 3-12. Simple model of execution of PROLOG program.

Finally, to understand the above issues better, let us look into Figure 3-13, which presents how the PROLOG program (see also back into Figure 3-9) is executed. Dotted lines represent the flow of execution over the tree of possibilities.

The major computational model for a PROLOG program on a single-processor platform is the so-called Warren Abstract Machine (WAM) (272,273).

It is important to take a look at the concept of WAM and later review parallel models of computations for PROLOG, because the Random PROLOG Processor that is used for *collective intelligence* is one more such model of computations — now based on Brownian movements of information.

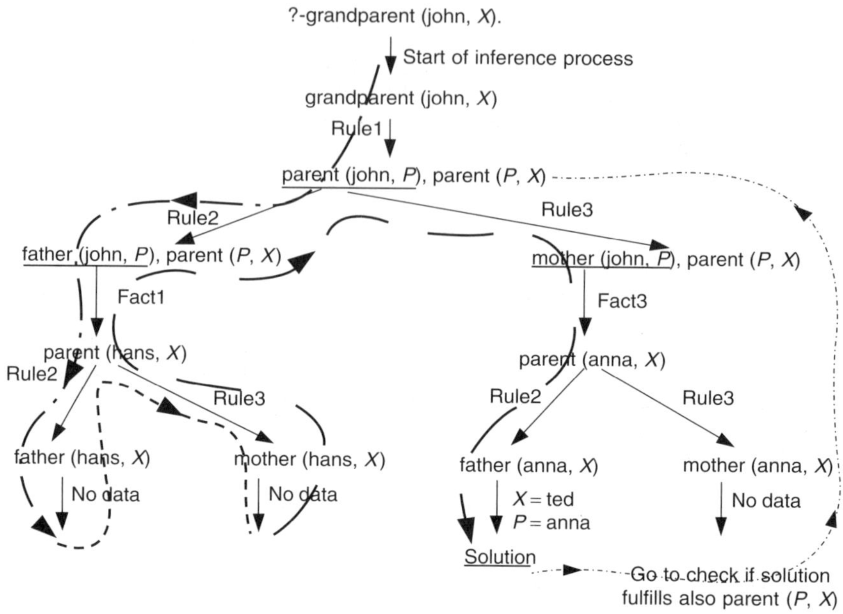

Figure 3-13. Run of execution of example grandparent problem.

At the end of this chapter, we should mention that standard PROLOG is implemented as a *backward-inferring system*, that is, chaining inferences from goals (hypotheses) toward facts (or a failure of the inference process).

Libraries in PROLOG — Built-In Predicates[22]

Basic PROLOG, as it is usually described in the introduction of a textbook, provides very poor programming (problem-solving) facilities. This is because such a PROLOG describes a mathematical logic-based methodology of building into the program the global inference about the problem to be solved, rather than providing powerful (but "taken from other disciplines of mathematics" tools), sophisticated, problem-oriented algorithms widely used in other programming languages.

Moreover, most widely used numerical methods that are required for efficient programming are based on higher level calculus than on first-order predicate calculus, which is used to define the kernel PROLOG.

Examples of this include the arithmetic required for efficient programming, input–output procedures, database-manipulation functions, and so forth. It would be torturous for PROLOG compiler size and efficiency if, for example, deriving numerical solutions were done through pure logic inferences[23]

To bypass this problem, all implementations of PROLOG use clauses working like a "black box," which in the foreground provides a logical response of the

[22] ISO/IEC DIS 13211-1: 1995(E) part 8 is on built-in predicates.

[23] Simple addition will be defined in logic as a recursive PROLOG program:

```
plus(X, Y, Z) :- succ(W, X), plus(W, Y, V), succ(V, Z).
plus(0, X, X).
```

type fail/(success + instantiation of variables) to the execution control level after being activated. Moreover, in the background (in case of success), such a clause also provides other action(s) on the basis of sophisticated implemented algorithms, which are too tedious for the simple logic of PROLOG.

According to the ISO standard dictionary, the built-in predicate is "a procedure whose execution is implemented by the processor[24]."

Available in different implementations of PROLOG are problem-oriented built-in predicates:

- Input–output predicates
- Built-in predicates for arithmetic
- Comparing objects in PROLOG
- Predicates for managing a database of facts and rules in PROLOG
- Control predicates

Let us make a brief, selective review of some of these, trying to capture the "soul" of PROLOG for its later application to computational *collective intelligence*. The input–output predicates are not discussed here, because they are too oriented toward and dependent on the specific available hardware (monitor, keyboard, mass-storage devices) of the digital computer; thus, it is doubtful if this methodology and experience would be useful for *collective intelligence* purposes.

Our "logical behavior — decisions" are frequently dependent on the results of the quantitative evaluation of different elements in our environment. It requires us, for example, to calculate distances (e.g., to another being), volumes (e.g., of an object to be moved), speed, areas, and so forth. For all such applications, there are efficient numerical procedures available that can be expressed at the PROLOG language level as follows.

ARITHMETIC

The arithmetic is incorporated into the "mathematical logic-based structure" of PROLOG through the use of the infix operator *is/2* (i.e., with two arguments).

The second argument is evaluated numerically and succeeds if it matches the first argument. For example, a simple query:

```
?- X is 2 + 3 * 4 – 5.
        success
         X = 9
```

PROLOG Arithmetic Expressions Include the Following Functions:

N + N	Addition
N − N	Subtraction

[24] Here a (PROLOG) processor is defined as "a compiler or interpreter working in combination with a configuration."

N * N	Multiplication
N / N	Floating-point division
I // I	Integer division
I rem I	Remainder
I mod I	Modulo
N ** N	Exponentiation (result is floating-point)
−N	Sign reversal
abs(N)	Absolute value
atan(N)	Arctangent (in radians)
ceiling(N)	Smallest integer not smaller than N
cos(N)	Cosine (argument in radians)
exp(N)	Natural exponentiation, e^N
sqrt(N)	Square root
sign(N)	Sign (−1, 0, or 1 for negative, zero, or positive N)
float(N)	Convert to floating-point
floor(X)	Largest integer not greater than X
log(N)	Natural logarithm, $\log_e N$
sin(N)	Sine (argument in radians)
truncate(X)	Integer equal to the integer part of X
round(X)	Integer nearest to X
. . . and so forth.	

In the above description, symbols I or J denote integers; X denotes floating-point numbers, and N denotes numbers of either type.

For number comparisons, PROLOG uses the following infix operators of two arguments:

=:=	for numerically equal
=\=	for numerically unequal
<	for less than
>	for greater than
=<	for less than or equal
>=	for greater than or equal

The preceding listed comparisons are implemented in such a way that both sides of the operator are evaluated before the comparison is made, which gives a "foreground" logic result. For example:

```
?- 4 > 3.
   success
?- 4+3*5 =:= 20 - 1.
   success
```

It should be noticed that =:= is a very different thing from =, because the latter is matching (to be discussed), and the former is numeric.

A very simple example of use of both types of arithmetic operators in the recursive definition of a factorial is given here.

```
factorial(N, Result) :-
          N =:= 0,
          Result is 1.
factorial(N, Result) :-
          Result is N*factorial(N-1, Result).
```

COMPARING OBJECTS IN PROLOG

An interesting language property of PROLOG is the ability to compare composed data structures represented by terms.

It is useful for the computational *collective intelligence* applications that in PROLOG, we can compare "flexible" objects, that is, terms with variables inside.

Let us look at an example of two terms describing two triangles, defined by three vertices:

```
triangle(point(2,2), B, point(3,4)
triangle(Y, point(5,Z), point(3,U))
```

and their tree representation given in Figure 3-14. These triangles have the following unifier:

$$\theta = \{Y \leftarrow point(2,2), B \leftarrow point(5,Z), U \leftarrow 4)\}$$

These triangles can be considered equal after some modifications computed by the unification algorithm, as it is given in the lower part of Figure 3-14.

Let us now look at two basic term-comparison facilities in PROLOG. Comparing the simplest form of terms, that is, arithmetic expressions, has been discussed earlier. PROLOG expresses term comparisons with these basic operators:

$$\text{Term1} == \text{Term2}$$

Term1 and Term2 are tested if they are strictly identical, that is, without any attempt at unifying them. For example:

```
?- f(a,b) == f(a,b).
     success
?- f(a,X) == f(a,b).
      fail
```

In the second example the difference is in the occurrence of the constant and variable at the corresponding position.

If "elastic" comparison is required, as in the example from Figure 3-14, unification is used, and term comparison is denoted:

```
Term1 = Term2
```

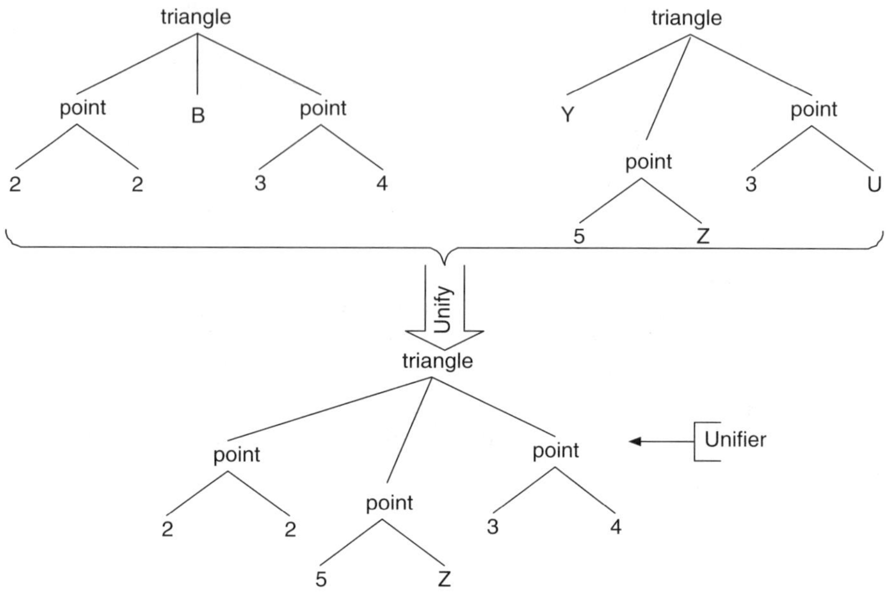

Figure 3-14. Example equalizing terms through unification.

The terms X and Y are unified to provide a logic answer for this predicate. For example:

```
?- triangle(point(2,2), B, point(3,4) = triangle(Y,point(5,Z),
                                          point(3,U)).
                        success
                  ?- g(X) = f(f(X)).
                         fail
                     ?- X = a(X).
                      undefined
```

There is also a variety of derived operators to compare and order terms, but they are based on alphabetic ordering of subelements of compared terms and thus, are too specific for general considerations of PROLOG for computational *collective intelligence*.

Now let us look at another interesting capability of a PROLOG program, that is, to dynamically modify its own structure during execution.

BUILT-IN PREDICATES TO MANIPULATE THE KNOWLEDGE BASE

The most common perception of a computer program is static, that is, the program changes data (which it is working with), but it is not allowed to change its own structure during execution.

Thus, only a programmer is allowed to create and modify program structure but not the program itself. This is especially obvious on the assembly programming level, for example, when we look at the concept of dividing programs into code, data, and working memory, that is, into code, data, and stack segments (274).

Only a few programming systems, like LISP and PROLOG, have programs that are allowed to alter their own structure as a result of its execution process.

If we analyze, over a certain span of time, our individual or group "intelligent behavior," it is obvious that our individual and group experience is changing and affecting the "algorithms of our behavior" in the consecutive time period. Thus, this programming option is very interesting from a computational *collective intelligence* point of view and should be discussed here.

In PROLOG, the implementation of this self-modification option is done through permission to add and remove facts and rules during run time. The applied programming methodology is as follows.

PROLOG predicates are classified into static and dynamic ones. Only dynamic predicates can be manipulated (changed). Static predicates are compiled into a form that is inaccessible to some or all of the built-in predicates described here. Nonetheless, some implementations may treat static predicates as dynamic. The declaration of a dynamic predicate should have the form:

```
:- dynamic(Pred/Arity).
```

For example, if we expect that, a rule `new_rule` with a head with two arguments will be modified (added, removed) on run time, it is necessary to declare it in advance:

```
:- dynamic(new_rule/2).
```

Digital computers are sequential devices, so a list of facts or rules is searched for matching clauses in a sequential, top-down way. Consequently, it is necessary to have two versions of the general assert[25] able to add a new fact or rule to the top or to the end of the predicates of those names. They have following form:

```
asserta(Clause)
```

Predicate `asserta( )` adds clause at the beginning of the internal list of clauses for its predicate. If there are no clauses for that predicate, the predicate is created and declared to be dynamic. If such a predicate already exists as some clauses and is static, an error is raised. An example of use of `asserta( )` for asserting facts will have the form:

```
?- asserta(raining), asserta(fog).
```

[25] Predicate `assert( )` is not supported by ISO Standard and must be replaced by either `asserta( )` or `assertz( )`.

For another example, if we want to assert a new rule into our PROLOG program stating that "if it is a bird, must have two legs."

```
asserta(legs(Bird_name, 2) :- bird(Bird_name))
```

Notice that there is no terminating dot after the description of a rule inside `asserta()`.

```
assertz(Clause)
```

Predicate `assertz(Clause)` will assert `Clause` at the bottom of the database.

Working with `asserta()` and `assertz()`, we can significantly speed up the program execution when, for example, important new facts or rules are immediately discovered for matching, without a redundant search through the whole listing of a PROLOG program.

To remove facts or rules, PROLOG uses a `retract()` clause.

```
retract(Clause)
```

This removes from the knowledge base any dynamic clause that matches the `Clause` (which must be at least partly instantiated). This gives multiple solutions upon backtracking, because we should keep in mind that there might be multiple occurrences of the same fact or rule we intend to retract.

To appreciate the ability of building programs that learn (or self-modify), let us look into the student's problem of computing Fibonacci numbers. The recursive definition looks trivial, that is,

$$F_n = F_{n-1} + F_{n-2} \quad \text{with} \quad F_1 = F_2 = 1$$

However, a direct application of recursion will give the situation presented in Figure 3-15.

Observe that in the recursive approach, F_4 will be computed twice and F_3 three times. Thus, either it is necessary to replace recursion with bottom-up computations, that is, step-by-step computing ascending Fibonacci numbers

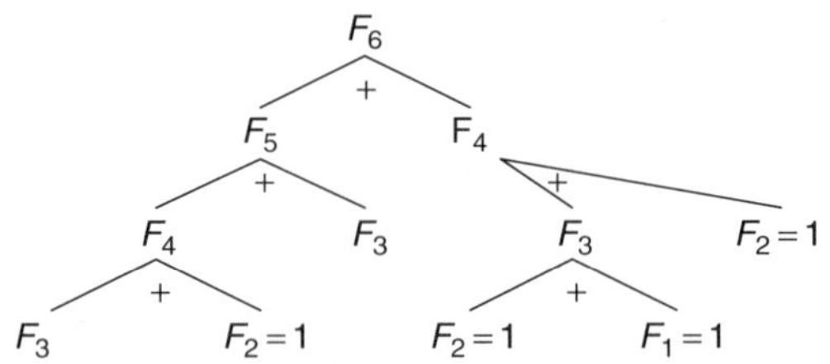

Figure 3-15. Computing simple Fibonacci numbers.

until the destination number is reached, or the program (when computing recursively) should build a database of temporary results that are themselves lower Fibonacci numbers. Such an "optimized" recursive program will have the form:

```
fibonacci(1,1) :- !.
fibonacci(2,1) :- !.
fibonacci(N,Result):- N1 is N-1, fibonacci(N1,Result1),
                      N2 is N-2, fibonacci(N2,Result2),
                      Result is Result1 + Result2,
                      asserta((fibonacci(N,Result) :- !)).
```

Cut is necessary to prevent noxious backtracks.

CONTROL PREDICATES

When we write a program in imperative language, we create a direct flowchart showing how the execution must go, but even with this "imperative power" at hand, we cannot predict all the values of variables that can make decisions in the execution of the program. Thus, control structures like `if-then`, `if-then-else`, `while-do`, and so forth are necessary.

In a declarative language like PROLOG, the situation regarding flow of execution is more complicated, because variants of facts and rules are allowed. This increases nondeterminism and consequently, the importance of control clauses.

Later, we will see that with the chaotic model of computations based on PROLOG, which has been designed for *collective intelligence*, the situation is deteriorating even more.

As has been mentioned before, there is a metacontrol of the Operating System "over" programs written in classical imperative languages and over standard PROLOG, whereas with chaotic-inferring systems, there is no possible external control — control must be built into the process of inferences and computations. Thus, strong inferring subsystems devoted to stabilizing (controlling) the main flow of inferences are required to take them in the direction of a desired result.

Therefore, look at the control facilities of standard PROLOG.

The necessity of a reasonable discussion on backtracking in PROLOG has forced us to present the basic control predicate, that is, cut (**!**) in the last section. Now let us look at the remaining control predicates available in PROLOG.

`fail`

Predicate `fail` (with no arguments) is used when we want to force the inferring system to backtrack for organizational reasons (e.g., loop) or when our metaknowledge on the basis of temporary results informs us that backtracking is necessary.

Perhaps, the simplest example of the use of the `fail` predicate is the definition of the property `different`:

```
different(X,X) :- !, fail.
different(X,Y).
```

During the execution of this clause (to check the difference between two arguments), the first clause containing cut (!) will be tried and will fail. Thus, if the first and second arguments for clause `different()` are the same, and the first variant matches, then the offset on the tree of variants informing about the second variant, that is, `different(X,Y)` will be disposed off by the cut clause, and the `fail` will be imposed.

If the two arguments are different, only the second variant will match, and the property of being different will be successfully concluded.

Let us look at other control predicates.

In general, the structure of clause `h: -`$g_1, \ldots, g_n$. is the conjunction of lower level goals, and this conjunction is built with the help of the comma (,). However, in some cases it is necessary to have a goal; let us say g_i subdefined as a local alternative (either/or) of some goals. Such alternatives of goals can be constructed in PROLOG with the help of semicolons (;). The goal composed of alternatives is successful if at least one goal is to be successful. For example:

```
cube_volume(Edge, V) :- (integer(Edge) ; real(Edge)),
                        !,
                        V is Edge * Edge * Edge.
```

To implement **if-then** control structure in PROLOG, that is, **if** $goal_1$ **then** $goal_2$, a construct is used with (—>) symbol, that is,

```
goal1 —> goal2.
```

for example:

```
color(X), X = yellow  —>  write(X).
```

In PROLOG, we can also easily construct the user's defined structure analogous to **if** $goal_1$ **then** $goal_1$ **else** $goal_3$, which in PROLOG will have the form:

```
x :- goal1, !, goal1.
x :- goal3.
```

where `x` stands for a procedure name, but to improve the programming work, there is the language construct that combines (->) and (;), that is,:

```
goal1 -> goal2 ; goal3.
```

for example:

```
X=b, X=a -> write(a) ; write(b).
```

It is also relatively easy in PROLOG to have loops; for example, **repeat-until** that are implemented with the predicate `repeat`. This predicate succeeds repeatedly and indefinitely. Thus, loops, which are defined with `repeat` should be finished with a cut (!), because otherwise the loop will be repeated infinitely. If a predicate called after `repeat` always fails, the indefinite loop will occur. If `repeat` follows after a conjunction (,) the part left of it would not be backtracked anymore.
An example of a simple loop with `repeat` can have the form:

```
repeat_until :- N is 1,          % initialize counter
                repeat,          % initialize repetition
                 write(a),       % action to be repeated
                N is N + 1,      % increase counter
                N < 20,          % again ?
                !.               % cut and exit loop
```

Now let us discuss the main computational model for PROLOG, that is, Warren abstract machine (WAM) (272,273).

Basic Sequential Model of Execution for PROLOG — The Warren Abstract Machine (WAM)

The WAM defines the instruction set and memory organization for an abstract computer, which should allow easy compiling of the PROLOG program. This instruction set (given in Fig. 3-16) is low-level enough to allow efficient emulation[26] and/or consecutive translation into the assembly language of a target computer designed to run PROLOG programs.

WAM can be realized efficiently on a wide range of hardware and serves as a target for portable PROLOG compilers. It is in fact the accepted standard base for implementing PROLOG (275).

Let us look at the design of WAM, that is its instruction set, memory organization, and how it works.

The complete instruction set for WAM according to Kaci-Aït (275) has the form given in Figur 3-16. However, we should keep in mind that WAM has given inspiration to a variety of similar and more advanced abstract machines for PROLOG, for example, the Berkeley abstract machine (BAM) for the Aquarius PROLOG (276), PAM (277), BinWAM (a simplified WAM) (278), and others.

Although PROLOG is a declarative language, implementation requirements impose a stack-based architecture on the WAM machine. This implies similarities with imperative language implementation schemes, for example, WAM[27] uses of call–return instructions and frames for maintaining a procedure's local environment. However, to support features specifically required by the nature of logic programming, the WAM instruction set has been extended with instructions to support unification and backtracking.

[26] Two WAM emulators are available at WAM related to the Aquarius Project: *ftp://gatekeeper.dec.com/pub/plan/prolog/ucb/*

[27] WAM at the Computer Science Department at Uppsala University: *ftp://ftp.csd.uu.se/pub/*WAM-emulator/

Put instruction	Get instructions
put_variable *Xn*, *Ai*	get_variable *Vn*, *Ai*
put_variable *Yn*, *Ai*	get_value *Vn*, *Ai*
put_value *Vn*, *Ai*	get_structure *f*, *Ai*
put_unsafe value *Yn*, *Ai*	get_list *Ai*
put_structure *f*, *Ai*	get_constant *c*, *Ai*
put_list *Ai*	
put_constant *c*, *Ai*	
Set instruction	**Unify instructions**
set_variable *Vn*	unify_variable *Vn*
set_value *Vn*	unify_variable *Vn*
set_local_value *Vn*	unify_local_value *Vn*
set_constant *c*	unify_constant *c*
set_void *n*	unify_void *n*
Control instruction	**Choice instructions**
allocate	try_me_else *L*
deallocate	retry_me_else *L*
call *P*, *N*	trust_me
execute *P*	try *L*
proceed	retry *L*
trust *L*	
Indexing instruction	**Cut instructions**
switch_on_term *V*, *C*, *L*, *S*	neck_cut
switch_on_constant *N*, *T*	get_level *Yn*
switch_on_structure *N*, *T*	cut *Yn*

Figure 3-16. Warren abstract machine instruction set according to Kaci-ït (275) (with the permission of Hassan Kaci-Aït)

The memory used by WAM (see Fig. 3-17) is divided into the following major data areas serviced by specific WAM machine registers:

CodeArea

This is used to store the compiled code of the program; associated with this area are two registers:

P–instruction pointer, that is, next instruction to execute

CP–to store the return address, that is, where to resume execution after a successful call defined by P

Heap

This is used to store the complex data structures (lists and PROLOG's compound terms) created during the execution; associated with this area are three registers:

S–contains the address on the Heap of the next subterm to be matched.

HB–is assumed to contain the value of H at the time of the latest choice point.

H–always contains the next available address on the heap.

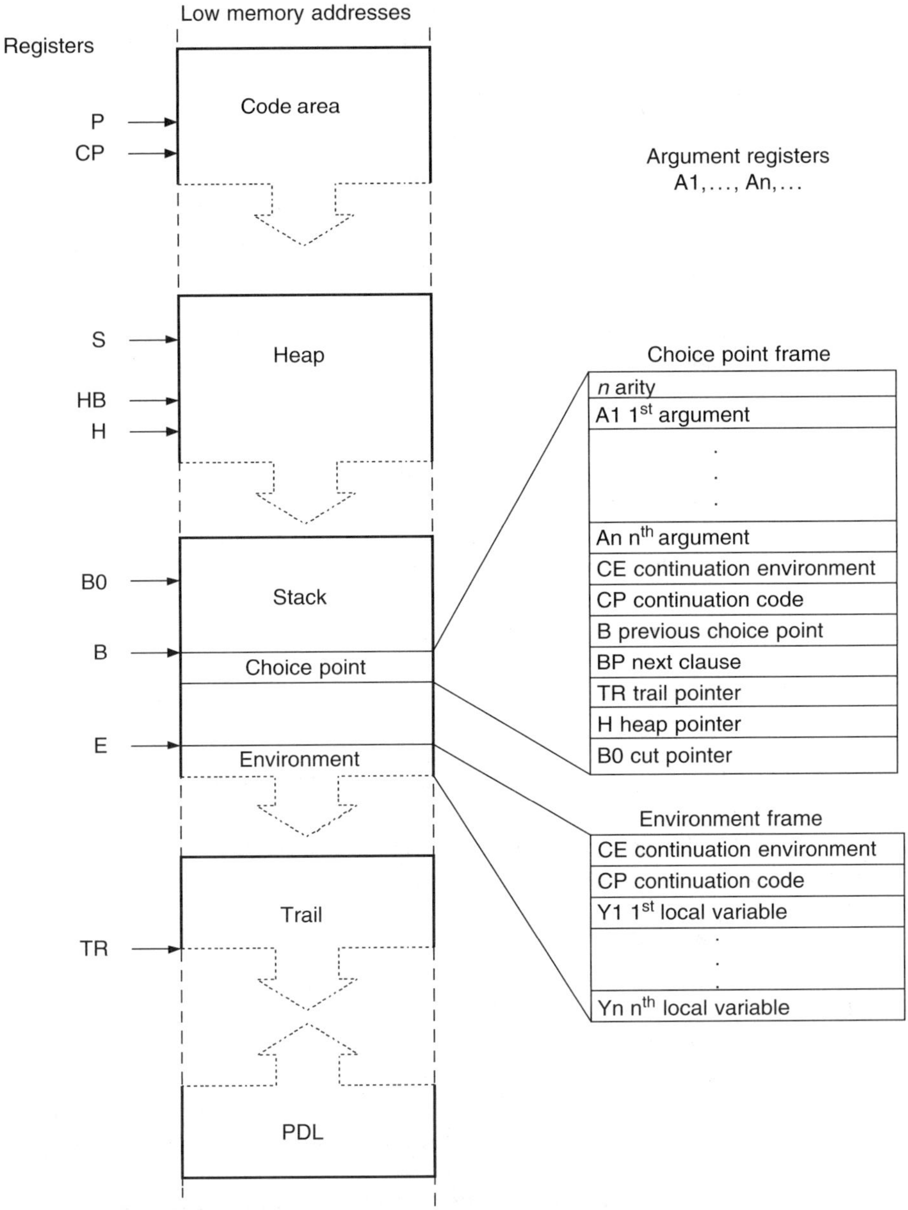

Figure 3-17. Memory & Register organization in WAM (with the permission of Hassan Kaci-Aït.

Stack

This is equivalent to the control stack in the implementations of imperative languages — it contains control frames, called here *environments*, which are created upon entering a new clause (a new procedure) and are used to store the local variables of the clause and the control information required for returning from the call.

Choice points encapsulate the execution state for backtracking purposes. A *choice point* is created whenever a call having multiple possible solution paths (i.e., more than one clause successfully matches the call) is encountered. Each *choice point* should contain sufficient information to restore the status of the execution at the time of creation of the *choice point*, and should keep track of the remaining unexplored alternatives. Associated with this area are three registers:

B0–is the cut register; the value of B0 must be set to the address of the choice point that is current at the time a procedure call is made.

B–keeps the head of the list corresponding to the latest choice point.

E–keeps the address of the latest environment on the top of the stack.

Trail

During execution, variables can be instantiated. Nevertheless, during backtracking, these bindings need to be undone (to restore the previous state of execution). To make this possible, bindings that can be subject to this operation are registered in the trail stack. Each choice point records the point of the trail where the undoing activity needs to stop. Associated with this area is one register:

TR–is the current trail pointer, and informs where the boundary is to "unwind" the trail upon backtracking. It is the address in the trail to which all variables must be reset.

PDL

The push-down list is a stack of pairs of addresses for the unification procedure.

Now let us briefly discuss[28] how some elements of a PROLOG program are translated into data and instructions of WAM, and how they later are used for execution of the PROLOG program.
The concept of WAM is based on two pillars:

- PROLOG is a backward-inferencing system; thus, the starting point for inference is a query, and facts + rules are used to match it and to build the tree of inferences.
- PROLOG is a declarative language in which the alternative facts and rules create independent "logic units"—more-or-less complicated procedures.

As a consequence, a query from a PROLOG program is translated into data and put on the WAM heap, but facts and rules from this PROLOG program are translated into pieces of code using WAM's instruction set.

[28] This presentation is derived from a book by H. Kaci-Aït: The Warren Abstract Machine. MIT Press. 1991. The Internet version of this book is available under the web address: *www.isg.sfu.ca/~hak/documents/wam.html*. Good descriptions of WAM can be also found by Newmarch (19) and by Kogge (17).

These pieces of code are later used for "execution of the PROLOG program," which results in variable instantiation and building of the tree of variants.

The first step in explaining WAM is to present how a term that will be used in specification of a query, for example, `?-p(Z,h(Z,W),f(W)).` is stored in the memory (*heap*).

PROLOG is a dynamically typed language; thus, the type information is associated with each data object that is stored in the memory of WAM. PROLOG terms are represented as tagged words. Each word is composed of a tag identifying the type of object, namely, variable, structure, and so forth, and by a value, namely identifier, pointer to the first element of a structure, and so forth.

If we keep in mind that a *heap* is not organized as a *stack*, and that a *heap* allows interspersing of data structures, then the term

```
p(Z,h(Z,W),f(W))
```

could be represented in the WAM heap as given in Figure 3-18.

Now suppose that our PROLOG program is composed of a query (as discussed before) and just one fact. For easier unification let us assume that the fact has the form:

```
p(f(X),h(Y,f(a)),Y).
```

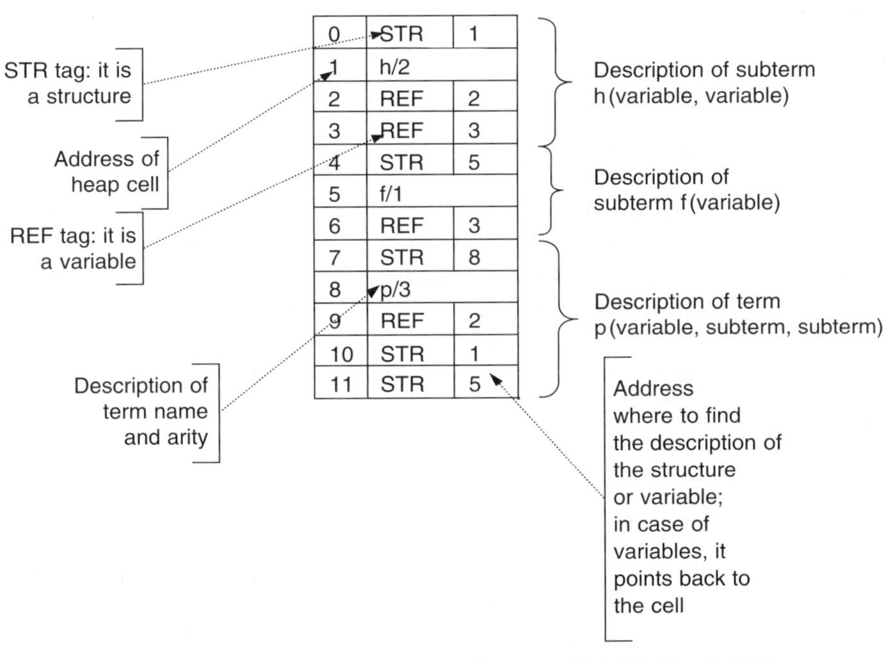

Figure 3-18. Heap representation of term `p(Z,h(Z,W),f(W))`.

This fact will be compiled into a piece of the WAM program built by a sequence of instructions:

```
get_structure p/3,X1
unify_variable X2
unify_variable X3
unify_variable X4
get_structure f/1,X2
unify_variable X5
get_structure h/2,X3
unify_value X4
unify_variable X6
get_structure f/1,X6
unify_variable X7
get_structure a/0,X7
```

For a clear understanding of the structure of this small program representing the above-mentioned fact, the concept of the "flattened form"of the term should be explained.

In WAM, terms are compiled down to a machine representation wherein each term is of the form X or f(X1, X2,. . .,Xn). Thus, the flattened term is either a variable or a structure containing only variables. For instance, the term:

```
f(a,b(a,c))
```

becomes like the set of equations:

```
f(X1,X2),
X1 = a,
X2 = b(X1,X3),
X3 = c
```

Thus, while compiling the fact `p(f(X),h(Y,f(a)),Y).` into the program, registers `Xi` are assigned to subterms as follows: `X1` is for the whole term, `X2` for `f(X)`, `X3` for `h(Y,f(a))`, `X4` for `Y`, `X5` for `X`, `X6` for `f(a)`, and `X7` for a. Observe that they are translated top down instead of bottom up. First, the whole term is processed and then its subterms and so on. This provides a direct, convenient procedure for unifying this term with something that is already on the heap. The unification algorithm starts at the top and goes down; thus, this form of fact perfectly matches the functional requirements of the unification process.
Now let us look at how rules are compiled into WAM's code. The rule:

```
p(X, Y) :- q(X, Z), r(Z, Y).
```

will be compiled into the code:

```
p/2 : allocate 2
      get_variable X3,A1
```

```
get_variable Y1,A2
put_value X3,A1
put_variable Y2,A2
call q = 2
put_value Y2,A1
put_value Y1,A2
call r/2
deallocate
```

Here, it is necessary to emphasize an important element of PROLOG, which later in the Random PROLOG Processor (RPP) will be dominant. Facts and rules create active units of code that are prepared to modify data, whereas a query in a PROLOG program is just an activation of the computational process. In the current versions of PROLOG, these facts and rules are still not autonomous—they must be externally activated. In the RPP, facts, rules, and goals are carried out by autonomous, quasi-Brownian-displacing *information molecules*, acting to change other *information molecules* at rendezvous, if preimposed logical conditions are fulfilled.

In case there are variants of facts or rules, as in the example given here:

```
p(X, a).
p(b, X).
p(X, Y) :- p(X, a), p(b, Y).
```

the WAM code will be created as follows:

```
p/2 : try_me_else L1
      get_variable X3,A1
      get_structure a/0; A2
      proceed
L1  : retry_me_else L2
      get_structure b/0,A1
      get_variable X3,A2
      proceed
L2  : trust me
      allocate 1
      get_variable X3,A1
      get_variable Y1,A2
      put_value X3,A1
      put_structure a/0,A2
      call p/2
      put_structure b/0,A1
      put_value Y1,A2
      call p/2
      deallocate
```

Now, assuming that we have a general perspective[29] of how the WAM is designed, let us specify some key elements of execution, that is, the concepts of *environment* and *choice point*, necessary for implementing the backtrack. For presentation purposes, let us follow Kaci-Aït's (275) example:

```
        a :- b(X),c(X).
        b(X) :- e(X).
        c(1).
        e(X) :- f(X).
        e(X) :- g(X).
        f(2).
        g(1).
query   ?-a.
```

The flow of execution, instantiation of variable X, and backtrack are shown in Figure 3-19.

Analyzing this picture, it is obvious that every call to a PROLOG procedure must be associated with information storage "about" the state of the abstract machine at that point, to allow the backtrack.

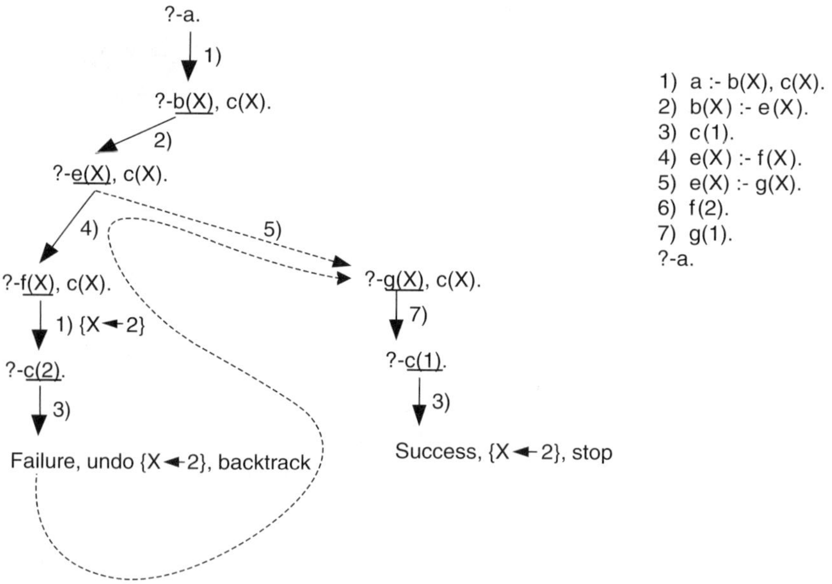

Figure 3-19. Flow of execution for WAM.

[29] The best tutorial on WAM is that of Kaci-Aït (275).

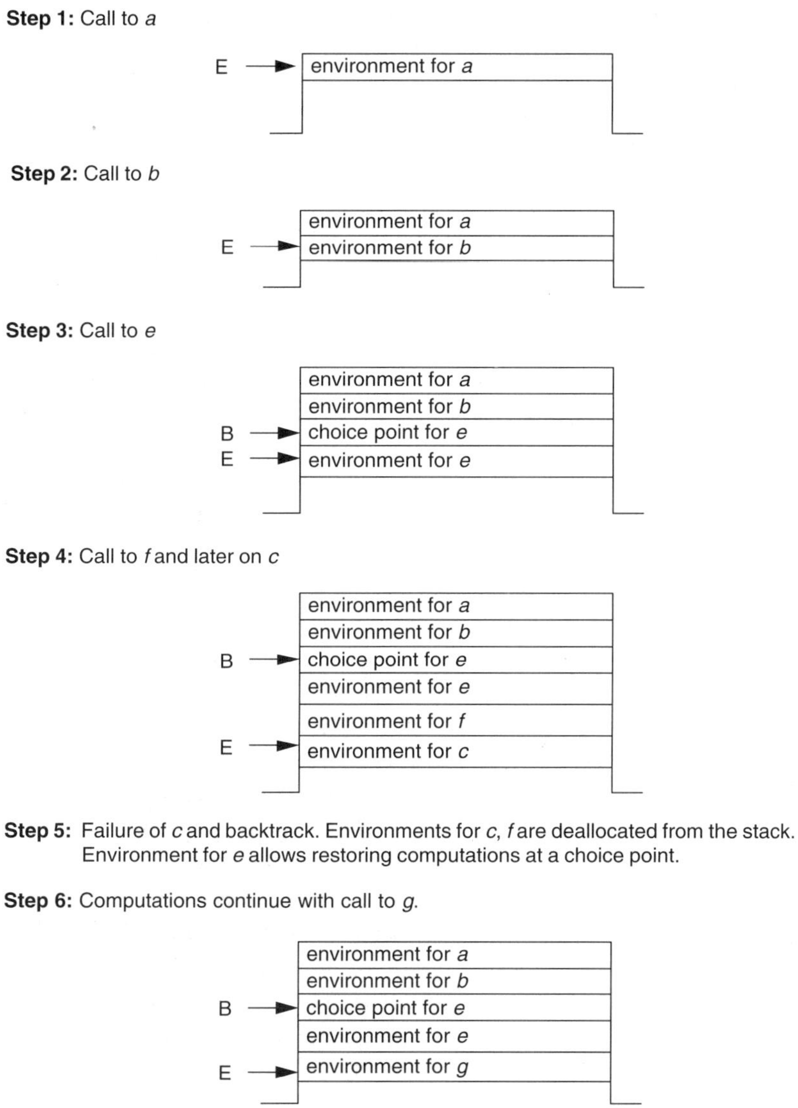

Figure 3-20. WAM activity on stack.

In WAM, such information is stored through the use of *choice points* and *environment* records. Their internal structure (data fields) is shown Figure 3-17. Now we will only present an example of the dynamics, showing how they are allocated and deallocated from the stack given in Figure 3-17. Observe that *choice points* and *environment* records share the same stack.

Remembering that B keeps the latest choice point and E keeps the latest environment on the top of the stack, WAM activity on the stack will be as illustrated in Figure 3-20.

Concluding the presentation of WAM, we should say that in the literature on PROLOG, there have been various other attempts to build WAM hardware, for example, the SLAM microprocessor (Southern California Logic Abstract Machine,) which is a 200 MHz high-performance PROLOG processor super-pipelined for symbolic computation.

Parallel PROLOGs

One of the most fascinating challenges of designing and implementing a PROLOG system is the problem of parallelizing the inferences (279).

There are several options more-or-less deterministic for parallelizing PROLOG on a system of deterministic processors. However, when we finally come to the concept of the Random PROLOG Processor (RPP), we find that with parallelization in quasi-chaotic systems quite new horizons are opened to exploit the "inborn parallelism-ready property of PROLOG."

Let us review the basic possibilities and approaches to parallelizing PROLOG available in the literature[30]. There are two basic possibilities with PROLOG:

- We can exploit the intrinsic opportunities to parallelize PROLOG, which come from its mathematical logic origins, and from the programming methodological fact that PROLOG does not allow destructive assignments (i.e., assignments are reversible until cut is done), and that in PROLOG, we can fully utilize control over the information (280).
- Another possibility for parallelizing is to develop PROLOG as a special programming system assumed for certain multiprocessor hardware platforms, that is, designing it by introducing programming and control constructs typical for parallel processing, for example,
  1. Equipping PROLOGs with message-passing primitives. Examples of such PROLOGs are the Delta Prolog (281) and CS-PROLOG (373).

     The basic idea here is that multiple PROLOG processes run in parallel and communicate with each other via messages.
  2. Designing PROLOG with blackboard[31] primitives. An example of such PROLOGs is Shared PROLOG (282). In this approach, multiple PROLOG processes are running in parallel and communicate with each other through the use of a common *blackboard system.*

[30] A very good survey on parallelizing PROLOG by Carlsson, Gupta, Ali, and Hermenegildo is available on the Internet: Parallel execution of Prolog programs: a survey. At *www.cs.nmsu.edu/IIdap/pub_para/survey.html*.

There is also an interactive Internet overview: Adventures in Parallel Logic Programming by Enrico Pontelli, Laboratory for Logic, Databases, and Advanced Programming, New Mexico State University. At *http://www.cs.nmsu.edu/ epontell/adventure/paper.html*

[31] *Blackboard communication systems* assume that the communication takes place through a shared knowledge structure of some type called a *blackboard*. Modules (agents) can post items on the *blackboard*, and they can read and act on messages that are posted by other modules (agents) (287).

3. PROLOG systems with guards, committed-choice[32] (see e.g. (17)), and data-flow synchronization. Examples of such PROLOGs include Parlog (283), GHC (284) and Concurrent Prolog (285).

For comparison purposes, when we consider procedural languages, parallelization can be done at six possible points (286):

1. Program level (multiprogramming)
2. Parallel procedures
3. Parallel statement execution
4. Arithmetic can be parallelized through independent addresses and operand calculations
5. Separate operator calculations
6. Pipelining (overlapping execution of instructions using redundant structures in a processor)

Another way to classify parallelism in general (17) is to define the following:

1. *Microscopic parallelism* (e.g., parallel adder)
2. *Fine-grain parallelism* (e.g., concurrent arithmetic operations in an expression)
3. *Medium-grain parallelism* (e.g., parallelizing loops)
4. *Large-grain parallelism* (e.g., parallelizing transactions)

However, with declarative logic programming, the situation is different. According to the specifications of M. Carlsson, G. Gupta, K.M. Ali, and M.V. Hermenegildo (280) (see also (288)), four different kinds of parallelism (given here) can be identified in logic programs. They are in general independent from each other, that is, one can be (theoretically) implemented without affecting the implementation of the other. Thus, it is (theoretically) possible to implement all of them simultaneously in one parallel PROLOG system. However, it should be remarked that no efficient parallel system has yet been built (despite attempts like the Andorra model and its successors) that achieves all of them at the same time. Let us list PROLOG parallelisms:

TYPES OF PARALLELISMS POSSIBLE IN THE STANDARD CONCEPT OF PROLOG

1. **Unification Parallelism.**

   The opportunity for this type of parallelism arises when arguments of a goal are unified in parallel with a clause head (after checking to see if

[32] The efficiency of implementing parallelism into PROLOG language can be increased by equipping the programmer with constructs to specify conditions under which to *commit* to a particular clause in advance of completing the entire right-hand side. Such specifications are called *guards*. In principle, they are similar to cuts because they indicate that as soon as all the literals to the left are satisfied, no other clause need be investigated for the same goal.

they have the same name and arity), as demonstrated on the diagram illustrated here. The different argument terms in proper clauses can be unified in parallel, and the different subterms in a term can also be unified. The greatest problem here is if and how variables are related between terms. Unification parallelism is considered very fine grained (17) and can be exploited optimally by building specialized processors with multiple unification units. Unification parallelism is not the major focus of research in parallel logic programming, and the speedup bound for two arbitrary literals with n arguments is guaranteed for n processors at level $log(n)$ (268). An example is given in Figure 3-21.

2. **OR-Parallelism.**

   The opportunity for this type of parallelism arises when more than one rule in a PROLOG program defines a given relation. In other words, at a certain moment of inference, the subgoal can be unified alternatively with more than one rule's head of such a relation. This implies that the corresponding bodies of rules can then be executed in parallel with each other, creating alternative directions for the inference process. OR-parallelism offers a convenient and efficient way for searching through alternative chances for a solution to the query. Example is given in Figure 3-22.

3. **AND-Parallelism.**

   The name comes from the fact that all (logical AND) goals must be resolved to success. An example to be given here can be a query or

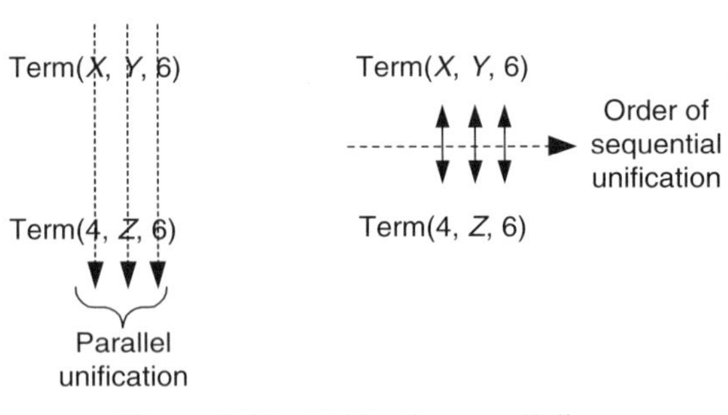

Figure 3-21. Unification parallelism.

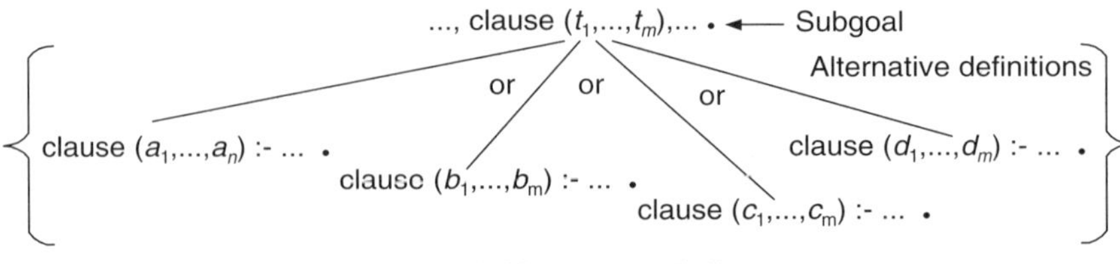

Figure 3-22. OR-parallelism.

body of procedures, since they are constructed with a *comma* operator that denotes the logical AND in PROLOG, whereas the OR-parallelism is concerned with avoiding interference among the procedure alternatives. AND-parallelism has to deal with problems of mutual dependence between goals in conjunction, which are created by common variables. We can define two subcases here:

(a) Independent AND-parallelism.

The opportunity for this type of parallelism arises in the inference process when more than one goal is present in the query or in the body of a procedure and goals are independent of one another. Two subgoals are defined as independent if either they do not share any unbound variables or the bindings produced by one for the common variables does not affect the computations of the other subgoal, that is, they either agree on the bindings for the common variables or the second subgoal simply does not access such variables during its execution. Such goals can be resolved in parallel.

Example:

```
?-grandfather(hans, X), salary(hans, Y).
```

(b) Dependent AND-parallelism.

This is a much more complicated case than the other one. The chance for this type of logic parallelism arises when two or more goals in the body of a procedure have common variable(s) and there is an attempt to execute them in parallel.

There are two ways to implement dependent AND-parallelism:

i. The two goals be executed independently until one of them accesses or binds the common variable. Now there are two options. It is possible to continue executing those two goals independently in parallel (i.e., executing each goal without regard to the other), even after the common variable has been accessed. Then, after the two goals finish, the bindings produced by each will have to be checked for compatibility (this compatibility check at the end is called *back unification*).

ii. Alternatively, once the common variable is accessed by one of the goals, it is bound to a structure or stream (the goal generating this binding is called the producer or generator), and this structure is read as an input argument of the other goal (called the consumer or checker).

Then, parallelism can be further exploited by having the consumer goal compute with one element of the stream, while the producer goal is computing the next element. Within this scheme, there is a large variety of proposals on how to manage the producers and consumers, for example, static vs. dynamic (289), consumers started a priori (290), or only after the producer has bound the variable (291).

Case (i) is very similar to independent AND-parallelism. Case (ii) is also referred to as *stream-parallelism*[33] and is useful for speeding up producer–consumer interactions. Note that *stream-parallelism* can also introduce a form of co-routining. *Stream-parallelism* is key for committed-choice languages, for example, Parlog (283) and Concurrent Prolog (285).

The next fundamental question that arises when discussing parallelization in PROLOG is the concept of implementation. This is because there is no one common, universal, parallel, computer architecture to be used — contrary to the existence of, for example, one almost universal, common model for personal, single-processor PC computers. As a result, there are parallel PROLOGs mainly exploiting only a few of the above opportunities for parallelizing but profiting from efficient and easier implementation. However, there have also been some attempts to create a general model of computations for parallel PROLOGs. Let us look into some of them.

The Basic andorra model (BAM) created by Warren (292) is a modification of the PROLOG execution that which exploits both OR-parallelism and dependent AND-parallelism.

OR-parallelism is natural in PROLOG because a PROLOG program usually delineates several alternatives for each procedure. Thus, alternative execution paths must be traversed. When a given path is successfully finished, proper information is stored for the next stage of execution. From a parallel execution point of view, the OR-parallelism allows different agents or workers or threads to traverse different paths in parallel.

The dependent AND-parallelism is, however, more difficult when we want to build a model of execution. The major achievement of the BAM was that it proposed a reasonable solution to this problem by modifying the order of PROLOG execution.

BAM execution of PROLOG goals assumes two phases:

- **Deterministic Phase**. Here, execution of a goal that matches several clauses (nondeterministic goals) is suspended and only deterministic goals (which match just one clause) are executed.

  Usually, such execution of deterministic goals results in changes of some nondeterministic goals into deterministic ones.

  The dependent AND-parallelism can be exploited during this (deterministic) phase, because executed goals are deterministic and just one flow of data exists. Therefore, those goals can be executed in any order, even in parallel, being synchronized by the flow of data.

[33] See Newmarch J. D.: *Logic programming — PROLOG and stream parallel languages*. Prentice Hall 1990. (19)

- **Nondeterministic Phase**. In this phase, assuming that in the deterministic phase before all the deterministic goals have been executed (i.e., each suspended goal is now nondeterministic), a nondeterministic goal is selected according to the PROLOG execution order (leftmost) and reduced within the non-deterministic phase. This will create a choice point that will make it possible to restart the computation state at that point in order to follow an alternative path at a later stage. These choice points are the key elements in the exploitation of OR-parallelism, because they define different paths that can be traversed in parallel (by different agents/workers/threads).

The nondeterministic phase provides the condition to start a new deterministic phase where new deterministic goals are reduced. Thus, the computational process can be cycled until all the goals have been reduced.

Now let us see how this concept is implemented in the Andorra-I model (293,294).

Andorra-I exploits the deterministic dependent AND-parallelism presented here that is, it executes deterministic goals first and concurrently. This execution order of deterministic goals can result in reducing the search space because unnecessary choice points are eliminated. A processing element that performs computations in Andorra-I is called a *worker*. In practice, each *worker* corresponds to a separate processor. Andorra-I is designed in such a way that *workers* are classified into *masters* and *slaves*. One *master* and some or no *slaves* constitute a *team*. Each *master* in a *team* is responsible for creating a new choice point, while *slaves* are managed and synchronized by their *master*. *Workers* in a *team* cooperate with each other in order to share available AND-work. Different *teams* of *workers* cooperate to share OR-work.

The Andorra-I system consists of several parts:

1. *Preprocessor:* responsible for generating a determinacy code and the sequencing information necessary to maintain the correct execution of PROLOG programs,
2. *Engine:* responsible for the execution of the Andorra-I programs,
3. *Two Different Scheduler Components:*
   a. The AND-scheduler is responsible for finding eligible AND-work, which corresponds to a goal in the run queue (list of goals not yet executed) of a *worker* in the same team
   b. The OR-scheduler is responsible for finding OR-work, that is, an unexplored alternative in the OR-tree
   c. The Reconfigurer is responsible for arranging the *workers* into *teams* in a way that allows both AND- and OR-parallelism to be freely exploited when they are available.

From this point of view, the Extended andorra model (EAM), which has been designed by D.H. Warren and coworkers as a concept of the *ideal system* (295) for PROLOG should be mentioned. Their intention was to provide the formal framework and an abstract computational model for logic programming in which can be described and compared different approaches to parallelism in logic. In EAM, computations are expressed through a set of rewriting rules acting on a state description.

The goal of the project in the Extended Andorra Model and followers of this idea (296,297), was to find a computational model for parallelizing PROLOG that would reach the following goals:

- The number of inferences should be minimized, and the related amount of computational work should be reduced to a minimum, which entails the following requirements:
  1. Branches in the tree of computations should be shared, without recomputing.
  2. So-called speculative computations should be avoided; it is the natural bias of parallelism to produce speculative computations.
- The percentage of actions run in a parallel way should be maximized despite the fact that minimizing the number of inferences and exploiting maximal parallelism is contradictory.
- Restrictions should not be imposed on the PROLOG language. For example, such a model should support language constructs developed in other PROLOGs that are also trying to optimize their concepts from a parallelization point of view.

The EAM execution model itself originates from work on the BAM (for better description see (296–298).

The ideal nature of the EAM arises from the fact that the model may achieve the best balance between the amount of parallelism exploited and the number of inference steps performed. On the other hand, as it is, the model is very abstract and far from a possible implementation. The major concern is that the abstract level of the model ignores many aspects involved with implementation (efficient management of environments, synchronization between agents, etc.). Nevertheless, the EAM is useful since it supplies a general framework for describing and comparing different parallel execution models, where emphasis is put on what can be done in parallel (without losing sight of the issue of efficiency) and outlining the "ideal" situation.

As has been mentioned, the EAM can be formally defined (299) using rewrite rules, which manipulate AND/OR-trees that are represented through AND-, OR-, and choice-boxes.

AND-boxes are created when launching a new clause; OR-boxes are created when launching a new goal. Choice-boxes are special OR-boxes created when the clauses defining a procedure include a pruning operator, %. The original EAM supports two pruning operators: cut and commit.

The Extended Andorra Model has four main operations:

1. *Reduction:* that expands a goal in an AND-box into an OR-box.
2. *Promotion:* that promotes constraints from an inner box to an outer AND-box.
3. *Substitution:* that applies a constraint on a variable.
4. *Forking:* that distributes a conjunction across a disjunction.

Execution in EAM is given in Figure 3-23 (from Lopes (299)).

Now let us look at Figure 3-24, that gives the example[34] of EAM execution originally presented by Lopes and Costa (300).
The set of facts and rules for the query `?-g(X).` has the form:

```
a(1).
a(2).
b(4).     b(X):- c(X).
c(1).
c(3).     g(X):- a(X),b(X).
```

Elements of Figure 3-24 should be interpreted as follows:

- OR-boxes are represented as black dots.
- AND-boxes are represented as a rectangle divided into three areas. The left area is reserved for local variables; the middle area for conjunctions of goals; and the right one is for the external variables.

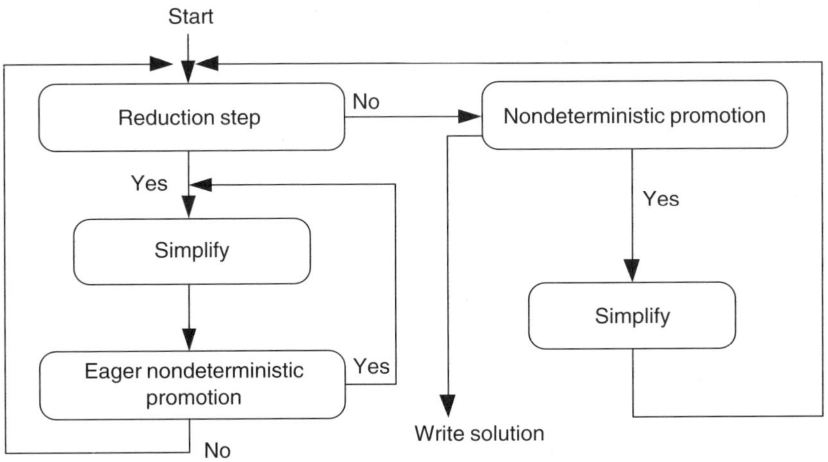

Figure 3-23. Execution in EAM (with permission from R. Lopes and V.S. Costa (299).

[34] With permission of Ricardo Lopes.

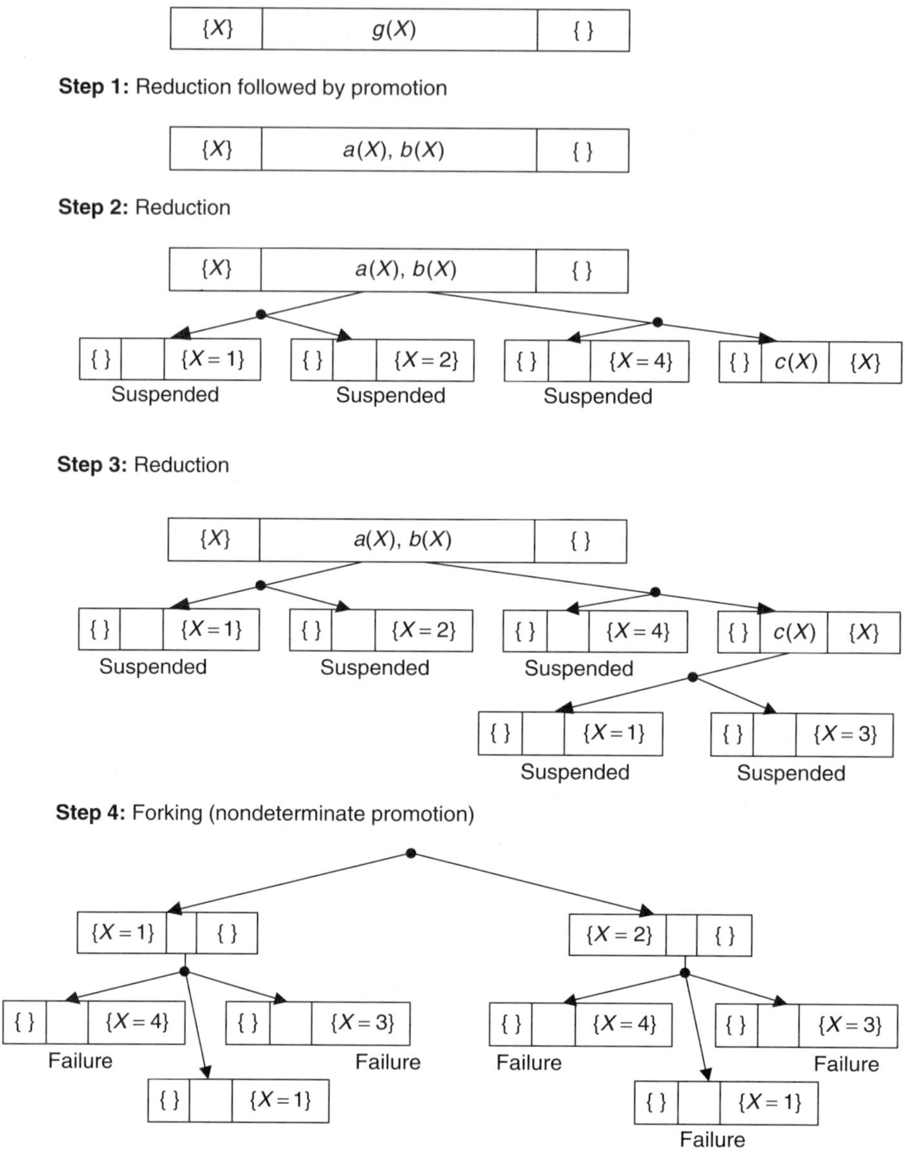

Figure 3-24. Example of EAM execution (with permission from (299)).

Steps of execution should be read as follows:

Step 1: After starting execution, the EAM will perform a reduction on `g(X)` followed immediately by a promotion since `g(X)` only has one alternative.

Step 2: A reduction is performed on both `a(X)` and `b(X)`.

Here there are two alternatives to `a(X)`:

1. to perform `X = 1`, which leads to suspension because `X` is an external variable.
2. The second alternative will also suspend when trying to make `X = 2`.

   There are also two alternatives to `b(X)`; however, the first one is suspended when trying to make `X = 4`.

Step 3: The system can work only on `c(X)`, because all the others are suspended. A reduction is applied, creating two more alternatives. Both of them are suspended immediately because they also try to assign a value to *X*.

At this point, all possible alternatives are suspended. This forces us to apply a nondeterministic promotion as the only rule. The system decides to choose the OR-box that is the leftmost on the tree.

After forking, the tree is divided into two, with an OR-box on top. The left side `X` binds to `1`; on the right side `X` is bound to `2`.

After reactivation of all the suspended AND-boxes, they fail immediately, with the exception of just one solution, which is *X* = 1 (on the left side of the tree).

In general, the Andorra-I prototype has demonstrated that the BAM concept can successfully use two forms of parallelism: OR-parallelism and dependent AND-parallelism in the same system, and that such a system can reduce the search space for a large category of PROLOG programs.

The drawback of the Andorra-I approach is that it depends on finding deterministic applications. If this cannot be efficiently accomplished, applications with strong parallelism are forced to run sequentially.

The Extended Andorra Model was the base for two directions of research. Warren and related researchers at Bristol concentrated on the development of an Extended Andorra Model with Implicit Control (295), where the goal was to obtain the advantages of the Extended Andorra Model with the least effort from the programmer.

The researchers at SICS[35] (Haridi, Janson) concentrated on the Andorra kernel language (AKL) (301). On the basis of advantages of the Extended Andorra Model, they tried to develop a new programming paradigm that could subsume both traditional PROLOG and the committed-choice languages. Research in AKL concentrated on including novel features such as ports, important for concurrent programming and on obtaining good performance through sequential and parallel implementations. The AKL researchers also worked with Oz (302), a language similar to AKL, developed at DFKI[36].

Research on the Extended andorra model with Implicit Control (EAM), followed a rather different approach. They started at first by trying to prove the feasibility of the model by developing the proper interpreter (303), showing that

[35] Swedish Institute of Computer Science (SICS)

[36] German Research Center for Artificial Intelligence (DFKI)

the EAM was indeed feasible. Warren proposed solutions such as *lazy copying* and *eager producers* to give finer control over search when required.

Lopes and Costa (299,300) reported on the successful design of a first implementation for the EAM. As a first step, they concentrated on the implementation of the main rewriting rules of the EAM. This subset of the EAM was implemented on the first prototype, the BEAM.

The authors of EAM assumed minimization of the amount of control information that the user is required to supply. This was considered later on as something of secondary importance in some systems originating from EAM. However, the concept of the Random PROLOG Processor (RPP) presented in this book took this issue to the level of the basic principle of the whole parallel PROLOG system.

The RPP PROLOG is a quasi-chaotic inferring system, and removal of any control (besides dynamical self-control) is considered as a "gate" to fascinating new opportunities.

At the end of this chapter, let us look into "the first" implementation of EAM, that is, BEAM designed by Lopes and Costa (300). First let us look at the execution model of EAM, which is given in Figure 3-25.

The execution model of BEAM has the following five main components:

- **AND-OR-Tree Manager**: This applies the EAM rewriting rules to the existing AND-boxes and OR-boxes until it can start WAM-like execution for the selected goal. The rewrite rules include the Reduction-rule, the Promotion-rule, and the Forking-rule.
- **Abstract Machine**: this runs a WAM-like code (see Section 3.4.1.5 for a description of WAM) to perform unification and setup goals. The unification code is similar to WAM. Control instructions follow a compilation scheme similar to WAM but with a different execution. The set of machine

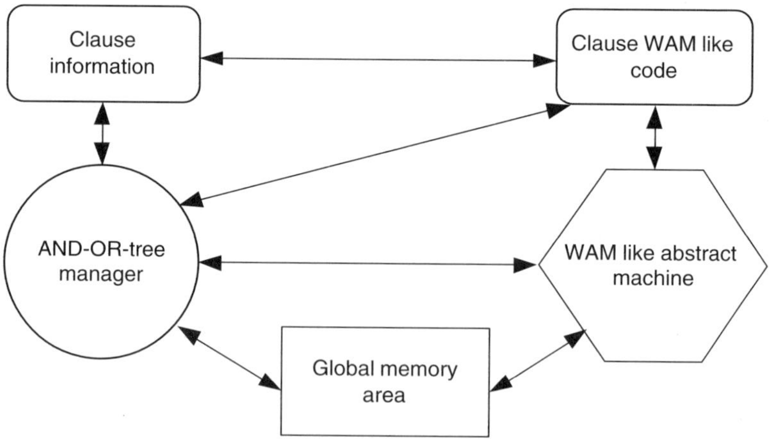

Figure 3-25. EAM execution model (with permission from Lopes and Costa (300).

instructions for BEAM contains WAM instructions: `get`, `put`, and `unify`. These instructions, however, slightly differ from corresponding WAM instructions. The main new instructions introduced in BEAM are for control purposes:

```
explore alternative i
prepare calls n
call pred
proceed
```

- **Clause Information:** Clause Information contains the program's code and support information.
- **WAM-like code:** WAM-like code forms a sequence of abstract machine instructions for each clause.
- **Global Memory Areas** Global Memory Areas operate in a similar way to a *heap* in the WAM model. Variables values, compound terms like lists and structures, and PROLOG atoms are saved here. This further serves requests for AND-OR-boxes.

The And-OR-Tree Manager handles most of the complexity in the EAM. It uses the *Clause Information* to know how many alternatives one clause has and how many goals one clause calls. Using this information, it constructs the tree and uses the EAM rewriting rules to manage it. It requests memory for the boxes in the *Global Memory Areas*. The *WAM-like Abstract Machine* is called by the And-Or-Tree Manager to execute and unify the arguments of the goals and clauses.

As an example of the preceding discussion, let us consider the clause:

```
p(X,Y):- g(X), f(Y).
```

When running this clause, the AND-OR-Tree Manipulation transforms the `p(X,Y)` into one AND-boxs and calls the *WAM-like Abstract Machine* to create the subgoals and OR-boxes for `g(X)` and `f(Y)`. Control then returns to the manager if the boxes need to suspend.

3.4.4.2 The Random Prolog Processor (RPP) The concept of the Random PROLOG Processor (RPP) originated with the author around 1993. The first, acceptable working simulation model with a three-dimension computer graphics interface, on a eight-processor SGI computer emerged around 1996 (56).

The basic research goal of building the RPP was not to measure *collective intelligence* but to check feasibility of an inferring system, for example, PROLOG without upper level control, implemented by an Operating System and an AND/OR-tree manager. The idea of using this model of chaotic computations in logic for *collective intelligence* emerged unexpectedly during a “hot” discussion between the author (who has been working and teaching AI for several years) and Dr. S. Chrobot (who was working in the domain of Operating Systems) on perspectives of such a nondeterministic system, in fact very inefficient from a general computational point of view. In retrospect, it can be said that we represented opposite points of view on computational processes.

Reviewing that discussion, let us recapitulate and justify the use of such a quasi-chaotic PROLOG for the computational *collective intelligence* problem.

Upon observing the social structures of, for example, humans, which are the most transparent for observation (at least in some respects), it is striking that the inferences emerging are parallel, chaotic, and at the same time different algorithms of inference are applied.

Moreover, it is difficult to separate messages from message-processing agents. The same being or agent can be the processor, the message carrier, and the message, from the point of view of different parallel-running processes. This is strange, but note how frequently we participate in the inference process and are not aware of it. A good example is the research area, where after a certain discovery is published and found as significant, many other researchers claim "copyrights" for some parts of the discovery.

The inferring processes emerging inside social structures, which create the *collective intelligence* phenomenon can be observed as global, but the role of specific elements cannot be easily identified and interpreted.

Thus, a mathematical logic-based representation of social structure behavior is necessary for analysis, separate from interpretation. We have to rely on only approximations of the inference process we observe, and we must be able to easily improve a given approximation; thus, declarative, loosely coupled inference systems are necessary after some modifications (which is be given later). The concept of PROLOG seems to best fulfill the requirements:

- PROLOG is declarative, that is, facts, rules, and goals can easily be real-time added or retracted in the inference system. Different independent variants of facts and procedures are allowed. This is basic for chaotic systems.
- Symbols and interpretation of clauses of facts, rules, and goals are independent because PROLOG is based on first-order predicate calculus. Thus, clauses can describe roughly observable aspects of behavior (e.g., of ants) without understanding them very well. A good example is describing a small social group of ants solving a maze problem, with the use of pheromones. They can be described as a simple inferring automata or as "micro-expert systems."
- Without changing the PROLOG dialect, it is easy to adopt a molecular model of computations, as has been done in the RPP.

Let us go through the concept and implementation of this model of computations.

Information Molecules (IM) and Computational Space (CS)

One of the fundamental concepts of our computational model of *Collective Intelligence* is the assumption that everything, that is, all the information from beings up to social structures is carried and approximated by stationary or displacing *information molecules (IM)*.

Information molecules exist in *computational space (CS)*; however, these two concepts are inseparable because higher level *information molecules* can also be *computational spaces* themselves from a more general point of view.

The concept of an *information molecule* is useful (and probably necessary) for the model of *collective intelligence* because it allows us to create a "continuum" of formal objects of all possible types, starting from a molecule of a pheromone in the real world up to an abstract message in a network, continuing through to the concept of encapsulated objects, including data structures and procedures to service them. In this continuum of types of *information molecule* there can also be formal (software) agents existing in a computer network, but live beings as well, such as viruses, bacteria, ants, humans, and so forth.

Ships, planes, and so forth, with a crew on board can be also considered as higher order *information molecules* (displacing). Social structures, families, villages, cities, nations, and so forth with their natural or artificial borders and their policy and behavior towards the environment or "objects outside" can be also considered as *information molecules* (motionless). They are usually not moving, but do not forget nomadic social structures — they move.

Let us look at Figure 3-26, which depicts the entry concept of *information molecule*.

It is important to note that we do not assume or impose any dimension to *information molecules* or the structure of membranes.

As has been mentioned earlier, the basic mathematical formalism supporting the concept of *information molecule* is predicate calculus — thus, a single clause of fact can be the simplest "legal" *information molecule*. However, there is no sense in speaking here about dimensions or membranes. Considering more complicated logical expressions, that is, clauses of facts and rules, which are

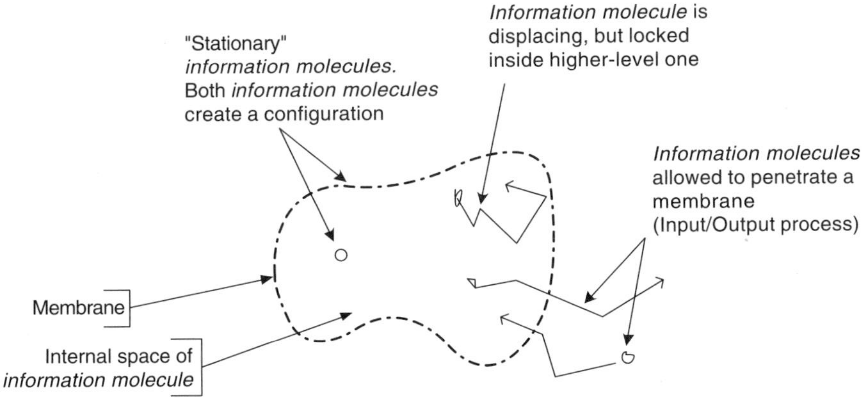

Figure 3-26. Initial concept of the *information molecule*.

composed of sequences (strings) of unit clauses, dimensions can be introduced (e.g., the order of processing when looking for a match from left to right - or the opposite), but there is no reason to introduce a membrane.

Probably the first reasonable use of a membrane is when we define software agents (encapsulation) or real world objects such as bacteria, ants, and so forth.

The precise specification of a dimension and a membrane for a given type of *information molecule* should reflect the specific properties of objects being modeled with our formalism (which will be given now).

Please note that *information molecules* will be abbreviated with *CS* (as *computational space CS*, not *IM*) for the reasons mentioned earlier because only the elementary *information molecules* do not create associated *computational space*.

The first-level *computational space (CS)* with internal quasi-random traveling or stationary *information molecules* of PROLOG facts, rules, and goals c_i are denoted as the multiset $CS^1 = \{c_1, \ldots, c_n\}$. Thus, clauses of facts, rules, and goals are themselves 0-level *CS*.

We do not assume any nature of *CS*. It can be any continuous or discrete space. For example, clauses of facts, rules, and goals can quasi-randomly displace in a three-dimension lattice.

Please note that a PROLOG program, stored in a computer memory with given memory locations of clauses, also subjects this formalism.

For a given *CS*, we define a membrane similar to that of the Chemical Abstract Machine (304) denoted by $|\cdot|$, which encloses inherent facts, rules, and goals. It is obvious that $CS^1 = \{c_1, \ldots, c_n\} \equiv \{|c_1, \ldots, c_n|\}$.

For a certain kind of membrane $|\cdot|$ its type p_i is given, which is denoted $|\cdot|_{p_i}$, to define which *CS* can pass through it.

Such an act is considered Input/Output for the given *CS* with a given $|\cdot|$ (i.e., membrane).

It is also allowable in the Random PROLOG model of computations to define *degenerated membranes* marked with $\cdot|$ or $|\cdot$. Such a membrane should be interpreted that a collision-free (with membrane) path that can be found going from the exterior to the interior of an area enclosed by such a membrane, for all types of *CS*.

The simplest possible application of degenerated membranes in the *CS* simulating a given social structure is to make, e.g., streets or other territorial boundaries.

If the given *CS* contains simple PROLOG clauses and other *CSs*, then it is considered a higher order one, depending on the level of internal *CS* existing inside.

Such internal *CS* will be also labeled with $\hat{v}_j$ for example,

$$CS^2 = \left\{|c_1, \ldots CS^1_{\hat{v}_j}, \ldots c_n|\right\} \quad \textit{iff} \quad CS^1_{\hat{v}_j} \equiv \{|b_1, \ldots, b_n|\},$$

$$\textit{where} \quad b_i \quad i = 1 \ldots m \quad \textit{and} \quad c_j \quad j = 1 \ldots n \quad \textit{are clauses}$$

Every c_i can be labeled with $\hat{v}_j$ to denote characteristics of its individual quasi-random displacements.

The general practice is that higher level *CSs* take fixed positions, that is, they create structures, and lower level *CSs* perform displacements. This is because we must keep in mind possible interpretations. Moving social structures are relatively rare cases (migrating nomads, ships, planes), whereas in most cases we observe only moving forms of encapsulated information, for example, bacteria, humans.

Most complex social structures take a fixed position, only their shape (boundaries or configuration) varies.

It is also allowed in this model of computations to have some specific (even low level) *CSs* "settling" in specific locations of the main *CS*, after a certain period of quasi-random displacements. Some inference processes require this because for inference, local unions are necessary that *emerge* (*evolve*) on the basis of *cooperation* or specific forms of *trade* between *computational spaces*. This can have even immediate practical applications in designing computer architectures through emergent regrouping and cooperation of a processor's modules (305).

Please note that the formal system given earlier uses only two primitives, *information molecules* and *membranes*, to build computational processes (spaces) of an arbitrary complexity. The binary system used in today's computers uses also only two primitives, 0/1 to build strings of data and programs of arbitrary complexity. This "binary" bias of computational processes of an extremely different nature should be analyzed with special research attention.

For a given *CS* it is useful to define a position function *pos*:

$$pos : O_i \rightarrow \langle position\ description \rangle \cup undefined, \quad where \quad O_i \in CS$$

On this basis, if there are any two internal *CS* objects O_i, O_j in the given *CS*, then there can be defined a distance[37] function $D(pos(O_i), pos(O_j)) \rightarrow \Re$ and a rendezvous distance d.

We say that during the computational process, at any time t or time period Δt, two objects O_i, O_j come to rendezvous if $D(pos(O_i), pos(O_j)) \leq d$.

The rendezvous act is denoted by the rendezvous relation ®, for example, O_i ® O_j, which is reflexive and symmetric, but not transitive. For another definition of rendezvous as the λ-operator, see Fontana et al. (306).

A rendezvous relation is necessary to decide if two or more *CSs* are candidates for the inference process.

Rendezvous and inferences (if any) can be depicted by adoption of so-called *Feynman diagrams* (307) used in physics for graphical representations of particle interaction, as is in Figure 3-27.

The computational PROLOG process for a given *CS* is defined as the sequence of frames F labeled by t or Δt, interpreted as the time (given in standard

[37] In organizational behavior, the concept of distance is termed "*proximity*", and is used for the purpose of analyzing of communication networks (see "Theories of Physical and Electronic Proximity" in social structures (159)).

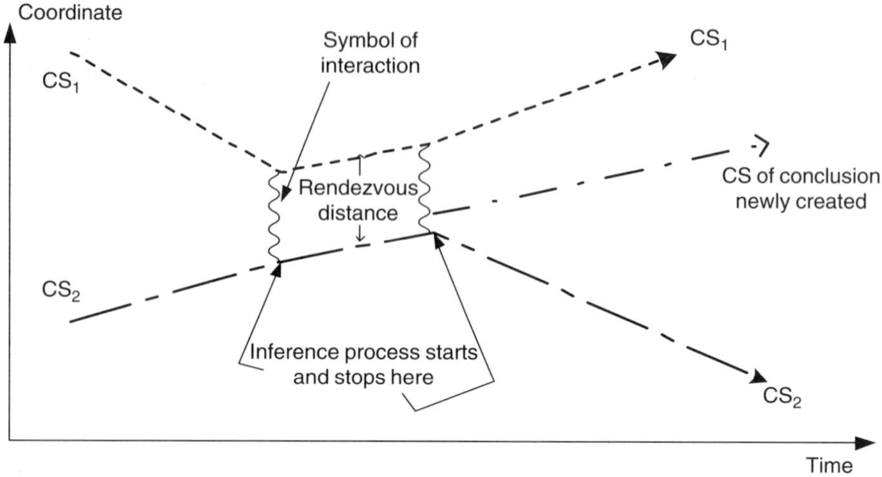

Figure 3-27. Rendezvous and inference process presented in the Feynman diagram (307).

time units or simulation cycles) with a well-defined *start* and *end*, for example, $F_{t_0}, \ldots, F_{t_e}$.

For every frame the multiset $F_j \equiv \{|c_1, \ldots, c_m|\}$ is explicitly given, with all related specifications: *pos(.)*, membrane types *p*, and movement specifications v if available.

The simplest case of *CS* for the RPP used in our simulations is the three-dimension cube with randomly traveling clauses of facts, rules, and goals inside.

The RPP is initialized to start the inference process after the set of clauses, facts, rules, and goals (defined by the programmer) is injected into this *CS*.

More advanced examples of the *CS* for the RPP include a single main CS^2 with a set of internal CS^1, which take fixed positions inside CS^2, and a number of CS^0, which are either local for a given CS_i^1 (because the membrane is not transparent for them) or global for any subset of $CS_j^1 \in CS^2$.

While modeling the *collective intelligence* of certain closed social structures, interpretations in the structure are given for all CS_n^m, that is, "this *CS* is a message"; "this is a single human"; "this is a village, a city," and so forth.

The importance of properly defining $\hat{v}_j$ for very CS_j^i should be emphasized. As has been mentioned, the higher level CS_j^i takes a fixed position to model substructures such as villages or cities. If we model a single human as CS_j^1, then $\hat{v}_j$ reflects displacement of a human being. Characteristics of the given $\hat{v}_j$ can be purely Brownian or can be quasi-random, for example, in lattice, but it is profitable to subject it to the present form of CS_j^i. When $\hat{v}_j$ has the proper characteristics, there are the following essential tools:

- The goal clause, when it reaches the final form, can migrate toward a defined *Output* location. This can be a membrane of the main *CS* or even a specific, local *CS*. Thus the appearance of a solution of a problem in the *CS* can be observable.

- Temporarily, the density of some *CMs* can be increased in a given area of *CS* in such a way that after a given low level CS^i_j reaches the necessary form, it migrates to a specific area(s) to increase the speed of selected inferences in some areas.

Figure 3-28 gives a summary of the concept of *computational space* in two-dimension and the *information molecules* existing inside it, and the rendezvous and inference process.

Now let us discuss the issue of *configuration* of a given logical expression, which is a natural extrapolation of the concept of *membranes* and *computational space*, down to the single (PROLOG) logical expression in the Random PROLOG Processor concept.

In general the dialect of PROLOG required for the RPP is the same as the syntax of "traditional PROLOG" given in section 3.4.4.1.
When we look at section 3.4.4.1 for the syntax of a body of rules or goals:

$$\ldots \wedge c_1 \wedge c_2 \wedge \ldots \wedge c_n \bullet \text{ where } c_i \text{ are unit clauses}$$

we can conclude that the definition of the logical operator AND as a connector for unit clauses does not impose any further restrictions on representation or ordering of elements (i.e. unit clauses) in such a logical expression.

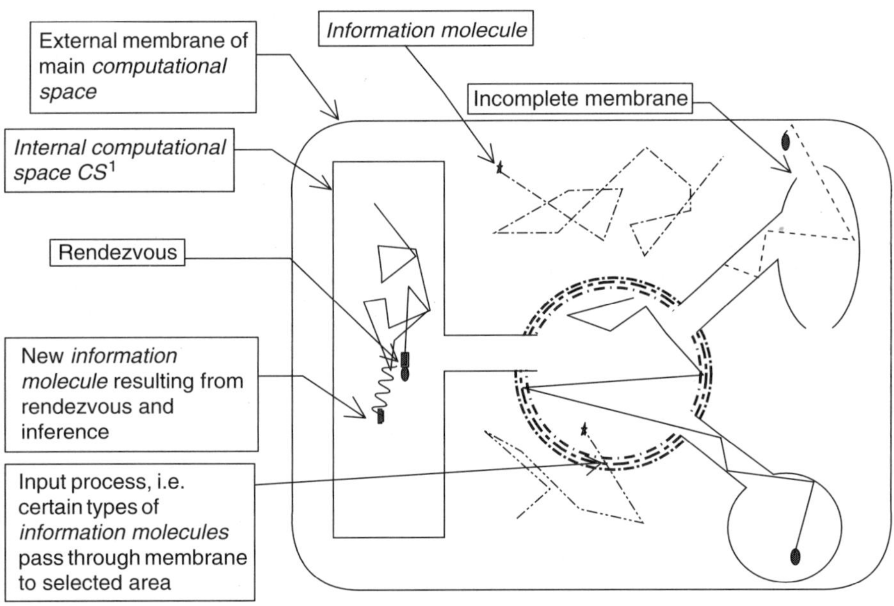

Figure 3-28. Example of structured *computational space* CS^1 in 2-D with *information molecules*.

It is our system and tradition of writing down and processing a text from left-to-right, line after line with line breaks—instead, for example, of writing top–down or in other two-dimension or three-dimension spatial ways on the page or any display device.

The body of the rules and goals in the Random PROLOG Processor can be freely considered as any set $S(\ldots)$ of unit clauses bounded by AND, in contrast to that in standard PROLOG where there is additionally an ordered list of unit clauses.

Such a set can even be considered a local, invariable *CS* associated with rules containing unit clauses, as illustrated in Figure 3-29.

This concept also allows us to define *logical clusters*, for example, to construct sets of related facts enclosed by membranes, which are traveling through any *CS*. Please keep in mind how "boring" the problem of matching facts with rules is, when the database is large (see the Rete Algorithm for Expert systems (14).
For some simulated problems, it is necessary to introduce the *configuration*, to somehow order (even spatially 3-D) the unit clauses in the set $S(\ldots)$. A good example is the concept of a stack with its through-top-only-access, used here to force a certain sequence of inferences for a specific rule (see Fig. 3-30). This provides a certain form of *guarding* in a natural way.

Although it can be argued that we can always redefine the logical expression of clauses in such a way that information about the spatial shape of that clause is included as some of its arguments (terms) inside (e.g., at the start)—this approach should be profitable.

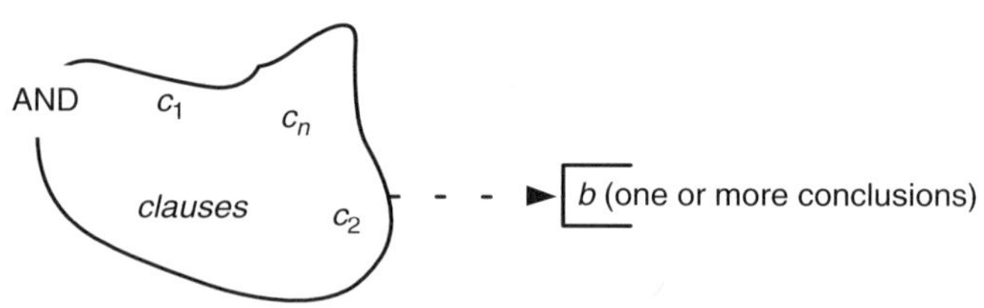

Figure 3-29. Rule b:- $c_1, \ldots, c_n$• defined with the use of *computational space*.

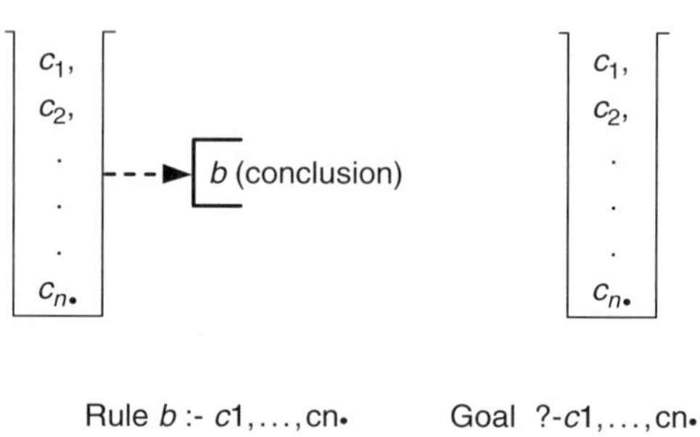

Figure 3-30. Stack as *CS* for guarding the specific sequence of processing a rule or a goal.

Please finally note again how well the "hierarchical concept" of *CS* and membranes fulfills the requirements of the concept of encapsulation in object-oriented programming languages.

General Inference Model of the RPP

After the concepts of *information molecules* and *computational spaces CS* have been discussed, we can give a definition of inference in the Random PROLOG Processor. The pattern of inference in the RPP generalized for any *CS* has the form:

DEFINITION 22: GENERALIZED INFERENCE IN CS^N

Assuming that $CS = \{\ldots CS^i_j \ldots CS^k_l \ldots\}$, we can define CS^i_j Ⓡ CS^k_l and $U(CS^i_j, CS^k_l)$ and C(one or more CS^m_n of conclusions) $\vdash$

---

one or more CS^m_n of conclusion, $R(CS^i_j$ or $CS^k_l)$

The preceding description should be interpreted as follows:

CS^i_j Ⓡ CS^k_l denotes a rendezvous relation;

$U(CS^i_j, CS^k_l)$ denotes that unification of the necessary type can be successfully applied;

C(*one or more* CS^m_n *of conclusions*) denotes that CS^m_n are satisfiable.

Notice that the reaction $\rightarrow$ in *CHAM* (304) semantics is equivalent to $\vdash$ inference here.

$R(CS^i_j$ or $CS^k_l)$ denotes that any parent(s) are retracted if necessary. ■

The definition given earlier is constructed on the basis of the fundamental mathematical logic definition of *inference* or *logical consequence* (16,17), which says that:

> A wff G is an inference from a set of axioms $\{A_1, \ldots, A_n\}$ if any interpretation that simultaneously satisfies all of the axioms also satisfies G.

The standard PROLOG inferences are simple cases of the preceding definition. Later, when discussing the N-element inference, we are only interested in "constructive" inferences, that is, when a full chain of inferences exists.
Thus the previous diagram will be abbreviated as

$$CS^i_j; CS^k_l \xrightarrow{RPP} \sum_n CS^m_n$$

without mentioning the retracted *CSs* given by $R(CS^i_j$ or $CS^k_l)$.

In general, successful rendezvous can result in the "birth" of one or more child *information molecules*, which must then fulfill a $C(\ldots)$ condition; otherwise, they are aborted.

EXAMPLE CS^0 Ⓡ CS^0 inference: fact with rule

```
a(1).                        (fact)
Ⓡ
answer(Y) :-  a(X),          (rule)
          greater(X, 0),
          sum(X, 5, Y)
          retract(a(X).),
          assert(message(''molecule a(X). is killed'').).     ⊢
--------------------------------------------------------------------
answer(6).                   (logical result)
```

Therefore, after the rendezvous, the following process takes place:

Step 1:
Unification of clauses `a(1)` and `a(X)` $\Rightarrow \{X/1\}$ — *matching*;
Step 2:
Logical evaluation of `greater(1,0)` $\Rightarrow$ True — *evaluation of*
numerical calculation of `sum(1,5,Y)` $\Rightarrow \{Y/6\}$ — *built-in predicates*
Step 3:
`retract` and `assert` control actions:
retract one parent — - " -
and fire the message molecule into the RPP — - " -
Step 4:
Logical expression (parent rule) reduces to unit clause, that is, fact `answer(6).` (because there are no evaluations into False, and all built-in predicates are executed successfully). An information molecule `answer(6).` can be considered a "legal child." The message molecule is the "background child."

Summary of example Now only one parent *information molecule* exists (rule remains, fact is retracted), so the rule undergoes further random travel and inferences; a child *information molecule* emerges, that is, `answer(6).` and starts to random travel. Then the new `message(...)` *information molecule* is fired into the solution.

Because our proposed RPP is designed to evaluate the inference power of closed social structures, simplifying assumptions based on real life observation can be made.

It is difficult to find cases of direct rendezvous and inference between two CS_i^m *and* CS_j^n *if* $m,n \geq 1$ without an intermediary involved CS_k^0 $k = 1, 2, \ldots$ (messages, pheromones, observation of behavior, e.g. the bee's dance, etc.).

Even in Genetic algorithms (7), the crossover of genes can be considered the inference of the two genomes, CS_i^0 *and* CS_j^0.

Only if we consider CS^n on the level of whole nations, where mutual exchange (migration) of humans takes place, can such a case be considered as an approximation to such higher level rendezvous and inferences.

This is, however, just approximation because eventually this exchange is implemented at the level of personal contact of humans, which are just rendezvous and inferences of two CS_i^0 *and* CS_j^0 with the help of CS_k^0 $k = 1, 2 \ldots$.

Thus, rendezvous and direct inference between two CS_j^i *if* $i \geq 1$ is not discussed in this book. We only make use of a single CS_{main}^n *for* $n > 1$ as the main CS.

Single beings such as humans or ants can be represented as $CS_{individual}^1$. Such beings perform internal inferences (in their brains), independently of higher level, cooperative inferences inside CS_{main} and exchange of messages of the type CS^0.

It is allowable to have internal CS^k inside the main CS, but only as static ones (taking fixed positions) to define substructures such as streets, companies, villages, cities, and so forth.

For simplicity, however, we try to approximate beings as CS^0; otherwise, even statistical analysis are too complicated.

It is also important to assume that the results of inference are not allowed to infer between themselves after they are created. Products of inference must immediately disperse; however, later inferences between them are allowed (J. Giarratano and G. Riley call this *refraction* (14)).

Now after defining a single inference we have to also define the chain of inferences or better said, the network. We should have in mind that the inference process in the Random PROLOG Processor, which finally produces a conclusion is a *net* spanned over time and a given *computational space* of parallel inferences connected by predecessors and successors.

N-Element Inferences in CS

To specify the global inference process composed of elementary inferences (see Def. 22) in the Random PROLOG Processor we have the following definition:

DEFINITION 23: N-ELEMENT INFERENCE (NEI) IN CS^N

There is a given CS at any level $CS^n = \{CS_1^{a_1}, \ldots CS_m^{a_m}\}$, and an allowed set of inferences SI of the form $\{set\ of\ premises\ CS\} \xrightarrow{I_j} \{set\ of\ conclusions\ CS\}$, and one or more CS_{goal} of a goal.

We say that $\{I_{a0}, \ldots, I_{a_{N-1}}\} \subseteq SI$ is an N-element inference in CS^n, if for all $I \in \{I_{a0}, \ldots, I_{a_{N-1}}\}$ the premises are present in CS^n at the moment of firing this inference, all $\{I_{a0}, \ldots, I_{a_{N-1}}\}$ can be connected into one tree by common conclusions and premises, and $CS_{goal} \in \{set\ of\ conclusions\ for\ I_{a_{N-1}}\}$. ■

To correctly interpret the above definition, let us look at Figure 3-31, which presents the basic conceptual elements of this definition. It is assumed there that the main CS is just a line segment on the Y-axis, where few *information molecules*

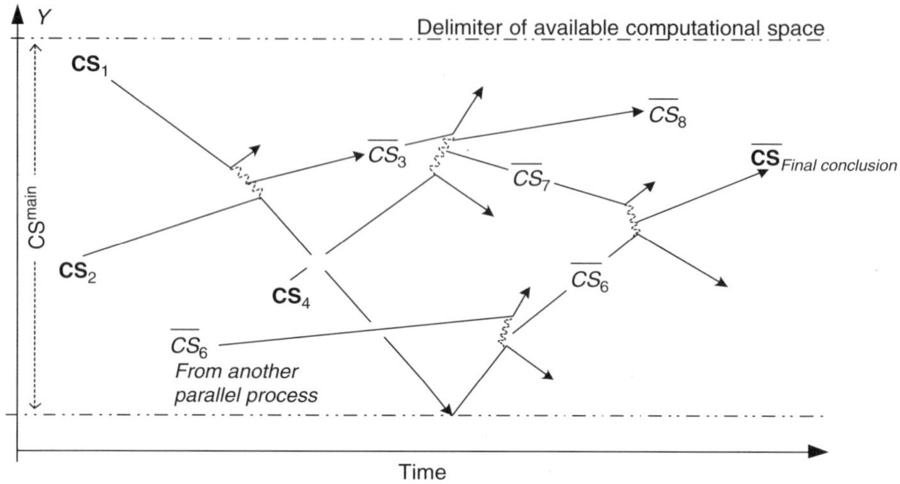

Figure 3-31. Illustration for definition of N-element inference.

exist, displace (in one-dimension), rendezvous, and infer. To make the picture clear, not all *information molecules* are presented, that is, it is assumed that at a specific time a new *information molecule* ($\overline{CS^6}$) emerges. This is the result of input or another, run in parallel inference process; however, this *information molecule* takes an active part in our N-element inference (NEI). For simplicity Brownian components of movements are not given. *Information molecules* of temporary conclusions (not facts) are marked as $\overline{CS_i}$.

The preceding definition fulfills all the basic requirements for defining an inference process of necessary complexity for the purpose of evaluating *collective intelligence*:

- An NEI may be interpreted as any problem-solving process in a social structure or mental process inside a single being in which N inferences are necessary to get a result, or any production process in which N-technologies or elements have to be found and unified into one final technology or product.

  This allows us to model inferring processes within a social structure in the same uniform way as production processes.

  This is very important because some inference processes can be observed only through resultant production processes or specific logical behavior, for example, of ants, bees, and bacteria.
- Simulating NEI in the RPP allows us to easily model the distribution of inference resources between individuals, their dissipation in space or time, displacements, and temporary concentration in the *CS*.

  This clearly reflects the dissipated, moving, or concentrated resources in a social structure of any type.

- With this approach, cases can be simulated very easily where some elements of the inference chain are temporarily not available, for example, the chain of inference can be temporarily broken, but at a certain time *t*, another inference running in the background or in parallel produces the missing components.

  Such situations are well known in human social structures, for example, when a given research or technologic discovery is blocked until missing theorems or sub-technology is discovered.
- Humans infer in all directions:
  - Forward, for example, improvements of existing technology
  - Backward, for example, searching for a way to manufacture a given product going back from a known formula
  - Generalization, for example, two or more technologies can be combined into one more general and powerful technology or algorithm
  - Directions of inference are frequently mixed together.

  The N-element inference simulated in the RPP reflects all these cases clearly.
- It has been widely observed that the inference process is noncontinuous; different threads of the same inference or different inferences are mixed in together.

We must remember that in general the computational process in the Random PROLOG Processor has the following components:

1. Main *computational space* CS^{main}, where the Input/Output, that is, "programming" and initialization for the run of inferences and computations takes place.
2. Local *computational spaces* CS_i^j of different levels to run local computational processes.
3. *Information molecules* CS_k^0 or even moving local computational spaces to implement transfer of information.

In general, *computational spaces* can exit even in one-dimensional space, as shown in Figure 3-32, in two-dimension (see Fig. 3-28), in three-dimension (see Fig. 3-32), and there are no formal objections to define *computational spaces* in any "abstract space of higher dimension."

Input/Output Process for CS

Every computational system, computer, or model of computations requires definition of proper Input and Output to initialize computations, and later on to capture the results required.

In general, Input and Output are considered complementary tasks for gathering data for a computer or a program or a simulated model of computations to work with (Input), and for making the results of the these systems' activities available to the user or to other computer processes (Output). Special hardware and software are usually necessary to implement Input/Output functions.

Example in one dimension (a): Single molecule performing Brownian motion in space enclosed by two membranes.

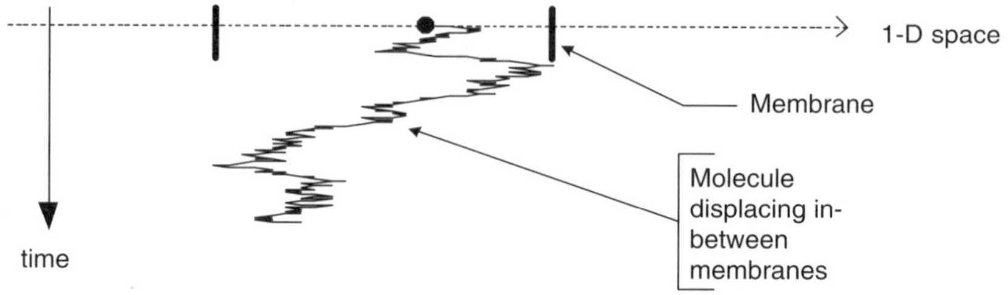

Example in one dimension (b): Two molecules performing Brownian motion in space enclosed by three membranes, one of them is degenerated (transparent for specific molecule).

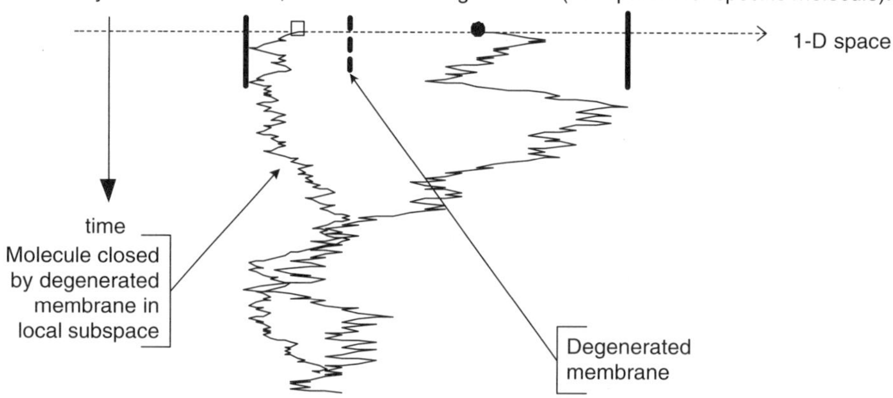

Example in two dimensions: Structured computational space CS with *information molecules*

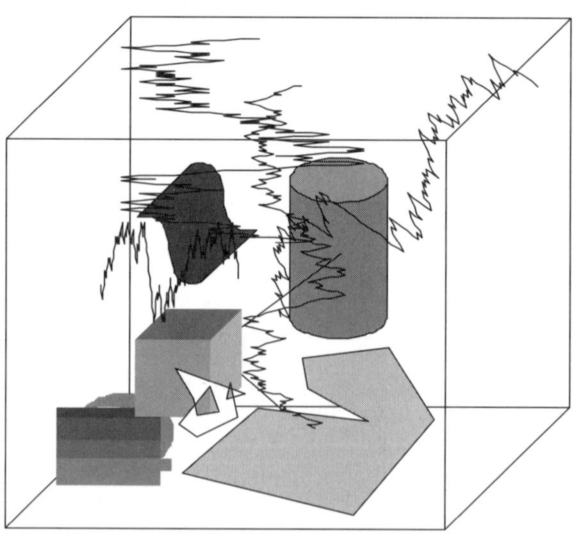

Figure 3-32. Examples of *computational spaces* in one dimension and two dimensions.

This makes definitions of Input/Output fuzzy and inseparable from the definitions of "kernel" computers or programs or simulated models of computations. The Input/Output process can be perceived in a narrow sense as well as a more general process. Let's follow a more general approach because we face different types of computational systems.

For digital computers the general Input process can be considered as consisting of the following:

1. Allocation of a compiled program (i.e. translated from a problem-oriented language to machine code) into, for example, a *code segment* of computer RAM memory and with allocation of proper data into, for example, a *data segment* of RAM memory (274)
2. The basic registers (in a CPU) necessary for computations are initialized, for example, addresses are set in the *instruction pointer, stack pointer*, and so forth.
3. The modes of a processor are set (*flags register*) to define the future method of execution.

Finally, the computational process in a digital computer can be started. Later on, when the process halts in a natural or artificial way, the Output can be considered as the contents of a specific memory location (which alternatively can be displayed - such a memory is widely referred to as a frame buffer; or, for example, printed from the printer's buffer, or at least forwarded into the network).

For the analog computer, as presented in section 3.4.3, the Input process can be considered a manual or automatic wiring of analog elements to create the desired configuration, followed by setting parameter values for simulation. After this, the analog computational process can be started. The Output of the computational process for an analog computer can be seen as the run of voltage(s) recorded at specific point(s) of circuitry (or sent to any controller), given as a function of time that represents the function which is a solution to a problem (usually it is differential equation(s) to be solved).

With the DNA computer (this model of computations is discussed in 3.4.5.2) to implement an Input there should be a macro–micro interface unit, that transforms input information into a corresponding distribution of molecular components. For Output of results of computations, the micro–macro interface unit of the DNA-processor should be a system capable of detecting the nature and measuring the distribution of molecular component concentrations corresponding to the final result of the computation.

With the Random PROLOG Processor model of computations, the Input/Output concept is in principle similar to DNA one; however, some differences exist.

The RPP model also has apparent similarities to the analog model of computations regarding configuring computational space, which is similar to the configuring elements of the analog computer.

The structure of Input–Computations–Output for the RPP is given in Figure 3-33.

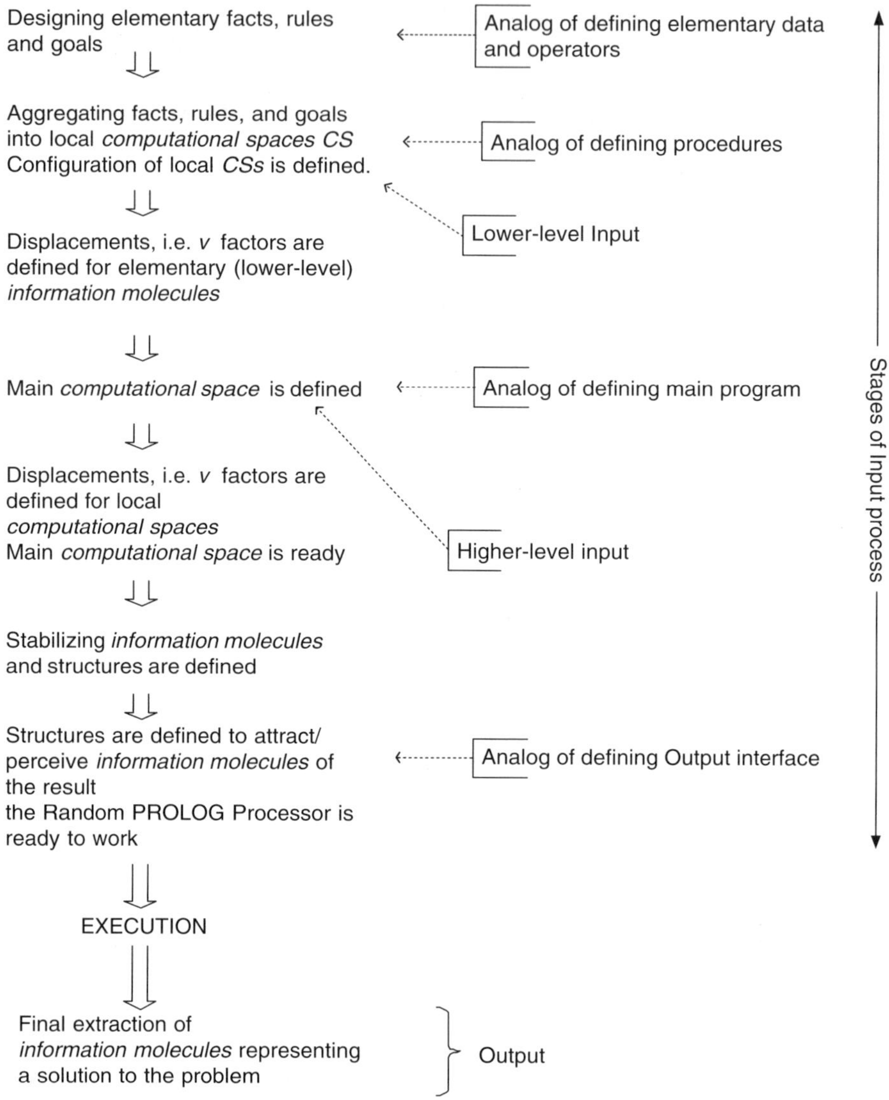

Figure 3-33. Input–Execution–Output for the Random PROLOG Processor.

Properties of Computations in the RPP

The model of computations represented in the Random PROLOG Processor displays specific, new, and exciting behavior as well as properties of a parallel, quasi-random inference process.

These properties, when discovered (56,), were an inspiration and allowed us to build the concept and computational model for measuring *collective intelligence* (308).

Let us list and discuss the most important of them:

1. *Information molecules* infer randomly and are independent, which implies full parallelism. This full parallelism is the consequence (among others) of the fact that there is no operating system as a supervising factor over the process. There is nothing like memory allocation or memory address. The function of an operating system is partially taken (imitated) by *control molecules* (which are discussed later on) and proper structuring (with membranes) of *computational space*. Molecules move around local or global *computational spaces* quasi-randomly in multiple copies. The only restricting factors are the membrane and the individual molecule's displacement abilities. *Information molecules* infer randomly.
2. The inference process automatically "splits" into concurrent and "cooperating" forward, backward, and rule–rule inferences.

   This is an exciting phenomenon for anybody who has had difficulties with arrangement and synchronization of forward and backward inference in any AI system. To illustrate how an inference process behaves in the Random PROLOG processor, let us look at simple simulations of a ten-step inference as defined here.

   There exists one starting fact:

   $a_0(1).$

   Our goal is to know the value of $a_9(X)$ in the query:

   $?answer(X), a_9(X).$

   There are 9 rules:

$a_1(X)$:- $a_0(X)$.	$a_4(X)$:- $a_3(X)$.
$a_2(X)$:- $a_1(X)$.	...
$a_3(X)$:- $a_2(X)$.	$a_9(X)$:- $a_8(X)$.

   To find a solution (which has the form $a_9(1)$, which implies that $X = 1$), it is necessary to make a minimum of ten inferences in this simple system.

   Because *information molecules* are moving randomly, independent of each other, there are the following possible kinds of inferring processes:

   (a) From facts toward a goal (forward reasoning), for example after rendezvous and unification:

   $a_1(1).\ ;\ a_2(X):\!-\ a_1(X).\ \vdash a_2(1).$

(b) Inferences between rules produce new rules (descendant rule inference), namely after rendezvous and unification:

$$a_4(X) :- a_3(X). ; a_5(X) :- a_4(X). \vdash a_6(X):- a_4(X).$$

(c) From goal back toward root fact (backward reasoning), for example, after rendezvous and unification:

$$a_{n-1}(X) :- a_{n-2}(X). ; ?answer(X), a_{n-1}(X) \vdash ?answer(X), a_{n-2}(X).$$

additionally, results of the (b) type inferences amplify backward reasoning, for example:

$$a_{10}(X):- a_4(X). ?answer(X), a_{10}(X). \vdash ?answer(X), a_4(X).$$

This is clearly demonstrated in Figure 3-34 as a "snapshot" of the temporary state of inferences in the RPP suddenly stopped after a certain period of time. In Figure 3-34. PROLOG notation is used.

The inference process behaves here a bit like "growing ice flowers on a wet window": there are multiple centers of activity, and suddenly the flowers are done. This is a surprising property of the inference process; however,

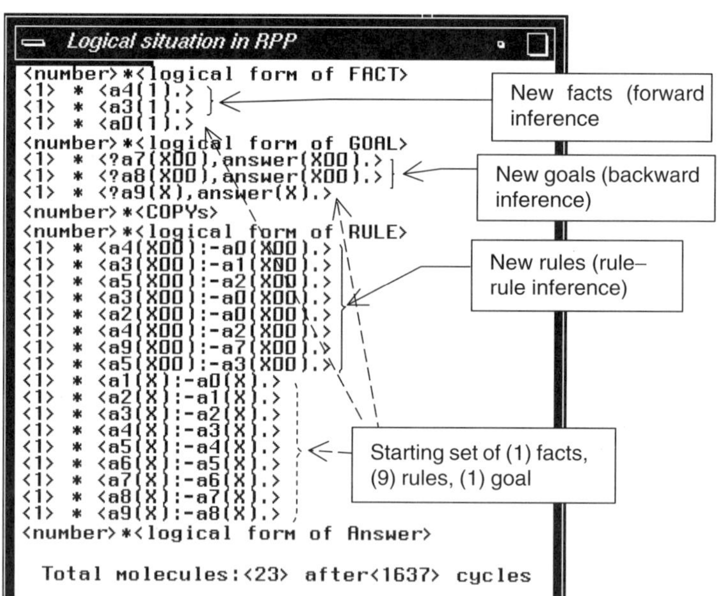

Figure 3-34. Example inference in the RPP.

it is very profitable because the low frequency of rendezvous is highly compensated by such quasi-chaotic, "joined" parallelism.

There are systems such as ART and KEE Expert systems that use both forward and backward inference (14), but it seems to be a dominant feature of AI systems that integrating different diagrams of inference is too complicated.

3. In the RPP it is possible to implement more inference patterns than in standard PROLOG, where an inference is backward only from the formula of the goal toward the facts.

   However, the next restricting factor in PROLOG is the demand to translate the original problem using Horn clauses only. The request to use only Horn clauses in inferring systems originates from the following (17):

   - Constraints can be placed on the syntax of the well-formed formulas *(wff)* of logical expressions that guarantee that each *wff* that is introduced into an inferring system converts into exactly one clause.
   - For the axiom set built of Horn clauses, reasonably complete and efficient decision procedures, feasible for today's digital computers can be defined.
   - For practical problems, restrictions imposed by Horn clauses can be avoided with some additional constructs in the program.
   - Horn clauses create clear and distinct forms of facts, rules, and goals which correspond well to the human way of representing and manipulating knowledge about the surrounding world (see section 2.1.3.2 on Expert systems).

   In the Random PROLOG Processor we are much less restricted, which results in a chance for more inference patterns, for example, through dropping the requirement to use only Horn clauses.

   From definition 22 of the generalized inference in CS^n, along with the possibility to configure clauses in the *information molecule*, it is clear that the requirement for Horn clauses can be dropped from the RPP. As a result, we can have, for example, an inference pattern[38] similar to that given below.

   An example of an RPP inference pattern:

   (a) A clause of rule C_1 rendezvous with another clause of rule C_2
   (b) Unification between strings of unit clauses $\mathbf{a_n}, \ldots, \mathbf{a_r}$ and $\mathbf{a'_n}, \ldots, \mathbf{a'_r}$ in C_1 and C_2 respectively, is possible.
   (c) After the binding of variables, there is no clause in the conclusion on the left-hand-side of :-, which would be evaluated to false.
   (d) As a result, a modified rule is produced, that is using the presentation convention from the last example:

[38] A review of inference rules can be found in Kogge (17), L. Wos et al. (309), etc.

$$b_m \ :- \ c_1, \ldots, c_i, \mathbf{a_n}, \ldots, \ \mathbf{a_r}, c_j, \ldots. \qquad (C_1)$$

Ⓡ

$$\mathbf{a'_n}, \ldots, \mathbf{a'_r} \ :- \ d_1, \ldots, d_s. \qquad \vdash \qquad (C_2)$$

$$b_m \ :- \ c_1, \ldots, c_i, d_1, \ldots, d_s, c_j, \ldots. \qquad (\text{conclusion rule } C_3)$$

Most probably careful research will reveal many more such inference opportunities because now in the RPP it is allowed to configure the logical information for matching and inference even spatially.

4. With simple stabilizing methods (e.g., self-destruction of inconsistent clauses) the RPP is surprisingly resistant to inconsistent sets of clauses.

   To demonstrate this, let us look at a simple simulation (Fig. 3-35) of an inconsistent system, that is, in the *CS* the same time rules of the pattern, for example, $a \to b; a \to \neg b$ are allowed.

   Moreover, we allow infinite loops of inferences of the form $a \to b; b \to c; \ldots; \to a$.

   Such inferring systems are observable in real life (e.g., committees), which we will show after the presentation of simulations.

   In our experiment there is a ten-element inference with one starting fact, a set of ten rules of the form $a \to b$, and the goal. Here we have simple one-element inferences, as well as very favorable ones, which jump far ahead

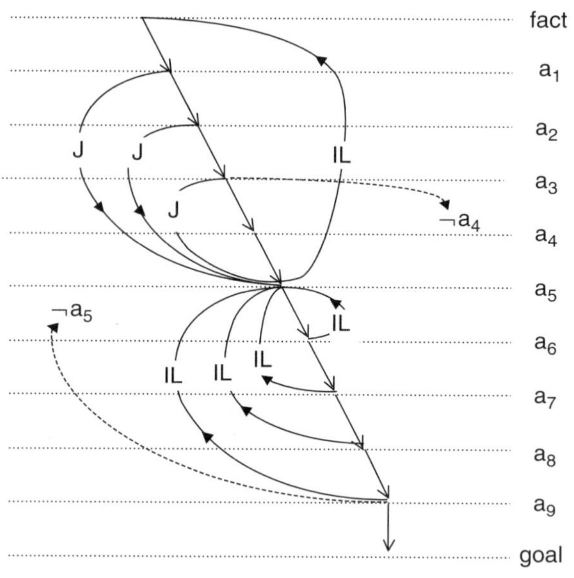

Figure 3-35. System with infinite loops and inconsistent inferences.

over elementary inferences, but we also have inferences that go back to conclusions already proven.

Simple stabilizing measures have been used in this example, such that when rendezvous occur with "inconsistent" *information molecules* like b ® ¬ b, the result is a retraction of both.

The following rule can be used for implementation of this stabilization.

```
retract(X(Y).),retract(¬X(Y).):-
                    molecule(X(Y).),molecule(¬X(Y).).
```

Notice that this is a non-Horn clause, as discussed before; the retract process occurs when any two *information molecules*: `molecule(X(Y)).` and `molecule(¬X(Y)).` rendezvous one after another with the preceding rule.

The number of cycles necessary to reach a conclusion for the inference here (Table 3-12) is surprisingly not very far from the speed of the ten-element inference in a non-structured environment (see previous example), where there are no inconsistent rules, jumps, or loops; 17,643 cycles were necessary in the previous example (310).

This example has a very straightforward interpretation in the group dynamics theory of sociology. Shaw (145) writes: *"group judgments reduce error of judgment"*; however, this is a very complex problem because incorrect leadership can force the group to *output* incorrect evaluations.

Group judgment is usually better because the individual can make false conclusions on the basis of incorrect use of inferring rules or because of incomplete databases, and nobody will correct it. This means that at the same time in the group, rules of inconsistent logically pattern such as $a \rightarrow b; a \rightarrow \neg b$ are allowed.

Our simulations can model, for example, a case of the social structure of a committee where there is no leadership, that is inferences are not prioritized, and all inferences are "context free."

TABLE 3-12. Inconsistent Inferences with Loops

RENDEZVOUS DISTANCE $d = 0.025$ SIZE OF CS: $1 \times 1 \times 1$ NO STRUCTURES IN CS BROWIAN MOVEMENTS: GAUSSIAN DISTRIBUTION WITH $\mu = 0$ $\langle \nu \rangle = 0.124$ NEI = TEN-ELEMENT INCONSISTENT INFERENCE	
CONCLUSION REACHED AFTER CYCLES	25436
FINAL NUMBER OF *information molecules* IN CS	108

It is a well-known fact that committees (or groups) have problems reaching agreement because during the meeting the same doubts are raised repeatedly by some members. This case can be simulated by introduction of infinite loops of inference as in our example earlier. Some members of a committee are able to infer only one step at a time; others can jump ahead with inferences.

The earlier simulation confirms the hypothesis that a group has a higher probability of giving a correct judgment than any single member, even if the group is obstructed by inconsistencies and redundant loops of inferences.

5. Proper and efficient run of an inference process usually requires the use of *control molecules*, as has been partially presented in an earlier example.

   This is such an important issue that the next part of the book addresses this problem. As mentioned before, in the Random PROLOG processor there is no operating system, but there cannot be a "vacuum"—something must replace the operating system with its tasks and duties in such a "highly dynamic system". A proper system of *control molecules* do this job.

6. Appropriate structuring of *computational space* with membranes can provide sufficient control over probabilistic displacement of *information molecules*.

   Especially useful are degenerated membranes because they can work as filters for whether or not to allow certain classes of *information molecules* into some areas.

   Along with the ability to control parameter $\hat{v}_j$, and *control molecules*, the structuring of *CS* with membranes is a third major tool to control the inference process.

7. Parallel threads of inferences can be run at the same time in the RPP.

   This is a consequence of the fact that an inference occurs only between specific *information molecules*, upon rendezvous. If no mistake is made (i.e., different inferences use the same *information molecules*) and until *information molecules* do not conflict for locations in the *CS*, we can have as many parallel threads of inference in the RPP as we want.

   It is obvious that a social structure "is thinking" at the same time in parallel about major and minor issues—refereeing problems of individuals and problems of society.

   We should again emphasize that the Random PROLOG Processor is proper tool for modeling *collective intelligence*.

8. Parallelism of multiple inference diagrams highly compensates for the low efficiency of the random inference process.

   For example, when the N-element inference of the form

$$\frac{a_0 : a_0 \rightarrow a_1; \ldots : a_i \rightarrow a_{i+1} : \ldots ; a_{n-1} \rightarrow a_n}{\text{N-element inference}}$$

is repeatedly simulated for various values of n (see e.g. in Fig. 3-34), to measure and graph a time $t_{a_n}(n)$ when the last element of the inference chain emerges in *CS*, it seems that the time to reach the conclusion a_n is almost the same, and does not clearly depend on n —as long as parameters of *CS* remain unchanged.

Figure 3-36. gives some unpublished initial results of simulations of $t_{a_n}(n)$ dependency for a simple cube-shaped *CS*, as specified in Table 3-12.

The relationship between the length of inference n and the time t_{a_n} necessary to conclude the inference is not clear and difficult to evaluate. It is the result of multiple interacting "crystallization points of inference," which produce growing numbers of multiple copies and boost speed of inference. It is something like the fact that the size of a window (distance between vertices) does not affect the time it takes to cover the window with frost.

This process has built-in positive feedback, which can lead to a combinatorial explosion of the number of *information molecules* in *CS*.

At the time of writing this book, the mathematical analysis and evaluation of this process was not available to the author. However, it seems necessary to analyze this phenomenon because something similar appears in social structures: sometimes complicated conclusions take the same time as simple ones.

The discussion presented here has demonstrated the importance of the problem of stabilizing a dynamic, quasi-chaotic inference process in a given *CS*. This problem is discussed now.

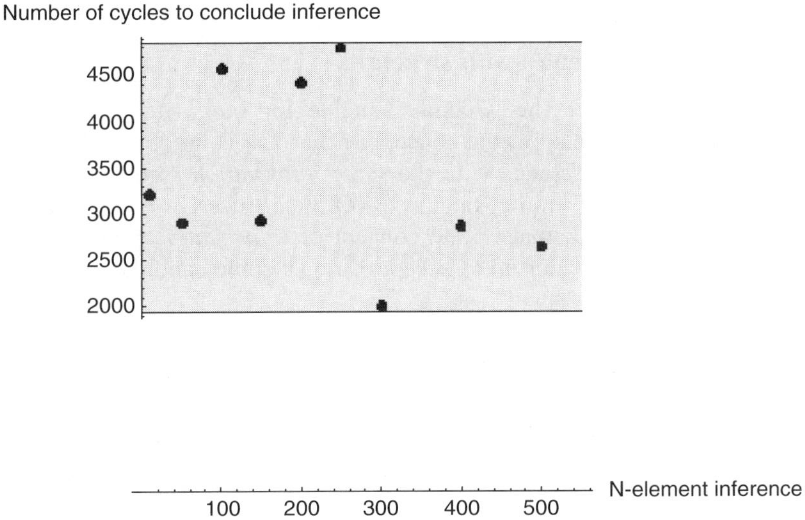

Figure 3-36. Dependency between length of inference and time necessary to conclude it.

Stabilizing and Controlling Measures in the RPP

The Random PROLOG Processor is a dynamic nondeterministic system; thus a fundamental issue is to "keep" the inference processes under control, and so there are the certain requirements:

- *Stabilization* is needed to avoid combinatorial explosion. During run time it is difficult to see if combinatorial explosion is coming because some types of computations may temporarily require a large increase in (specific) *information molecules*, for example, if huge numbers of variants must be created for a check, later on a reduction of items have to occur. This closely resembles problems with stack overflow in digital computers.
- *The inference process must be constantly directed (focused) toward a desired conclusion.* This is an especially sensitive issue in such a molecular model of computations because the processes here are nondeterministic, and cases are allowed in the Random PROLOG Processor only when certain properties of future solutions are a priori given — not only the direct specifications, for example, if the form of the solution is not known in advance, such as production arrangement in a dynamic programming problem.

The two problems, that is *stabilization* and *focusing*, are inseparable. This has been demonstrated before in the computational process given in Figure 3-35. Usually, an applied *stabilization* or *focusing* remedy helps in both cases.

Stabilizing and controlling measures in the Random PROLOG processor are currently defined on three levels, for CS^{0} (i.e., only for *information molecules* carrying facts, rules, and goals). Cases with $CS^{n>1}$ are left for later research, as too complicated.

Before a detailed discussion can begin, we should briefly list some of the most basic and useful stabilization and focusing measures:

1. Information molecules with structure.

There should be a specific structure suitable for *stabilization* and *focusing* activity. In Expert systems (14) the concept of *time tag* is used to avoid so-called "refraction" (repeated inference with the same *information molecule*, leading to combinatorial explosion). In the Random PROLOG Processor we have proposed a more powerful concept, that is, the concept of *information molecules* with a *heap*[39] to memorize and later on to accept or reject some candidate "partners" if rendezvous happen.

2. Control Information molecules.

There should be a system of *control information molecules* in a given *computational space* CS or subspaces to stabilize the number of *information molecules* of a certain type inside a certain population range. A good example

[39] Please remember that in the discussed model of computations, information is also itself a processor.

from real life is mutual stabilization of the population of rabbits and wolves on any island.

> It can be claimed that such a system is an analog of the operating system in a digital computer—at least some operating system functions, for example, Watchdog procedures are implemented—but with different technology. We (305) proposed the concept of a wide family of control *information molecules* for organization and management purposes including, for example, transportation of some of them to specific areas.

3. **User implemented control and stabilization functions.**

In almost all nondeterministic programs, there are certain strategies for support or restriction of conclusions, and also parent *information molecules*, which programmers can implement themselves.

> A good example is the immediate retraction of parent *information molecules* carrying a certain fact, for example, when a successor *information molecule* is born, which from now on carries an updated fact in *computational space*.

Now let us look closer at these methods.

INFORMATION MOLECULES WITH STRUCTURE.

During various simulation experiments (56) it has been found that for stability and focusing of computations every *information molecule* must have its own memory (heap), for example, to remember the previous partners in the inference. The same rule and fact should not go into trivial loop inferences with the same partners in a short time period of evolution. Furthermore, such a heap can be also used for other purposes. In the RPP implementation designed by the author and his colleagues, a *heap* for a maximum of ten clauses has been found sufficient.

Some proposed built-in predicates to service heap of information molecules

`remember_partner();` clause of partner recently met in *computational space* is pushed to the top of the *heap*. If later the consecutive clause has to be pushed onto the *heap*, and the *heap* is full (ten clauses have been remembered so far) then the bottom clause is removed. Every time a new *information molecule* is born the heap is cleaned to NIL.

`known_fact(0/1);` to see if a *heap* of *information molecules* contains a clause matching the clause of the present partner. Value `0/1` can be later used for logical computations, for example to force *fail* (inconsistency) or to continue with another action.

CONTROL INFORMATION MOLECULES.

Good methodology in the design of the inference/computational process for the RPP includes a definition of a proper system of *information molecules* for the kernel of the inference process (inference itself), and a system of control *information molecules* to supervise this inference. The simplest control *information molecule* is just a "killer" of redundant ones.

The typical pattern for so-called "killer" *information molecules* used to remove unnecessary clauses from *CS* has the form:

```
retract(<clause>) :- <clauses defined to check if given
                     information molecules matches condition>,
                     <additional computations to confirm or
                     drop case, if necessary>.
```

An example of how such a "killer" *information molecule* can be useful is given in the next section with the process of finding maximum or minimum value in a set.

For control purposes, it is required to somehow label the *information molecules*. The labeling action simply adds to the clause body of the *information molecules* a certain `<marker clause>`, which later on can be checked and will trigger (or not) certain actions of this or other control *information molecules*, when rendezvous happen again.

Some proposed built-in predicates used by control *information molecules* for marking

```
mark(<marker>);           adds marker clause to the
                          body of the information
                          molecule
remove_mark(<marker>);    removes marker clause from
                          the body of the information
                          molecule
```

CONTROL AND STABILIZATION FUNCTIONS TO BE IMPLEMENTED BY THE USER.

While designing a given *information molecule* for a specific function in the *CS*, the programmer must specify the following:

- Computational (logic) functions, which *information molecule* will performs. Its behavior regarding other *information molecules* with which it eventually rendezvous. This can be either simple retraction (killing) of *information molecules* if certain conditions are met, or modification. For implementing modification, it is sufficient to combine functions to `retract(<information molecules>)` and immediately after this to `assert(<modified information molecules>)`.
- Its own behavior must be specified in the assumed time span. This is especially useful when it is somehow necessary to use the analog of

"aging and expiring *information molecules*". Such an *information molecule* automatically vanishes after a certain, predefined time.

Another possibility is when an *information molecule* should automatically vanish after performing some specified actions. A good example is computing 3-CNF feasibility, when the *information molecule* must vanish (becomes useless from a logic point of view) after giving birth to two alternatives: *True* and *False* for certain variables (see the next section for an example).

Another example of the behavior of an *information molecule* that is targeted to stabilize the computational process, is when the *information molecule* "finds itself *useless*" or "out of abstract resources, for example, *energy, money*, and so forth, which causes its automatic death. An example of the computational process when this approach has been used is the evolutionary design of the hardware architecture of a computer graphics workstation (305).

To service the user's defined control and stabilization functions we propose some built-in predicates:

`self_destroy(<condition>);`	to destroy *information molecules* if a condition is met
`retract(<clause>);`	to retract an *information molecule* identified by its clauses
`assert(<clause>);`	to create new *information molecules* with given clauses

Now several examples are given of computational processes of level CS^1 in the Random PROLOG Processor.

Examples of RPP Programing and Simulations

Now is the time to present several examples of PROLOG processor written for the Random PROLOG Processor, to discuss what they can calculate or simulate, and to show behavior (dynamics) of computations and inferences as the process goes on.

CALCULATIONS OF RANDOM TIME.

An interesting problem to ponder is whether efficient information on internal time, that is *random time*[40], can exist in such a quasi-chaotic processor, for example, to be used by other, parallel processes.

[40] Suppose that in the morning rush you forgot your watch. Obviously, from time to time (randomly, at rendezvous) you ask somebody what time it is, or you look for a clock to update your knowledge about the present time.

This is also a test for frequency of rendezvous of any two given *information molecules* in a given *computational space* or *subspace CS*.

To test it, let us suppose that in the cube of the RPP there are two random traveling molecules. The first one "keeps" information (subjective!) on present time; the other advances (updates) time +1 after a rendezvous.

This is something like a logical description of a random clock. The first clause (fact) states that time is 0 (at the beginning). The second clause (rule) states that "if (your knowledge about present time is X) then compute (Y = X + 1), retract molecule `time(X)` and assert molecule `time(Y)`." The proper program for the RPP has the form:

```
time(0).
assert(time(Y).),retract(time(X).):-time(X),sum(Y,X,1).
```

Here one parent molecule defining current time should be destroyed, and a child molecule with a new time value should be inserted into the space of the RPP.

Let us see the importance of this idea:

- It is a run-time control of how many times the two well-defined molecules rendezvous in a given time period.
- It is a logical method to start and stop other parallel inferences in the function of random time. A given process may be made sensitive to a *time molecule* carrying a predefined value. This way a programmer can control the behavior of the random logical process from the logical level of the program.

We may have as many random clocks in the RPP as we want, with different kinds of precision and time units. Precision is defined by the number of rules advancing the time value randomly. More molecules means the rendezvous takes place more frequently (on average) for time advance.

In the example that follows we have two random clocks with different precision: in the first clock the time unit is 1, and there are five rules for `time 1`, and in the second clock the time unit is 10, and there is one rule for `time 2`.

The program code for the RPP to implement such clocks have the form:

```
time1(0).
assert(time1(Y).),retract(time1(X).) :- time1(X),sum(Y,X,1).
assert(time1(Y).),retract(time1(X).) :- time1(X),sum(Y,X,1).
assert(time1(Y).),retract(time1(X).) :- time1(X),sum(Y,X,1).
assert(time1(Y).),retract(time1(X).) :- time1(X),sum(Y,X,1).
assert(time1(Y).),retract(time1(X).) :- time1(X),sum(Y,X,1).
time2(0).
assert(time2(Y).),retract(time2(X).) :- time2(X),sum(Y,X,10).
```

Calculation of random time in the RPP is also an interesting example of the inferring process, where the number of molecules is stable over the whole period. For every created molecule, one is destroyed. In this example, annihilating the parent molecule is permitted.

FINDING MINIMUM/MAXIMUM VALUE IN THE SET

The problem of finding the minimum (or maximum) value in the set can be easily translated into a parallel evolutionary program suitable for the RPP, where the "fitter" value (smaller or bigger, respectively) retracts any weaker value when they rendezvous.

J. Blazewicz (311) discusses a mirrored problem of finding the maximum value in a set of $n = 2^k$ integers for some integer k in a multiprocessor computer. The algorithm is given in the form:

```
for  r:= k−1  downto 0
  begin
    par[2^r ≤ j ≤ 2^(r+1)] a_j := {max a_2j, a_2j+1}
end
```

where **par**[$1 \leq i \leq z$] s_i means that instruction s_i has to be executed in parallel for the given scope of i. Execution time is $O(log\ n)$ for $n/2$ processors.

If at the beginning every processor there gets $log\ n$ numbers to be checked for the maximum in a sequential way, then the execution time is still $O(log\ n)$, but only $\lceil n/log\ n \rceil$ processors are necessary.

This algorithm can be used as a reference point for our results, because it actually does in fact the binary comparing and mutually reducing in the set of integers.

In the RPP we can introduce smarter algorithms based on the idea of reproducing "killer" *information molecules* during the evolution of computations. In the above algorithm a given integer can be used to eliminate the maximum $log\ n$ of other integers.

In the RPP, a given integer, after rendezvous with a rule, produces killer *information molecules*. Therefore, even if eliminated later on by other killer *information molecules*, its child, the killer *information molecule* exists to work and eliminate other *information molecules* carrying bigger integers.

Observe how short the program is for the RPP to calculate such a minimum (just one *information molecule* for one rule + data *information molecules* carrying integers):

```
/* data for program, for example, 200 integers */
   val(a1).
   ...
   val(a200).
/* Rule representing program */
   retract(val(Y).) := val(X),val(Y),greater(Y,X).
```

Such extremely short programs are characteristic for nondeterministic systems, which is also confirmed by other authors (31).

Let us briefly discuss what happens with such a solution of *information molecules* during the evolution of computations. Let us suppose now that an example of a rendezvous takes place, and an inference molecule pointed to by ⊢ is produced:

```
val(49).
retract(val(Y).)    :- val(X), val(Y), greater(Y,X).       ⊢
---------------------------------------------------------------
retract(val(Y).)    :- val(Y), greater(Y,49).              (*)
```

Such an inferred molecule will be a killer later on for all rendezvous molecules carrying values greater than 49.

Thus, in the early stages of the evolution process, the number of killers grow very fast, but it is well-balanced by a decrease in the global amount of `val()` *information molecules*.

After some time only minimum a_n and a set of jobless rules of the form (*) are left. At this moment the process of evolution is stabilized; no more inferences can be done. Figure 3-37 shows (on the basis of an experiment) how the number of *information molecules* decreases.

However, such a nondeterministic algorithm can face "problems" with a final conclusion, that is, the problem to stop (halt) with just one highest or lowest value. If the main computational space is of a size that probability of rendezvous is small, it can happen that the last few *information molecules* remain with a low probability of being found and retracted.

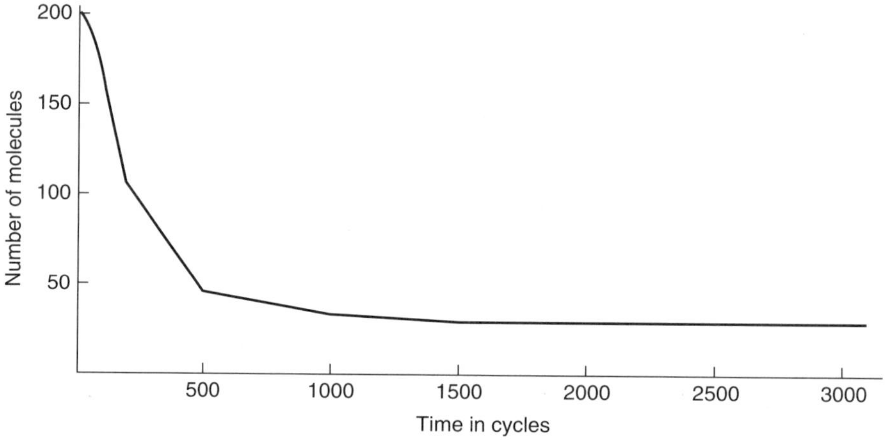

Figure 3-37. The number of *information molecules* during a computational process of finding min/max value. There are 200 facts and 1 rule at the beginning.

The remedy for this is to structure the computational space in such a way that after a certain time, such remaining *information molecules* should start to gradually migrate to any small *sub-space* or one side of the *computational space*, where the rendezvous probability is be much higher, and the process concludes with just one *information molecule* carrying the highest or lowest value.

Another problem is that at the end of the process mentioned earlier, the *computational space* is "overcrowded" with useless "killer" *information molecules*.

A remedy for this was proposed while discussing *stabilizing* and *focusing* remedies. It is sufficient to equip every newborn "killer" *information molecule* with the property that it expires "if no more food or work"—except for the first, *information molecule* of program.

3-CNF FEASIBILITY.

This problem was introduced in Section 3.4.2.1 while discussing theoretical advantages of the Nondeterministic Turing Machine.

It is well known that feasibility of logical expressions is one of the key problems in the complexity of algorithms. This is a difficult problem for computations (from a time and memory consumption point of view) because in every logical expression tested for feasibility, any variable can exist as: *still free variable, or* 1 (True), *or* 0 (False). This implies that for the expression with n variables, the 3^n possible nodes in the search tree should be produced (and later on remembered in the memory or pruned).

Let us check how the RPP deals with this.

Algorithm for 3-CNF ((31) discussed in Section 3.4.2.1) has the form:

```
repeat while there is still a clause Cᵢ = f(x,y,z) that
                                               is not satisfied
    x ←   choice[T, F]
    y ←   choice[T, F]
    z ←   choice[T, F]
  if Cᵢ = F  then FAIL
end repeat
if all clauses are satisfied  then SUCCESS  stop;
```

Please observe that in the preceding algorithm FAIL means that a given process is "killed," that is, no longer produces successors.

It is much easier to find a satisfying substitution if a logical formula is satisfiable than to prove that it is unsatisfiable.

In the first case any message (output) can be generated to inform (the output) if any process finds a satisfying substitution.

If a formula is unsatisfiable, then one symptom of this is that all processes eventually FAILs. The preceding observations are important because this symptom is be completely obvious in our RPP.

The greatest problem here is the combinatorial explosion of processes. Therefore, in the program below for the RPP, three strategies to restrict clauses are used.

1. First, it is obvious that if any variables binding to 1 or 0 imply that, for example, expression $E(q_1, q_2, q_3, q_4) =$ False, even if free variables still exist, then a corresponding *information molecule* should not be produced. This strategy can be implemented simply by evaluating the resultant logical expressions.
2. Secondly, we can see that if for any variable q_i the given parent molecule (rule) produces two child ones with $\{q_i/0\}$ and another with $\{q_i/1\}$, then such a parent rule can be retracted, as it is no longer necessary for the global inference process. To implement this strategy it is necessary to equip the *information molecule* with a memory (heap).
3. Thirdly, a rule should not infer again with the same fact (the stack is used again to avoid *refraction*).

For this purpose in the RPP program there are three stabilizing and control predicates:

```
remember partner;
false_if_known_fact;
self_destroy(if_double_checked);
```

Now let us analyze an example of how the RPP can solve a problem of logical feasibility of expressions. Suppose that the typical (31) logical expression has the 3-CNF form:

$$E(q_1, q_2, q_3, q_4) = (q_1 \vee \neg q_2 \vee \neg q_3) \wedge (q_1 \vee q_2 \vee q_4) \wedge (q_3 \vee \neg q_4) \wedge (\neg q_1)$$

Program for the Random PROLOG Processor[41]

```
/* facts which define proposed alternative substitutions of
      1/0 for variables q1, q2, q3, q4 */
   p(q1,1).
   p(q1,0).
   p(q2,1).
   p(q2,0).
   p(q3,1).
   p(q3,0).
   p(q4,1).
   p(q4,0).
/* rule */
```

[41] Symbol $\neg$ is replaced by $\sim$ in PROLOG program.

```
assert(answer(Q1,Q2,Q3,Q4).) :-
     p(q1,Q1),      unit clauses where proposals
     p(q2,Q2),      of bindings Qi to 1 or 0 are              (1)
     p(q3,Q3),      incorporated
     p(q4,Q4),
     remember_partner,
     known_fact(X),
     equal(X,0),
     self_destroy(in heap remembered partners p(XX,0),
     or(Q1,~(Q2),~(Q3)),     E(q1, q2, q3, q4)      p(XX,1)),
     or(Q1,Q2,Q4),           logical expression
     or(Q3,~(Q2)),           denoted as PROLOG
     or(~(Q1)).              clauses
```

Let us analyze the basic inference as described by the above PROLOG like program. Rules in form (1) rendezvous with facts, for example, `p(q1,1)`. In the program for the RPP more than one copy of the same fact can be used to speed up the inference process. As a result, after the rendezvous, the temporary working form of (1) is be produced with binding $\{Q1/1\}$ for further evaluation:

```
assert(answer(1,Q2,Q3,Q4).) :-
          p(q2,Q2),
          p(q3,Q3),
          p(q4,Q4),
          remember_partner,
          known_fact(X),
          equal(X,0),
          self_destroy(in heap remembered partners p(XX,0),
                                                   p(XX,1),
          or(1,~(Q2),~(Q3)),      this subformula is
          or(1,Q2,Q4),            False
          or(Q3,~(Q2)),
          or(~(1)).
```

After this inference the child is not produced because the formula

$$\text{or}(\mathbf{1}, \sim(Q2), \sim(Q3)),\ \text{or}(\mathbf{1}, Q2, Q4),\ \text{or}(Q3, \sim(Q2)),\ \text{or}(\sim(\mathbf{1})) = \text{False}.$$

There is only one background result that the given parent molecule (rule) remembers on its heap: the `p(q1,1)`. Please observe that the parent *information molecule* does not “die” after giving birth to a conclusion; thus, a combinatorial explosion can be sparked because the same parent can produce the same

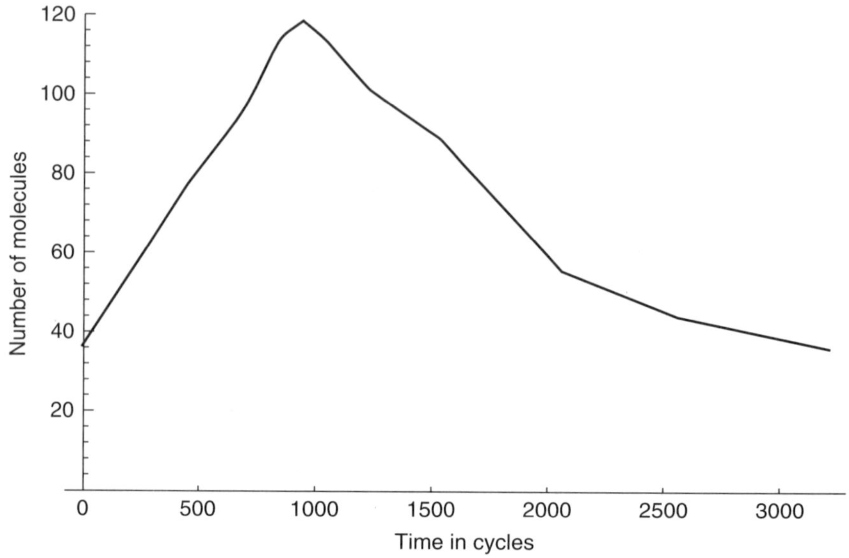

Figure 3-38. The number of *information molecules* during the computational process for the 3-CNF feasibility problem. Every fact has three copies. The formula is not feasible and has the form: $(q_1 \vee \neg q_2 \vee \neg q_3) \wedge (q_1 \vee q_5 \vee \neg q_6) \wedge q_4 \vee \neg q_4$ After an average of 3140 cycles, the process reduces itself to 36 facts only.

conclusion *information molecules* again and again. To avoid this, a parent remembers its partners, and as result, it does not generate children with the same variable bindings again. Moreover, if two children *information molecules* are generated with both 0 and 1 setting for the same variable, the parent *information molecule* will self-destroy. The justification is that it has generated two "alternative offsets" and is no longer necessary from combinatorial point of view.

In Figure 3-38 an example is given of how the number of *information molecules* grows fast at first and later slows down for a unfeasible expression with six variables.

If the example of a logical expression is feasible (see below), a built-in predicate is executed and removed from the formula. Also logical or expressions are True and are removed.

```
assert(answer(s1,s2,s3,s4).) :-
                remember partner,
                false_if_know_fact,
                know_fact(X),
                equal(X,0),
```

```
or(s1,~(s2),~(s3)),
or(s1,s2,s4),
or(s3,~(s2)),
or(~(s1)).
```

logical subformula is True

Finally, this logical expression simplifies to

```
assert(answer(s1,s2,s3,s4).):-.
```

Now `assert(...)` can be fired and produces molecule (fact):
`answer(s1,s2,s3,s4)`, where (`s1`, ..., `s4`) denote satisfying substitutions.

If a logical formula is not feasible, then (with the strategies mentioned before) after a given time period only molecules of facts are left in the RPP, while molecules carrying rules undergo self-destruction.

The problem is how to get the message that our global process is in such a stable holding state. As a closing comment to Figure 3-38, it can be mentioned that the RPP is programmed for feasibility computations for a formula[42] with 6 variables of the form:

$$(q_1 \vee \neg q_2 \vee \neg q_3) \wedge (q_1 \vee q_2 \vee \neg q_6) \wedge (\neg q_2 \vee q_3 \vee q_4) \wedge (\neg q_1 \vee q_5 \vee \neg q_6)$$

The RPP "was producing" the first *information molecule*

```
answer(s1,s2,s3,s4).
```

surprisingly quickly, after an average of 322 cycles of simulations only!, where every cycle is considered as resulting with new moves (displacements) of all *information molecules*, and only a single resulting inference (per molecule), if successful rendezvous and unification have happened.

Simulating feasibility calculations in the RPP in a computer, even a multiprocessor, start to be difficult for unfeasible logical formulas with more than 8 variables because the number of *information molecules* can go over 1000. Therefore, such computations most probably are more reasonable in some chemical machine based on the CHAM idea (304), or in a specially designed computer.

EXAMPLE OF A DYNAMIC PROGRAMMING PROBLEM.

Now let us analyze a case, that is, how the RPP can solve problems such as those in dynamic programming. The data for the experiment has been taken from Lauriere (31).

[42] This formula is feasible.

The PROLOG program for the RPP has the form:

```
/* facts describing variants of production in
  January, February, and  March */
  prod(jan,10,0).  prod(feb,10,0).  prod(mar,10,0).          (1)
  prod(jan,12,1).  prod(feb,14,1).  prod(mar,12,1).
  prod(jan,15,2).  prod(feb,16,2).  prod(mar,17,2).
  prod(jan,20,3).  prod(feb,19,3).  prod(mar,19,3).
                   prod(feb,23,4).
/* rule to define production schedules for a given time
   period */
   assert(cost(Xw,Y1,Y2,Y3).) :-                            (2)
     prod(jan,X1,Y1),
     prod(feb,Y2,Y2),
     prod(mar,Y3,Y3),                                       (3)
     sum(Ya1,Y1,Y2), not(greater(Ya1,4)),                   (4)
     sum(Ya2,Y1,Y3), not(greater(Ya2,4)),
     sum(Ya3,Y2,Y3), not(greater(Ya3,4)),
     sum(Y,Y1,Y2), sum(Yw,Y,Y3), equa_um(Yw,4),             (5)
                              sum(X,X1,X2), sum(Xw,X,X3).
/* the pattern for a ''killer molecule'' to retract
   production schedules that have a higher cost for the
   same time period */
   retract(cost(Y,A,B,C).) :-                               (6)
     cost(X,A,B,C), cost(Y,A,B,C), greater(Y,X).
/* pattern for a ''killer molecule'' to retract multiple
   copies of the same solution  */
   retract(cost(Y,A,B,C).) :-                               (7)
     cost(X,A,B,C), cost(Y,A,B,C), equal_num(Y,X).
```

```
Fact (1) should be decoded as follows:
   production(<month=January>,<production cost=10>,<how many
                                       pieces=0>).
```

Rule (2) should be decoded as follows. In line (3) there are patterns for binding the different productions in January, February, and March. In line (4) there is something like a condition: if the sum of production in any two months is greater than 4, then a False clause appears — which later interrupts any inference.

Remember that during two rendezvous, the proposed production may be greater than 4 – such a case should not produce a new molecule.

In line (5) final production and cost are calculated. Rules (6) and (7) are to stabilize the number of molecules. The idea is the same as in the previous example, where a minimum integer value was sought.

For this example a solution `cost(41,1,2,1).` has been found after around 35 molecules were produced (starting with 16 molecules) after a period of about 4112 cycles of the RPP.

Summary of Differences between the Standard PROLOG Approach and the Random PROLOG Processor

At the end of this discussion, let us state what distinguishes the just-discussed Random PROLOG Processor (RPP) from other PROLOGs.

> *The fundamental difference is that the RPP is "anchored" to quite a different model of execution (computation), compared to the digital computer, which is based on the Deterministic Turing Machine.*

Moreover, every programming system to claim optimality must refer in a direct or at least implied way to the most fundamental model of execution and to an intermediate implementation methodology; otherwise it is quite inefficient (or an emulator).

A program in standard PROLOG must be translated into a process of rewriting binary strings of the form . . .01110110. . . located in the computer memory.

Surprisingly, however, the program for the Random PROLOG Processor also must be translated into dynamics of three-dimensional structures constructed with two primitives only, that is, *information molecules* and *membranes*.

While writing programs for both systems we need to have these differences in mind. Let us look at what consequences result from these fundamental differences.

1. The dialect of the RPP is in general the same; however, it is not necessary to be restricted in the RPP to expressions having a pattern of Horn clauses only. It is expected that further progress with the RPP introduces more significant syntax differences.
2. While thinking about execution of standard PROLOG, it is useful and natural to consider it in terms of a growing and changing *tree of variants*, hidden in the description of the user's program. In principle this tree is built by the behavior (run) of the user's PROLOG program, under supervision of the operating system. With the Random PROLOG Processor we have to think in terms of an evolving, parallel inference process nested in a certain computational space. For a description, it is better to use here the *phase space* or *state space*, as discussed in Section 3.4.3; however, some forms of graphs can be also used, for example, Feynman diagrams.

   There is in principle no need for any Operating System in the RPP; however, control *information molecules* are necessary because the inference process could eventually face a combinatorial explosion.
3. Standard PROLOG is potentially nondeterministic in the sense that from a given point of inference, several alternative offsets can usually be derived. However, the deterministic nature of digital computers "cut this off on implementation level," that is, inferences when repeated are done in the same way, giving the same conclusions.

In the Random PROLOG Processor, nondeterminism is further strengthened compared to standard PROLOG because the model of execution is based on the nondeterminism of the quasi-Brownian behavior of *information molecules*. Thus, even simulations of the RPP on digital computers are nondeterministic if random generators used for simulations are properly set.

4. Finally, it looks like the Random PROLOG Processor is attracted by quite different applications than standard PROLOG is covering now. These applications are so potentially lucrative (see Section 5 of the book) that the Random PROLOG Processor can start to diversify more and more from his "natural father"—the PROLOG.

We now review some other models of computation similar to the RPP. This discussion should provide a more comprehensive *acceptance* of the RPP idea by the reader.

3.4.5. Review of Computational Models Similar to the RPP in Concept

The Random PROLOG Processor as a model of computations is not the only such model available in the research literature. There are several similar models of computations;[43] the most important are these two:

- The Chemical Abstract Machine (CHAM) of G. Berry and G. Boudol (304)
- The DNA computer of Adleman (5)

So what is the difference between the Random PROLOG Processor model of computations described in this book and the models mentioned earlier, since they all apply the four fundamental metaphors (marked with italics):

1. Information exists in the form of *molecules*.
2. Computations are implemented by *reactions*.
3. Computational space is structured with *membranes*.
4. Computations are *nondeterministic and quasi-chaotic*.

When these models appeared, the scientific world got very excited with the idea of a hot, new computational technology (after analog and digital technology) for building a computer, based on chemical reactions in liquids.

[43] There are many individual and "group" webpages rich with literature on this topic. Among others, we could suggest these:

"Artificial Chemistry Research" at *http://ls11-www.informatik.uni-dortmund.de/people/dittrich/alife/prj-binsys-rel.html* maintained by Peter Dittrich at the University of Dortmund, Department of Computer Science, Germany

"A Bibliography of Molecular Computation and Splicing Systems" webpage at *http://www.wi.leidenuniv.nl/~pier/dna.html* Maintained by Frisco Pierluigi at the Theoretical Computer Science Department at Leiden University, The Netherlands.

If we look at Section 5.1 of the book where the relationship between *Life* and computational processes for *intelligence* are discussed, we can make the somewhat obvious statement:

> *every computational process is restricted to specific problems and has computational limits*

"Purely chemical computers", such as those related to the Chemical Abstract Machine, do not allow such advanced computations, as those using DNA will, because of the problem of constructing (defining) and processing complex data structures. Thus, perhaps at the advent of *collective intelligence* on Earth, the "purely chemical computers" were introduced and successfully used, but later on, for the requirements of *Life*, "all computations" were moved to the DNA platform.

Notice that the "live beings" on earth are all of a chemical nature, but at the same time to transmit information for a longer distance, for example from brain to hand, beings use electrical signals, not molecules.

Also, our fascination with the "very deterministic" digital computer can be explained by the fact that this device "introduces the needed balance" into our inborn chaotic inference processes, providing us with a way to "keep them (the inference processes) as a whole on the required and safe quasi-chaotic level."

Measuring *collective intelligence* requires a computational model which covers the spectrum of all known cases, for example inferring colonies of simple bacteria, social insects, and human social structures.

Thus, such a model must be abstract from any technological details such as "chemical reactions" or "transformations of DNA" and must allow construction of any inference pattern, according to the nature of the beings and the specifications of their environment.

For this reason, the Random PROLOG Processor has been developed as a formal model, and it seems that the goal of universality has been achieved, with the preceding requirements fulfilled through our definition of the N-element inference.

An unexpected result of this approach is that this model is also abstract from the concept of *Life*, which has extended the validity of this model into the domain of digital computer systems.

We do not intend to build the Random PROLOG Processor with any present or future technology because at this point it is only a tool for analysis.

Thus, there also exists no conflict between the Random PROLOG Processor and computational *collective intelligence* on the one hand, and today's digital computers on the other.

Moreover, digital computers are required here, but as very robust multiprocessor systems able to simulate social structures with the Random PROLOG Processor.

Let us start our review with the most abstract approach, that is, with the Chemical Abstract Machine, abbreviated by its originators as CHAM.

3.4.5.1. The Chemical Abstract Machine The literature on CHAM is relative rich, including many easily available papers: (304, 312–314), and so forth.

In general, the CHAM model of computations is built on the basis of a *chemical* metaphor, which was first proposed by Banâtre and Le Métayer (229) to illustrate an implementation possibility of their Gamma (Γ) formalism of parallel programming.

In this concept, programs are executed through transformations of multisets — thus before presenting CHAM, let us look into their concept of GAMMA (228,229).

The *multiset M* is the same as a set, except that it may contain multiple occurrences of the same element. Notation $M = \{\ldots\}$ is also used to represent multisets, for example, a multiset of pairs $M = \{(4, 8), (2, 5), (3, 9), (1, 13), (5, 9)\}$. Multisets are defined as intrinsically unordered.

The basic control structure (also called a multiset transformer) associated with the multiset is the Γ operator, which is in general defined according to the following pattern:

$$\begin{aligned}
&\Gamma\left(\left(R_1, A_1\right), \ldots, \left(R_m, A_m\right)\right)(M) = \\
&\quad if \quad \forall i \in [1, m], \forall x_1, \ldots x_n \in M, \neg R_i\left(x_1, \ldots x_n\right) \\
&\quad then \quad M \\
&\quad else \quad let\ x_1, \ldots x_n \in M\,[1, m]\, such\ that \quad R_i\left(x_1, \ldots x_n\right) \quad in \\
&\quad \Gamma\left(\left(R_1, A_1\right), \ldots, \left(R_{m1}, A_m\right)\right)\left(M - \{x_1, \ldots x_n\}\right) + A_i\left(x_1, \ldots x_n\right)
\end{aligned}$$

In this definition (R_m, A_m) are pairs of closed functions (without global variables), which are specifying reactions in such a way that R gives the conditions for a reaction, and A specifies the result of this reaction over the multiset M.

Please keep in mind that usually more than one reaction can take place at the same time in nondeterministic order in the given multiset M.

In the first section the earlier specification is saying that if no conditions are fulfilled for any reaction (i.e., $\neg R_i$), then M will stay unchanged. Otherwise, reactants $\{x_1, \ldots x_n\}$ necessary for one or more reaction(s) R_i will "be taken", and product(s) $A_i\,(x_1, \ldots x_n)$ of a reaction emerge in M, i.e., $(M - \{x_1, \ldots x_n\}) + A_i\,(x_1, \ldots x_n)$.

If one or several reaction conditions hold for several subsets at the same time, the choice, which is made among them, is not deterministic.

If the reaction condition holds for several disjoint subsets, the reactions can be carried out independently and simultaneously.

Now, let us look for a very simple example. Suppose that we have to define Γ to transform given multiset M to have at the end of computations only *prime numbers* there. Only one reaction R is sufficient for this problem, with the condition that "x is a multiple of y." In such a case (if the condition is fulfilled), the x is retracted. The full specification has the form:

Example of GAMMA programming and run of computations:

prime numbers(N) = Γ ((R,A))
({2,...,N}) where
R(x,y) = multiple(x,y)
A(x,y) ={y}

One among the many possible paths of reactions leading to the solution of this problem is given in Figure 3-39. Lines between numbers mark where in the multiset reactions take place in this specific path of reaction. The leftmost circle is an initial state of M, and the rightmost is the final one where no more reactions can take place.

Remarks on GAMMA:

- We can say that a Γ computation can be considered as a set of transformations or reactions that consume elements of the multiset and produce new ones, according to the rules that constitute the program. Because reactions on disjoint subsets can take place in any order or even simultaneously, the Γ model of computations is inherently parallel. It is also nondeterministic, as has been mentioned before.
- Berry and Boudol (304) say that Petri-nets are a well-known example of the multiset transformation style of programming. Markings are multisets of places, and each transition of the net can be seen as a reaction rule to transform the markings.

However, there are also disadvantages of Γ computations:

- With a GAMMA program it is difficult to express computations as a collection of local operations.
- It is also difficult to program problems where we have to rely on control decisions involving the whole state of computations.

Now, let us look at the concept of the Chemical Abstract Machine (CHAM).

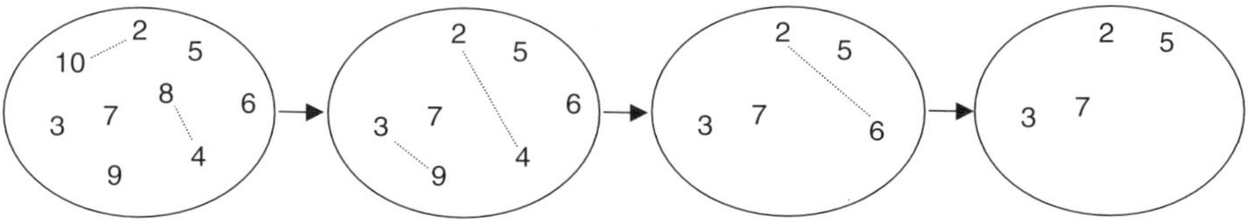

Figure 3-39. Example of Gamma programming.

Boudol (312) says that the CHAM concept has been efficiently demonstrated as a modeling tool for different areas — from graph reduction to concurrent language definition and implementation.

It has also been shown (304) that CHAM formalism has the power of classical process calculi and has the behavior of concurrent generalizations of lambda calculus.

CHAM BASICS.

In general the Chemical Abstract Machine can be specified by defining the following objects:

molecules: *m, m'*,... and

solutions: *S, S'*,... of molecules.

Molecules constitute the basic elements of a CHAM, whereas solutions are multisets of molecules that can be interpreted as describing the transition states of a CHAM during the computational process.

Different authors provide different detailed descriptions of CHAM and its elements due to their requirements, that is, what they use the CHAM concept for.

A typical definition of molecules (304) could have the form in BNF notation: if p, a are molecules, then

<molecule> $::= 0|\alpha\cdot p|(p|p)|p\backslash a$ <solution in membrane> | $p \lhd S$

where "0" is inaction (e.g., remainder of molecule after reaction);

"α" is called valence and expresses ability to react with another molecule;

"|" denotes parallel (e.g., aggregate of two molecules);

"\" denotes restriction;

"$\lhd$" denotes airlock.

Molecules can be defined as terms of a syntactic algebra derived from a set of constants and a set of operations specific to a given application of CHAM.

Solutions S, S′, . . . are finite multisets of molecules, each denoted as a comma-separated list of molecules:

$$m_1, m_2, \ldots, m_n$$

Solution can be built from other solutions by combining them through the multiset union operator $\uplus$. For example, let there be given solutions S and S':

$$S = m_1, \ldots, m_n \quad \textit{and} \quad S' = m'_1, \ldots, m'_k$$

$$\text{then} \quad S \uplus S' \quad \text{is another solution, and}$$

$$S \uplus S' = m_1, \ldots, m_n, m'_1, \ldots, m'_k$$

Any subsolution can be transformed into a single molecule with respect to other solutions by means of an encapsulation construct $\{|, \ldots, |\}$ called a membrane, e.g.,

$$m_1, \ldots, m_n, m'_1, \ldots, m'_k$$

after encapsulation with the use of the membrane

$$m_1, \ldots, m_n, \left|m'_1, \ldots, m'_k\right|$$

a new molecule has been created $\left|m'_1, \ldots, m'_k\right|$

What is important is that the membrane concept allows the effects of transformations to be localized within that membrane. In other words, the solutions inside a membrane can freely evolve independently of other solutions.

Another important thing is that membranes can be defined as semi-permeable, allowing certain molecules to enter and leave the membrane.

A reversible operator called an airlock is used to selectively extract molecules from a solution and place the rest of that solution within a membrane. We can also say that the airlock is acting as a membrane constructor.

The reversibility of the airlock allows molecules to be *reabsorbed* into the original solution.

$$\{|m, m_1, m_2, \ldots, m_k|\} \xrightarrow{airlock} \left\{\left|m \triangleleft \{|m_1, m_2, \ldots, m_k|\}\right|\right\} \quad \text{the airlock builds}$$

a new molecule $m \triangleleft S$ out of molecule m and solution S

$$\left\{\left|m \triangleleft \{|m_1, m_2, \ldots, m_k|\}\right\}\right| \xrightarrow{airlock} \{|m, m_1, m_2 \ldots, m_k|\} \quad \text{the inverted airlock}$$

The second important element in the CHAM specifications are transformation rules $T, T', \ldots$ which define transformation relations $S \rightarrow S'$ describing the way solutions evolve; in other words, how states of CHAM change.

In CHAM we can distinguish two major types of rules:

- *General laws* (valid for all CHAMs)
- *Specific rules* (depending on the particular implementation)

The specific rules must be elementary rewriting rules that do not involve any premises. In contrast, the general laws are permitted premises.

<u>*CHAM General Laws*</u>

CHAMs obey four general laws:

The Reaction Law — Specification of the Reaction Law is the same as the definition of Γ in GAMMA. An instance of the right-hand side of a rule can replace the corresponding instance of its left-hand side in the solution.

let (R_i, A_i) be a reaction with condition R and result A
if molecules $\mathrm{m}_1, \ldots m_n \in S\,[1, n]$ are such that $R_i\,(m_1, \ldots m_n)$,
then a new solution is created on the basis of S such that
$S' = (S - \{m_1, \ldots m_n\}) + A_i\,(m_1, \ldots m_n)$

The Chemical Law—This law states that reactions can be performed freely within any solution, which has the form:

$$\frac{S \rightarrow S'}{S \uplus S'' \rightarrow S' \uplus S''}$$

In other words, we can say that if subsolution S evolves into S', the supersolution in which it is contained also evolves.

A solution is said to be *inert* if no reaction rule can be applied to it.

The Membrane law—A subsolution can evolve freely within any context C,[44] which has the form:

$$\frac{S \rightarrow S'}{\{|C\,[S]|\} \rightarrow \{|C\,[S']|\}}$$

The Airlock law—A molecule can always be extracted from and reabsorbed into a solution at the same time, and its identity as an individual molecule is preserved. This has the form:

$$m \uplus S \leftrightarrow m \triangleleft \{|S|\}$$

CHAM Specific Rules

At any given point, a CHAM can apply as many rules as possible to a solution, provided that their premises do not conflict—that is, no molecule is involved in more than one rule. In this way it is possible to model parallel behaviors of different real processes by performing parallel transformations.

When more than one rule can apply to the same molecule or set of molecules, then we have nondeterminism, in which case the CHAM makes a nondeterministic choice as to which transformation to perform.

Berry and Boudol in their original works (304,312) discuss three specific kinds of rules that appeal to our intuition about chemical reactions:

1. heating rules, denoted as (*dec* means decomposition)
$$p|q \xrightarrow{dec} p, q$$
2. cooling rules, (*reb* means rebuild)
$$p, q \xrightarrow{reb} p|q$$

[44] We denote by C[T] the term we get by filling the holes in the context C by the term T.

3. reaction rules with the concept of valences

$$a.p, \quad \overline{\alpha}.q \xrightarrow{\alpha} p, q$$

where in a reaction α, molecules $a.p$, $\overline{a}.q$ participate with suitable valences a, $\overline{a}$

A rule is the heating type if it decomposes a molecule into its constituents. Conversely, a rule is a cooling type if it composes a compound molecule. Finally, a rule is a reaction if it actually changes the nature of the solutions. Please notice that the concept of consecutively heating and cooling provides an analog of the steps of computations in a digital computer.

Following the intuition further, a solution is said to be hot (frozen) if no heating (cooling) rule is applicable.

It is interesting to note that, given the right set of rules, a possibly infinite amount of effort can be spent by a CHAM unproductively looping between heating molecules and then cooling them back down. This is apparently a drawback of the CHAM approach to behavior specification.

3.4.5.2. Adleman's DNA Model of Computations The concept of a biologic processor is relatively old, but a real breakthrough was made in 1994 when Adleman published his groundbreaking paper in the science journal, entitled "*Molecular computations of solutions to combinatorial problems*"(5).

This article sparked a real wave of research papers and books, for example, (315–317) on the idea of a DNA computer.[45]

Adleman's paper has the following significance:

1. This paper has pointed to a class of problems that could theoretically be solved faster with such a computer because they are difficult to solve on digital computers.
2. Adleman has defined almost entirely the technology that should be used.
3. His paper presented a complete, successful experiment with a real example of such computations (finding a path on a Hamiltonian graph).

Adleman (5) showed how to use the unique possibilities of information coding with DNA molecules (in combination with biochemical techniques for transforming this information) to solve the problem (Hamiltonian Path). It is well known that from a theoretical complexity point of view this problem is NP-complete, and therefore that presumably there is no effective (polynomial time) algorithm for solving it using digital computers.

Later on we briefly, but in a comprehensive way, try to present Adleman's approach, since it has defined the direction for all DNA computer-based research up to now.

[45] There is a very rich bibliography on this subject, which can be found at http://www.wi.LeidenUniv.nl/~pier/dna.html.

Even formal models of computations such as *formal splicing systems*, which originated with T. Head (318,319) in 1987, before Adleman's paper was published—also finally now refer to Adleman's approach.

First, let us present the nature of the basic assumed carrier of information in DNA computers, that is, the DNA molecule.

At the start of this discussion, however, it should be mentioned that despite the passing of several years, the final form of the DNA computer has not yet been crystallized, both from a carrier of information point of view, as well as from the point of view of its actions and architecture. Adleman and most researchers suggest the use of DNA as an information carrier, but DNA has many forms that could be suitable, and there are also other molecules similar to DNA that could be applied in molecular computations using the DNA concept.

For example, either single-stranded or double-stranded DNA can be used as a carrier for information, but partially double-stranded DNA (320), nonlinear DNA (321), and even circular DNA (322), and so forth have also been proposed.

However, double-stranded DNA appears to be the preferred form, mainly from a *reaction* point of view, and the use of other DNA structures has only been considered theoretically (323) so far in the literature available to the author at the moment.

Some researchers have also speculated on the use of artificial DNA-like polymers, such as PNA,[46] either as more stable information carriers or for intermediate use in operations (320).

Another strong candidate (related to DNA) for molecular computations is RNA,[47] which is also suitable as an information carrier. In nature, RNA is more often manipulated and rewritten than DNA. It has been observed that DNA's function in vivo is mostly that of a rather passive, nearly read-only, long-lived instruction tape, whereas RNA is more of a short-lived scratch memory used in protein synthesis. RNA is the main inspiration for the abstract CNA[48] model by S.A. Kurtz et al. (330).

As has been mentioned, the biologic cells genetic information is stored in strands of DNA (deoxyribonucleic acid). DNA is a polymer—a large molecule consisting of repeated smaller units (monomers)—with a linear structure at the lowest level.

DNA is built of four different monomers known as nucleotides: adenine (A), guanine (G), cytosine (C) or thymine (T). All of these consist of a nitrogenous base, a phosphate molecule, and a sugar molecule. The phosphate and sugar

[46] PNA is a molecule of synthetic origin that binds to single-stranded nucleic acids. Instead of a repeating sugar-phosphate backbone, it has a repeating polyamide structure to which the purine and pyrimidine bases are attached in a fashion that confers the ability to bind to RNA and DNA in a highly efficient manner.

[47] RNA is similar to DNA, but it has a slightly different sugar in its backbone, which makes it more flexible. Moreover, thymine, denoted in DNA by T, is replaced by uracil (denoted U). Uracil binds to A, similar to T. With few exceptions, RNA is observed in vivo as a single-stranded polynucleotide.

[48] CNA stands for Computational Nucleic Acid, to denote a *computational molecule*.

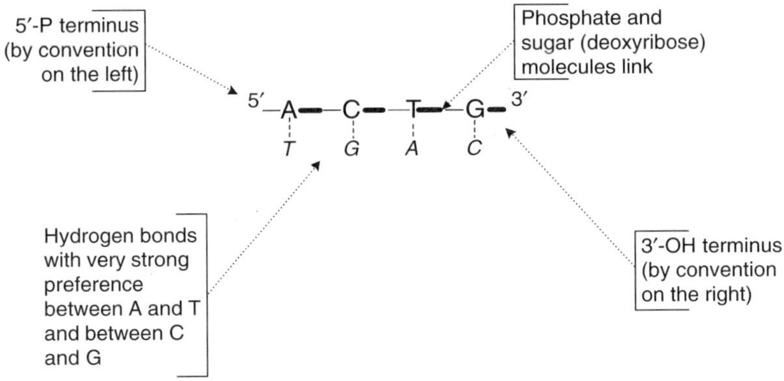

Figure 3-40. Linear example of DNA structure.

molecules link together in a linear structure, thus forming DNA's linear backbone, as given in Figure 3-40.

The backbone has two distinct ends, known as 3′ and 5′ respectively (or more precisely 3′-OH and 5′-P or 5′-phosphate), giving it a direction. This is also referred to as polarity, or that DNA is antiparallel, as given in Figure 3-41.

DNA can thus abstractly be viewed as a string over a four-letter alphabet, such as ...ATGGTCAACTG... . In the real world DNA strings create gigantic lists (15) ranging from 0.7 μm (15 plasmid) to 40000 μm (4 cm) (human).

The chemical structure of DNA building blocks implies, that DNA can create very complex structures, starting immediately on the lowest level of a string, up to more complex structures in two dimension and three dimension:

1. Structure in one-dimension

The first step of the increasing complexity of the DNA molecule starts with basepairing in 1-D, which occurs because of a very strong chemical preference

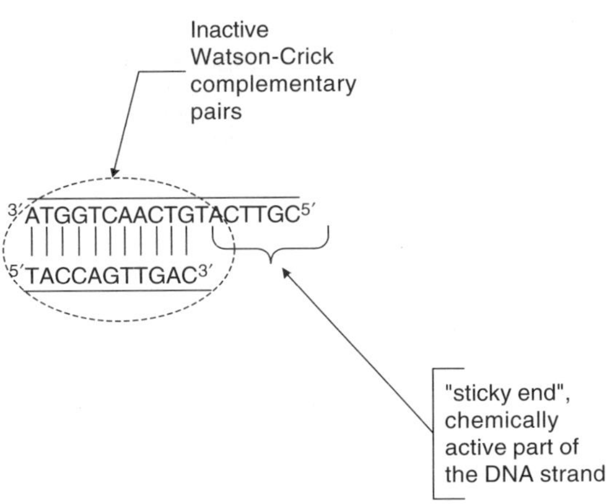

Figure 3-41. DNA strand with a sticky end.

between A and T and between C and G. The bases in these pairs are said to be Watson–Crick complementary. Thus, DNA can exist as single or double stranded. The two strands in double-stranded DNA are each other's complement: the base sequence of one is enough to determine the base sequence of the other.

2. Structure in two-dimension

As a consequence of the existing sticky ends, which selectively recognize and bind each other even partially, the single stranded DNA can fold and create stable patterns in two-dimension of a variety of complex shapes, for example lines or circles, (see Fig. 3-42), where selected areas are double stranded, but other regions are not.

3. Structure in three-dimension

In three-dimensional space, DNA also creates complex spatial structures because it creates a so-called double-helix and spatial structures with specific proteins, for example for replication purposes.

The structure of DNA, shown in Figure 3-42, existing in a cell of an organism makes its replication relatively easy. As mentioned before, the DNA in a cell is normally double stranded, and it forms a double helix of two intertwined strands that are bound together by hydrogen bonds. Theoretically, DNA replication is implemented by splitting the double helix of DNA into its two strands (of single stranded DNA) and next through rebuilding their complementary strand onto them. As result, two copies of the double-stranded DNA emerges. For this process the existence of free bases (to be building blocks) in the solution as well as specific enzymes to drive the replication process is also required (some more details are given later on).

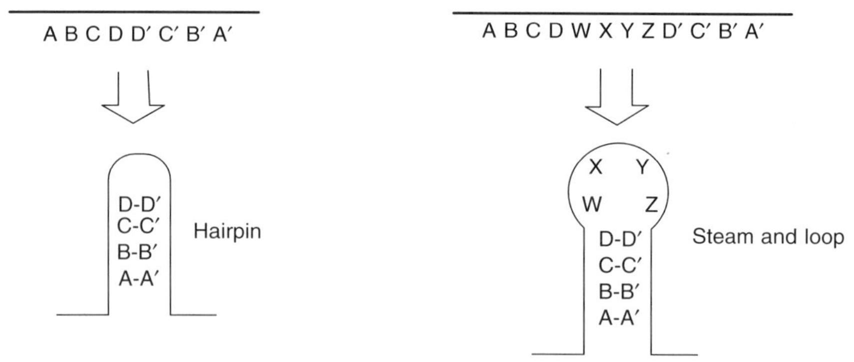

Figure 3-42. Characteristic forms of DNA

The "palette" of basic difficulties in designing a computational process with the use of DNA and it's properties can be given as follows:

1. **How to code information in a DNA computer**

   If DNA is used to code proteins, then the question is what should be the structure of the "expressions" constructed with DNA — to provide a general and uncomplicated system to encode any information we want to process later on in the intended DNA computer.

   In digital computers this problem also exists, such as in different "existing data formats" to code, store in memory numbers, and to process these numbers, which also exist in a variety of forms, for example, signed or unsigned integers, integers in twos-complement form, IEEE floating-point standard 754 (324), and so forth. With the DNA computer, this problem appears to be much more complicated. It becomes clear if we look at how much more complex DNA is in three-dimension, where it is uses code based on four symbols, compared to the linear 0/1 code used in digital computers. We should also keep in mind that originally DNA "was designed" to store data about proteins, not human data.

   To partially illustrate this difficulty, let us look at Figure 3-43, based on the results presented in a paper by S. Roweis, E. Winfree et al. (320), which describes an attempt to build a coding system with DNA for a universal model of computations. They assumed binary coding as a basis (as in digital computers), but it was carried by "*DNA regions, each with M bases*." Thus, depending on the size of the problem, the 0/1 bit can be five-bases long, as given in the example below, or even 20-bases long as proposed for breaking the DES code.

   Thus, we can say that coding with this concept is done in two steps: from a real problem → to 0/1 code → DNA carrier.

   In contrast, in his original experiment Adleman applied direct coding of the underlying problem into the DNA carrier, as demonstrated in Figure 3-44,

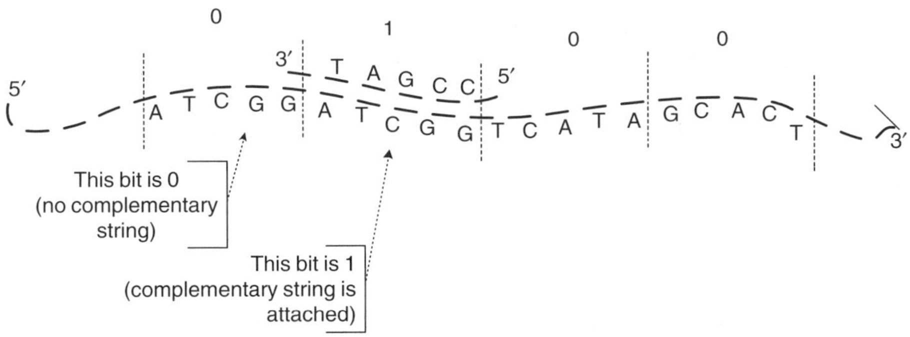

Figure 3-43. Proposed concept of coding . . .01001110. . . with strings of DNA. Bits are coded with five bases each.

using specific properties of DNA to process data, but at the cost of reduced generality, to have a really universal molecular computer. Now let us look at his concept.

The main objective of Adleman's work was to replace the *consecutive* generations of all possible paths (e.g., by digital computer) while solving the Hamiltonian path problem with a *simultaneous parallel* generation of all possible paths, by exploiting the well-known behavior of DNA oligonucleotides.[49]

He used the following method:

The individual forms of nucleotides O_j consisting of random 20-mer sequences of bases (A, T, C, G) were correlated with each vertex j of the initial graph. The individual forms of oligonucleotides O_{ij} were created for each edge i–j. They were 10-mer of O_i followed by 10-mer of O_j. In addition, 20-mer oligonucleotides O_j with sequences that are Watson–Crick complementary to the O_j were chosen.

On the basis of these oligonucleotides, the first logical step of solving the problem consists of ligation reactions, resulting in the formation of DNA molecules that encode all random paths through the graph.

Adleman suggests that the DNA computational process has a basic operator: ligation of DNA strands, which have "sticky ends" (or cohesive ends) of mutually complementary sequences of oligonucleotides. The forming of hydrogen bonds between such sequences is known as *annealing* or *hybridization*.

Thus, Adleman's approach can be applied to specific problems only. It was shown fairly rapidly after Adleman published his paper that the proposed concept could be used for solving the SAT problem, which is finding satisfying inputs to a Boolean formula of the size N; the 3-colorability problem, which is to color a graph into red, blue, and green in such a way that after coloring there are no two vertices which are connected by an edge having the same color, and some other problems, including molecular implementation of Turing Machines.

Here we come to the first restriction of Adleman's approach.

In a digital computer . . .010100. . .sequences serve in general both as data and program determining the behavior of a processor. On the level of programming languages, it is more restrictive (to use interchangeable data and program) , but some programming systems, for example, LISP, allow this, that is, it is allowed to build specific data and eventually to activate this data as a program for execution. Even loops: data → program → data → and so forth, are allowed.

In a DNA computer, DNA strings serve mainly as data, and only partially as active objects, as are discussed in the following section.

Now let us address the next problem: of how to build a DNA computer.

[49] A short polymeric chain of two–ten nucleotides.

2. **What are the necessary operators in a DNA computer?**

The next problem while thinking about the design of a DNA computer is "what kind of operators should be used in the computational process (equivalent to machine-level instructions in digital computers) and how they should be carried out by such a DNA computer."

There are natural, fundamental, directly available operators:

- Self-assembling of DNA Strands having Matching Sticky Ends.

  In his PhD Thesis[50] entitled, "Algorithmic self-assembly of DNA," Winfree distinguishes at least eight types of possible annealing reactions in two dimension between DNA strands, but there are most probably many more possible schemes due to the complexity of DNA and the various methods "discovered by the nature in vivo" of different organisms. We can to some extent say that this is an equivalent of the operator for finding matching pieces of information.

- Amplification of certain DNA sequences in a PCR reaction (DNA polymerase chain reaction).

  This is some kind of a "copy" operator. The PCR reaction requires primers, that is, short sequences from the start and at the end of the sequence to be replicated. The active element for this copying process is an enzyme called DNA polymerase, which "reads" bases on one strand, and attaches complementary bases to the second, growing strand. The growth process takes place only in one direction $5' \rightarrow 3'$ (the growing end of the polymer must have a free $3'$-OH group).

- Recognizing specific locations (sequences of bases) and cutting DNA by restriction enzymes.

  The cutting of a DNA strand can be done at or near recognized sites defined by specific sequences of bases, with the help of specific enzymes (called restriction enzymes or restriction endonucleases). According to D. Freifelder (15) there are nearly 2000 different restriction enzymes known to be purified from various organisms. There are two basic types of restriction enzymes:

  a. Type I enzymes recognize a specific sequence but make cuts elsewhere.
  b. Type II enzymes make cuts only within the recognized cleavage site, which can have sticky-ends or not.

3. **What kind of high level architecture is needed for a DNA computer? How should the run of computations, i.e. "the program" be executed?**

The computational process based on DNA is parallel in general, and the simplest possible architecture of the DNA computer is just a *tube* (chemical reactor), where DNA molecules of input data react in the presence of some

[50] Also available at: *http://dope.caltech.edu/winfree/DNAresearch.html*

enzymes, that is, join again and again, change shape, replicate, and are cut—until the *solution* (i.e., a chemical solution) obtains a steady state, or somehow an output is generated successfully, detected, and "extracted outside the tube" for the programmer.

It is obvious that in such a chemical reactor, specific actions must be implemented *automatically or manually in a preassumed order*, to pass from input data to results, separating reactions from each other, because it seems to be extremely difficult to have a solution in the tube behaving "automatically," because we prefer to have more reactions run at the same time in the same space. In Adleman's paper he has demonstrated how such a sequence of manual actions can be implemented for a very specific problem. His DNA computer has no internal structure—it is just a *tube*. Thus, let us look at a summary of his experiment.

In fact his approach was a brute force solution to the problem, to generate all possible candidate solutions "chemically," and later on to apply the "chemical" verification algorithm to each of them, gradually filtering until the only real solution to the problem remained. The whole brute force search was performed in parallel because of the specific chemical reaction.

The general algorithm used by Adleman consists of the following steps. For a system of N points (the directed graph with designated vertices V_{in} and V_{out}):

Step 1: All possible random paths through the graph were generated.

Step 2: Only those paths that began with V_{in} and end with V_{out} were kept.

Step 3: Only those paths that entered exactly N vertices were kept.

Step 4: Only those paths that entered all of the vertices of the graph at least once were kept.

To implement the steps of the algorithm, Adleman used generally accepted techniques of genetic engineering:

(i) Amplification of chosen DNA species by polymerase chain reactions

(ii) Chromatographic extraction methods

(iii) Affinity purification with a biotin–avidin magnetic beads system

Assuming that the problem to be computed is coded into DNA molecules as given in Figure 3-44, the computations have the form of states defined by the contents of consecutive *tubes* (biochemical reactors) after specific reactions.

Stage 1: All paths through the graph are generated on the basis of spontaneous chemical reactions between DNA molecules having matching sticky ends. From step 3, one can see that it is sufficient to generate all paths of length n; the mechanism used here also produces other paths; however, they will be filtered out in step 3. To generate all candidates, super-exponential time is required on a deterministic computer, but here they are done in parallel using chemical reactions, which is much more efficient. For all nodes i except the *start* and *end* node, and all edges, $O_{i\to j}$ ligate with $O_{h\to i'}$ and $O_{j'\to k}$ where $i - i'$ and $j - j'$ are complementary. This results in a new $O_{h\to k}$.

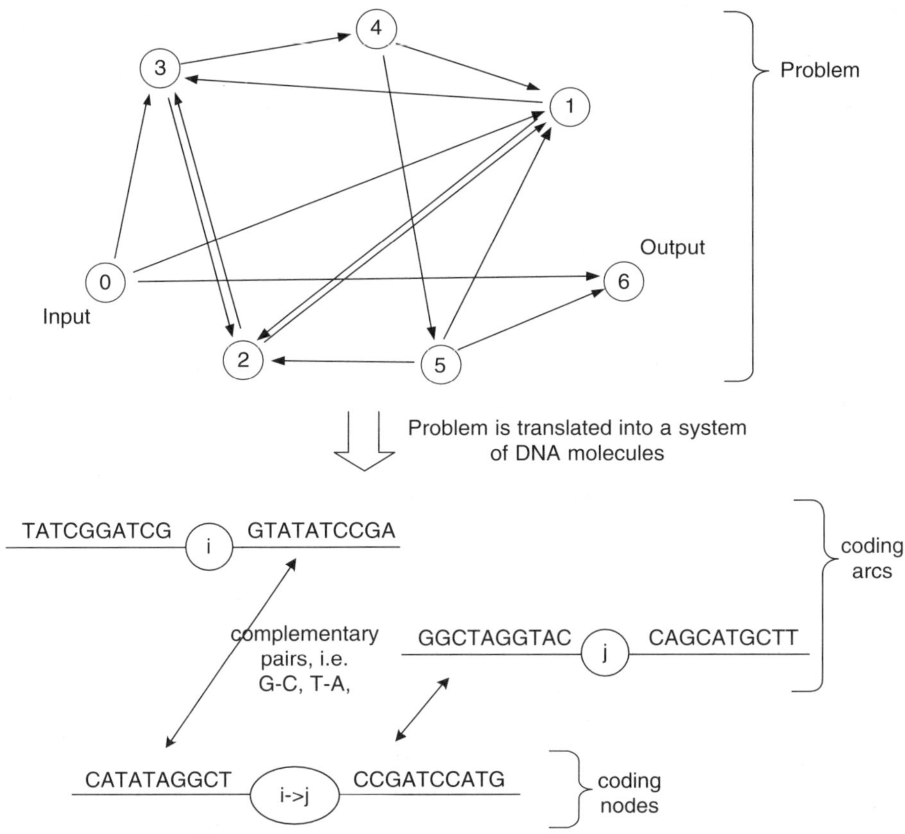

Figure 3-44. Adleman's approach to solve the Hamiltonian path problem with a DNA process.

Stage 2: PCR amplification is done by using O_{start} and O_{end} as primers, resulting in amplification of those molecules that encode paths with the desired start and end node.

Stage 3: The separation in length is done using gel extraction by running the molecules through a gel. The speed with which a molecule runs through the gel depends on its weight. The molecules are thus sorted into bands of molecules with the same weight. The molecules in the 20·n band (corresponding to paths with length n) are excised from the gel to be used in the next step.

Stage 4: The product of step 3 is purified first, and single stranded DNA is generated from it. Next, repeated extraction—once for each node i—is done using a magnetic beads system: $O_{i'}$ conjugated to magnetic beads is added, and allowed to anneal to strands containing Oi. These are extracted and retained for the next iteration. As a result, in the solution only DNA strands remain "going" through all the required vertices. With the connection of the previous step, it has been guaranteed that the remaining strands go through every vertex only once.

Stage 5: The readout (output), that is extracting the answer to the problem, is done by first PCR amplifying the remaining solution and detecting the presence of DNA using gel electrophoresis. This answers the problem of the Hamiltonian path. If a solution path is desired, one of the strands detected can be sequenced.

In the practice, in the test tube for each vertex 1, 2, 3, 4, 5 and each 14 edges, 50 pmol of DNA were used (50 pmol = 50 mm^3 of 0.06 g/liter concentration, which gives 3×10^{13} copies of each vertex and edge). The test tube was $\approx$15.7 cm^3 (the computational space). It is worth noting that the experiment took seven full days of work in Adleman's laboratory.

The question is how to make such a *tube(s)* work as efficiently as, for example, Pentium processors with their internal network of *buses* to transport information between functional units (two integer processors and a floating point unit) and storage areas (registers, stacks, and caches).

Roweis, Winfree, et al. (320) have even proposed an architecture for a DNA computer like the following:

> *The machine is a sort of parallel robotic workstation for molecular computation in which various robotic and fluid flow apparati are controlled by a central programmable electronic computer. It contains a rack of many test tubes, a small amount of robotics, some fluid pumps and heaters/coolers, and some conventional microelectronics. For each of the operations in the model, we have made a specific choice of physical procedures to implement it.*

In 1996, L.M. Adleman (325) made an attempt to clarify a way for practical implementation of the concept of the DNA computer. He considered the possibility of excluding the stage of enzymatic amplification and reducing the sets of biochemical operations to two groups, which he called the *unrestricted model* and the *restricted model.*

Adleman defined the notion of *tube* (T), representing a volume of a reagent containing a set of molecules of DNA, that is a multi-set of finite strings over the alphabet (A, C, G, T).

The unrestricted model consisted of the following steps:

1. Separate operation

Given a tube T and a string of symbols S over (A, C, G, T), produce two tubes +(T, S) and −(T, S), where +(T, S) are all of the molecules of DNA in T which contain the consecutive subsequence S, and −(T, S) entails all of the molecules of DNA in T that do not contain the subsequence S.

2. Merge

Given tubes T_a and T_b, pour T_b into T_a thereby making $T_a \leftarrow T_a \cup T_b$. Tube T_b is destroyed.

3. Detect operation

Given a tube T, say *Yes* if T consists of at least one DNA molecule, and say *No* if it consists of none. Tube T is preserved.

4. Amplify operation

Given a tube T, produce two tubes $T'(T)$ and $T''(T)$ such that $T = T'(T) = T''(T)$.

For the restricted model Adleman used only the first three operations presented earlier: separate, merge, and detect.

Adleman pointed out that the restricted model makes it possible to solve a number of important problems, though it has more restricting features. At the end of the discussion about possible architectures of a DNA computer, a fast-developing approach should be noted[51] (326), which can be characterized as "DNA computing on surfaces." In most papers, the DNA computations are *envisioned* in *test tubes*, and the appropriate DNA molecules are removed from the solution by hybridization to complementary DNA strands affixed to magnetic beads. The number of different types of beads required for a particular mathematical problem scales as the number of operations in the algorithm, and can reach into the thousands. The goal of the *DNA computations on surfaces* approach is to design high density, chemically complex surfaces (usually gold) that can replace the test tube or magnetic bead methodology and simplify the task of performing the thousands of successive separations by hybridization that would be required in any DNA computing scheme. The general concept of this approach is given in the Figure 3-45.

As has been said, there is no doubt that Adleman's approach does open the door for solving combinatorial problems of not very high magnitude in a quite different way.

In the early outbreak of enthusiasm, the evaluation of the computational power of a DNA computer was estimated by D. Boneh, C. Dunworth, and J. Sgall (327) as given in Table 3-13.

In this table, the reaction carried out in a single test tube is considered as a single bio-step (single computational step).

Where: s- size of the computation (formula, circuit, etc.) being simulated
ref. (2) c- degree of each vertex
ref. (8) t- time, N- number of nondeterministic bits used in the Turing Machine

However, soon it was found that the DNA computer brought with it not only great promises but also technical and theoretical difficulties. Some of the technical difficulties have been discussed before, in "the "palette" of basic difficulties...". J.H. Reif (328) for instance, found restrictions inherent in the practical use of the DNA computer idea. He ascribed the main restrictions to the following factors:

1. Total number of aggregates in a test tube T
2. Time duration of each lab step

[51] It is expected that this technology will also have diagnostic and *computational value*.

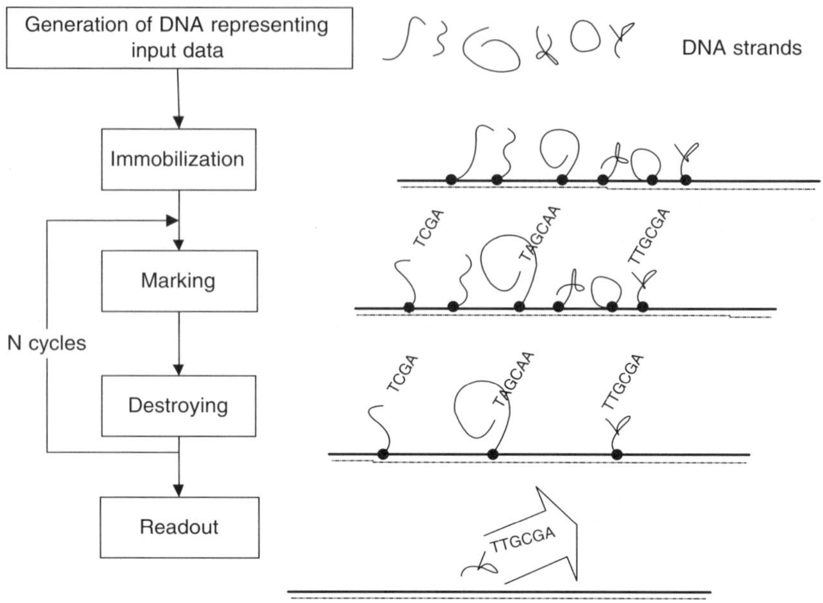

Figure 3-45. DNA computing on surfaces — main executin cycle.

3. Number of lab steps
4. Length of complementary matching in DNA strings
5. Energy

It should be also noted that many researchers do not really consider the DNA processor as a molecular processor but rather as "a chemical reaction information processing device." Thus, molecular mechanisms that control the functioning

TABLE 3-13.

Problems	Decreasing Volume Algorithms	Bio-Steps	Strands
(1)	Directed Hamiltonian path	O(n)	n!
(2)	Any NP problem via (1)	O(n^c)	2^{n^c}
(3)	CNF-formula satisfiability	O(s)	2^n
(4)	MAX-CNF-Satisfiability	O(s)	2^n
	Constant Volume Algorithms		
(5)	Circuit satisfiability	O(s)	2^n
(6)	Circuit with ROMs satisfiability	O(s)	2^n
(7)	MAX-Circuit-Satisfiability	O(s)	2^n
(8)	1-tape NTM	O(t)	2^N
(9)	Circuits via (8)	$\Omega(s^2)$	2^n
	Mixed Algorithms		
(10)	Contact network satisfiability	O(s)	2^n
(11)	PSPACE	O(s)	2^{n}
(12)	Polynomial Hierarchy	O(s)	2^n

of the DNA processor are mechanisms of chemical reactions between different molecular forms of oligonucleotides. They are based indirectly on molecular information-processing mechanisms.

Because the DNA-processor is a chemical reaction device based on giant multi-component reaction media, some restrictions to its practical possibilities should be considered.

- First of all there are *mass* restrictions. D. Beaver (329) estimated the volume of the reagent, which it is necessary to use for solving the problem of factoring a 1000-bit number. It can be reduced to a Hamiltonian Path Problem having 10^6 nodes. In this case the number of different nucleotides used should be approximately equal to the number of possible paths, which is greater than $2^{1000000}$. Thus on the order $>10^{200000}$ liters or more are needed. Nonetheless, mass restrictions represent only one of the aspects of the problem discussed.
- Second, mixing hundreds of different nucleotides in one reaction (chemical reactor or tube) would lead to enormous decreases in the concentrations of each of these nucleotides in the reaction media. This in turn would give rise to sharply decreasing rates of chemical reactions between the different nucleotides, and to additional increases in computational time.
- Third, mixing the many different groups of nucleotides required for complex, multi-step computations, increases the risk of unexpected series of calculations.

S.A. Kurtz et al. (330) presented a discussion of the Hamiltonian Path Problem based on a detailed chemical kinetic analysis. They showed that Adleman's algorithm requires at least quadratic time even with the simplest problems, much worse than naive expectations would suggest. Given more complicated cases, the analysis shows that the yield of Adleman's algorithm can fall off exponentially with problem size.

They concluded that these results are not an objection to the DNA-computing approach in general, but rather difficulties to be overcome in its development.

CHAPTER 4

Computing a Collective Intelligence Quotient (IQS) for Social Structures of Beings

Defining *collective intelligence* formally and defining how it should be efficiently measured are two different problems. There are many examples of processes that are well defined, but there are serious formal difficulties with a proper evaluation measure for them and how the measuring process should be eventually implemented.

There are several reasons why measuring *intelligence* is a difficult process. Some of them were partially discussed in Section 2.1, but a brief summary is given here:

1. As a result of every test, the being is learning (getting experience) how to work with intelligence tests. Even if later the results are not given to such a being (for positive or negative feedback), it would have learned how to process the "format of the test," and as a result, with the next test, such a being is more efficient, usually less stressed and therefore, has more chance to get better scores.
2. It is difficult to define a battery of tests with a proof that the tests included are fully equivalent to allow multiple and uncorrelated evaluation of the same abilities of the being.
3. Beings change during their lives and even over a span of a week or a day. It is difficult to arrange the same environment and the same "internal mode" of the being for a repeated test.
4. Bacteria or even, for example, ants can be considered automata with fixed repertoires of abilities; thus, they are easy to "measure." Humans are complex beings with multiple abilities spanning over a large domain of problems. This implies obvious difficulties with defining proper IQ tests, as has been discussed in Section 2.1.2.1 and 2.1.2.2.
5. Social structures representing the accumulated abilities of their members (*collective intelligence*) will be even more complex objects from an *intelligence* evaluation point of view. This becomes less deterministic and covers more abilities than with a single being.

Coming back to the problem of measuring the *collective intelligence* of social structures, the author's belief is that difficulty 1. and consequently difficulty 2. are not serious for social structures, because tests can be better hidden in social activities than in the case of a single being. Because single beings participate only partially and accidentally in the group problem-solving, there is a much lower probability that they will discover that in the midst of a battery of everyday problems, one more problem to be solved has been inserted—an IQS test.

As has been maintained throughout the entire book, a social structure is a powerful but highly nondeterministic system. Thus, for efficient IQS testing of social structures, we have assumed the following pillars:

- □ The probability that certain problems can be solved should be used as an IQ for social structures.
- □ No single value or vector should be used for measuring *intelligence*, as was discussed in Section 2.1.2.2 for humans, but rather a probability function over a span of time and the domain of problems. This will give a solution for the difficulties mentioned in 3. and 4 listed earlier. In addition to the assumption that an IQ test can be given to a social structure several times "under cover," the proposal of the IQS test (discussed later) is theoretically justified and reasonable from an implementation point of view.

4.1. A FORMAL DEFINITION OF A *COLLECTIVE INTELLIGENCE* QUOTIENT (IQS) AND ITS PROPERTIES

The starting point for defining the *collective intelligence* quotient (IQS) is "Definition 23: N-element inference in (NEI) CS^n."

Let us find a problem essential for *intelligence* testing that can be logically described as an NEI in a certain environment.

DEFINITION 24: ELEMENTARY *COLLECTIVE INTELLIGENCE* QUOTIENT (IQS)

An elementary IQS for a social structure over a problem represented by a given NEI with a certain goal is measured by the probability P that after time t, the conclusion CS_{goal} will be reached from the starting *state of* CS^n, as a result of the assumed NEI. This is denoted IQS $= P(t, N)$. ■

Remarks

- In general, there are no contradictions for this definition if it also covers a single being, which is "a one-member social structure" as well.
- The IQS defined in such a way is a two-dimensional function over t and N. This means that, for example, a certain social structure or being can be

superior for short problems to be solved in a short time, whereas another one may prevail for long inferences if time is sufficient. In this way, our proposed definition resolves the problem of time in IQ testing.

- Using probability resolves the problem of, for example, a temporarily low "frame of mind" affecting the result of the IQ test.
- This is the precisely defined problem(s) underlying the IQ test. It theoretically gives the opportunity to use the equivalence of problems here, that is, if they are reducible into the same NEI. However, we should keep in mind that translating one problem into another is difficult (even if they both are NEI). Because we use probability for IQS, theoretically it is possible to evaluate the chance that if we are able to solve a certain problem requiring an NEI we will also easily be able to solve the equivalent problem.

Let us define an IQS for a social structure over a domain of problems.

DEFINITION 25: COLLECTIVE INTELLIGENCE QUOTIENT (IQS) OVER DOMAIN *D*

Let there be given a domain of problems D as a set of proper NEI with their goals, that is,

$$D = \{(\text{NEI}_1, CS_{\text{goal1}}), (\text{NEI}_2, CS_{\text{goal2}}), \ldots\}$$

The IQS_D is defined similarly to IQS as a function $IQS_D = P(t, D)$ ■

Remarks

Note that N is no longer necessary in the definition, because it has been replaced by $\text{NEI}_i \in D$.

This definition results in a relatively complicated probability function describing the *collective intelligence* of a social structure.

However, if we take into account some possible equivalences between problems having the same NEI, it is possible to think about computing an approximation of such a function on the basis of selective sampling of the abilities of the given social structure and how it solves specific problems and hence build an approximation in this way.

To define and evaluate *collective intelligence*, the preceding two definitions (24 and 25 together with 23) fulfill all the basic requirements (mentioned before in Section 2.2 and 3.1):

- An NEI can be interpreted as any problem-solving process in a social structure or inside a single being where N inferences are necessary to get a result, or any production process, where N-technologies/elements have to be found and unified into one final technology or product. This allows us to model and evaluate inferring processes within a social structure in the same uniform way as production processes. This is very important because some inference processes can be observed only through resultant production processes or specific logical behavior, namely of ants, bees, bacteria.

- Simulating NEI in the RPP allows us to easily model the distribution of inference resources between individuals, dissipation in space or time, or movement (or temporary concentration) in the *CS*. This clearly reflects the dissipated, moving, or concentrated resources in a social structure of any type.
- With this approach, cases can be simulated very easily in which some elements of the inference chain are temporarily not available, for example, the chain of inference can be temporarily broken, but at a certain time t, another inference running in the background or in parallel will produce the missing components. Such situations are well known in human social structures, such as when a given research or technological discovery is blocked until missing theorems or subtechnology is discovered.
- Humans infer in all directions: forward, for example, improvements of existing technology; backward, for example, trying to manufacture a given product by going back to a known formula, and also through generalization, for example, two or more technologies can be combined into one more general and powerful technology or algorithm. NEI simulated in the RPP reflect all these cases clearly.

As a result, we have a descriptive tool for measuring *collective intelligence* that should be universal and feasible from a computational (simulations and analysis of data) point of view.

Now let us look into some immediate, logical consequences of the previous definitions (way of thinking).

The proposed measure of *collective intelligence* allows us to easily give formal definitions of the properties of social structures, which are obvious in real life, and immediately point to some simple theorems.

DEFINITION 26: LEVELS OF *COLLECTIVE INTELLIGENCE*

Let there be given social structures S_a and S_b, which are characterized by their IQS_D expressions $P_{S_a}(t, D)$, $P_{S_b}(t, D)$ over a common domain D.

Social structure S_a is said to represent a higher level of social intelligence than the compared social structure S_b, which is denoted

$$S_a \overset{IQS_D}{\rhd} S_b \quad \textit{iff} \quad \forall_{t, NEI_i \in D}(P_{S_a}(t, D) \geq P_{S_b}(t, D)). \qquad \blacksquare$$

Example the *collective intelligence* of parents versus the *collective intelligence* of their children. However, it can be difficult to prove that at the level of teenagers it will still be true.

It is more interesting and plausible in real life that a given social structure is better than another in some selected areas only. Our concept of IQS defines this easily.

DEFINITION 27: SPECIALIZATION OF SOCIAL STRUCTURES

Let there be given social structures S_a and S_b, which are characterized by IQS_D expressions $P_{S_a}(t, D)$, $P_{S_b}(t, D)$ in a certain common D where they are both active.

Social structure S_a is said to represent a higher level of specialization in a given domain $D_a \in D$ than the compared social structure S_b which is denoted $S_a \overset{IQS_D}{\underset{D_a}{\rhd}} S_b$ *iff* $\forall_{t,N}(P_{S_a}(t, N) \geq P_{S_b}(t, N))$ such that NEI are taken from domain D_a. ■

Example A social structure of musicians is compared to a social structure of nonmusicians.

With the preceding definitions, we can try to propose some theorems; however, the goal of this book is not to develop a "sophisticated" mathematical theory of computational *collective intelligence* but rather to propose a tool suitable for applications resulting from this theory.

Section 2.2.3 of discusses how *configuration* and *communication* in a social structure affects its behavior and performance. Assume that it is possible to formally define the configuration of a social structure, and let us denote this in a general way as *Conf.* This term should be understood as the organizational configuration and the communication system as well as the various roles carried out in the social structure by group members.

The configuration symbol used as a superscript will denote that for a given social structure S, we have proper information about it, that is S^{Conf}.

HYPOTHESIS 1. INDIVIDUAL VERSUS SOCIAL STRUCTURE

Let I denote individual and S denote an existing social structure such that $I \notin S$. There exists a configuration *Conf* for a new social structure $S' \equiv \left\{ S \overset{inc}{\cup} I \right\}$, which emerges after *inclusion* (denoted by operator $\overset{inc}{\cup}$ of I into S, such that S' represents a higher level of intelligence than I does, that is $S' \overset{IQS}{\rhd} \{I\}$ and $S' \overset{IQS}{\rhd} S$ for $D_I \cup D_S$. ■

People try to join groups because their individual performance is in most cases higher or even "opened up" after inclusion into a group—we can say that they are catalyzed by the facilities of the group. In most cases, the rest of the group will profit from the inclusion of a new member. However, it has been widely observed that "positive" inclusion in many cases is not easy and takes time or is sometimes even impossible. The problem is in finding a configuration *Conf* for the new group, which will be good, both for the individual and for the group itself.

Hypothesis represents an "optimistic belief of the author on the positive nature of the social behavior" of humans.

The preceding definitions also allow us to speak about equivalence of social structures.

DEFINITION 28: CARDINAL EQUIVALENCE OF SOCIAL STRUCTURES OVER DOMAIN *D*

Let there be given social structures S_a and S_b, over a certain D which are characterized by IQS expressions $P_{S_a}(t, N)$, $P_{S_b}(t, N)$.

Social structures S_a and S_b are said to be equivalent in a given domain D which is denoted as:

$$S_a \underset{D}{\overset{IQS}{\equiv}} S_b \textit{ iff} \quad \textit{cardinal numbers are equal } n(D_a) = n(D_b)$$

$$\textit{where } D_a, D_b \in D \textit{ and}$$

$$N\textit{—element inference belongs to } D_a \textit{ iff } \forall_{t,N}(P_{S_a}(t, N) \geq P_{S_b}(t, N))$$

$$\textit{and respectively,}$$

$$N\textit{—element inference belongs to } D_b \textit{ iff } \forall_{t,N}(P_{S_a}(t, N) \leq P_{S_b}(t, N)) \quad \blacksquare$$

From formal considerations on *collective intelligence* measures, let us move to the practical problems of how to compute the IQS function for a specific social structure existing in a specific environment.

As has been mentioned several times, most probably, only simulations followed by *mathematical identification* (estimation) of the IQS function will be reasonable.

Let us explain this difficulty on the basis of a very simple example. First, we will map an abstract human social structure into an RPP model of computations for a specific NEI (4-element inference) representing a problem to be solved. Later, we will discuss the difficulties with computing the IQS for this problem.

4.2. TYPICAL MAPPING OF HUMAN SOCIAL STRUCTURES INTO RPP STRUCTURES FOR COMPUTING THE *COLLECTIVE INTELLIGENCE QUOTIENT IQS*

To demonstrate the concept of mapping a social structure into the RPP for further *collective intelligence* evaluation, let us consider a given human social structure suffering from cold weather.

For this social structure, we will make the following assumptions:

- There is one person with matches, who is moving somewhere inside the social structure. This person owns resources.
- Another has a matchbox, that is, owns resources.
- A third person has an idea of how to use the matches and matchbox to make a fire if both components are at hand. This person has knowledge (technology).
- A fourth person is conscious that heat from fire is a solution for the cold weather problem in this social structure. This person can be a manager, organizer, politician, or perhaps a businessman looking for a new product required by the market, that is, has knowledge/abilities.
- Other humans are void from this logical problem point of view.

Assume also that nobody in the social structure has total knowledge of all the necessary elements and their present position; everybody can infer only locally.

For this social structure the *CS* for the RPP is simple and can be easily defined as follows:

$$
\begin{array}{lll}
CS^1 = \{\texttt{matches.} & \texttt{fact,} & CS^0_{\texttt{matches}} \\
\quad\;\;\; \texttt{matchbox.} & \texttt{fact,} & CS^0_{\texttt{matchbox}} \\
\quad\;\;\; \texttt{matches} \wedge \texttt{matchbox} \rightarrow \texttt{fire.} & & \\
 & \texttt{rule,} & CS^0_{\texttt{matches}\wedge\texttt{matchbox}\rightarrow\texttt{fire}} \\
\quad\;\;\; \texttt{fire} \rightarrow \texttt{heat.} & \texttt{rule,} & CS^0_{\texttt{fire}\rightarrow\texttt{heat}} \\
\quad\;\;\; \texttt{?heat.}\} & \texttt{goal,} & CS^0_{\texttt{?heat}}
\end{array}
$$

Now It is necessary to make the following qualifications:

- The displacement abilities are assigned to the *information molecules* defined earlier. We can use pure or quasi-Brownian movements when, for example, humans involved in problem solving run around on foot in chaotic (e.g., panicky) ways looking for the necessary components.

  If transportation is available, the characteristics of displacement are different. Virtual displacement by telephone or by Internet search can also be defined.
- Traveling may be periodic on a daily, weekly or yearly scale.
- The internal structure of *CS* that can affect rendezvous probability should be defined (internal membranes reflecting boundaries, e.g., streets).
- Various artificial restrictions can be imposed, for instance, to restrict unification, for example different languages, existence of casts, racial conflicts, and so forth.

The above system is a 4-element inference, as can be seen in Figure 4-1, presented with the help of the Feynman diagram (see 3.4.4.2). The IQS can be computed

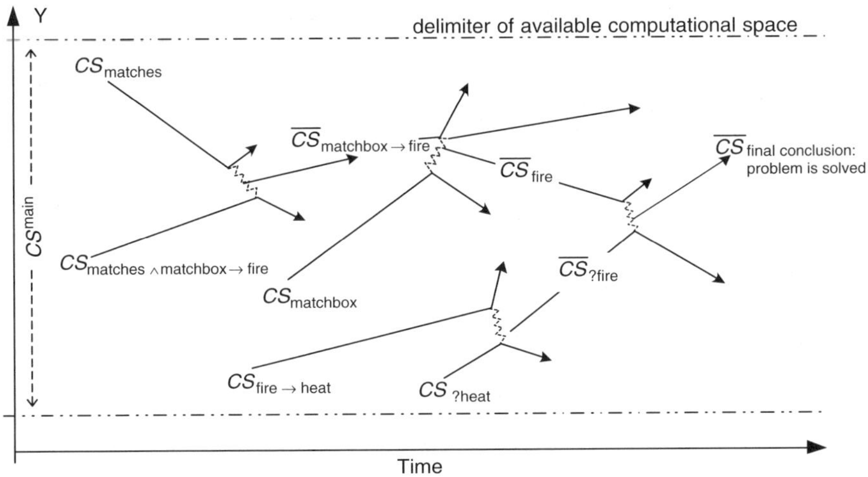

Figure 4-1. A possible run of a 4-element inference for the "cold weather problem".

for this problem in this social structure on the basis of simulations as a curve showing how probability changes in a given time period, or as a general analytical function $P(4, t)$, if we can manage to derive it.

If we assume that *computational space CS* is just a bounded plane, there is a chance to have an analytic solution for $P(4, t)$; however, a real social structure would not be so simple, even for this problem of cold weather. The following section will try to extract and summarize the major computational difficulties just mentioned.

4.3. COMPUTATIONAL DIFFICULTIES WITH THE IQS

To provide a basis for discussion of the difficulties in computing IQS, let us assume that a problem such as the "cold weather problem" is identified in a given social structure, and we have to compute a proper IQS. The major goal of IQS computations can be, for example, for the, purpose of optimizing this social structure or for comparison reasons (versus other social structures) or as an emergency drill, and so forth.

Analyzing the social structure, the problem, and later related computing problems with the IQS, we will face several analytical and computational difficulties, which can be identified as follows.

Difficulty I: Identification of Real, Virtual, and Void Members of the Social Structure

In our example of the "cold weather problem" there are only four essential members of the social structure, which are "creating–defining" the whole *collective intelligence* of the structure, and the other members are void.

Even in a simple problem such as that mentioned earlier, it is difficult to agree that only one person exclusively has a specific resource such as a "matchbox"; that only one has "matches," and similarly that only one has an idea of how to use them, and so forth. In most cases, resources and information occur in multiple copies. The problem is to estimate the size of each set of occurrences for all resources.

For advanced evaluations of IQS, we also have to take into account those apparently void members of the social structure who in specific, for example, emergency situations can become active members (e.g., supporting other, critical members).

Difficulty II: Identification of the Structure of the *CS*

The inference process usually takes place in complex environments defined by the geographical structure of the city (see again Fig. 2-63), the structure (geographical) of the company, the structure of buildings, geographical structure of the department, and so forth.

Moreover, the next level of structuralization, the "virtual structuralization," can be indirectly generated by the organizational (also informal) structure of the company, such as those given in Figure 2-43 in Section 2.2.3 of the book.

Proper identification of the structure of a *computational space* may require analyses such as those given in Figure 2-63, or can even require the use of special identification procedures such as those used for identification of "communication matrices" described in Section 2.2.3.3.

Difficulty III: Description of Quasi-Brownian Displacements of Beings and Information Inside a Social Structure

With "live beings," there can be displacements of two types:

- Real (personal displacements)
- Virtual (communication) displacements (e.g., telephone calls).

Additionally, some types of communication (e.g., by letter, company documents, messages, etc.,) will require introduction to *computational space* (so far populated by live *information molecules*) of some new types of *information molecules* representing them. Consecutively, it will require identification of how they are displaced, and of how they are processed (i.e., how they participate in the inference process).

Difficulty IV: Defining Inferences in *Computational Space*

Definition 22 of "Generalized Inference in CS^N" provided in Section 3.4.4.2 gives only a general concept of building a specific molecular inference system on first-order predicate calculus. It is a problem similar to the "knowledge engineering problem" in Expert System design (14), where certain knowledge about the process must be translated into an adequate set of rules, which in most cases is accompanied by probability-related parameters such as CF (Certainty Factor). Such rules are later compiled by an Expert System Shell into a ready-to-work system, able to run inferences and to provide explanations.

Difficulty V: *CS* as a Closed System

There are, for example, of bacterial colonies that can exist in interleaved mode (symbiosis) in different social structures. Such a phenomenon has been widely observed in the real world. For example, it can be observed in human social structures, that in some places around the world, different nationalities, religious groups, and social structures differing in language live "together but apart," interacting with each other nevertheless.

The difficulty here is to convert the *open system* in the proper way into a *closed system* (see Section 2.2.3.1) for the purpose of analysis and simulations.

Difficulty VI: How to Initialize

Finally, if the analysis is done, and we are heading toward simulations, we have to define the *initial conditions for the process* of *collective intelligence*.

This can even be a major subject of research, for example, when it would be necessary to analyze the question of "distribution and allocation of resources around a specific social structure, for example, a company will affect its IQS measure for solving a specific class of problems."

Difficulty VII: Simulation Difficulties

Simulating a set of displacing and inferencing objects requires in practice the use of powerful multiprocessor computers. Experiments conducted by the author and described in the book show that, for example, an eight-processor computer (each processor equipped with a coprocessor) is still only able to simulate a set of around 300 beings in an environment that is not very complicated (e.g., with only one central capital city). For such experiments, simulation time was in the range of single hours. Bigger social structures in more complex environments will require more powerful computers, for example, for "analysis of the influence of the Internet on the IQS of specific social structures."

Due to the complexity of the behavior of chaotic processes, an advanced graphics interface is required, both for tuning simulations to present final results.

To illustrate the need for advanced graphics in *collective intelligence* research, there is an example given in the next section of the book of an artificial social structure elaborated in three-dimensional space by certain behavior motivated by *collective intelligence*.

This means that the quest for computational power would be very great when working with *collective intelligence.*

Difficulty VIII: *Collective Intelligence over a Domain of Problems D*

All the preceding difficulties have referred to the problem of evaluating elementary *collective intelligence* as described by Definition 24. However, in many cases, it may required to eventually measure the IQS over a certain domain D of problems.

In such a case, the entry point for evaluating *collective intelligence* will be to find a representative of NEIs (sample of problems) in the given domain D that can be effectively evaluated and will cover all D in such a way that all other problems from D can be solved with the probability well approximated by the probability of solving "adjacent" representative NEIs (sample problems).

CHAPTER 5

Applications of Collective Intelligence — Toward Collective Intelligence Engineering

The theory of *collective intelligence* proposed in this book provides us with at least two basic *GATES* into possible theoretical and practical applications:

- The computational model used for *collective intelligence*, that is, the Random PROLOG Processor (RPP), provides a surprisingly powerful but simple theoretical tool, which can be used in other research disciplines for other theoretical or even philosophical considerations there.

  Binary 0/1 calculus has grown from elementary Boolean algebra through the concept of the Turing Machine, has used the discovery and application of silicon technology, and has finally come to fruition with the present shape of digital computers. Similarly, with the RPP, there are only two elementary terms: the *information molecule* and the *membrane*, which allows us to define a powerful, specific hierarchy of quasi-random computational processes and a hierarchy of *CS* hosting such computations.

  However, the interpretation of the *information molecules* and the *membranes* in this model of computations is totally different from the True/False or 1/0 interpretation of Boolean logic in digital computers.

  Just as the various interpretations and related processing of . . . **01110100010** strings provide almost unrestricted possibilities of "computing" the underlying process, the *information molecules* and the *membranes* provide proper structuring so that interpreting them should provide us with a computational model of probably comparable computing possibilities. Some examples given in this part of the book will confirm this.

  Section 5.1 will be our first example of how powerful and fruitful this theoretical approach is. The model of computations based on the concept of *information molecules* and *membranes* originally used for *collective intelligence* can be easily interpreted and used for general, almost philosophical (but partially formalized) considerations of the nature and processes of *Life*.
- When we consider applications at a higher level, that is, directly at the *collective intelligence* level of any social structure, we immediately see a rich

bonanza of possible areas where given social structures can be described, modeled, analyzed, and compared (and eventually perhaps optimized) through the use of the computational model of *collective intelligence*.

In this domain, there is a wide spectrum of social structures such as: bacterial colonies, immunology systems, colonies of ants, honeybees, and rats, and so forth — ending with groups of people.

THESE ARE OPPORTUNITIES FOR *COLLECTIVE INTELLIGENCE* ENGINEERING

In a later part of this chapter, some examples that have emerged and sufficiently crystallized before this book was ready for printing are given.

Only a few applications of *collective intelligence* are discussed here. The reason is that, according to the author, every such application requires substantial analyses of the environment, followed by the extraction of specific *collective intelligence* naturally existing there, and concluding with the analysis and design of a possible application. In most cases, it entails an in-depth research project.

Just to give an example of how complicated a problem it is, look at Section 5.3. We know that most probably there exists a specific "hidden *collective intelligence*" in the economy. People often talk, for example, about "Adam Smith's invisible hand"[1]. We can say, most probably, that we know of a *tool* used by this "hand," that is, *money*, and we also know of an elementary goal, that is, *individual profit*, but business and the economy are a *wild jungle* where everybody is trying to *devour* everybody else; thus, we cannot talk about willful cooperation in the area of the economy. So, what is the "*global idea of this hand?*" We have no idea, but this *hand* has a connotation for almost all of us who live at a higher standard in countries driven by the economy than by any other force, even those driven by ideals such as "freedom, equality, and brotherhood." For these reasons, the discussion on *collective intelligence* in Section 5.3. is limited to the problem of *money*.

For alternative discussions on *collective intelligence* from the application point of view, readers are encouraged to look at the 96-page NASA Ames Tech. Report by Wolpert and Tumer, "*An introduction to Collective Intelligence*" (331).

Full list of publications of this research group is listed separately (for convenience) at the end of the bibliography.

5.1. THE COMPUTATIONAL MODEL OF COLLECTIVE INTELLIGENCE SUGGESTS THAT INTELLIGENCE EMERGED FIRST BEFORE LIFE ON EARTH

Periodically, perhaps, we ask, "What is the relationship between *Life* and *intelligence?*" Especially if somebody is working with or teaching *artificial intelligence* (AI), this question is becoming importunate in a related form: "we can now build almost intelligent computers that, for example, are able to win

[1] Adam Smith (British philosopher and economist 1723–1790) coined the principle of the "invisible hand" in which every individual is led, as if by an invisible hand, to achieve the best good for all. (From The Encarta® 99 Encyclopedia).

chess matches against top human masters," or at least computers can emulate most intelligent behavior in animal or human problem solving, but we do not attribute *Life* to such artificially *intelligent* computers.

There are several "vectors[2]" of research efforts that could tackle this problem. Here are the two major ones:

- Analysis of *Life* through its complexity, for example, Lewin (332).
- Attempts to define and simulate *artificial life*[3] (AL).

> According to C.G. Langton (333,334) "artificial life is a field of study devoted to understanding *Life* by attempting to abstract the fundamental dynamical principles underlying biological phenomena, and recreating these dynamics in other physical media — such as computers — making them accessible to new kinds of experimental manipulation and testing."

Such attempts are increasing the depth of our knowledge, but the question "*How are Life and intelligence related?*" still remains.

The use of the formal definition of *collective intelligence* and the computational model of *collective intelligence* (8,57,308,335) will perhaps shed some light on this problem.

The formal definition of *collective intelligence*, as we have seen before, has only three basic requirements:

1. *Information molecules* must emerge in a certain *computational space*. Such *information molecules* can be almost anything: chemical molecules, software agents, ants, humans, or even social structures at an arbitrary level such as cooperating villages.
2. Later or in parallel, some interaction (at a higher level: cooperation) must emerge between abstract *information molecules*, which in a given environment results in the ability to solve specific problems.
3. The emergence of *collective intelligence* is viewed in terms of the probability that specific inferences will result.

It has been demonstrated in this book that as a result of this restricted set of formal assumptions, we can build a suitable theory, and we can analyze the problem of the *collective intelligence* of human social structures (e.g., with the group dynamics of Shaw (145), also (142)), where individuals are highly intelligent and also the problem of the *collective intelligence* of ant or bee colonies (see Sections 2.2.1.2), where individual intelligence is doubtful (individuals are "like automata" (9)). Nevertheless, their *collective intelligence* is high (10,11,106). We can even go down to the edges of *Life*, to biofilms

[2] Vector has direction and length but no location. Thus, this metaphor is appropriate to *label* research efforts of different intensity done at different centers in the same research direction.

[3] Some interesting lectures (also .ps file) and an entry level study on *artificial life* on the Internet can be found at: http://www.c3.lanl.gov/~rocha/ss504_02.html

of interaction in bacterial colonies (see Section 2.2.1.1), where the individual property of being alive begins to be doubtful. The colony is alive, but presently there is growing evidence that such a bacterial colony is collectively intelligent (96–98). At this moment we cannot provide evidence that viruses or prions cooperate and create any *collective intelligence*; however, we can prove it indirectly by referring to the DNA computer of Adleman (5,6). *Information molecules* in such a system are able to run inferences (computations) like a digital computer running an Expert System (14), but the *information molecules* are not alive at all. Moreover, the "conclusions" in such a DNA computer are active chemical molecules, thus, able to output, that is, implement a solution to the problem discovered by this *CS*.

If we look at our present perception of *Life* (336,337) and *intelligence* through the complexity of individuals and the social structures they create, it is obvious that it is a dynamic system and that *Life* and *intelligence* are interleaved. The question is, how does it happen?

Using the model of computations designed for considerations on *collective intelligence*, we can try to prove or pose for further discussion the following hypotheses:

- **Precedence Hypothesis:** *collective intelligence* first emerged (perhaps accidentally) as a result of interacting chemical molecules on earth.
- **Hypothesis on Origin:** *Life* emerged later, perhaps (probably) as a "product" of *collectively intelligent* activity "looking" for a method to attain stabilization and to develop or propagate itself.
- **Hypothesis on Cycles:** The codependency between *Life* (at different levels of complexity) and *intelligence* (individual and collective) is the consequence of a spiral (development cycle) of evolution fired at that time and still active.

We will try to present and defend these hypotheses on the basis that *collective intelligence* is less complicated and therefore could emerge more easily on a primeval earth. Other theories also support our hypotheses, such as those discussed in Section 2.2.1.1, for example, the *Proliferation Theory*, which tries to extrapolate "what happened at that time" on the basis of our present knowledge.

We will try to present a draft of a proof for the PRECEDENCE HYPOTHESIS.

THE BASIC PROPERTIES OF THE MODEL OF COMPUTATIONS APPLIED FOR *COLLECTIVE INTELLIGENCE*

Now let us give a brief, concluding summary of the most important properties of the model of computations used for *collective intelligence*. It will be given in the form of presenting "what is necessary" or supplementary, but also "what is not necessary." The second set should also be mentioned here because we frequently (unconsciously) assume many properties of a "subject under discussion" by default, which later are contradictory to the whole concept—especially when we compare the terms *Life* and *intelligence*.

Fundamental, necessary elements for the definition of *collective intelligence* (nc stands for necessary):

nc1. *Information molecules must emerge* in *CS*. In other words, temporarily stable processes, chemical molecules, beings, agents, and so forth, must emerge in a given environment. Let us call this requirement ***IM(emerge)***[4].

nc2. *Information molecules must displace* somehow, that is, they must possess the ability to move; there must be some "hand or demon" or force moving them, for example, Brownian movements (13), where permanent bombardment by gas molecules chaotically moves particles of, for example, perfume in the air. Let us call this requirement ***IM(displace)***.

nc3. *Information molecules must interact* if they rendezvous, and certain conditions must be fulfilled. Notice that the term rendezvous requires definition of the rendezvous distance. Depending on this subdefinition, it can be direct or remote interaction. Let us call this requirement ***IM(interact)***.

nc4. The problem to be solved must be specified. It can be anything: to locate food, to create antibiotic resistance, to carry a heavy prey, and so forth. This is a problem of natural selection or "filtering," that is, only such cases of *collective intelligence* are accepted that solve the required problem — others are wiped out. Let us call this requirement ***Filter(CI)***.

nc5. For an assumed time period, the probability for solving the above problem must be $\gg 0$. In other words, *collective intelligence* must have a chance to complete an inference. This can happen, for example, if some processes are repeated in a given environment with slight variation, or in similar environments in parallel, in different locations, the same or a similar process occurs. Let us call this requirement ***Chance(CI)***.

Note that the above conditions nc1.–nc5. are very basic.

Elements not necessary (redundant) for the definition of *collective intelligence* (nn stands for not-necessary):[5]

nn1. It is not necessary to use any definition of *Life*.

nn2. It is not necessary to assume that beings are somehow individually intelligent. Higher individual intelligence can boost *collective intelligence* but not necessarily ... We can define a negative value of the *collective intelligence* measure (see part 3.1), such as "when beings fight, for example, two fighting deer are easy prey for humans or wolves;

[4] Interpret this as a logic predicate ***Information Molecule*(emerge)**

[5] Most of these elements are redundant to the basic definition but can play a major role in acceleration or optimization of *collective intelligence* in a social structure. Thus, frequently, they are considered as necessary and inseparable for a basic definition.

however, usually two or more deer cooperate and are very difficult to approach."

nn3. Beings can be considered as "black boxes" defined in terms of logical interaction. It is not necessary to understand the internal structure of the beings or processes involved in the *collective intelligence* process.

nn4. It is not necessary to have homogeneous social structures. The social structure can be created by beings of different natures, for example, a hunter and his dog, some cooperating fish.

nn5. It is not necessary to assume "conscious or willful" cooperation among beings. Cooperation among beings in a social structure can be "hostile," for example, two hostile shoemakers observing each other and improving their production.

nn6. *Collective intelligence* is a probabilistic process that can emerge and vanish. Even if it continues, it can vary in time and change its IQS value (see Chapter 4) if parameters of the social structure are changing, for example, the internal structure of the *CS* (environment) changes.

Thus, for example, if "transistors" somehow got the ability to move and "wire or join together like LEGO blocks" and accidentally configured a structure of a processor—"a certain computational ability" could temporarily emerge in the environment of such "transistors." Such an emerged computer could be a *collective intelligence* of transistors, which themselves are not alive. From an external point of view, such a computer would display the abilities of a single, intelligent being. More intelligent components could imply higher-level *collective intelligence* but not necessarily. The example of medieval shoemakers was given earlier (335). Now let us look at the ancient Roman war galley with, for example, 100 or more slave oarsmen and 20 hoplites (todays marines). Such a galley displayed specific military intelligence, but it was the *collective intelligence* of the ruling crew without taking the slaves into account. Their intelligence was not utilized at all—chains and whips forced their cooperation. From a battle point of view, this was just one factor, that is, an *information molecule*.

5.1.1. Comprehension and Definition of Life

Traditionally, *Life* has been defined as a material organization that fulfills certain lists of properties or requirements (336,337).

It is interesting that the distinction between *living* and *nonliving* forms in the environment around us has emerged as a result of "Cartesian" thought in science. Before that, humans considered all processes for example, clouds as alive. This way of thinking is still observable in so-called "personification" of environmental processes, attributing them to humanlike behavior.

Despite accelerating progress in science, we still have problems defining *Life* in an efficacious way. The basic properties for a process or being to be attributed with *Life* can be listed as follows:

1. *Metabolism* is defined in biology as the complex of physical and chemical processes occurring within a living cell or organism that are necessary for the maintenance of *Life*. In metabolism, some substances are broken down to yield energy for vital processes, whereas other substances, necessary for life, are synthesized. Metabolism can be also defined in biology as the functioning of a specific substance within the living body, for example, *water metabolism*.
2. *Adaptability* is defined as becoming suitable for a new use or situation.
3. *Self-maintenance* (in the sense of autonomy).
4. *Self-repair*
5. *Growth* is defined in biology as development from a lower or simpler to a higher or more complex form; an increase, as in size, number, value, or strength; extension or expansion.
6. *Replicability* is defined in biology as the ability to reproduce or make an exact copy or copies of, for example, genetic material, a cell, or an organism.
7. *Evolution* is defined in biology as either the theory that groups of organisms change with passage of time, mainly as a result of natural selection (338), so that descendants differ morphologically and physiologically from their ancestors or as the historical development of a related group of organisms, that is, phylogeny (339).

Other properties can also be subattributed to be properties of *Life*.

Most living organisms, such as viruses, adhere to these requirements; however, there are material systems that obey only a subset of these rules. There are also processes such as candle flames, which fulfill most of these rules, but scientists do not attribute them as life. As a result, we can say that *Life* is still a fuzzy concept. Even the properties listed above closely overlap.

To help us understand *Life*, we should look again at Section 2.2.1.1. about how *Life* emerged. According to the *Proliferation Theory* (97).

> "... biological organization arises through the association of evolving systems and through the mutation and genetic recombination of these systems. Higher levels of order thus gradually emerge from lower levels ..."

The *Proliferation Theory* assumes that the sequence of development of *Life* on Earth is as has been shown in Figure 2-27. Figure 5-1 recapitulates the early stages of the emergence of *Life*.

5.1.2. Ordering *Collective Intelligence* and Life

Our proposed draft of a proof that *collective intelligence* emerged first on earth, before *Life*, will be demonstrated in the following way:

1. First, we will formally define the complexity order for *computational spaces*.

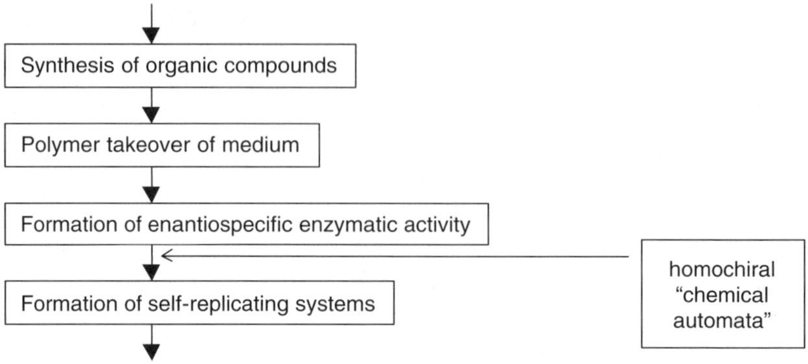

Figure 5-1. Main stages of prebiologic evolution (based on Goldanskii (340).

2. With the help of the previous definition on a complexity axis, we will order all possible CS_i^j that are interesting or could be turning points from a *collective intelligence* and/or *Life* point of view.
3. Finally, looking back at properties one to seven required for attributing something as alive, we will point out that it is not probable that *Life* emerged directly, skipping various simple evolutionary steps[6] where *collective intelligence* was present.

DEFINITION 29: STRONG[7] ORDERING OF *COMPUTATIONAL SPACES* CS^J

Assume that there are given CS_i^j and CS_k^l composed of elements:

$$CS_i^j = \{CS_{(\ldots)}^{a_1}, \ldots, CS_{(\ldots)}^{a_n}, |\cdot|_{(\ldots)}^{p_1}, \ldots, |\cdot|_{(\ldots)}^{p_m}\}$$

$$CS_k^l = \left\{CS_{(\ldots)}^{b_1}, \ldots, CS_{(\ldots)}^{b_r}, |\cdot|_{(\ldots)}^{q_1}, \ldots, |\cdot|_{(\ldots)}^{q_s}\right\}$$

where

$(\ldots)$ *denotes an unspecified identification number for a given object*

and $a_{i,}, \ldots, b_i, \ldots, p_i, \ldots, q_i$ *are types*

We say that $CS_i^j \underset{strong}{\overset{complexity}{>}} CS_k^l$ *iff* CS_k^l can be constructed solely of some but not all subsets of elements that are available in CS_i^j. ■

[6] Our discussion does not take into account hypotheses about "extraterrestrial" origins of life.
[7] The condition for ordering can be weakened, for example, if we require only that elements of the same type must be used, not necessarily in the same quantity.

Comment This definition is oriented toward ordering *collective intelligence* and *Life* in a maximally convincing way, which is quite rigorous.

Examples

$$CS_{u1}^1 = \{c_1, c_2, |\cdot|^{p1}\} \ \textit{and} \ CS_{u2}^1 = \{c_1, c_2, c_3, |\cdot|^{p1}\} \rightarrow CS_{u2}^1 \underset{strong}{\overset{complexity}{>}} CS_{u1}^1$$

reason: more *information molecules* c_3

$$CS_{w1}^2 = \{c_1, c_2, c_3, CS_d^1, |\cdot|^{p1}\} \ \textit{and} \ CS_{w2}^1 = \{c_1, c_2, c_3, |\cdot|^{p1}\} \rightarrow$$

$$CS_{w2}^2 \underset{strong}{\overset{complexity}{>}} CS_{w1}^1$$

reason: CS_{w1}^2 *has* CS_d^1 *inside which is not available in* CS_{w2}^1

Let us order *computational spaces* along the complexity scale defined here, and let us look at where the inference processes required for *collective intelligence* can begin and where *Life* can begin. The best way is to make a graphics display (see Fig. 5-2). Some comments are appropriate here.

The key problem is how to locate the point where property 6 (Replicability) could emerge. It is well known that many even simple chemical molecules can selfreplicate in a favorable environment (15). However, we should remember that selfreplicating molecules also take "building components" from their environment, thus absorb and process other molecules. Pure selfreplication cannot happen in the real world; otherwise the fundamental principle of "constant mass" will be violated. There is the following turning point in the *computational space* of the structure:

$$CS^1 = \{|c_1, c_2, \ldots|\} \ \textit{that is, information molecules are inside the membrane}$$

because according to the inference processes, various types CS^1 there can also be ordered by Definition 29, that is, based on how they affect CS^1. An inference process can *either* reduce the number of c_i that automatically moves CS^1 down on the complexity scale (analog of natural selection), *or* stabilize it *or* even expand it.

Collective intelligence as a computational process can also exist as a reduction process, for example, computing minimum–maximum value by mutual reduction or proving contradiction by decreasing to NIL (16). *Life* with requirement 6 (Replicability) cannot go beyond this point.

This validates our PRECEDENCE HYPOTHESIS given before.

However, the real *Replicability* can start as early as:

$$CS^2 = \{|c_1, c_2, \ldots, CS_1^1, CS_2^1, \ldots|\} \ \text{that is } \textit{the first local computational spaces } CS_{(\ldots)}^1 \textit{ emerge}$$

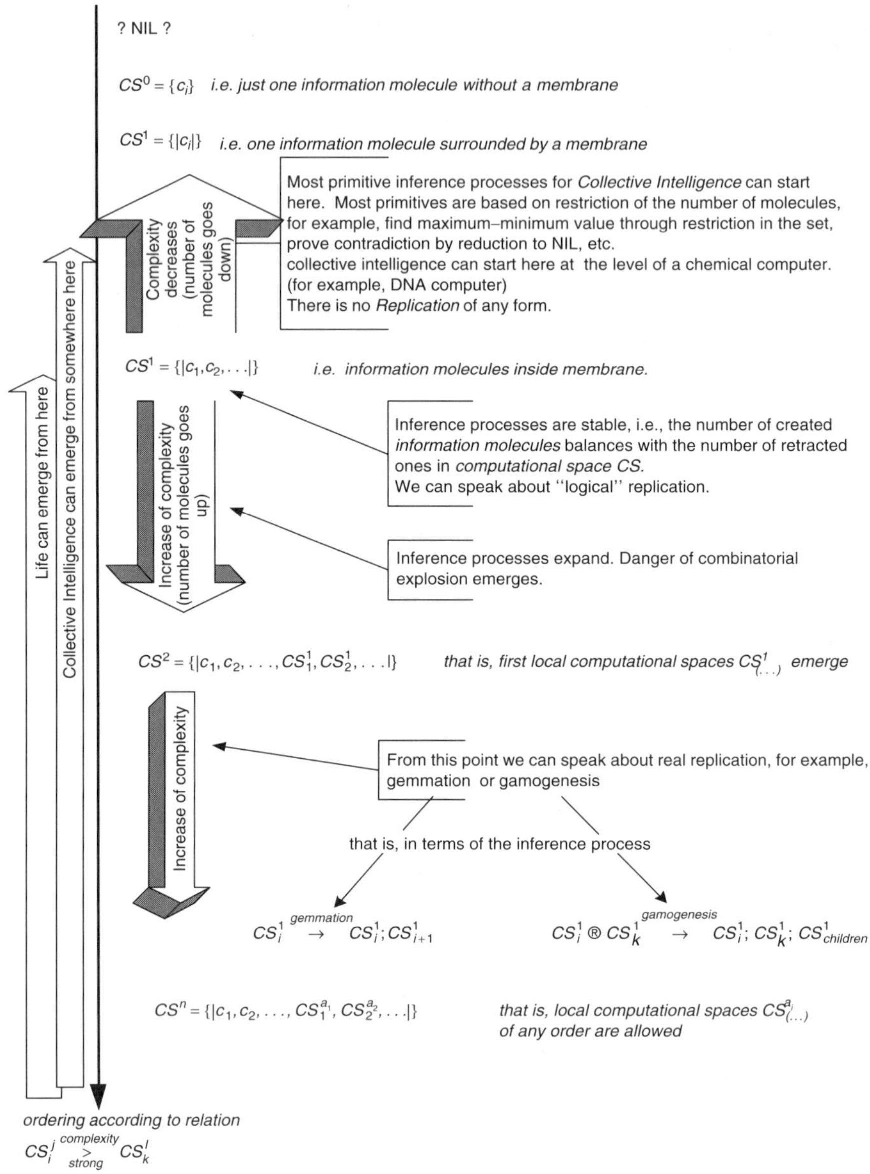

$$CS^1_i \xrightarrow{\text{gemmation}} CS^1_i; CS^1_{i+1} \qquad CS^1_i \circledR CS^1_k \xrightarrow{\text{gamogenesis}} CS^1_i; CS^1_k; CS^1_{children}$$

$$CS^j_i \overset{complexity}{\underset{strong}{>}} CS^l_k$$

Figure 5-2. Ordering computational spaces *CS* according to their level of complexity.

From this point on the complexity scale we can speak about gemmation and gamogenesis.

It is perhaps surprising that we can extrapolate *collective intelligence* back in time beyond the point when *Life* emerged, but there can also be other surprising extrapolations. A structure, such as a "B-52 bomber with its crew on board" also does not fulfill the requirements for being alive. The components of this social structure are alive but not the structure itself. Metabolism, adaptability, self-maintenance (autonomy), self-repair, perhaps growth, and even evolution but NOT replicability are fulfilled, and this object is *collectively intelligent*. However, for example, a company like IBM can also replicate and fulfill the definition of a live and (collectively) intelligent being.

At the time of writing this book, we were not able to conclude a draft proof of our HYPOTHESIS ON ORIGIN or the HYPOTHESIS ON CYCLES, that is, that *collective intelligence* as a model of inference processes implies *Life*, and that later such a metalogical process should behave in cycles. We consider them both as highly probable and as subjects for future discussion.

CONCLUSION

This section has been written in an attempt to use the formalism of *collective intelligence* to establish a formal relationship between the concept of *Life* and *intelligence*. We have proposed a draft of a proof on the basis of the complexity of computational processes that simple *collective intelligence* emerged before *Life* did on earth.

We have also proposed two hypotheses that *Life* (as a process) is a logical consequence of emerged *collective intelligence* processes in the environment of the earth. The second hypothesis states that since that time, a cyclic process developed during which more and more complex forms of *intelligence* and *Life* have propagated each other.

5.2. ARTIFICIAL COLLECTIVE INTELLIGENCE WITH AN EVOLUTIONARY DESIGN OF A PROCESSOR STRUCTURE FOR COMPUTER GRAPHICS[8]

As has been mentioned before, the *collective intelligence* theory does not require its components to be alive in the common sense. Thus, we can create any *artificial system* of *collective intelligence*, for example, of software agents, and we can try to use such an *artificial collective intelligence* to solve some of our, for example, engineering problems.

Let us look into one proposed opportunity of this type.

When "a production structure" is observed over a long time span, for example, the architecture of a computer for certain applications, it is clear that such a structure evolves to fulfill and optimize the requirements imposed by the nature of that class of computational processes. Normally, optimization is just used to

[8] This research project involves the following research colleagues: A. Y. Zomaya at the Parallel Computing Research Lab., in the Department of Electrical and Electronic Engineering at The University of Western Australia, and R. Straś from the Mathematics and Computer Science Computer Center at Kuwait University.

increase the speed of processing, that is, the number of instructions or other computational primitives (e.g., "Goraud shaded polygons" in computer graphics applications) that can be processed (will pass through) per second by a given system (242).

This *diagram* of "hardware optimization by evolutionary process" has been realized by the "external, live *collective intelligence* of human teams" (e.g., in the Silicon Graphics, Inc. research center) who are observing and analyzing the performance of working systems on a specific assignment and are introducing speedup modifications. As a result, we are provided with generation after generation of new hardware architectures for specific applications, which are claimed by the producers to be optimal; however, it is not possible to confirm this optimality. This is because the structure of the processor is too complex to be described and analyzed for optimization with any previous, formal tools.

Here, we present the belief that for the problem of processor design, we can build *artificial collectively intelligent systems*, which later can be modeled to see which "internal processor structure" will emerge. As a result, architectural suggestions for specialized graphic workstations can be given.

The idea of evolving hardware and software is relatively old; the inventors of the computer and the founders of cybernetics first broached it. Presently, this idea is developing under the headings of *evolutionary computing* or *reconfigurable hardware* and is growing in the field of *bioinspired systems* and *evolvable hardware*. The first workshop in this domain, "Towards Evolvable Hardware," took place in Switzerland, in October, 1995. The first international conference on *evolvable systems*, "From Biology to Hardware" (ICES96), was held in Japan in October, 1996. The second international conference on *evolvable systems*, "From Biology to Hardware" (ICES98), was held in Switzerland, in September, 1998 (341–344). The last one was in April 2000, in Scotland (ICES2000).

The novelty of the approach presented in the following text is that the paradigm of *collective intelligence* is being used for this purpose. On this basis, we propose to coin the new term and discipline *artificial collective intelligence (ACI)*, with the suggestion of potential industrial applications.

Our basic idea is to make intelligent *information molecules* the functional components of the computer architecture. Additionally, let us equip them with the abilities required for *collective intelligence*, and finally, let us see how their *collective intelligence* will drive them into a specific, final organization of *computational space*. It can be assumed that such an architecture will be quasi-optimal for a specific class of computational problems, because it will emerge through evolution.

It should be noted that the property that distinguishes the concept of *information molecules* for *collective intelligence* from *cooperating intelligent agent* approaches (185,345–348) is that their instinctive (fundamental, starting) behavior is chaotic. However, under certain environmental "pressure," driven by social abilities and properly arranged "intrinsic" *collective intelligence*, they eventually can shift to quasi-chaotic or even "settled" and organized behavior. This property will be designed here for the hardware.

Most of todays computer systems and even processors are internally complex architectures, composed of computational elements selected and organized into specific structures. This can even be seen in such basic structures as the Pentium processor, which has several functional units working in parallel; some of which are duplicated. There are characteristic internal substructures, such as, pipelines. Tasks (processor instructions) are transported between them until they are fully executed. Some instructions creating the program can be independent, whereas others must be executed in a specific order.

For a given processor's architecture, we must raise some general questions:

- □ Are the processing assignments of the functional units proper and optimal ones?
- □ Is the number of functional units correct?
- □ Is the internal organization, that is, location of functional units, links (bus structures), method of cooperation, and so forth, correct and optimal?—perhaps alternatively, do better structures exist for such a processor?

The difficulty of these problems from arranging the configuration is illustrated by Figure 5-3, which presents some examples of advanced multiprocessor workstations. More detailed considerations on principles of architecture for computer graphics are discussed later in Section 5.2.1.

As has been mentioned before, *artificial collective intelligence* is expected to be the tool that will allow the emergence of some evolutionary alternative architecture. For our considerations and simulations, we will use the domain of computer graphics for the following reasons:

1. Computer graphics workstations require extremely high computational power, especially when three-dimensional animated graphics is used for virtual reality (VR) helmets. For VR, two views, left and right must be calculated in real time under the time pressure of changing scenes and unexpected movements of the helmet when the user changes his focus.
2. Three-dimensional dynamic objects such as a *human face speaking* (see Fig. 5-5) are usually approximated by mesh, and thus, generate a huge number of homogenous graphic primitives (polygons) that must undergo the same processing patch passing through the workstation. This is a flow of tens of millions of primitives per second.
3. Mutual dependence between subtasks can be easily controlled a priori through assumption of certain illumination dependencies between primitives and through analysis of the shape of the three-dimensional object to be processed by a workstation.
4. For advanced, multiprocessor workstations designed for graphics, specific tree-like architectures have been elaborated, because requirements for computational speed are growing rapidly as the *token of computations*

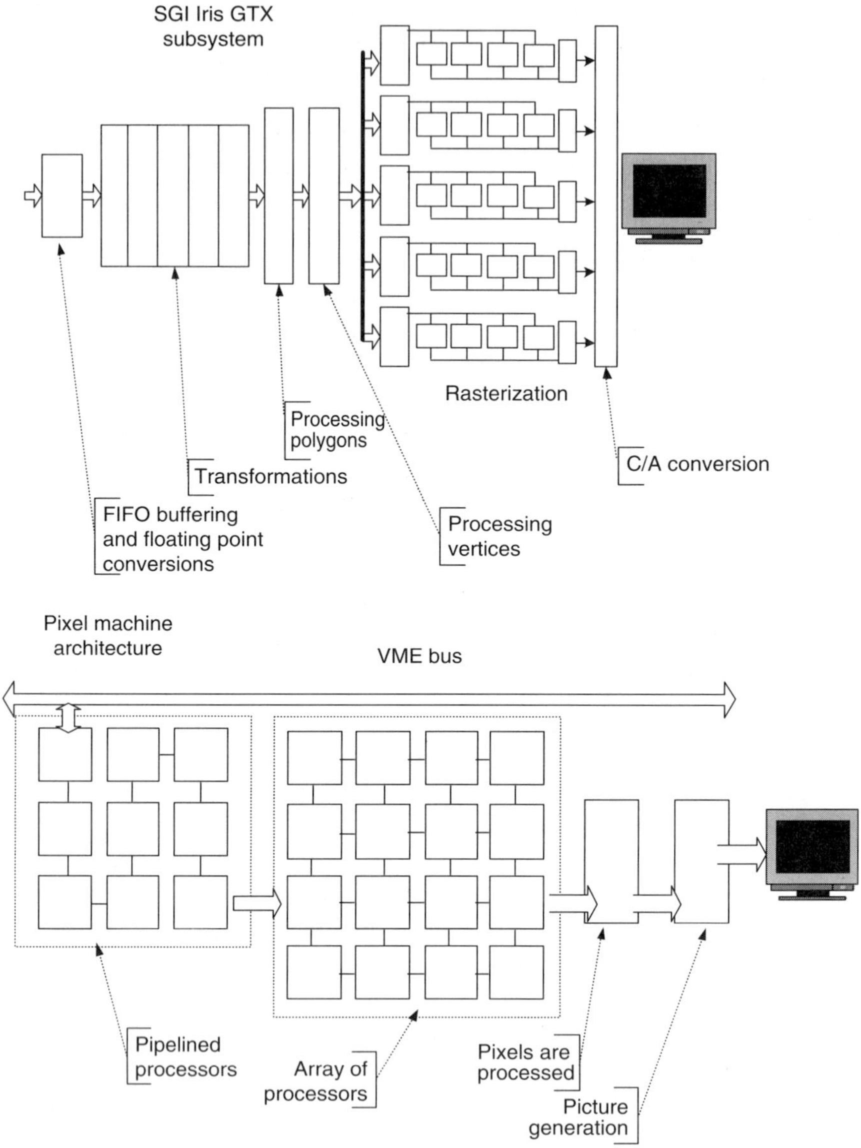

Figure 5-3. Examples of multiprocessor architectures in graphics workstations.

comes near an output device, that is, a monitor. This provides us with "a reference architecture" for our experiments.

The discussion we present here will have the following form. The next part will give an overview of the principles of computer graphics processing, and will present the basic concept of architecture for multiprocessor workstations.

The following part will present the concept of *artificial collective intelligence* on the basis of the basic theory of general *collective intelligence*. The last part will be a presentation of a specially designed simulation model with experiments, and finally, some conclusions will be given.

5.2.1. Data Processing in Computer Graphics

First, let us describe the primary sequence of computations for three-dimensional computer graphics. The basic picture is given in Figure 5-4.

The elementary computational steps for computer graphic problems, (simplified for an *object-order* approach) presented in Figure 5-4, require at least the following steps of processing:

Step 1: Database Traversal

The database containing formal or programming descriptions of three-dimensional objects (which create the scene) is "traversed" to extract polygons. They are described in a local coordinate system.

Step 2: Clipping Planes

The polygons are analyzed if they are inside the volume (fully or partially) created by the clipping planes. If not, the polygons are rejected from the display list or reduced (if only partially inside the clipped volume).

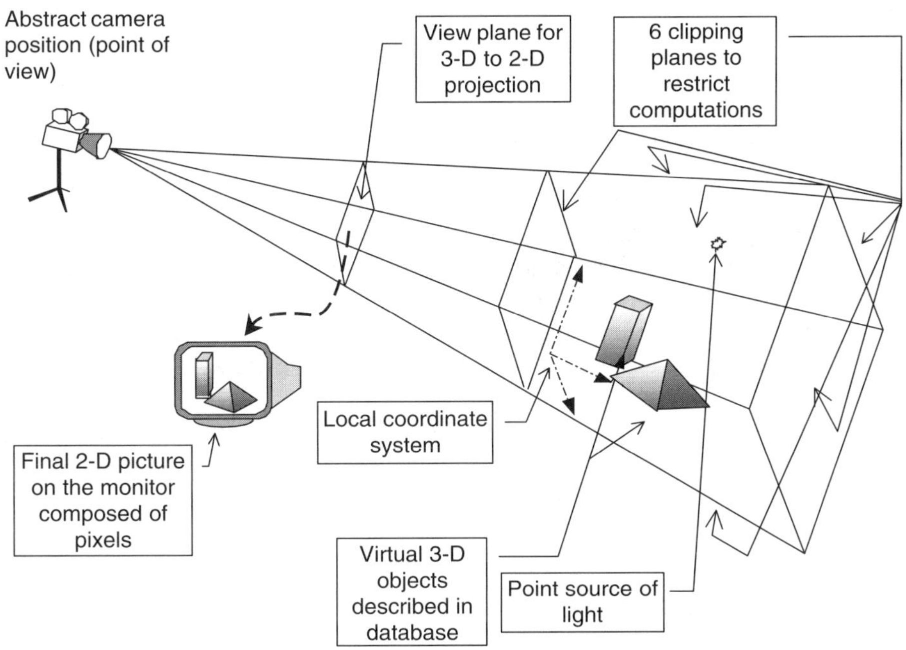

Figure 5-4. Basic concepts of calculations for three-dimensional graphics.

Step 3: Light and Shadow

The illumination problems are solved, and the polygons are colored.

Step 4: Projection from three-dimensions to two-dimensions

The polygons are projected into the view plane. Visibility problems are resolved, for example, on the Z-buffering base.

Step 5: Rasterization

The polygons projected into the view plane are converted (approximated) into a set of pixels in screen coordinates. Descriptions of pixels are sent to the screen controller for final display on the monitor.

The above sequence of processing is the conventional one (approximated) for analysis and modeling of experiments on evolving computer architecture for computer graphics purposes. Real sequences are more complicated (242).

Presently, we should keep in mind that a high-end computer graphics workstation should be able to process at least 30 frames per second, perhaps in virtual reality mode (left and right views) with even hundreds of moving and morphing objects such as those shown in Figure 5-5, for example, in a specific movie sequence.

Let us look at how parallel architectures can be organized for computer graphics workstations.

The basic issue is that at the database traversal level, computational requirements are relatively low and are restricted to a generation of polygons. Later, the required computational power rapidly grows, reaching a maximum at "pixel bus" where the required speed and flow of data is so high that a picture must be displayed column by column in interleaving mode. Otherwise, the required frequency in electronics would be too high. For considerations on how the number of computations grows at every step in a graphics pipeline, see J.D. Foley et al. (242).

There are many ways to design parallel multiprocessor architecture for robust computer graphics workstations, either using a sequence of fast, dedicated processors for execution of specific actions (pipelining) or processing several, for example, polygons in parallel at the same time, as shown in Figure 5-6. In some cases, matrices of processors must be used, for example, for transformations. As a result, we can have a variety of implementations like those illustrated before in Figure 5-3.

When parallelizing computer graphics computations from an algorithmic point of view, we should have in mind that computations for rasterization can be run either in *object-order* or in *image-order*:

object-order

```
for each primitive P do
  for each pixel q within P do
   Update frame buffer based on color and visibility of P at q;
```

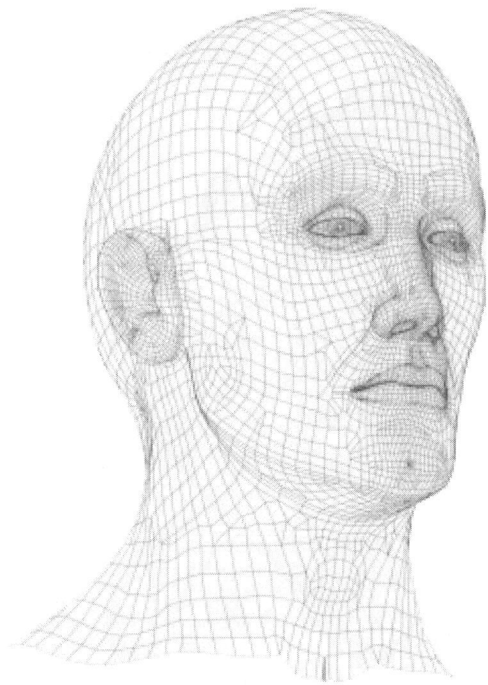

Head, Male 3 – R
Vertices – 6638
Polygons – 6639

Figure 5-5. Human face in three-dimensional graphics.

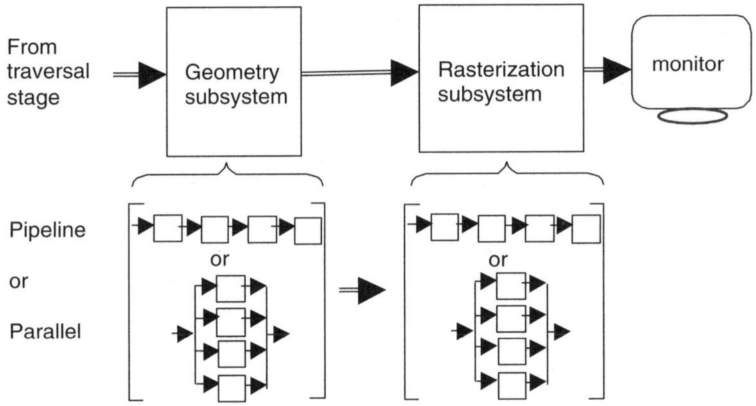

Figure 5-6. Basic concept of parallel, multiprocessor robust computer graphics architecture (according to Foley et al. (242)).

image-order

```
for each pixel q do
  for each primitive P covering q do
     compute P's contribution to q, outputting q when
                                                  finished;
```

The different *object-order* or *image-order* approaches highly affect hardware, because, for example, for *object-order*, the most suitable hardware is based on Z-buffering, whereas for *image-order*, the best architectures are optimized for *scan-line algorithms*. An example of a scan-line algorithm is the famous *ray-tracing algorithm*.

Note here that the problem of architecture design is similar to the problem of organizing *beings* into cooperative production structures at different levels and how to settle them around a production space to get maximum overall performance in that social structure.

Now we should define tools for our approach to designing multiprocessor architecture for a computer graphics workstation.

5.2.2. Artificial Collective Intelligence

The basic idea of *artificial collective intelligence* is creativity (to build artificial systems with the *collective intelligence* property) and not the analysis of existing systems to evaluate or improve their *collective intelligence*, which has been the dominant approach so far in this book.

There are three possible approaches:

Modeling: in this approach a simulation model (not necessarily an exact one) of a certain environment or process is created with some form of *collective intelligence* nested there to solve a specific problem. An example is our system for designing a multiprocessor architecture of a graphics workstation.

Attributing: it is possible to expand the abilities (attribute new abilities) of certain existing objects, for example, servers in the computer network, so that they can collectively and intelligently solve certain problems, for example, traffic jams on the web, the hunt for viruses, and so forth.

Creating: this possibility is still at the level of consideration. It could be any system of *collective intelligence* created from scratch.

When we intend to apply *artificial collective intelligence* to solve a specific problem in a specific environment with a special focus on designing architectures for computer graphics workstations, we can propose the following functional steps:

Step 1: An analysis of the existing environment should be done to find *destructive and constructive* forces. We must be aware that the classification into *destructive and constructive* depends on the point of view. For general *collective intelligence*, chaos is a *constructive force* and not a *destructive* one (at the early stage of development, and later for the introduction of variations). Later, the definition of *information molecules* will depend on these forces.

Almost anything can be taken as an environment, for example, computer networks or virtual, abstract *computational space* of any nature, for example, war-games.

Step 2: The goal of the overall process must be defined. In our problem, the goal is to obtain a processor structure that can be claimed as optimal or quasi-optimal for a computer graphics workstation. The start or initial state is "an empty" environment without *information molecules* (agents).

Step 3: *Information molecules* must be defined with *collective intelligence* ability. This will require the following subdefinitions:

1. The basic structure of *information molecules* includes displacement abilities, memory and computational abilities as well as communicational and perceptual abilities, if necessary.
2. Social abilities include individual goals, instinct bias to create families, unions, bands, and societies. The trading system can also be defined.

Information molecules can be defined at any required level of complexity, equivalent (or not) to:

I. Viruses
II. Bacteria
III. Beings with vision and systems of effectors
IV. Beings equipped with any *artificial intelligence* problem-solving abilities.

Step 4: In most cases, the environment must be "tuned" to somehow control the behavior of the *information molecules*, for example, to restrict unlimited (explosive) growth of some types or structures.

Step 5: In the authors experience, it seems to be practically impossible to get the desired results without long sequences of iterations (simulations). Systems of *artificial collective intelligence* are extremely complex and usually display unexpected behavior (305).

5.2.3. An Evolvable System for Computer Graphics Based on Artificial Collective Intelligence

Let us define how *artificial collective intelligence* can be created for the evolving architecture of a computer graphics system. The model of computer graphics computations used for our considerations is as described in Section 5.2.1. Our proposal to construct an evolvable system can be summarized as follows:

- In contrast to the majority of papers on evolvable hardware (341–344), we do not assume the existence of any hardware in the background. At the beginning, the functional elements of "future" hardware are carried out by *information molecules CSs* (of operator type) in the main *computational space* CS^{main}. They are fully chaotic: displace, replicate, expire, and self-evolve (i.e., change their abilities). Gradually, they should settle, define their mutual relations, and redefine "personal abilities"—until the *computational space* starts to be organized or rather becomes stabilized. After this, the hardware organization (e.g., silicon hardware structure) of the assumed future computer graphics workstation can be derived (or mapped) on the basis of analysis of the structure emerging from *computational space*.
- At the beginning of the proposed evolvable system, we assume that main *computational space* is simple, first level, that is, CS^1 and contains the following:
    1. Five types of *information molecules CSs* representing operators: $CS^{traverse}$, $CS^{clipping}$, $CS^{light\ and\ shadow}$, $CS^{projection}$, $CS^{rasterization}$. Let us denote members of this class as $CS^{operator}$. These are assumed as ancestors of replication for more components (functional), according to future processing needs.
    2. In addition, we assign some *information molecules CSs* with the ability to "store" and to deliver *information molecules CSs* of data type to other *information molecules CSs* of operator type. Let us denote members of this class as $CS^{transport}$.
    3. For such a model of computations, so-called *control information molecules CSs* are necessary, mainly to stabilize and control computational processes (310,335).

    In *computational space* CS^1, there will also be a rapidly changing (usually according to a bell curve) set of *information molecules CSs* representing all temporary forms of data required by the steps of processing, given in Section 5.2.1. Let us denote members of this class as CS^{data}. For example, if just a four-sided pyramid should be displayed, evolution of CSs would be like this ($\rightarrow$ means transition to state of CS):

    $CS^{pyramid} \rightarrow$

    $\{CS_1^{side}, CS_2^{side}, CS_3^{side}, CS_4^{side}\} \rightarrow$

    if each side is composed of 100 pixels then $\left\{CS_1^{pixel}, \ldots, CS_{400}^{pixel}\right\}$
- The hardware structure of a computer cannot be more than three-dimensional; thus, for our experiments main *computational space* CS^1 will have the form shown in Figure 5-7.
- To provide a chance for stabilization of such an evolvable system, and as a result of the emergence of the internal structure, optimal or quasi-optimal from a processing point of view, it is necessary to equip *information molecules CSs*

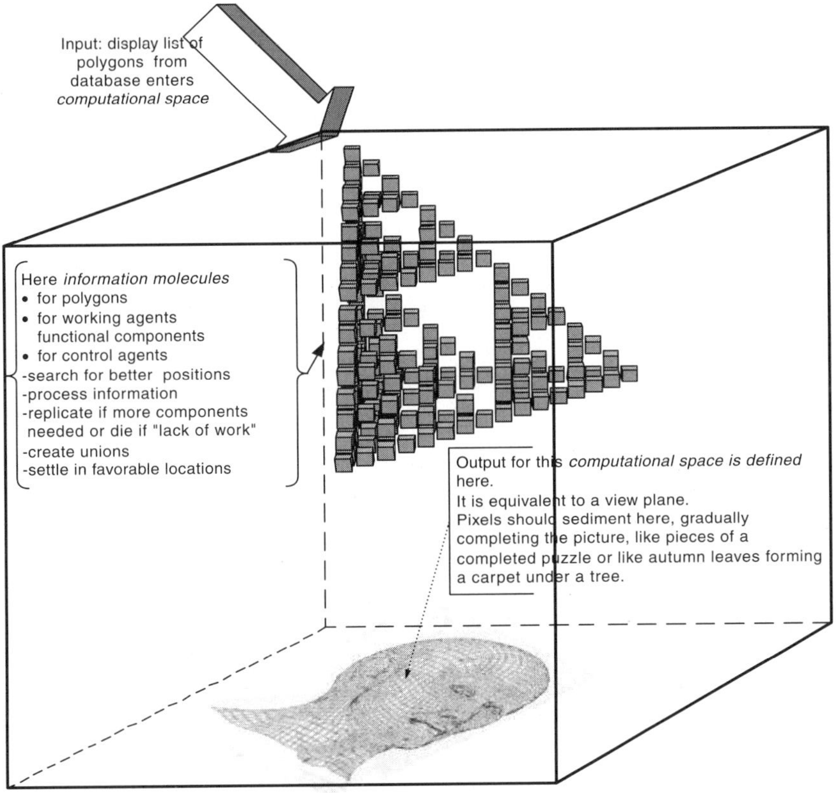

Figure 5-7. *Computational space* for designing architecture of graphics workstations.

representing operators with a social and settlement bias of behavior. Thus, the strategy of their behavior will have the form (note that not all elements of behavior have been implemented yet in our simulation model):

(a) *Information molecules* representing operators must process data; otherwise, they will expire. Every processing act will give (award) some credits to these *information molecules.* A lack of credits will initialize the expiration process for a molecule after a certain delay. We can interpret Brownian movements as a process of looking for the proper *information molecules* of data. If such a one is found and processed, the $CS^{operator}$ will "settle for the time being," assuming that this location is good for more CS^{data} of the proper type.

(b) The $CS^{operator}$ will try to cooperate with others in the following way. A given $CS_a^{operator}$ after processing given CS^{data} can either release it to CS or can look for another $CS_b^{operator}$ seeking this type of CS^{data}. This transfer, if successful, will be awarded with some credits transferred from *information molecule* "*a*" to "*b*." This should provide the emergence of social structures similar to pipelining, where *information molecules* representing operators settle together and cooperate.

It is interesting that use of abstract currency (as mentioned before) is the easiest way to impose cooperation in such a quasi-chaotic system *of information molecules* (agents).

This observation will be the pivotal element of the discussion given in the next Section, where a *collective intelligence* point of view will be presented on the origins and possible definition of "money or currency" used by human social structures.

5.2.4. Description of Simulation System and Results

Let us describe the simulation system that was built in 1999 by Dr. R. Straś (305) for our project. The simulation system was coded in C language and run on a Sun SPARC-1000 multiprocessor. At the moment of writing this text, a more advanced simulation system is under development.

The simulation system allows defining scalar or structural *data types*, such as integers, arrays, or strings of characters. On this basis, we can create *information molecules CSs* carrying data of a specified type, and for the needs of the simulation model, *data sets* containing *information molecules. CSs* can be created (new), destroyed, modified, copied, or moved between *data sets.*

An arbitrary number of types of $CS^{operator}$ can be defined. The $CS^{operator}$ definition consists of an operator descriptor, time needed to complete it, idle time if work cannot be done, input and output of CS^{data} sets, and the number of consumed and produced CS^{data} molecules. An arbitrary number of working *information molecules CSs* of each type can be created. If a working *CS* can acquire all its input CS^{data} molecules, it processes them and returns its output CS^{data} molecules; otherwise, it stays idle for a specified period of time. If a working *CS* stays busy for a specified number of subsequent work cycles, it creates a new working *CS* of the same operator type. On the other hand, if a working agent encounters a specified number of subsequent idle cycles, it is destroyed. A simulation ends when either the simulation time reaches its limit, or there are no more working agents or no more input CS^{data} molecules in the system.

The graphical processing problem is stated as follows. Given is a three-dimensional object defined as a set of edges, a set of vertices, and a set of surfaces. These data must be transformed into a set of three-dimensional polygons by *traverse* operations. Every polygon is then processed by *clipping*, and then by *light and shadow* operations. The next operation, called *projection*, transforms three-dimensional polygons into two-dimensional ones. Finally, the *rasterization* operation transforms each two-dimensional polygon into a number of pixels that can be displayed on the screen. The time needed to complete each of the five operations above is well defined and constant. The number of input CS^{data} is also known. The number of produced CS^{data} items, however, for some operations cannot be predicted. For example, if the entire figure is placed beyond the displayed area, the *clipping* operation will not produce any CS^{data}.

To run the graphical processing in our simulation system, we defined six working CS^{data} sets for each possible stage of processing. We defined a figure by creating a mesh. We have also given five $CS^{operator}$ types: *traverse, clipping, light and shadow, projection*, and *rasterization*, with input and output CS^{data} sets defined in such a way that they comprise a pipeline with mesh as input and pixels as output CS^{data} set. Initially, we created one working agent of each type. With the present version of the simulation system, every agent is duplicated after three subsequent work cycles, and after three subsequent idle periods, it is destroyed.

Let us now look at simulation results available at the moment of completing this book. This project is being continued, and new results are expected; however, even entry one is to some extent surprising. The emerging structure of the processor resembles a fractal pattern, but regularities are visible as shown in Figure 5-8a. Because results are three-dimensional, the most representative section of the *computational space* according to the approach presented in Figure 5-8a is shown in Figure 5-8.

Figure 5-8b presents typical simulation results. They are difficult to show clearly without color and three-dimensional representation, because they are fractal-like, with interleaving populations of settled functional elements. Arc lines express the fact that as we move away from the input, characteristics

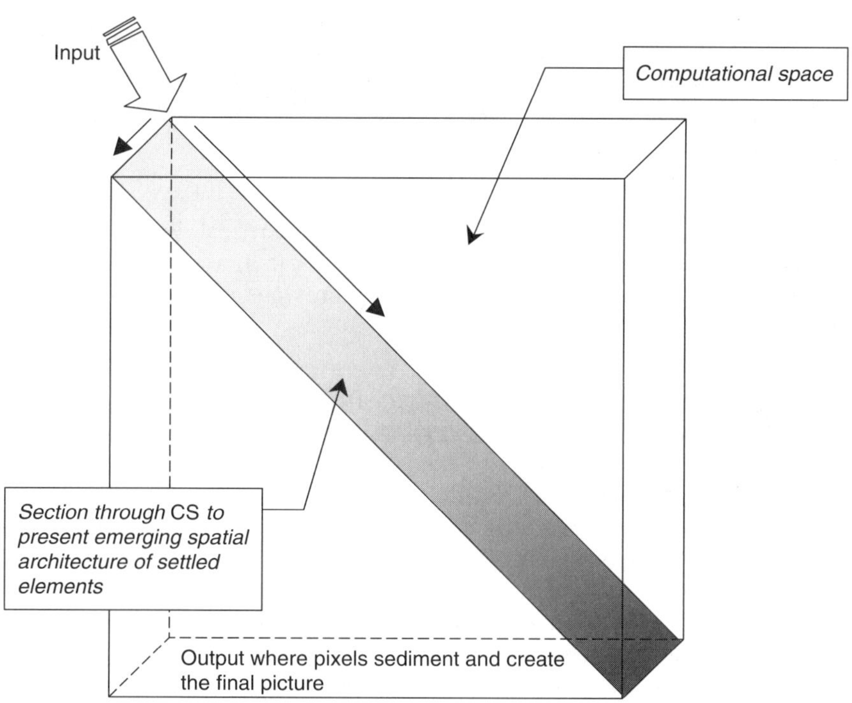

Figure 5-8a. Method of presenting simulation results on emerging architectures.

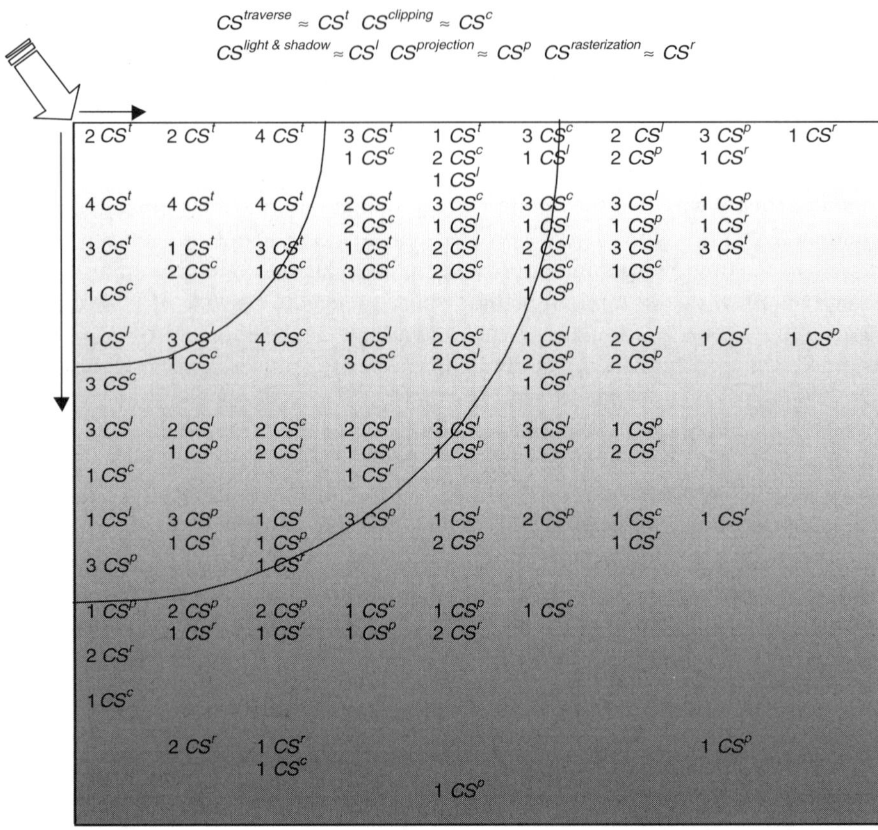

Figure 5-8b. Arrangement of settled components in simulation of hardware organization.

of settlement are changing in an approximately spherical way, in terms of overlapping populations. Even in areas where some functional elements are dominant, some elements can be found from a previous group or elements that should be in a spherical layer later.

5.3. CAN MONEY (CURRENCY) BE CONSIDERED AS AN ELEMENT (DISCOVERY) OF HUMAN *COLLECTIVE INTELLIGENCE*?

The concept of the Random PROLOG model of computations applied to *collective intelligence* allows a growing number of applications — some of which are obvious, such as analyzing or optimizing social structures or building *artificial collective intelligence* systems for engineering applications. However, in some cases, applications of *collective intelligence* are emerging in unlikely domains, for example, investigations of the origins of Life discussed in Section 5.1.

Now we want to point out one more such domain, where the *collective intelligence* concepts discussed in this book can be applicable, because the concept of *money* (currency) can also be viewed and analyzed from the formal *collective intelligence* perspective. It is not intended here to target an engineering application or a "product" that could be useful in, for example, stock trading or, for example, like *fractals* that were used in stock market analysis (349), but rather, we are interested in the general relationship between *money* and *intelligence*, in a very wide sense.

R.M. Starr (350) writes "why is there *money* ..." and that "*money*, like language and the wheel, is one of the fundamental discoveries of civilization." Computational economics, as we discuss later, is able to show in a mathematical (formal) way "how it has happened," but the question remains "why it has happened" that money exists in civilization.

The simulation model described in Section 5.2, designed to build a specific hardware equipped with *artificial collective intelligence*, has demonstrated that the agents created there (represented by *information molecules*) will behave in more organized ways and also will more quickly create social structures to solve computer graphics problems if they are designed to be able to *buy* resources for "personal input" and are able to *sell* (trade) their output to other agents. In other words, in the background of certain activities (production in this case) trade exists, and they use *money*.

The ability of agents to displace and settle in a certain space when looking for locations in a *computational space* rich with the required input resources and the ability to reproduce, are still not enough in a specific environment for efficient emergence of stable *collective intelligence* for solving specific problems.

We must remember that in such an artificial environment of computer-simulated agents, there are no natural *threats* or *critical necessities* imposing and stabilizing social structures of agents and their collective behavior, such as the problems of foraging, mating, defense or hunting, and so forth, (see Section 2.2.1 on the *collective intelligence* of animals).

To expand a simulation model with "wild animals," a "harsh winter" or "famine" is too complex, even to give a chance for a reasonable definition of those terms for a computer and to simulate them in an inexpensive or time-consuming way.

To compensate this lack, we must use or create some other mechanism, copied from nature or devised, and it must be a simple one to allow easy and efficient implementation in a computer-simulated model.

Looking at the most recent literature on agents (not related to computational economics) such as those of, for example, G. Weiss (351), it seems that the problem of cooperation between agents "suffers" a serious lack of any clear, general idea of how to define, organize, and implement it.

It seems that use of the mechanism of trading based on the use of money is probably the easiest and best way to define and impose a stable advanced cooperation between agents in a system of *distributed intelligence*.

This hypothesis seems strange — however, if we look deeper into this conclusion, it should be not a surprise — when observing what a powerful force in humans "the need for profits is, finally measured by earned or conquered *money*" (it does not matter if these human beings are individually considered as intelligent or not).

The simplicity and power of the concept of the mechanism of *money* imposing cooperation between *information molecules* (without any additional requirements, e.g., good will which can be difficult to implement), and clear results in the rapid creation of social structures bring us directly to perhaps the most fundamental question:

> "*is money* an inevitable concept in *collective intelligence*"?

However, it has not been observed that, for example, bacteria or ants use money; thus, perhaps a certain complexity is required[9], for example, of individual intelligence and/or size of the social structure. This problem will be addressed in the conclusion to this section of the book.

We can start our considerations with the question:

> "can we formalize any simple concept of *money* for use in computational *collective intelligence*"?

It is interesting that in the area of Computational Economics, the concept of agents is widely used for the purpose of analyzing economic processes. Research results from the area of Agent-based Computational Economics[10] (ACE) should especially be mentioned.

Let us quote the sentence found in the homepage on ACE, which we find very important from the point of view of our considerations on *collective intelligence*:

> *A central concern of ACE researchers is to understand the apparently spontaneous formation of global regularities in economic processes, such as the unplanned coordination of trade in decentralized market economies that economists associate with Adam Smith's invisible hand.*

Note that this is a "no more, no less" statement about the existence of certain, unspecified *collective intelligence* in or behind a trade.

To equip our *information molecules* (agents) with a trading nature for *collective intelligence*, the model of a trade between agents has been assumed to be slightly different from those available in ACE because we are not interested in analyzing a *trade*, but in strengthening (amplifying) the *collective intelligence* of a certain social structure through the use of *money*-based trade.

[9] For this reason, we will depart from our principle that "everything is an *information molecule* of the proper level," and to make the text more clear, in some cases, we will say agents but other times *information molecules*.

[10] There is an excellent website on Agent-based Computational Economics maintained by Prof. Leigh Tesfatsion from the Department of Economics, at Iowa State University, at *http://www.econ.iastate.edu/tesfatsi/ace.htm*. Resources available at this site include an annotated syllabus of readings, surveys, software, teaching materials, and pointers to individual researchers and research groups.

In our *collective intelligence* form of exchange with the use of abstract *money*, agents (*information molecules*) will earn *money* when selling output or services, (products of *information molecules*) but will also expend *money* when purchasing for input or services. If an *information molecule* (agent) does not "possess" any *money* (is bankrupt), the termination process for this *information molecule* will be started. In contrast, if an *information molecule* earns a sufficient number of credits, such an agent will reproduce.

This means that the widely known saying "those who trade, live and reproduce" will be applied here as a metarule.

Before we try to develop and discuss this process, let us look into the concept and history of *money* for humans, as presented in the literature related to economics (352).

5.3.1. Brief Summary of the Idea and History of Money and Humans

If we ask "what is money?"—obviously there are many possible definitions; thus, let us look at some fundamental sources, such as D. Glyn (352) on the history of money.
In general, money can be defined according to the encyclopedia as follows:

DEFINITION 30: MONEY[11]

A commodity, such as gold, or an officially issued coin or papernote that is legally established as an exchangeable equivalent of all other commodities, such as goods and services, and is used as a measure of their comparative values on the market. ■

To explain this definition, let us look at what Glyn (352) has to say: "Money is anything that is widely used for making payments and accounting for debts and credits," and he goes on to say that the functions of any particular form of *money* may change over time, which makes definition difficult.
According to Glyn (352), the basic functions of *money* are the following:

1. Specific functions (mostly microeconomic)
2. General functions (mostly macroeconomic and abstract)
3. Unit of account (abstract)
4. Common measure of value (abstract)
5. Medium of exchange (concrete)
6. Means of payment (concrete)

[11] Encarta 1998 CD-ROM Encyclopedia.

7. Standard for deferred payments (abstract)
8. Store of value (concrete)
9. Liquid asset
10. Framework of the market allocative system (prices)
11. A causative factor in the economy
12. Controller of the economy

It is interesting to note that for the purposes of computational *collective intelligence*, scientists are convinced (352) that "*money* originated very largely from noneconomic causes (from)":

- Tribute
- Trade
- Blood-money
- Bride-money
- Barter
- Ceremonial and religious rites
- Commerce
- Ostentatious ornamentation
- Acting as the common drudge between economic men

Since ancient civilizations, *money* has been considered as a method of *accumulating* and *exchanging* resources required for activity.

Glyn quotes linguistic evidence from a variety of languages to show how ancient and widespread the association between cattle and *money* was. For example, "pecuniary" comes from the Latin word which means "pecus," cattle however, other *names* of simple goods available to primitive civilizations have also been used to create words related to *money*. In the Polish language (slavonic group of languages), the term "to pay" originates from the term "linen," that is, pieces of linen were used as a form of currency. Both terms are still pronounced similar to the original form.

From a cooperation or *collective intelligence* point of view, another interesting "application of *money*" discovered in early civilizations, was the replacement of penalties for some forms of crimes or violence by *money* compensation. Blood-money is perhaps the most impressive example.

Glyn notes that the word "pay" is derived from the Latin word "pacare" originally meaning to pacify, appease, or make peace with—through an appropriate unit of value, customarily acceptable to both sides.

Similar to this was the payment for brides to compensate the head of the (her) family for the loss of a daughters services because, for example, in nomad families, every member contributed in global power, safety, and productivity of the group, represented by the *father*.

These functions provided significant stabilization (easier methods of avoidance of conflicts or wars) between ancient societies—and thus, amplified cooperation (or at least chance for willful cooperation), allowing them to raise cooperation above the level of the social structure of the *family*.

More advanced forms of *money* emerged with banking in ancient Mesopotamia. The royal palaces and temples provided centralized and secure places for the safekeeping of grain and other commodities. This required the introduction of receipts, which came to be used for transfers not only to the original depositors but also to third parties. A natural consequence was decentralization — when private houses in Mesopotamia also got involved in these banking operations. The laws regulating such exchange were included in the code of Hammurabi.[12]

Notice that with this approach, there were high-level social structures emerging, controlled and driven by the introduction of abstract objects (*money*) with varying interpretation (rate of converse) into real goods.

Money also can be defined in a formal way, assuming a certain *trade model*, for example, like the model that is most widely known under the name the "Kiyotaki-Wright trade model" (353).

We should, however, keep in mind that models like those of Kiyotaki and Wright are very simple compared with real trade, for example, such models consider a few agents trading with a few goods under some very formalized rules.

According to H. Gintis (354), the following definition can be given on the "existence of a medium of exchange" in certain environments populated with agents exchanging goods, that is, what are the conditions required so that certain objects m from a list of all the goods, g will begin to be considered as *money* by a group of agents A in a certain environment.

DEFINITION 31. THE EXISTENCE OF A MEDIUM OF EXCHANGE

We say that a specific good $m \in G$ (i.e. *money, Goods*) will become a universal medium of exchange in certain society A of agents, if there is a positive probability of trade of a good m in the time period, and m is accepted in trade by all the agents against all other available goods, that is, $g \neq m \;\; and \;\; g \in G$.

For a universal medium of exchange m, it is required that a good $m \in G$ has lower storage costs, that is, for each agent $\alpha \in A$, $\text{storage\_costs}(\alpha, m) \leq \text{storage\_costs}(\alpha, p_\alpha)$, where p_a are goods produced by agent α, that is, $p_\alpha \in P_\alpha$.

This definition is simple and convincing and is not imposing any conditions forbidding us to have *money* at any level of *collectively intelligent* behavior, for example, if either *money* and *trade* is built (programmed) into the nature of agents in an artificial way or agents are intelligent enough to collectively compare storage costs of goods, which are consumed, produced, and exchanged.

[12] Hammurabi, king of Babylonia (1792–1750 BC.) primarily remembered for his codification of the laws governing Babylonian life.

Simulations demonstrate (355) that if artificial agents are equipped (or born) with the ability to trade goods they consume and produce, then some commodities will emerge as *money* among them according to the definition given earlier. The trading and consumption pattern will converge to a stationary Nash equilibrium,[13] even if agents start with random exchange rules (355).

Thus, the emergence of *money* can be viewed as a *natural* process (formal consequence) of trade in a specific environment of agents. Note that, what is important is that it has been assumed that agents did not discover trade — trade was inherited as a part of their nature (social life).

Now let us take another point of view — let us see from the point of view of our formal RPP model of computations given in Section 3.4.4.2 of the book, if *money* as certain objects in a certain space fulfills the properties required to be considered as *information molecules* of any level — that is, if this model (RPP) can be applicable for considerations on *money*.

5.3.2. Can Money be Considered in Terms of the Random PROLOG Processor (RPP)?

If we look into the nature and the use of *money* as certain objects and as a whole, *currency* almost perfectly fits the concept of the RPP. This is proven because they both fulfill the following specifications:

1. Simple *currency* in various forms can be considered as "low-level" *information molecules* (of level CS^0) being transferred between higher order CS^n *information molecules*, where some of them (i.e., CS^n) will be interpreted as live beings using *currency*, and some of them will be interpreted as structures or institutions in *computational space*, using or processing and transferring *currency*.

   However, there are known cases where cattle or even slaves were used as *money*; thus, *money* can be any *information molecule* of any level.
2. Different forms of *information molecules* of *money or currency* can have different interpretations, namely, gold coins, cattle, camels, pieces of amber, banknotes, checks, and so forth, — but they can be abstract objects as well, for example, electronic *money*.

   Such *real* interpretations of *information molecules* of *money* can be consequently considered as their carriers, for example, coins, messages of transfer, and so forth.
3. The flow of *money* is nested in the structured space of trading centers, banks, and so forth; moreover, transfers of *money* undergo regulations — but the general behavior of *money* is quasi-chaotic.

   Other formal models of trade similar[14] to the Kiyotaki–Wright trade model, assume random matches of agents for trade; thus, we can say that they are

[13] A Nash equilibrium is a point where neither players gains by moving unilaterally.

[14] There are also other models that assume the existence of a central authority (so-called auctioneer).

the equivalent of "random rendezvous" of *information molecules* that have been applied in the RPP model of computations.

In general, the global quasi-chaotic nature of the money market has several causes:

- The individual quasi-chaotic behavior of humans in local social structures performing their daily routines.
- The behavior of individuals and companies gambling in the stock market for profit. As a result, all regularities "in market chaos" are immediately discovered and consequently applied for individual or company profit, which in the long run annihilates any such regularity.

As a net result (remembering that from the point of view of the dynamical systems theory, *chaos* means irregular fluctuations in a deterministic system), we can say that the stock market systems behave irregularly (quasi-chaotic) because of their own internal logic and not because of random forces acting from outside.

This phenomenon is widely recognized (356–358), and attracts the attention of many scientists and simple gamblers in expectation of extraordinary profits from some symmetry or regularity that aids in stock market prediction.

However, *chaos theory* seems better at explaining financial markets than predicting them (359).

The discovery of fractal patterns in stock indexes and the use of fractal models to describe quasi-chaotic behavior of the stock market appeared as the most successful way from a theoretical point of view for analyzing the stock markets through *chaos*.

B. Mandelbrot (360) defines a fractal in the following way:

A geometric figure or natural object is said to be fractal if it combines the following characteristics:

- o Its parts have the same form or structure as the whole (selfsimilarity), except that they are on a different scale and may be slightly deformed.
- o Its form is extremely irregular, or extremely interrupted or fragmented, and remains so, whatever the scale of examination.
- o It contains *distinct elements* whose scales are very varied and cover a large range.

However, we should be careful when relating *fractals* too much with the *chaos*. Often chaotic, dynamical systems exhibit fractal structures in phase space[15]; nevertheless, there is no direct relation. There are chaotic systems that have nonfractal limit sets (e.g., Arnold's cat map), and there are also fractal structures that can arise in nonchaotic dynamics (361).

In many cases, the behavior of a stock market can be analyzed with fractals, as was summarized in a widely refereed paper of Mandelbrot's, *a*

[15] Phase space is the collection of possible states of a dynamical system.

multifractal walk down Wall Street, published in the Scientific American, February 1999.

4. Units of *money* (*currency*) are created (issued), can be retracted (canceled, lost), converted, and finally stored or transferred. The same is assumed for *information molecules*.
5. Models of trade like the Kiyotaki–Wright model also assume the existence of "global economic" (to a given environment) chains of goods that agents produce and consume.

   They can be easily interpreted as N-element inferences (NEI), if we analyze the phenomenon of *money* with the RPP.

   Such chains of goods in models of trade similar to the Kiyotaki–Wright model are defined according to Gintis' specifications (354):

   - Each agent $a \in A$ consumes a nonempty set of goods $C_a \in G$ and produces a nonempty set of goods $P_a \subset G$ where $C_a \cap P_a = 0$.
   - Each agent $a \in A$ has an increasing, nonnegative, and bounded utility function $u_a : Z_+[C_a] \to \Re$ where R is the real number, and $Z_+[S]$ is the set of nonnegative integral multiples of elements of the set S.
   - Each good $g \in P_a$ also has a production cost $\kappa_{ag} > 0$.
   - It is assumed that an agent participating in trade has at least one production good whose cost of production is less than the utility of consuming c_a, which can be denoted as $\forall c_a \in C_a, u(c_a) > \min_{g \in P_a} \kappa_{ag}$.
   - Each agent $a \in A$ suffers a storage cost $s_{ag} > 0$ in each trading period for each unit of a good g held in inventory.
6. The generalized inference in CS^N given before in Definition 22 (in Section 3.4.4.2) can also be easily found (implemented) in the Kiyotaki–Wright model in such a way (354) that each agent has an *exchange strategy* specifying which trades are acceptable from a given pretrade inventory, and a *production–consumption strategy* specifying what the agent consumes and produces from a given post-trade inventory. When agents meet randomly with their pretrade inventories, they deploy their exchange strategies to identify a mutually acceptable trade. If such a "business unification is successful," they then produce and consume, given their post-trade inventories, according to their production and consumption strategies.

   Notice how well the generalized inference CS^N fits the requirements of the Kiyotaki–Wright model. This is also a significant example of the implementation of the generalized inference CS^N that emerged before the RPP did.
7. Trying to consider *money* as a *collective intelligence* category allows us to have a more general look at economic phenomena, that is, we can consider them as a certain part of interleaving logical processes run in certain social structures. For example, we can consider *money* as a component necessary or useful to "glue together," let us say, the broken chains of an NEI. Not

to be trivial, we can give as an example a case, "I will think for you, but pay me well." This high-level NEI can have many other interpretations unrelated to *money*.

On this basis, we can state the hypothesis that *money* (and the way it is processed) can also be (without any formal obstacles) considered and analyzed in terms of *collective intelligence* as certain *information molecules* existing in *computational-space* in which the *collective intelligence* process(s) take place.

5.3.3. Money-Driven Artificial Collective Intelligence

Let us try to define the simplest configuration of the RPP required for money-driven *collective intelligence*. We will try to look at the required internal and behavioral complexity of beings or agents in using money, and for money itself (perhaps also environmental), in such a way that such currency will be the fundamental force driving such agents individually and globally to some maximum of joined *collective intelligence*—for the purpose of solving a specific problem or class of problems.

First, let us assume that there exists a *closed system* (to exclude the influence of external factors) with the following characteristics:

1. Environment E of any nature, enclosed in a *computational space* CS^E.
2. Let there exist in CS^E a varying set of agents $A = \{CS_1^n, \ldots, CS_m^n\}$ carried by *information molecules* CS^n of a certain complexity. Assume that CS_i^n agents are equipped with the following intrinsic abilities:
   - Mobility to displace in a quasi-Brownian way inside CS^E according to the sum of internal decisions of an agent (e.g., any strategy) and the influence of the environment E.
   - Ability to reproduce if a certain amount of "money assets" are available to a given CS_i^n. Here we come to the first general benefit of having a concept of money with agents. It is not even necessary to specify the nature and amount of such resources required for reproduction, because if they can be traded, it is sufficient to give only a *money*-based approximation of their value to trigger reproduction. This approximation will be just a number (representing a value of assets), not the complex data structure with a detailed specification of the requirements for "reproduction assets." Thus, abstract *money* significantly simplifies the description of the agent in this area as well.
   - If the number of "assets" measured by local currency goes below a certain level, the termination (retraction) period will be initialized for the agent. Thus, the sum of mechanisms of (reproduction, expiration, money) creates for our computational system a simple but powerful evolutionary

mechanism for creating and controlling the population of agents, which are necessary in the system at a certain moment for specific functions.

However, this mechanism causes a reasonable implementation problem, because in some unfavorable situations, all agents of a given type could expire, and later they would be required again. As a result, the whole system could fail. There are probably at least two natural solutions here:

(a) The ants approach: there is a Queen agent laying eggs all the time providing more and more new waves of agents of all types.

(b) The human approach: after a certain time (of being jobless and facing a shortage of money) agents should be able to transform (metamorphose) into other types of agents, which are required by CS^N at the time.

(c) Other possibilities probably exist.

- Agents must have the ability to earn money.

The basic assumption is that earning *money* is a utility function of the agent for the whole *computational space* CS^E. Let us denote this function as

$$U(CS^N, \mathit{time}, \mathit{agent}) \rightarrow \mathit{money}$$

Notice that this function depends on the general task of *computational space* CS^E (see Section 5.1) and time because agents necessary, for example, at the beginning will be redundant later. This is clear from the point of view of the dynamics of social structures (see Section 2.2.3).

The nature of "earning ability" should not be specified because there are too many possibilities here, for example:

- Earning money through transforming other *information molecules* not necessary at a lower level. It can be a production–assembly process or, for example, a "teaching" process where we can say that, for example, the "internal state" of an *information molecule* "for example, the student" is changed.
- Earning money can be done through transporting other *information molecules* from one location to another in CS^N. The basic trade is based on displacement of certain objects from an area of surplus to an area of deficit; thus, workers paid for the transporting are also necessary for any production–assembly process. This is a significant departure from the producer–consumer approach applied in Kiyotaki–Wright trade models.
- There can be money paid for a workers presence, for example, a security man, in a certain location, that is, certain abstract (virtual) service is provided. This is another departure from the producer–consumer approach applied in Kiyotaki–Wright trade models.

It is important that the result here will be an exchange of *money* assigned to a specific agent CS_i^n in CS^N.

3. Assume in CS^E the existence of a set of *information molecules* M of money $M = \{CS_M^0, \ldots, CS_M^0\}$ with the following properties:
   - M can be a variable in the sense that the number of elements and their description can change spontaneously or as a result of the action of elements in the RPP. This will allow, for example, handling of certain processes related to currency such as *inflation*, producing coins or banknotes, loss of money, assets, and so forth.
   - For every $CS_j^k \in A$ and $CS_{M_i}^0 \in M$ there exists a function f defining the ownership rights to a given unit of currency, that is, defined as: $f(CS_{M_i}^0) \rightarrow CS_j^k$ and $f^{-1}(CS_j^k) \rightarrow CS_{M_i}^0$.

     This is the most important element in designing our RPP for a "money-driven *collective intelligence* system."

     The problem is how to implement this function in the RPP; to be consistent with what we observe in the real world of money, there are several possible methods:
     1. The Individual Purse

        It is assumed that the *information molecules* that are creating agents CS_i^n can also create temporary aggregates with a certain number of *information molecules* CS_M^0 of money. This can be interpreted: as "the agent carries money with him." This concept covers the classical use of cash.
     2. The "Right to certificate"

        The *information molecules* CS_M^0 of money are in some location in CS^N with a "*marker* who is the owner" and an agent CS_i^n who has a "right to certificate," that is, can initialize any process in CS^N that will terminate with the modification of the "*marker* who is the owner." This concept covers the use of all transfers, credit cards, remote banking, and so forth.

        Notice that the two cases are not mutually exclusive, that is, they can exist and function in parallel in a given CS^N where the *collective intelligence* process is partially or fully driven by money.
   - *Information molecules* of money can displace only in a deterministic way, as the result of actions of *information molecules* of agents.

Now let us try to discuss if such a system can be driven by the "Invisible Hand of the market" into a configuration or state that we require.

There are several streams of theoretical works considering this problem from the human economy and human social structure point of view under various key words, for example, "The Invisible Hand and Modern Welfare Economics" (362).

However, from our point of view, the use of those theories is restricted because they rely on the assumption of "human rights of individual beings." For example,

for formal considerations, there is the idea of a "Pareto[16] improvement" (363), which is defined as "a change in a social structure that benefits one person and injures nobody." Consequently, a system is defined as *Pareto efficient* if there is no way for the next *Pareto improvement*. This means that the social system has reached some kind of local optimum.
In our case, we are free of such "humanitarian" restrictions:

I. The *collective intelligence* of CS^N is used to service (achieve) the imposed computational task(s) of the whole system, for example, to build the architecture of a computer graphics workstation of maximum performance in an evolutionary way (measured, e.g. by throughput of polygons from database to display)—not to provide a benefit of any form to agents.
II. Agents displace in a quasi-chaotic way to find a location in which they are most necessary.
III. Agents are "liquidated" if they are not "lucky" enough to find a proper location or to convert into another kind of agent that is needed more or they are not able to create a social structure providing them with sufficient income to stay alive.

5.3.4. Conclusions on the Function of Money in *Collective Intelligence*

Our conclusion from this part of the book (and our hypothesis) is that as a category, *money* can be considered as a *functional* discovery of *collective intelligence*.
The basic advantages of this mechanism and explanations as to why it has been found so useful for *collective intelligence* can be summarized in the following way:

1. *Money* as a system creates a universal, overwhelming mechanism that imposes cooperation without regard to the level of the *information molecules* CS^n participating in the process; however, a certain critical, minimal n is required (see Section 5.3.5.). CS^n can be a single being and a social structure (or a company). The mechanism of *money* penetrates all levels of a social structure and all aspects of its activity. Even in some popular sentences about *money*, it is called *a language of communication*.

2. **Hypothesis: *Money* requires at least a minimal level of individual intelligence of the beings (in the real world)**

   But later the "financial mechanism based on *money*" very strongly "awards or prefers/supports" individuals and social structures with a high level of individual or *collective intelligence*.

[16] Named after the Italian economist Vilfredo Pareto (from Microsoft® Encarta® Online Encyclopedia 2000).

This is probably why *money* is not observably used among animals and why *money*, as a mechanism emerged among humans only at a certain stage of human progress on the individual and *collective intelligence* scales. Perhaps, an example could be how children at a certain age "discover" the existence of *money* in the surrounding world and how they start to be *intelligent* in "getting/earning/saving" some *money* for their own use. Notice that this age is above the mental age that can be reached by chimpanzees.

In the Kiyotaki–Wright trade models, *money emerges* spontaneously from the set of commodities used by agents, but in such models, agents are artificially created with the intrinsic ability to rendezvous, to trade, and to evaluate if the trade should be achieved or not. Thus, probably, the conditions for money to emerge are quite simple.

Growth of individual intelligence has somehow increased individual productivity, creating the human as a complex producer and consumer, and intelligence also triggered the emergence of the ability to evaluate, allowing us to compare costs and decide what to trade and when to trade (355).

Notice that ants and monkeys are not complex producers or consumers. Only the ant nest as a whole reaches this level. Thus, a trade can emerge between nests and/or intelligent individuals but not between single ants.

3. Hypothesis: *Money* requires at least a minimal complexity of a social structure (in the real world)

Very small human societies do not use *money* because mutual settlements can be made more easily on the basis of personal local relations, than when using *money*. A queen with pheromones can also efficiently control an ant nest or a bee hive from one central point. However, if the social structure starts to get too big, and the individuals too intelligent, combinatorial problems of mutual relations will probably impose the use of *money*.

In the Kiyotaki–Wright model, responsibility for this phenomena lies with at least two key factors:

- Agents must rendezvous frequently with other agents in attempt to trade. Many needs are temporary (e.g., tools, services, food), and some products expire (e.g., food) after a short time.

  To increase the frequency of rendezvous between agents to open up a chance for a trade, there are some possibilities:

  I There may be a very dense population of agents, but this can be difficult to achieve, for example, if a certain living space is required for a single agent or its "family." In case of foraging based on primitive assembling, or in desert-based stock-breeding, such a great distance between agents can be required that rendezvous frequency will be low.

  II Communication abilities can allow distance communication. This communication replaces the need for "personal rendezvous" for trade, with, for example, message-passing or any real-time, for example, telephone rendezvous.

III Cities or market places periodically visited by, for example, villagers or nomads living far from each other can also provide an increase of frequency of rendezvous.

IV Most probably there are also other methods.

Early experiments of the author showing how efficient the Random PROLOG Processor (RPP) is for evaluating the *collective intelligence* of social structures (310) have demonstrated that the speed of NEI rapidly increases if a City is created in a social structure.

This simulation experiment provides strong evidence that social structures that managed to create a City have also improved their *collective intelligence* significantly.

Let us look at the following results of simulations and the related discussion.

It has been assumed that there also exists a central local *computational space* (representing a City) in the main *computational space* (CS^2). *Information molecules* representing beings periodically (on a random basis) visit this City, stay there for 50 simulation cycles, and go back to the main CS^2. Have a look at Table 5-1 showing how rapidly the speed of a typical 10-step inference improves—by a factor of almost 10. This is a surprising result, because, for example, an increase in communication abilities (see Section 5.4) increases *collective intelligence* only linearly.

This can be interpreted as a demonstration of the importance of structuralization for a social structure.

If we look at this more generally, it is obvious that the hordes of nomadic humans were more efficient at hunting and defense than individuals were, but at a certain stage of development, cities emerged. This probably happened when the ability to produce or store food and to use language improved

TABLE 5-1. Impact of City on *Collective Intelligence*

Rendezvous Distance $d = 0.025$ Size of Main $CS^2 : 1 \times 1 \times 1$
Size of City CS^1 : *sphere at* $(0, 0, 0)$ $R = 0.2$
Brownian Movements: Gaussian Distribution with
Variance $v = 0.124$, $\mu = 0$, NEI = 10-Element Inference

	CS without City	With City (50 Cycles Inside)
Number of Cycles before conclusion	17643	1436
Final Number of *information molecules* in CS^2	69	74

Even now the percentage of the population that is living in Cities all around the world is still growing.

The definition of the NEI does not strictly impose how it should be interpreted; thus, it can be interpreted, for example, as any real life N-element technical assembly process or as a purely mental NEI process in this structure. This means that the mental ability of a social structure, and its production ability grows by a factor of ten! when the social structure discovers the City in any form. This also confirms our observations of real life — life in a City is easier in many ways.

- As mentioned before, in the Kiyotaki–Wright model, each agent $a \in A$ consumes a nonempty set of goods $C_a \in G$ and produces a nonempty set of goods $P_a \subset G$ *where* $C_a \cap P_a = 0$.

  As we know, some goods are fundamental for the existence of a single agent (e.g., food). Thus, for such development of a social structure, it is required that $P_a \subset G$ is minimalized and tuned on the basis of individual decisions or an "order from some ruling level" according to the individual abilities of the agents and/or the division of labor in a social structure. $C_a \in G$ can be unchanged or even expanded (higher consumption).

  This means that characteristics of agents should be able to evolve to allow efficient emergence of *money*.
- Other factors probably also exist.

4. A financial system can be quasi-chaotic and does not require any "centralized control." Certain forms of control over the *money* market are useful but are also criticized as obstructing activity in many cases.

   This century provides an impressive example of catastrophic results for the social structures of humans, when attempts were made to reduce the function or even to remove *money* from social structures of communistic nations. No other equivalent (other than money) mechanism to impose efficient cooperation was found by communistic theoreticians nor did one emerge spontaneously in communistic societies. No such mechanism has been found, on small, local levels or even on the level of trade between communistic nations. Borders between them were securely closed for individuals, for trade, and other forms of exchange.
5. The size and type of the partner as well as the number, for example, of beings in a specific social structure is not essential from a *money* point of view. However, it may have decisive importance on the quantitative level of *money* transactions.
6. *Money* provides a force to impose, continued, stable cooperation for social structures that are no longer under any external threat. Human beings are rarely threatened by "wild animals" or problems with foraging these days.
7. *Money* does not require any *personal relationship* between subjects of exchange. Even "enemies" usually cooperate in certain ways through the mechanism of exchange.

There are widely known examples of hidden trade between hostile organizations or nations and examples of using certain currencies secretly, even if they are excluded and strongly prohibited officially (e.g., there were laws in many countries calling for capital punishment for possessing U.S. dollars).

However, good will, honesty, and so forth, immediately provide higher efficiency for the exchange mechanism.

8. *Money* (currency) can be continuously developed into more advanced and more various other forms, adapting their form to present needs and the technological level of the social structure.

At the conclusion of this part of the book discussing the relationship between *money* and *collective intelligence*, it seems inevitable to infer that *money* is one of the key-control mechanisms in analyzing "living *collective intelligence*" from a certain level up as well as being necessary to nest the concept of *money* into *artificial collective intelligence* systems.

5.4. IS IT POSSIBLE TO GLOBALLY EVALUATE THE *COLLECTIVE INTELLIGENCE* OF A GIVEN NATION?

For a long time the author, as a young student in Poland, and later more conscious of socioeconomic problems while teaching there, was in a position to observe the "Cold War" between communistic eastern Europe and capitalistic Western Europe, and the United States of America. The United Soviet Social Republic led the communistic countries with imperialistic methods, using their resources and coordinating their economies, and until the 1970s eventually managing to equal and sometimes even surpass the United States of America, leader of the capitalistic nations, in such crucial areas as nuclear science, space research, and the defense industry.

Countries can be compared in various ways, but for such a competition between nations, (besides the size of the army, which can be a "giant with a clay legs") the most suitable and widely accepted index now for a competition is the gross national product (GNP), because it defines the real potential power of a country. However, it is only power from a production point of view.

Sometimes for specific purposes, there are different measures used, for example, evaluations of the intellectual abilities of a specific country: the number of patents issued yearly, the number of research papers published in renowned journals by scientists, and so forth. Such measures are, however, not representative and are not widely recognized.

Now, with the formal model of *collective intelligence* in hand, and the computational concept of the *collective intelligence* quotient (IQS) for arbitrary social structures, we can a risk asking the question:

- Is it possible to estimate the (*collective*) *intelligence* of a given nation?
- Is it possible to compare, for example, two nations based on their *collective intelligence*?

Notice that answers to such questions, even partial, approximated or questionable (like the conclusions, are sometimes questionable regarding, e.g., change of GNP) can have a real political value or can be used to analyze the impact of certain political or investment actions/decisions affecting the nation.

> The general hypothesis proposed here is that it is possible and feasible to estimate and compare the *collective intelligence* of whole nations—however, it can be difficult, and can require very serious, time-consuming research and analysis.

Let us try to sketch out how the *collective intelligence* of a whole nation can be estimated.

The general idea is to build an (approximated) RPP-based model of quasi-chaotic inference processes in the nation and then to estimate the proper IQS function for a battery of NEI representatives for such inference processes in the nation.

Later, such a function can be used for comparisons against another nation or for any form of *social engineering* run by a government (e.g., to analyze the impact and necessity of huge, nationwide investments to provide free Internet for all residents).

Notice that the nature of the RPP model allows the gradual addition of consecutive components (such as in approximating functions with a power series), providing us with better and better levels of accuracy and credibility of the model.

According to the author, to build such a model for a nation, we should apply the following steps:

Step 1. Defining a Battery of N-step Inferences (NEI) for Testing National IQS

The first step is to set a proper "benchmark." It should be a representative set of NEIs of different sizes, which are optimal logical representatives of real problems.

Notice that NEI abstracts from interpretation; thus, it is not necessary to know and name the real problems, but rather, it is necessary to know what percentage of problems are those requiring, for example, 50-step inference, and so forth.

Most probably, proper sociological data is not available presently, and such an analysis must be done from scratch.

Step 2. Defining the Configuration of a Nation

In the previous section, some results of simulations have been mentioned, showing that the speed of the inference process grows by a factor of approximately 10, if a City or a marketplace emerges in a social structure, which is regularly (on a probability basis) visited by agents that will stay there for a certain period.

Thus, at the beginning a proper *computational space* CS^N must be built, which will reflect basic distribution and local concentration of people around the country for evaluating rendezvous distances.

However, we should keep in mind here that not all the population is "logically active" from the point of view of problem-solving in the social structure — the percentage of children, elderly people, and so forth, should be taken into account here.

However, even though they do not participate directly in NEI, they can affect it. For example, a professional woman will seriously reduce her activity after the birth of a baby. Here also specific, problem-oriented sociological analyses should be done.

Step 3. Defining the Mobility of a Nation

People constantly displace between home, place of work, and places such as, for example, markets, less frequently around cities, and also around the nation with the help of highways, railways, planes, and so forth. Data and studies for such displacements are available from Geography Information Systems (GIS). Thus, the structure of a transportation system for a given nation and the probability model of human displacements should be taken into account in this step of developing the CS^N.

As an interesting remark, it should be mentioned here that in some former communistic countries there were artificial barriers created to reduce the mobility of people, for example, through introduction of "obligatory permission" to travel to remote areas.

Mobility of people can also be affected by the density of networks, for example, of bus systems, railways, and also by cost, comparing the budgets of different people.

Step 4. Defining the Communication Abilities of a Nation

For solving problems, it is not necessary to rendezvous face to face with another human or object or place. In most cases, it is sufficient to send or receive a message: fax, telex, e-mail, to have telephone contact, and so forth.

Such virtual traveling can also be evaluated and introduced into the description of the *information molecules* representing humans in CS^N before starting simulations for evaluating the IQS of a nation. Here, there are at least two formal possibilities:

- To extend the description of the *information molecules* representing humans with abstract displacement through a given communication channel to certain places on the basis of an abstract: *go-and-return*, for example, when calling for information.
- The second possibility is to assume that *information molecules* representing a human, temporarily generate other *information molecules* representing agents which, for example, travel through a telephone line and return with

information. After a human perceives the information, such an agent is annihilated.

Step 5. Defining the Availability of Resources for Members of a Nation

Let us look at the following example: a certain description of a technology or component is necessary to connect or finish a certain N-step inference. Usually there are two requirements: to get information about where this component is located, and finally to get (import) it for an inference.

In a country with a highly developed network of libraries, information systems, and e-mail shopping, such a component can be "in the hand" of the researcher, designer, and so forth, within, for example, 10 days after starting the search procedure.

In contrast, in the last century, or even presently in some countries, the same problem can take several months and will require, for example, costly personal trips.

CHAPTER 6

Conclusions

At the end of this book but at the beginning of the summary of findings and results, some things very important to our computational *model of collective intelligence* should be said, which have been proposed and justified in this book.

1. Our model does not impose any restrictions on the environment where computational processes can take place for *collective intelligence*.

   We have focused on "solid" *information molecules* with *membranes*, which could suggest the necessity for the *collective intelligence* of any form of beings that are perceptible objects, for example, chemical molecules, bacteria, human, planes, and so forth.

   This is not a must, at least from the theoretical point of view — *information molecules* and *membranes* can be redefined (generalized) with the help of fuzzy sets or even redefined as quantum objects in any continuous space.

   In such a case a certain *being* will be more a *probability* of existence over a given domain (space) than a *solid object* existing in a certain deterministic location.
2. Moreover, the process(s) responsible for the emergence of *collective intelligence* may be very specific, temporary, not continuous or recurring (i.e., can stop and resume), and finally can be oriented to solve very specific problem(s), which can also exist only temporarily and in a noncontinuous way in an environment.

   We should keep in mind that *collective intelligence* is based on the quasi-chaotic behavior of groups of individuals. Quasi-chaotic processes are themselves very difficult to observe and analyze.
3. As a result, *collective intelligence* as a process can be very difficult to observe without very precise analyses, without simulations (to extract what is natural in a given environment and what is extraordinary), or without a focus on specific problems or phenomena.
4. To answer the question (or rather hypothesis) on the existence (or emergence) of *collective intelligence* processes in certain environments, it will be necessary:

1. To build a model of this environment and a model of individuals to test them when acting alone
2. To analyze given environments with individuals, to check if for a specific problem, they create a *collective intelligence* process, that is, if according to the definition of *collective intelligence* given in Section 3.1, "there is significant progress in problem solving."

While writing this book, a student evaluating my manuscript asked me the question:

> "Why don't you put open questions at the end of sections?—like some other authors or lecturers do"?

Addressing this remark, I should mention that, according to a well-known proverb:

> "To pose a good question, half of an answer should be known to the person asking."

Therefore, as the author, I was afraid to pose such questions at the end of sections, despite the fact that such questions were emerging in large numbers when writing the book, and still some of them trouble me off and on in different ways, for example, "suggesting to be an interesting topic for future research and papers."

Rather, I tried to elaborate on some such questions (which emerged before or during writing this book) in the form of small paragraphs, which were presented in Section 5 of this book. They are presented in the form of a statement of the problem supported by the author's "vision" of how they should be tackled.

However, to fulfill this tradition, at the end of the book, let us pose several such questions, not defined nor elaborated on, because as everything, this book has its limits.

CHAPTER 7

Open Questions and Ideas

- **The Random PROLOG Processor is also a Binary System**

  It is very interesting to observe that the Random PROLOG model of computations (RPP) used to construct the computational model of *collective intelligence* is in fact a binary system like those of 0/1 used in today's digital computers.

  Digital *deterministic* computer strings of the `0100111010. . .` form are stored in the memory, transferred from one functional unit of the computer (processors) to another, and converted to other strings. They do not have an interpretation inherent in them: the same string can be data, program, address, and so forth, from the processor point of view. They are rewritten mechanically. The human engineer who designs the computational process and operates a computer with programs makes the interpretation, gives the meaning, and even attributes *intelligence* to complex, for example, *artificial intelligence* (AI) programs.

  It is astonishing that the *nondeterministic* model of computations of the RPP also requires only two objects: the *information molecule* and the *membrane*, which are also without intrinsic interpretation. They are also configured into increasingly complicated structures; however, the difference is that the binary 0/1 system is constructed in a two-dimensional (linear) way (0/1 strings), whereas the molecular system of the RPP "is born" to configure *information molecules* and *membranes* in a three-dimensional way, that is, in a spatial way. In such a processor, the human also defines the functioning and interpretation of such an inferring system.

  The paradox is why such three-dimensional binary computational systems emerged in a natural way on the earth but the binary two-dimensional system (based on 0/1) did not.

- **The Internet affects the Collective Intelligence of Nations or even of our Civilization**

  The emergence in recent years of a cheap and widely accessible Internet (even for children) has suddenly and dramatically changed and expanded our human communication and accessibility options. Just to say (due to the author's experience) that suddenly it got easy (even sitting at home) to learn about a geographical place, to reserve hotels (directly!—thus, cheaper), to get advice and warnings from other explorers, and finally to have a fantastic overland trip through deserts and mountains of such exotic countries like the Sultanate of Oman. On the other hand, even a few years ago, to find another researcher working in a specific, narrow domain anywhere around the world and to get reprints of his papers required a lot of work with abstracts in university libraries and even half a year (in total) to get the longed for reprint in the mail. Presently, it takes just a couple of minutes to have a .ps or .pdf file downloaded through the Internet or maybe a week to contact the author by e-mail and to ask him to mail an old paper from the preinternet era. Also, to find, e-mail, order, and to have on the desk, for example, new computer hardware is barely a matter of a week nowadays!

Also, the Internet, with common, standard English language in use and common formats of files, has reduced most of the personal, racial, compatibility, and so forth, barriers—providing a "unification tool" that is even difficult to evaluate.

Thus, according to our definition of *collective intelligence*, the Internet is increasing the *collective intelligence* of social structures of probably all types and sizes up to civilizations, but the question is how to analyze this phenomenon efficiently.

The tools of computational *collective intelligence* should allow at least an entry point into such an analysis.

- **The RPP Model of Computations Analyzes Unconscious Thinking**

  Probably, the RPP can be used to model, analyze, and explain the phenomenon of unconscious inference processes[1] at the "back" of a human mind.

  It can be claimed on the basis of considerations on the RPP that behind the conscious (foreground) level of our minds, where we can control and trace all our inference processes, there also exists a second level in our mind, an unconscious, quasi-chaotic inference process at the "back" of our minds.

  Such a process is running nonstop (it is easily allowed by the RPP) and is "fed" all the time with new facts, rules, and goals from our perception and mind.

  This subconscious level contacts the conscious level only when some N-step inference is concluded. Thus, such a contact is an accidental process.

  We consider this contact as a sudden "enlightening" with a solution of a problem or a new idea, and so forth.

[1] W. Sulis also argues in (389) that the *collective intelligence* can be used to explain *unconscious*, but on the level of an ant nest.

- **Analysis and Simulation of Collective Intelligence to Evaluate and Predict the Response and Collectively Acquired Resistance of Bacterial Colonies against Drugs**

  The problem of the *collective intelligence* of a bacterial colony has been discussed before, but let us mention one more symptom.

  It has been evident (since the nineteenth century) that a higher survival ratio depends on the size of bacterial colony[2] (however, until a certain point usually defined by environmental factors).

  Normally, an experiment has groups with varying numbers of cells, example, 250, 500, 750, 1000 cells, all plated in the same size Petri dish in drug and radiation studies (364) because the interaction of the cells is a factor. Some scientists even do "half-feeding," replacing only half the media at a time to preserve the presence of cell secretions that support cell life.

  Bacterial colonies should allow in vitro analysis of their interaction, and in this way computational–simulation models can be built defining their *collective intelligence* against drugs, such as, antibiotics. Bacteria are "theoretically" so simple that the computational model of their *collective intelligence* should be well within the range of our present research abilities.

- **Can Collective Intelligence Analyze the Collective Behavior and Power of an Immune System?**

  Prof R. King and graduate student V. Hamilton (Department of Electrical and Computer Engineering, Mississippi State University) have recently initialized some research entitled, "A Collective Intelligence Model Inspired by the Mammalian Immune System." The abstract of the research is given below.

  Abstract: Biological inspiration has long been the basis for computer architecture, algorithms, and network designs. The mammalian immune system's process of recognition and resolution as well as its judicious use of resources are traits sought in many different computer applications. When examined through the template of *collective intelligence* theory, the immune system becomes a viable application. This work describes the modeling of the key constituents of the immune system in a hierarchical adaptive resonance theory (ART) and artificial neural network (ANN) architecture. This will result in a computer recognition system that is able to learn in an unsupervised manner, be capable of discarding irrelevant inputs or interactions, and have the ability for self-organization to judiciously use limited resources. It would also have the capability of being inoculated to known patterns. This work will show how an ANN-implemented artificial immune system can be seen as an application of *collective intelligence*.

[2] Virginia Hamilton from Mississippi State University has provided date on this issue to the author.

- **Hypothesis on the Cyclic Development of Forms of Life and Intelligence**

  This hypothesis has been discussed briefly in Section 5.1 of this book, but not sufficiently, so let us return to this problem again as an idea and a question.

  The hypothesis posted by the author in this book claims that a dependency exists between *Life* (at different levels of complexity) and *intelligence* (individual and collective), and this dependency can be illustrated or interpreted as a evolutional spiral:

  1. First, *collective intelligence* emerged among nonliving chemical molecules. This form of *intelligence* was probably alternatively emerging and vanishing because of temporary forms and harsh environmental circumstances.
  2. At a specific moment under favorable circumstances, this primitive *collective intelligence* must have "discovered" a primitive form of *Life* as a "method" to survive and proliferate. At this moment, our hypothetical spiral started to spin faster.
  3. Life as a "carrier" of *intelligence* (or rather "computational processes responsible for *intelligence*") was becoming increasingly complex until sufficient, (effective) individual *intelligence* emerged — at first, at a very primitive level.
  4. Progress in individual *intelligence* providing autonomy, after a certain time or in parallel, again allowed emergence of a higher level of *collective intelligence* of, for example, ants, cooperating predators, and finally humans.
  5. This spiral is still active.

     Most probably the individual *intelligence* of humans is increasing (see the Flynn effect discussed in Section 2 of the book), and *collective intelligence* is also evolving, which can be claimed, for example, on the basis of the emergence of the Internet, which involves live beings (humans) and nonliving computers.

- **It is a Widely Known Fact that Darwin's Hypothesis on Evolution does not Explain Why Evolutionary Processes are so Fast**

  There are several hypotheses on this under the common name of Holistic Darwinism (365), but they are not commonly accepted.

  Our results suggest that evolution can be viewed as *something* much more complicated than a simple trial-and-error process but as a computational process of a complexity, which can be even now difficult to estimate.

  This concept provides an open research window both for studies on evolution and as a new application for our model of computational *collective intelligence*.

BIBLIOGRAPHY

1. J.P. Das, J.A. Naglieri, and J.R. Kirby, *Assessment of Cognitive Processes—The PASS Theory of Intelligence*, Allyn & Bacon, Needham Heights, Mass., 1994.
2. A.P. Goldstein and L. Krasner, Handbook of psychological assessment. *Pergamon Gen. Psychol. Ser.* **131**, (1990).
3. L.E. Epstein and W.A. Carnielli, *Computability, Computable Functions, Logic, and the Foundations of Mathematics*, Wadsworth & Brooks/Cole, 1989.
4. P.J. Hayes, *Computer Architecture and Organization.* 3rd ed., McGraw-Hill, New Hill, 1988.
5. L.M. Adleman, Molecular computations of solutions to combinatorial problems. *Science*, (1994).
6. J.H. Reif, Parallel Molecular Computation—Models and Simulations. http://www/cs.duke.edu/~reif/paper/paper.html
7. Z. Michalewicz, GA + *Data Structures = Evolution Programs*, Springer-Verlag, New York, 1992.
8. T. Szuba, and R. Stras, Parallel evolutionary computing with the Random PROLOG Processor. *J. Parallel Distributed Comput., Spec. Iss. Parallel Evol. Comput.* **47**, 78–85 (1997).
9. Ant Colony Optimization. Homepage managed by Marco Dorigo. http://iridia.ulb.ac.be/dorigo/ACO/ACO.html#Bib
10. J.L. Deneuborg, ed., The Dynamics of Collective Sorting, Robot-Like Ants, Ants-Like Robots, *From Animals to Animats*, MIT Press, Cambridge, Mass., 1991.
11. M. Dorigo, V. Maniezzo, and A. Colorni, The Ant System—Optimization by a Colony of Cooperating Agents, IEEE Trans. on SMB-Part B, 26, 1, 29–41, 1996.
12. R.A. Alberty, *Physical Chemistry*, 7th ed., Wiley & Sons, New York, 1987.
13. C.A. Whitney, Random Processes in Physical Systems, *An Introduction to Probability-based Computer Simulations*, Wiley & Sons, New York, 1990.
14. J. Giarratano and G. Riley, *Expert Systems*, 2nd ed., PWS Pubishers, 1994.
15. D. Freifelder, *Molecular Biology*, Jones and Bartlett Publishers Boston, Mass., 1987.
16. M. Ben-Ari, *Mathematical Logic for Computer Science*, Prentice Hall, New York, 1993.
17. P.M. Kogge, *The Architectures of Symbolic Computers*, McGraw Hill, New York, 1991.
18. M. Spivey, *An Introduction to Logic Programming PROLOG*, Prentice Hall, New York, 1996.
19. J.D. Newmarch, *Logic Programming—PROLOG and Stream Parallel Languages*, Prentice Hall, New York, 1990.

20. S. Taylor, *Parallel Logic Programming Techniques*, Prentice Hall, New York, 1989.

21. A. Takeuchi, *Parallel Logic Programming*, Wiley & Sons, New York, 1992.

22. R.E. Mayer: *Thinking, Problem-Solving, Cognition*. 2nd ed., W.H. Freeman, New York, 1992.

23. N. Brody, Intelligence, 2nd ed., Academic press, New York, 1992.

24. H.J. Butcher, Human intelligence — its Nature and Assessment, Harper, 1973.

25. P.H. Winston, *Artificial Intelligence*. 3rd ed., Addison-Wesley, Reading, Mass., 1993.

26. J.R. Flynn, Massive IQ gains in 14 nations — what IQ tests really measure. *Psychol. Bull.* **101**, 171 (1987).

27. R. Gregory, *Psychological Testing: History, Principles, and Applications*. 2/e Wheaton College, 1996.

28. R.J. Sternberg and D.K. Detterman (eds.), *What is Intelligence? — Contemporary View on its Nature and Definition*, Norwood, N.J., Ablex, 1986.

29. A. Newell, J.C. Shaw, and H.A. Simon, *Preliminary description of General Problem Solving Program-I (GPS-I)*, Report CIP Working Paper 7, Carnegie Institute of Technology, Pittsburg, Penn., 1957.

30. G.W. Ernst and A. Newell, *GPS — A case Study in Generality and Problem Solving*, Academic Press, New York, 1969.

31. J-L. Lauriere, *Problem Solving and Artificial Intelligence*, Prentice Hall, New York, 1990.

32. R.J. Schalkoff, *Artificial Intelligence — An Engineering Approach*, McGraw-Hill, New York, 1990.

33. A.M. Turing, Computing machinery and intelligence. *Mind* **59**, 433–450 (1950).

34. Z.W. Pylyshyn, *Computation and Cognition*, MIT Press, Cambridge, Mass., 1984.

35. H. Gardner, *Frames of Mind: The Theory of Multiple Intelligence*, Basic Books, New York, 1983.

36. D.T. Lykken, T.J. Bouchard, M. McGue, Jr., and A. Tellegen, The Minnesota Twin family registry — some initial findings. *Acta Genet. Med. Gemellologiae (Rome)*, (1990).

37. R.B. Cattell, Are culture fair intelligence tests possible and necessary? *J. Res. Dev. Edu.* **12**, 3–13 (1979).

38. R. Plomin and R. Rende, Human behavioral genetics. *Annu. Rev. Psychol.* **42**, (1991).

39. D. Wechsler, Intelligence defined and undefined: A realistic appraisal. *Am. Psychol.* **34**, (1975).

40. D. Hothersall, *History of Psychology*, Temple University Press, 1984.

41. C.E. Spearman, General Intelligence — objectively determined and measured. *Am. J. Psychol.* **15**, (1904).

42. C.E. Spearman, *The Abilities of Man*, Macmillan, London, 1927.

43. Hellendoorn, eds., *Fuzzy Model Identification*, Springer-Verlag, New York, 1997

44. P.E. Vernon, *The Structure of Human Abilities*, Methuen, London, 1950.

45. J.P. Guilford, The three faces of intellect. *Am. Psychol.* **14**, (1959).

46. J.P. Guilford, *The Nature of Human Intelligence*, McGraw-Hill, New York, 1967.

47. P.E. Vernon, Creativity and Intelligence. *Educ. Res.* **6**, (1964).
48. J. Hunt, *Intelligence and Experiments*, Ronald Press, New York, 1961.
49. A.M. Law and W.D. Kelton, *Simulation Modeling and Analysis*. 2nd ed., McGraw-Hill, New York, 1991.
50. J.L. Devore, *Probability and Statistics for Engineering and the Science*. 4th ed., Duxbury Press, 1995.
51. M.B. Harris, *Basic Statistics for Behavioral Science Research*, Allyn & Bacon, Needham Heights, Mass., 1998.
52. A. Newell and H. Simon, *Human Problem-Solving*, Prentice Hall, New York, 1972.
53. J. Piaget, *Biology and Knowledge*, 1967. Reedited by University of Chicago Press, Chicago, Ill., 1971.
54. N. Chomsky, *Rules and representations*, Columbia University Press, New York, 1980.
55. J.A. Fodor, *The Modularity of Mind*, MIT Press, Cambridge, Mass., 1983.
56. T. Szuba, Random parallelization of computations in the Random PROLOG Processor. *J. Kuwait Univ.* (1996).
57. T. Szuba, *A Molecular Quasi-random Model of Computations Applied to Evaluate Collective Intelligence*, IPPS/SPDP'98, Orlando, Fla., March 30–April 3, 1998.
58. K. Gunderson, ed., The Meaning of "Meaning", in *Language, Mind and Knowledge*, Minnesota studies in the Phylosophy of Science, University of Minessota Press, Minn., 1975.
59. J. Fodor, *The Language of Thought*, Tomas Crowell, 1975.
60. N. Chomsky, *Language and Mind*, Hardcourt Publisher, 1968.
61. F. Rosenbaltt, *Principles of Neurodynamics: Perceptrons and the Theory of Brain Mechanism*, Spartan Books, 1962.
62. D.J. Amit, *Modeling Brain Function*, Cambridge University Press, New York, 1992.
63. K. Knight and E. Rich, *Artificial Intelligence*, 2nd ed., McGraw-Hill, New York, 1991.
64. M. Minsky and S. Papert, Perceptrons — An introduction to Computational Geometry, MIT Press, Mass., 1969.
65. E.G. Boring, Intelligence as the tests test it. *New Repub.* **35**, 35–37 (1923).
66. R.J. Herrnstein and C. Murray, *The Bell Curve — Intelligence and Class Structure in Americal Life*, Free Press, New York, 1994.
67. R.L. Atkinson, R.C. Atkinson, E. Smith, and D. Bem, *Introduction to Psychology*, 10th ed., Harcourt Brace Javanovich, Orlando, Fla., 1990.
68. J.C. Raven, *Progressive Matrices*, H.K. Lewis, London, 1965.
69. S.E. Wood and E.G. Wood, *The World of Psychology*. 2nd ed., Allyn & Bacon, Mass., 1996.
70. M.K. Singley and J.R. Anderson, *The Transfer of Cognitive Skill*, Harvard University Press, Cambridge, Mass., 1989.
71. C.L. Forgy, Rete: A Fast Algorithm for the Many Pattern/Many Object Pattern Matching Problem, *Artificial Intell.*, (1985).
72. M. Neuilly et al., Evidence of early spontaneous chain reaction found in Gabon Mine, excerpts from press conference regarding Geological and Mineral Documentation published by Commissariat a l'Energie Atomique, 1972.

73. Hölldobler and E.O. Wilson, *The Ants*, The Belknap Press of Harvard University, 1990.

74. D. McFarland, *Animal behaviour: Psychology, Ethology and Evolution*, 2nd ed., Longman, 1993.

75. H.D. Giebel, Visual learning capacity in hoofed animals. *Zoologische Jahrbücher Abteilung für Allgemeine Zoologie* **67**, (1958).

76. B. Brooks, *Making Sense—Animal Perception and Communication*, Farrar Straus Giroux/Harcourt Brace Jovanovic Publishers, 1993.

77. R.A. Langworthy and J.W. Jennings, Oddball abstract olfactory learning in laboratory rats. *Psychol. rec.* **22**, (1972).

78. B.L. Whorf, Science and Linguistic, in J.B. Carrol, ed., *Language, Thought and Reality: Selected writings of B.L. Whorf*, MIT Press, Cambridge, Mass., 1956.

79. J.J. Gumperz and S.C. Levinson, *Rethinking Linguistic Relativity*, Cambridge University Press, New York, 1996.

80. R. Byrne, *The Thinking Ape—Evolutionary Origins of Intelligence*, Oxford University Press, New York, 1995.

81. R.A. Gardner and B.T. Gardner, Teaching sign language to a chimpanzee. *Science* **9**, (1969).

82. E.S. Savage-Rumbaugh, Language acquisition in nonhuman species: Implications for the innateness debate. *Dev. Psychol.* **26**, (1990).

83. I.M. Pepperberg, Cognition in African gray parrot (Psittacus erithacus): Further evidence for comprehension of categories and labels. *J. Comp. Psychol.* **104**(9), (1990).

84. L.M. Herman, Cognition and language competencies of bottlenosed dolphins, in Schusterman et al., ed., *Dolphin Cognition and Behavior: A Comparative Approach.* Lawrence Erlbaum Associates, Hillsdale, New York, 1986.

85. G. Viaud, *Intelligence—Its Evolution and Forms*, Harper & Brothers, 1960.

86. R.K. Thompson, D.L. Oden, and S.T. Boysen, Language-naive chimpanzees (Pan troglodytes) judge relations between relations in a conceptual matching-to-sample task. *J. Exp. Psychol. Animal Behav. Processes* **23**, (1997).

87. R.E. Passingham, Primate specialization in brain and intelligence. *Symp. Zool. Soc. Lond.* **46**, (1981).

88. S.J. Russel and P. Norvig, *Artificial Intelligence—A Modern Approach*, Prentice Hall, New York, 1995.

89. L.G. Mathieu and S. Sonea, Time to drastically change the century-old concept about bacteria. *Sci. Trib.* **8**, (1996).

90. D.E. Caldwell and J.W. Costerton, Are bacterial biofilms constrained to Darwin's concept of evolution through natural selection? in *Microbiología SEM* **12**, 1996.

91. E. Ben-Jacob, I. Cohen, and D.L. Gutnick, Cooperative organization of bacterial colonies—from genotype to morphotype. *Annu. Rev. Microbiol.* **52**, (1998).

92. E. Ben-Jacob, H. Shmueli, O. Shochet, and A. Tenenbaum, Adaptive self-organization during growth of bacterial colonies. *Physica A* **187**, 378–424 (1992).

93. W.C. Fuqua, S.C. Winans, and E.P. Greenberg, Quorum sensing in bacteria: the LuxR-LuxI family of cell density-responsive transcriptional regulators. *J. Bacteriol.* **76**, (1994).

94. R.M. Harshey, Bees aren't the only ones: swarming in gram-negative bacteria. *Mol. Microbiol.* **13**, (1994).
95. E. Ben-Jacob, Bacterial wisdom, Gödel's Theorem and creative genomic webs. *Physica A* **248**, 57–76 (1998).
96. D.E. Caldwell, E. Attuku, and D. Wilkie, Germ theory versus community theory in understanding and controlling the proliferation of biofilms. *Adv. Dental Res.* **11**, (1996).
97. D.E. Caldwell, D.R. Korber and G.M. Wolfaardt, Do bacterial communities transcend Darwinism? *Adv. Microb. Ecol.* **15**, (1996).
98. D.E. Caldwell, G.M. Wolfaardt, and D.R. Korber, Cultivation of microbial communities and consortia, in D. Stahl, et al., eds., *Manual of Environmental Microbiology*, American Society for Microbiology Press, Washington, D. C., 1996.
99. J.M. Pasteels and J-L. Deneubourg ed., *From Individual to Collective Behavior in Social Insects*, Birkhäuser Verlag, Basel, 1987.
100. E. Bonabeau, M. Dorigo, and G. Theraulaz, *Swarm Intelligence—From Natural to Artificial Systems*, Oxford University Press, New York, 1999.
101. M. Dorigo and L.M. Gambardella, Ant Colony—a Cooperative Learning Approach to the Traveling Salesman Problem, IEEE Trans. on Evol. Computations, April 1997.
102. O.E. Wilson, A chemical releaser of alarm and digging behavior in the ant *Pogonomyrmex badius* (Latreille). *Psyche* **65**, (1958).
103. R. Schoonderwoerd, O. Holland, J. Bruten, and L. Rothkrantz, Ant-based load balancing in Telecommunications Networks. *Adapt. Behav.* **5**, (1997).
104. G. Di Caro and M. Dorigo, *Mobile Agents for Adaptive Routing*, Proceedings of the 31-st Hawaii International Conference on System, IEEE Computer Society Press, Los Alamitos, Calif., 1998.
105. G. Bilchev and I. Parmee, The Ant Colony Metaphor for Searching Continuous Design Spaces, in T. Fogarty, ed., *LNCS 993*, Springer-Verlag, New York, 1995.
106. M. Dorigo and L.M. Gambardella, Ant colonies ... BioSystems, 1997.
107. T.D. Seeley, *The Wisdom of the Hive*, Harvard University Press, Cambridge, Mass., 1995.
108. P.S. Fisher and G.E. Mobus, Foraging search at the edge of Chaos, in D. Levine, V. Brown, and R. Shirey, eds., *Oscillations in Neural Networks*, Lawerence Erlbaum and Associates, Publishers, 1996.
109. T.D. Seeley, Honey bee foragers as sensory units of their colonies. *Behav. Ecol. Sociobiol.* **34**, (1994).
110. F.C. Dyer, Spatial memory and navigation by honeybees on the scale of the foraging range. *J. Exp. Biol.* **199**, (1996).
111. S.W. Zhang, K. Bartsch, and M.V. Srinivasan, Maze learning by honeybee. *Neurobiol. Learn. Memory* **66**, (1996).
112. R. Menzel, et al., The knowledge base of bee navigation. *J. Exp. Biol.* **199**, (1996).
113. A. Michelsen et al., How honeybees perceive communication dances, studied by means of a mechanical model. *Behav. Ecol. Sociobiol.* **30**, (1992).
114. A. Manning and M.S. Dawkins, An Introduction to Animal Behavior, 4th ed., Cambridge University Press, New York, 1995.
115. M. Penny, C. Brett, and G. Roslin, *Predators—Great Hunters of the Natural World*, Ebury Press, 1995.

116. J. Alcock, *Animal Behavior—An Evolutionary Approach*, 4th ed., Sinauer Associates, Sunderland, Mass., 1989.

117. R. Heinsohn, and C. Packer, Complex cooperative strategies in group-territorial African lions. *Science* **269**, (1995).

118. A. Newell, *Unified Theories of Cognition*, Harvard University Press, Cambridge, Mass., 1990.

119. W.T. Cockayne and M. Zyda, *Mobile agents*, Manning, 1998.

120. J.B. Smith, *Collective Intelligence in Computer-Based Collaboration*, Lawrence Erlbaum Associates, 1994.

121. M.S. Ackerman, *Considering an Organization's Memory*, ACM Conference on Computer-Supported Cooperative Work (CSCW'98), 1998.

122. J.P. Walsh and G.R. Ungson, Organizational Memory. *Acad. Manage. Rev.* (1991).

123. V. Bush, As we may think. *Atl. Month.* **176**, (1945).

124. D.C. Engelbart, R.W. Watson, and J.C. Norton, *The Augment Knowledge Workshop*, AFIPS Conference Proceedings, 1973.

125. S. Greenberg and M. Roseman, GroupWare toolkits for synchronous work, in Beaudouin-Lafon, ed., *Computer-Supported Cooperative Work: Trends in Software Series*, Wiley & Sons, New York, 1998.

126. L. Garton and B. Wellman, Social impacts of electronic mail in organizations—a review of the research literature. *Commun. Yearbook* **18**, 434–453 (1995).

127. Y. Shoham and M. Tennenholtz, *On the Synthesis of Useful Social Laws for Artificial Agent Societies—Preliminary Report*, Proceedings of the 10th National Conference on Artificial Intelligence, San Jose, July 1992.

128. T. Wagner, J. Shapiro, P. Xuan, and V. Lesser, *Multilevel Conflict in Multiagent Systems*, Proceedings of AAAI Workshop on Negotiation in Multiagent Systems, 1999.

129. K.D. Blakeley, The application of modes of activity to group meetings—a case study. Technical Report No. TR90-045, Chapel Hill, N.C., 1990.

130. D. Kasler and P. Hurd (Translator), *Max Weber—An Introduction to his Life and Work*, University of Chicago Press, Chicago, Ill., 1989.

131. T. Parsons, *The System of Modern Societies*, Prentice-Hall, New York, 1971.

132. M.K. Ahuja and K.M. Carley, Network Structure in Virtual Organizations. Special Issue on Virtual Organizations. *J. Comp-Med. Commun.* **3**, (1998).

133. M. Ahuja, D. Galletta, and K. Carley, *Individual Centrality and Performance in Virtual Groups*. Working Paper, Florida State University, Tallahassee, Fla., 1998.

134. J. Lipnack and J. Stamps, *Virtual Teams-Researching Across Space, Time, and Organizations with Technology*, John Wiley & Sons, 1997.

135. S.L. Jarvenpaa and B. Ives, The global network organization of the future: Information management opportunities and challenges. *J. Manage. Inform. Syst.* **10**, (1994).

136. J.P. Scott, The Evolution of Social Systems. *Monographs in Psychology Series*, Gordon & Breach, Hanghorn, Penn., 1989.

137. A.E. Emerson, *The Superorganismic Aspects of the Society*, Colloques Internationaux du Centre National de la Reserche Scientific, No 34, 1952.

138. R.L. Daft, *Organization Theory and Design*, 6th ed., South-Western Publishing, Cincinnati, OHio, 1998.

139. R.I. Dunbar, *Primate Social Systems*, Croom Helm, 1988.

140. J. Greenberg and R. Baron, *Behavior in Organizations*, Prentice-Hall, New York, 1997.

141. B. Tuckman, Developmental sequence in small groups. *Psychol. Bull.* **63**, (1965).

142. D.W. Johnson and F.P. Johnson, Joining Together—Group Theory and Group Skills, 7th ed., Allyn & Bacon, Needham Heights, Mass., 1997.

143. S.P. Robbins, *Organizational Behavior*, Prentice Hall, New York, 1998.

144. R.W. Napier and M.K. Gershenfeld, *Groups—Theory and Experience*, 4th ed., Houghton, 1989.

145. M.E. Shaw, *Group Dynamics*, 4th ed., McGraw-Hill, New York, 1971.

146. J.F. Nunamaker et al., Electronic meeting systems to support group work. *Commun. ACM* **34**, no. 7 (1991).

147. I. Zigurs and B. Buckland, A theory of task/technology fit and group support systems effectiveness. *MIS Quart.* **22**, (1998).

148. D. Cartwright and A. Zander, eds., *Group Dynamics—Research and Theory*, 2nd ed., Evanston, 1960.

149. J.E. McGrath, *Groups: Interaction and Performance*, Prentice-Hall, Englewood Cliffs, N.J., 1984.

150. M. Fishbein ed., *Readings in Attitude Theory and Measurement*, Wiley & Sons, New York, 1967.

151. V.P. Richmond and J.C. McCroskey, Management Communication Style, Tolerance for Disagreement, and Innovativeness as Predictors of Employee Satisfaction: A Comparison of Single-factor, Two-factor, and Multiple-factor Approaches, in D. Nimmo ed., *Communication Yearbook 3*, New Brunswick, N.J., 1979.

152. F. Herzberg, *Work and the Nature of Man*, Cleveland World, 1966.

153. J.R. Gordon, *A Diagnostic Approach to Organizational Behavior*, Allyn & Bacon. Needham Heights, Mass., 1991.

154. D.J. Cherrington, *Organizational Behavior—The Management of Individual and Organizational Performance*, Allyn & Bacon, Needham Heights, Mass., 1989.

155. R.E. Quinn and K. Cameron, Organizational life cycles and some shifting criteria of effectiveness—some preliminary evidence. *Manage. Sci.* **29**, (1983).

156. F. Dance, The concept of communication. *J. Commun.* **20**, (1970).

157. D.A. Level, Communication effectiveness—methods and situations. *J. Business Commun.* **28**, (1972).

158. N. Contractor, Self-organizing systems perspective in the study of organizational communication, in B. Kovacic, ed., *New Approaches to Organizational Communication Albany*, SUNY Press, New York 1994.

159. F.M. Jablin and L.L. Putnam, (eds.), *Handbook of Organizational Communication*, 2nd ed., Thousand Oaks, Calif, 1999.

160. D.J. Brass, A social network perspective on human resources management. *Res. Personnel Human Resources Manage.* **13**, (1995)

161. C. Stohl, *Organizational Communication—Connectedness in Action*, Thousand Oaks, Calif. *Sage Publications*, 1995.

162. S.P. Robbins, *Managing Today*, Prentice-Hall, New York, 1997.

163. M.J.J. Wolters and M.R. Hoogeweegen, *Management Support for Globally operating Virtual Organizations — The Case of KLM distribution*, Proceedings of the 32nd Annual Hawaii International Conference on System Sciences, 1998.

164. E.G. Freedman, *Scientific Induction — Individual Versus Group Processes and Multiple Hypotheses*, Proceedings of the 14th Annual Conference of the Cognitive Science Society, Hillsdale N.J. Lawrence Erlbaum, 1992.

165. L.K. Michaelsen, W.E. Watson, and R.H. Black, A realistic test of individual versus group consensus decision making. *J. Appl. Psychol.* **74**, (1989).

166. P.W. Yetton and P.C. Botger, Individual versus Group Problem-solving — an ampirical test of best member strategy. *Organizat. Behav. Human Perform.* **29**, (1982).

167. D.A. Kolb, I.M. Rubin, and J.M. McIntyre, *Organizational Psychology — A Book of Readings*, 3rd ed., Prentice-Hall, Sydney, 1979.

168. R.G. Golledge and R.J. Stimson, *Spatial Behavior — A Geographic Perspective*. The Guilford Press, New York, 1997.

169. O. Huisman and P. Forer, *Towards a Geometric Framework for Modeling Spacetime Opportunities and Interaction Potential*, IGU-CMGS Conference on Spatial Analysis and Environmental Processes, Lisbon, Portugal, 1998.

170. H.C. Berg, *Random Walks in Biology*, Princeton University Press, Princeton, N.J., 1993.

171. P. Schmid-Hempel, Foraging Characteristics of the Dessert ant Cataglyphis, in J.M. Pasteels and J-L. Deneubourg eds., *From Individual to Collective Behavior in Social Insects*, Birghaüser Verlag, Basel, 1987.

172. S-L. Shaw and L.P. Dass, *Geographic Variations in Travel Characteristics*, Proceedings of ESRI User Conference, 1996.

173. S-L. Shaw, Handling disaggregate spatiotemporal travel data in GIS, GeoInformatica. (forthcoming in 2000).

174. T. Hägerstrand, Space, time and human conditions, in T. Lundqvist, et al., ed., *Dynamic Allocation of Urban Space*, Saxon House Farnborough, 1975.

175. A. Leon-Garcia, *Probability and Random Processes for Electrical Engineering*. 2nd. ed., Addison-Wesley, Reading Mass., 1994.

176. O. Huisman and P. Forer, *Computational Agents and Urban Life-spaces — A Preliminary Realization of the Time Geography of Student Lifestyles*, Proceedings 3rd International Conference on GeoComputation, Bristol, UK, 1998. CD-ROM. Also http://www.ggy.bris.ac.uk/geocomp/cdrom/68/gc_68_paper.htm

177. ——— *Encyclopaedia of Mathematics on CD-ROM*, Kluwer Academic Press, Norwell, Mass., 1997.

178. Z. Kohavi, *Switching and Finite Automata Theory*, 2nd ed., McGraw-Hill, New York, 1978.

179. D. Chowdhury and A. Mookerrjee, Random walk and magnetization of spin clusters in spin glasses. *Am. J. Phys.* **3**, (1985).

180. B.D. Hughes, On returns to the starting site in lattice random walks. *Physica* **134A**, (1986).

181. A. Luria, Human Brain and Psychological Processes, Harper & Row, New York, 1966.

182. E. Ben-Jacob, I. Cohen, and D.L. Gutnick, Cooperative organization of bacterial colonies: From genotype to morphotype. *Annu. Rev. Microbiol.*, (1997).

183. M. Almulla and T. Szuba, *Toward a Computational Model of Collective Intelligence and its IQ Measure*, SAC'99 ACM, San Antonio, Texas, U.S.A., 1999.

184. J. Bates, The role of emotion in believable agents. *Commun. ACM* **37**, 122–125 (1994).

185. M. Wooldrige and N.R. Jennings, Intelligent Agents—theory and practice. in *Knowl. Eng. Rev.* (1995).

186. A. Drogoul and J. Ferber, Multiagent simulation as a tool for studying emergent processes in societies, in N. Gilbert and J. Doran, ed., in *Simulation Societies, the Computer Simulation of Social Phenomena*, UCL Press, 1994.

187. R.A. Eve, S. Horsfall, and M.E. Lee, eds., *Chaos, Complexity, and Sociology—Myths, Models, Theories*, Sage Publications, 1997.

188. D.L. Kiel and E. Elliot eds., *Chaos Theory in the Social Science-Foundations and Applications*, University of Michigan, 1997.

189. M.D. Hauser and M. Konishi, eds., *The Design of Animal Communication*, MIT Press, Cambridge, Mass., 1999.

190. S.L. Vehrencamp and J.W. Bradbury, *Principles of Animal Communication*. Sinauer Associates, Sunderland, Mass., 1998.

191. L.A. Zadeh, Fuzzy Sets. *Inform. Control.* **8**, (1965).

192. G.J. Klir and St. Clair, *Fuzzy Set Theory Foundations and Applications*, Prentice-Hall, New York, 1997.

193. H.T. Siegelmann, Neural Networks and Analog Computation—Beyond the Turing Limit, in *Series Progress in Theoretical Computer Science*, Birkhauser, 1999.

194. G. Agha, Actors: A Model of Concurrent Computation in Distributed Systems, *Artificial Intelligence Series*, MIT Press, Cambridge, Mass., 1986.

195. C. Hewitt, Viewing control structures as patterns of passing messages. *J. Art. Intell.* **8(3)**, (1977).

196. H. Nwana, Software agents—an overview. *Knowl. Eng. Rev.* **11**, (1996).

197. H. Nwana and D. Ndumu, A perspective on software agents' research. *Knowl. Eng. Review*, (1999).

198. M. Minsky, The society of mind. *Soc. Mind* (1985).

199. C. Varela and G. Agha, What after Java?—from objects to actors. *J. Comput. Telecommun. Network.* **4** (1998).

200. T. Berners-Lee, World-wide computer. *Commun. ACM*, (1997).

201. T. Berners-Lee, et al., The world-wide web. *Commun. ACM* **8**, (1994).

202. C. Callsen and G. Agha, Open heterogeneous computing in ActorSpace. *J. Parallel Distribut. Comput.* **21**, (1994).

203. S. Frølund, *Coordinating Distributed Objects—An Actor-based Approach to Synchronization*, MIT Press, Cambridge, Mass., 1996.

204. L. Floridi, *Philosophy and Computing—An Introduction*, Routledge, Chapman & Hall, New York, 1999.

205. E.J. Borowski and J.M. Borwein, eds., *Hilbert Problems*, in *The Harper Collins Dictionary of Mathematics*, Harper Collins, New York, 1991.

206. C. Boyer, U. Merzbach, *The Hilbert Problems—History of Mathematics*, 2nd ed., Wiley & Sons, New York, 1991.

207. K. Gödel, On Undecidable Propositions of Formal Mathematical Systems, in S. Feferman, ed., *Gödel's Collected Works*, 1986, pp. 1–36.

208. A.M. Turing, *On Computable Numbers, with an Application to the Entscheidungsproblem*, Proceedings of the London Mathematics Society, 1936.

209. D.G. Feitelson and D.C. Feitelson, *Optical Computing—A Survey for Computer Scientists*, MIT Press, Cambridge, Mass., 1992.

210. T. Thompson, When silicon hits it limits, what's next? *BYTE*, 4 1996.

211. P. Benioff, The computer as a physical system—a microscopic quantum mechanical Hamiltonian model of computers as represented by Turing machines. *J. Stat. Phys.* **22**, (1980).

212. W. Asprey, *John von Neumann and the Origins of Modern Computing*, MIT Press, Cambridge, Mass., 1992.

213. G.J. Myers, *Advances in Computer Architecture*, Wiley & Sons, New York, 1982.

214. J. Backus, Can programming be liberated from the von Neumann style? A functional style and its algebra of programs. *Commun. ACM* **8**, (1978).

215. M.R. Garey and D.S. Johnson, *Computers and Intractability—A Guide to the Theory of NP-Completeness*, W.H. Freeman, New York, 1979.

216. C.H. Papadimitriou, *Computational Complexity*, Addison-Wesley, Reading, Mass., 1994.

217. U. Hopcroft, *Introduction to Automata Theory, Languages and Computation*, Addison-Wesley Reading, Mass., 1979.

218. S. Cook, The Complexity of Theorem-Proving Procedures, Proceedings of the 3rd Annual ACM Symposium on Theory of Computing, 1971.

219. B. Soucek and M. Soucek, *Neural and Massively Parallel Computers the Sixth Generation*, Wiley & Sons, New York, 1988.

220. M.J. Flynn, *Computer Architecture—Pipelined and Parallel Processor Design*, Jones and Bartlett Publishers, Sudbury, Mass., 1995.

221. S.G. Shiva, *Pipelined and Parallel Computer Architectures*, HarperCollins, New York, 1996.

222. K. Miller, *An Assembly Language Introduction to Computer Architecture—Using the Intel Pentium*, Oxford University Press, New York, 1999.

223. B.E. Bauer, *Practical Parallel Programming*, Academic Press, New York, 1992.

224. —IRIS Power C User's Guide (007-0702-050), SGI Press.

225. M.J. Flynn, *Some Computer Organizations and their Effectiveness*, IEEE Trans. Computers. (9) 1972.

226. W. Chemij, Parallel computer taxonomy, M. Phil, Aberystwyth University, 1994. Also available at http://www.gigaflop.demon.co.uk/comp/chapt7.htm#7.5

227. A. Hodges, *Alan Turing–The Enigma*, Vintage, 1992.

228. J-P. Banatre, A. Coutant, and D. Le Metayer, A parallel machine for multiset transformation and its programming style. *Future Generat. Comput. Syst.* **4** (1988).

229. J-P. Banatre, and D. Le Metayer, Programming by multiset transformations. *Commun. ACM* (1993).

230. D.R. Simon, *On the Power of Quantum Computation*, Proceedings of the 35th Annual Symposium on Foundations of Computer Science, 1994.

231. H.T. Siegelmann, Computation beyond the Turing limit. *Science* (1995).

232. H.T. Siegelmann and S. Fishman, Computation by dynamical systems. *Physica.* (1998).

233. G. Dougherty, *Mathematical Methods for Artificial Intelligence and Autonomous Systems*, Prentice Hall, New York, 1988.

234. G.J. Klir, *Fuzzy Sets And Fuzzy Logic—Theory and Applications*, Prentice Hall, 1995.

235. A. Berthiaume and G. Brassard, Oracle quantum computing. *J. Mod. Opt.* **41**(12), (1994).

236. A. Berthiaume, Quantum Computation, *Complexity Theory Retrospective II*, Springer-Verlag, New York, 1996.

237. A. Hemmerling, Concentration of multidimensional tape-bounded systems of Turing automata and cellular spaces, in L. Budach, ed., *Fundamentals of Computation Theory*, 1979.

238. S. Lloyd: A potentially realizable quantum computer. *Science* **261**, (1993).

239. G.L. Baker and J.P. Gollub, *Chaotic Dynamics*. Cambridge University Press, New York, 1990.

240. E. Ott, *Chaos in Dynamical Systems*, Cambridge University Press, New York, 1993.

241. J.A. Yorke, K. Alligood, and T. Sauer eds., *Chaos—An Introduction to Dynamical Systems*, Springer-Verlag, New York, 1996.

242. J.D. Foley, A. van Dam, K.S. Feiner, and J.F. Hughes, *Computer Graphics—Principles and Practice*, 2nd ed., Addison-Wesley, Reading, Mass., 1992.

243. J.-P. Eckmann, et al., Liapunov exponents from time series. *Phys. Rev.* **A 34**, (1986).

244. H.G. Schuster, *Deterministic Chaos—An Introduction*, 3rd ed., Wiley & Sons, New York, 1995.

245. A.E. Rogers and T.W. Connolly, Analog Computation in Engineering Design, McGraw-Hill, New York, 1960.

246. H.T. Siegelmann, The simple dynamics of super Turing Theories. *Theor. Comput. Sci.* **2**, (1996).

247. I. Bratko, *PROLOG Programming for Artificial Intelligence*, Addison-Wesley, Reading, Mass., 1986.

248. D. Crookes, *Introduction to Programming in Prolog*, Prentice Hall, New York, 1988.

249. R. Kowalski, Search Strategies for Theorem Proving, *Machine Intelligence 7*, B. Beltzer and D. Michie eds., Edinburgh University Press, 1969.

250. A. Colmerauer, H. Kanoui, R. Pasero, and P. Roussel, Un systeme de comunication homme-machine en Francais, Rapport, *Groupe Intelligence Artificielle*, Universite d'Aix Marseille, Luminy, 1973.

251. A. Colmerauer and P. Roussel, *The Birth of Prolog*, HOPL Preprints, 1993.

252. A.J. Robinson, A machine oriented logic based on the resolution principle. *J. ACM* **12**, (1965).

253. D.H. Warren, *Generating Conditional Plans and Programs*, Proceedings AISB Summer Conference, Edinburgh, 1976.

254. W.F. Clocksin and C.S. Mellish, *Programming in Prolog*, Springer-Verlag, New York, 1981.

255. M.A. Covington, D. Nute, and A. Vellino, *Prolog Programming in Depth*, Prentice Hall, New York, 1996.

256. V. Weber, *Unification in Prolog by Connectionist Models*, Proceedings of the Fourth Australian Conference on Neural Networks, ACNN'93. 1993.

257. D. Maier, D.S. Warren, *Computing with Logic*, Benjamin/Cummings, 1988.

258. R.S. Boyer and J.S. Moore, *Computational Logic Handbook*, 2nd ed., Academic Press, New York, 1997.

259. J.W. Lloyd, *Foundations of Logic Programming*, 2nd ed., Springer-Verlag, New York, 1987.

260. A. Nerode and R. Shore: *Logic for Applications*, Springer-Verlag, New York, 1997.

261. J. Herbrand, *Travaux de la Soc. des Science et des Lettres de Varsovie* **33**(128), (1930).

262. J.A. Robinson, Computational logic: The unification computation. *Machine Intell.* **6**, (1971).

263. M. Venturini-Zilli, *Complexity of the Unification Algorithm for First-order Expressions*, Technical Report, Consiglio Nazionale Delle Ricerche Instituto per le applicazioni del calcolo, Rome, Italy, 1975.

264. G. Huet, Resolution d'equations dans les langages d'odre 1, 2, . . . , !. PhD thesis, Universit'e de Paris VII, 1976.

265. M.S. Paterson and M.N. Wegman, *Linear Unification*, Proceedings of the Symposium on the Theory of Computing, 1976.

266. J. Harland and J. Jaffar, On parallel unification for Prolog. *New Generat. Comput.* **5**, (1987).

267. H. Yasuura, *On the Parallel Computational Complexity of Unification*, Technical Report TR-027 ICOT, 1983.

268. C. Dwork, P.C. Kanellakis, and J.C. Mitchell, On the sequential nature of unification. *J. Logic Prog.* **1**, (1984).

269. J. Hager and M. Moser, *An Approach to Parallel Unification Using Transputers, Proceedings of the 12th German Workshop on Artificial Intelligence*, 1989.

270. P. Robinson, The SUM — An AI coprocessor, *Byte*, June 1985.

271. Y. Kaneda, et al., Sequential Prolog machine PEK. *New Generat. Comput.* **4**, (1986).

272. D.H. Warren, An abstract Prolog instruction set, Technical Note 309, SRI International, Menlo Park, Calif., 1983.

273. D.H. Warren, *Implementation of Prolog. Lecture notes*, 5th International Conference and Symposium on Logic Programming, Seattle, Wash., 1988.

274. K. Irvin, *Assembly Programming*, 3rd ed., Prentice Hall, New York, 1999.

275. H. Kaci-Aït, *Warren Abstract Machine*, MIT Press, Cambridge, Mass., 1991.

276. P. Van Roy and A.M. Despain, High-performance logic programming with the Aquarius Prolog Compiler. *IEEE Comput.* **1**, (1992).

277. C. Beierle and E. Börger, Specification and correctness proof of a WAM extension with abstract type constraints. *Formal Aspects Comput.*, (1996).

278. P. Tarau, *A Simplified Abstract Machine for the Execution of Binary Metaprograms*, ICOT'91, Tokyo. 1991.

279. G. Gupta, *Multiprocessor Execution of Logic Programs*. Kluwer, Academic Press, Norwell, Mass., 1994.

280. M. Carlsson, G. Gupta, and K.M. Ali, Parallel execution of Prolog programs: a survey. *J. Logic Prog.*, (1995).

281. N.J. Aparicio, J. Cunha, L. Monteiro, and L.M. Pareira, Delta-Prolog — a distributed backtracking extension with events, 3rd International Conference on Logic Programming. LNCS 225, Springer Verlag, New York, 1986.

282. P. Ciancarini, Blackboard Programming in Shared Prolog, in *Languages and Compilers for Parallel Computing*, MIT Press, Cambridge, Mass., 1993.

283. K. Clark and S. Gregory, Parlog — parallel programming in logic. *A.C.M. TO-PLAS* **8**, (1986).

284. K. Ueda, *Guarded Horn Clauses*, Ph.D. Thesis, University of Tokyo. 1986.

285. E. Shapiro, Concurrent Prolog — Collected Papers, MIT Press, Cambreidge, Mass., 1987.

286. P.C. Treleavan, *Exploiting Problem-Parallelism in Computing Systems*, Tech. Report 107, Computer Laboratory University of Newcastle upon Tyne, 1977.

287. E. Rich and K. Knight, *Artificial intelligence*, 2nd ed., McGraw-Hill, New York, 1991.

288. R.J. Douglass, *A Qualitative Assessment of Parallelism in Expert Systems. IEEE Software*, 5, 1985.

289. K. Shen, *Exploiting Dependent And-parallelism in Prolog — the dynamic dependent And-parallel scheme*, Joint International Conference and Symposium on Logic Programming, MIT Press, Cambridge, Mass., 1992.

290. H. Tebra, *Optimistic And-Parallelism in Prolog*, PARLE 87, Springer-Verlag, New York, 1987.

291. J.S. Conery, *Parallel Execution of Logic Programs*, Kluwer Academic Publishers, Norwell, Mass., 1987.

292. D.H.D. Warren., *The Andorra model*, Presented at Gigalips Project workshop, University of Manchester, March 1988.

293. I. Dutra, *Strategies for scheduling And- and Or-work in Parallel Logic Programming Systems*, Proceedings of ILPS'94, Ithaca, 1994.

294. I. Dutra, *Distributing And-work and Or-work in Parallel Logic Programming Systems*, Proceedings of HICSS'96, Hawaii, 1996.

295. D.H.D. Warren, *The Extended Andorra Model with Implicit Control*, Proceedings of the Parallel Logic Programming Workshop, ICLP'90, 1990.

296. V. Santos Costa, D. Warren, and R. Yang, *The Andorra-I engine — A Parallel Implementation of the Basic Andorra model*, Proceedings of Conference ICLP'91, 1991.

297. V. Santos Costa, D. Warren, and R. Yang: *The Andorra-I Preprocessor — Supporting Full Prolog on the Basic Andorra model*, Proceedings of Conference ICLP'91. 1991.

298. V. Benjumea and J.M. Troya, *A Static Implementation of the Basic Andorra Model for Distributed Memory Systems*, JICSLP'96 Workshop, 1999.

299. R. Lopes, V.S. Costa, *The BEAM-Toward a First EAM Implementation.* Workshop on Parallelism and Implementation Technology for (Constraint) Logic Programming Languages, Port Jefferson, New York, 1997.

300. R. Lopes, V.S. Costa, *The BEAM: A First EAM Implementation APPIA-GULP-PRODE'99* — Joint Conference on Declarative Programming. L'Aquila, Italy, 1999.

301. S. Janson and S. Haridi, *Programming Paradigms of the Andorra Kernel Language*, ILPS'91, 1991.

302. G. Smolka, The Oz Programming Model. *LNCS Vol. 1000*, Springer-Verlag, Berlin, 1995.

303. G. Gupta and D.H.D. Warren, An interpreter for the Extended Andorra Model, Bristol University Report, 1991.

304. G. Berry and G. Boudol, The Chemical Abstract Machine, *Theoretical Computer Science*, Elsevier, 1992, p. 96.

305. R. Straś, T. Szuba, and A.Y. Zomaya, An evolutionary parallel model of computations for computer graphics, based on the concept of Collective Intelligence, PDCS'99, 1999.

306. W. Fontana and L.W. Buss, The arrival of the fittest. *Bull. Math. Biol.* **56**, (1994).

307. B.R. Martin and G. Shaw, *Particle Physics*, Wiley & Sons, New York, 1992.

308. T. Szuba, *Evaluation Measures for the Collective Intelligence of Closed Social Structures*, ISAS'97 Gaithersburg/Washington D.C., 22–25 Sept. 1997.

309. L. Wos, R. Overbeek, R. Lusk, and J. Boyle, *Automated Reasoning—Introduction and Applications*, 2nd ed., McGraw-Hill, New York, 1992.

310. T. Szuba, A Molecular Quasi-random Model of Computations Applied to Evaluate Collective Intelligence. *Future Generat. Comput. J.* **14**, (1998).

311. J. Blazewicz, *Computational Complexity of Combinatorial Problems*, WNT Press, Warsaw, 1988, (in Polish).

312. G. Boudol, in *LNCS No 803*, "Proceedings of the REX School/Workshop A Decade of Concurrency", Springer-Verlag, New York, 1994 p. 5.

313. D.K. Campbell and G. Liam, *A Chemical Abstract Machine for Linda*, Technical Report YCS-282, Department of Computer Science, University of York, 1997.

314. P. Inverardi and A.L. Wolf, Formal specification and analysis of software architectures using the Chemical Abstract Machine Model. *IEEE Trans. Software Eng.* **21**, (1995).

315. T.M. Gramss, et al., Nonstandard Computation—Molecular Computation—Cellular Automata—Evolutionary Algorithms—Quantum Computers, Wiley & Sons, New York, 1998.

316. G. Pâun, et al., *DNA Computing—New Computing Paradigms*, Springer-Verlag, Berlin, 1998.

317. G. Pâun ed., Computing with Bio-Molecules—Theory and Experiments, *Springer Series in Discrete Mathematics and Theoretical Computer Science*, Springer-Verlag, Berlin, 1999.

318. T. Head, Splicing schemes and DNA, in G. Rozenberg and A. Salomaa ed., *Lindenmayer Systems—Impacts on Theoretical Computer Science, Computer Graphics, and Developmental Biology*. Springer-Verlag, New York 1992.

319. T. Head, *Splicing System and Molecular Processes*, ICEC'97 Special Session on DNA Based Computation, Indiana, 1997.

320. S. Roweis and E. Winfree, et al., *A Sticker Based Architecture for DNA Computation*, Proceedings of AMS'96 Conf. on DNA-based Computers, Princeton University, N.J., 1996. Available also from ftp://hope.caltech.edu/pub/roweis/DIMACS/stickers.ps.

321. E. Winfree, X. Yang, and N.C. Seeman, *Universal computation via self-assembly of DNA—some theory and experiments*, Proceedings of AMS'96 Conf. on DNA-based Computers, Princeton University Press, Princeton, N.J., 1996.

322. T. Yokomori, S. Kobayashi, and C. Ferretti, *On the Power of Circular Splicing Systems and DNA Computability*, Technical Report CSIM 9501, University of Electro Communications, Department of Computer Science and Information Mathematics, Tokyo, Japan, July 1995.

323. N.C. Seeman et al., *The Perils of Polynucleotides—The Experimental Gap Between the Design and Assembly of Unusual DNA Structures*. Proceedings of AMS'96 Conf. on DNA-based Computers, Princeton University, N.J., 1996.

324. A.S. Tanenbaum, *Structured Computer Organization*, 3rd ed., Prentice Hall, New York, 1990.

325. L.M. Adleman, On constructing a Molecular Computer, in *DNA-Based Computers, DIMACS: Series in Discrete Mathematics*, American Mathematical Society, Providence, R.I., 1996.

326. L.M. Smith and R.M. Corn, A surface-based approach to DNA Computation. *J. Comput. Biol.* **5**, (1998).

327. D. Boneh, C. Dunworth, and J. Sgall, *Discrete Appl. Math.* **71**, (1996), Also Technical Report No. TR-499-95, Princeton University, Princeton, N.J., 1995. Also at: ftp://ftp.cs.princeton.edu/pub/people/dabo/biocircuit.ps.Z

328. J.H. Reif, Parallel molecular computation—models and simulations. *Algorithmica* (1998).

329. D. Beaver, Computing with DNA. *J. Comput. Biol.* **2**, (1995).

330. S.A. Kurtz, S.R. Mahaney, J.S. Royer, and J. Simon, *Active Transport in Biological Computing*, AMS'96 Proceedings.

331. D. Wolpert and K. Tumer, An introduction to Collective Intelligence, Tech Report NASA-ARC-IC-99-63.
A shorter version of this paper is available in: M. Bradshaw, Jeffrey ed., *Handbook of Agent Technology*, AAAI Press/MIT Press, 1999.
On-line version including on extensive survey of related fields, at: http://ic.arc.nasa.gov/ic/projects/coin_pubs.html

332. R. Lewin: *Complexity-Life at the Edge of Chaos*, Macmillan Publishing, New York, 1992.

333. C.G. Langton, Artificial Life. *Artificial Life* **6**, (1989).

334. C.G. Langton, Life at the Edge of Chaos, in *Artificial Life II*, Addison-Wesley, Reading, Mass., 1992.

335. T. Szuba, *A Quasi-Chaotic Computational Model of Collective Intelligence and its IQ Measure*, CI&N'98, Research Triangle Park, N.C., October 23–28, 1998.

336. H. Pattee, Simulations, Realizations, and Theories of Life, in C. Langton ed., *Artificial Life*, Addison-Wesley, Reading, Mass., 1989.

337. R. Rosen, *Life itself: A Comprehensive Inquiry into the Nature, Origin, and fabrication of Life*, Columbia University Press, New York, 1991.

338. P. Calow, *Evolutionary Principles*, Chapman & Hall, New York, 1983.

339. S. Osawa and T. Honjo eds., *Evolution of Life—Fossils, Molecules, and Culture*, Springer-Verlag, New York, 1991.

340. V.I. Goldanskii, Tunneling, Chirality and Cold Prebiotic Evolution, in *Chemical Evolution—Self-organization of the Macromolecules of Life*, Proceedings of Conference on chemical evolution and the origin of Life, Trieste, 1993.

341. D. Mange, M. Tomassini eds., *Bioinspired Computing Machines — Toward novel Computational Architectures*, Presses Polytechniques et Universitaires Romandes, 1998.

342. M. Sipper, *Evolution of Parallel Cellular Machines: The Cellular Programming approach*, Springer-Verlag, New York, 1997.

343. M. Sipper, D. Mange, and A. Pérez-Uribe eds., Evolvable Systems — From Biology to Hardware, Proceedings of the 2nd International Conference on Evolvable Systems ICES'98. *LNCS Vol. 1478*, Springer-Verlag, Berlin, 1998.

344. E. Sanchez and M. Tomassini eds., Toward Evolvable Hardware, *LNCS*, Vol. 1062, Springer-Verlag, New York, 1996.

345. P. Kandzia and M. Klusch eds., Cooperative Information Agents, *Lecture notes in Artificial Intelligence*, Springer-Verlag, New York, 1997.

346. W. Wobcke and M. Pagnucco eds., *Agents and Multiagent Systems, Lecture Notes in Artificial Intelligence*, Springer, 1997.

347. W. Velde and J.W. Perram, eds., Agents Breaking Away, *Lecture Notes in Artificial Intelligence*, Springer, 1996.

348. C. Zhang and D. Lukose, eds., Distributed Artificial Intelligence, *Lecture Notes in Artificial Intelligence*, Springer, 1995.

349. B. Mandelbrot, A Multifractal walk down Wall Street. *Sci. Am.*, (1999).

350. R.M. Starr, *Why is there Money? — Convergence to a Monetary Equilibrium in a General Equilibrium Model with Transaction Costs*, University of California, San Diego, Working Paper no. 99–23. Also available at: http://weber.ucsd.edu/Depts/Econ/Wpapers/dp99.html#99-23

351. G. Weiss, ed., *Multiagent Systems — a Modern Approach to Distributed Artificial Intelligence*, MIT Press, Cambridge, Mass., 1999.

352. D. Glyn, *A History of Money from Ancient Times to the Present Day*, 2nd ed., University of Wales Press, Cardiff, 1996.

353. N. Kiyotaki and R. Wright, On money as a medium of exchange. *J. Polit. Econ.* **97**, (1989).

354. H. Gintis, A Markov model of money and trade — Theory and Artificial Life simulation. *Comput. Math. Organizat. Theory* **(3,1)**, (1997).

355. R. Marimon, E. McGrattan, and T.J. Sargent, Money as a medium of exchange in an economy with artificial intelligent agents. *J. Econ. Dyn. Control* **14**, (1990).

356. W.A. Brock, D.A. Hsieh, and B. LeBaron, *Nonlinear Dynamics, Chaos, and Instability — Statistical Theory and Economic Evidence*, MIT Press, Cambridge, Mass., 1991.

357. D.N. Chorafas, *Chaos Theory in the Financial Markets: Applying Fractals, Fuzzy Logic, Genetic Algorithms, Swarm Simulation, and the Monte Carlo Method to Manage Market Chaos and Volatility*, Probus Publishing, 1994.

358. B. LeBaron, Chaos and nonlinear forecastability in economics and finance. *Philosophical Transactions of the Royal Society*, Series A, vol. 348, Sept 1994.

359. R. Di Lorenzo, *A Chaotic Model of the Financial Markets (CSSP)*, 15th International Conference on Scientific Computation, Modeling, and Applied Mathematics, IMACS'77, Berlin, 1977.

360. B.B. Mandelbrot ed., *Fractals and Scaling in Finance — Discontinuity, Concentration, Risk — Selecta*, Springer-Verlag, New York, 1997.

361. C. Grebogi, et al., Strange attractors that are not chaotic. *Physica 13D*, (1984).

362. J. Stiglitz, The Invisible Hand and Modern Welfare Economics, NBER Working Paper No. 3641, Cambridge, Mass., 1991.

363. G. Busino, "Pareto, Vilfredo", in *The New Palgrave, A Dictionary of Economics*, Vol. 3, 1987, pp. 799–804.

364. G.P. Amorino, V.M. Hamilton, and H. Choy, Enhancement of radiation effects by combined docetaxel and carboplatin treatment in vitro. *Radiat. Oncol. Investigat.* **7**, (1999).

365. P.A. Corning, Holistic Darwinism—synergistic selection and the evolutionary process. *J. Soc. Evol. Syst.* **20**(4), (1997).

366. D. Deutsch, *Quantum Theory, the Church-Turing Principle and the Universal Quantum Computer*, Proceedings of the Royal Society, Series A, 400, 1985, pp. 97–117.

367. P. Bock, The Emergence of Artificial Cognition—An Introduction to Collective Intelligence, in H.P. Schwefel, ed., *Parallel Problem Solving from Nature*, Springer-Verlag, New York, 1991.

368. C. Dworak, P.C. Kaneakis, and J.C. Mitchel, *On the Sequential Nature of Unification*, MIT Report LCS/TM-257, March 1984.

369. J-L. Deneubourg, et al., Self-Organization Mechanism in Ant Societies—Learning in Foraging and Division of Labor, in J.M. Pasteels, J-L. Deneubourg, eds., *From Individual to Collective Behavior in Social Insects*, Birghaüser Verlag, Basel, 1987.

370. J. Duffy and J. Ochs, Fiat money as a medium of exchange—experimental evidence. (working paper, at http://www.pitt.edu/~jduffy/jduffy.html)

371. K. Fisher and M.D. Fisher, *The Distributed Mind—Achieving High Performance through the Collective Intelligence of Knowledge Work Teams*, Amazon Press, 1998.

372. D.R. Forsyth, *Group Dynamics*, 3rd ed., Brooks/Cole Publishing, 1998.

373. I. Futo, *Prolog with Communicating Processes—from T-Prolog to CSR-Prolog*, 10th International Conference on Logic Programming, 1993.

374. Z. Guessoum, *A Hybrid Agent Model—Reactive and Cognitive behavior*, IEEE, ISADS'97, Berlin, pp. 10–11, 1997.

375. J.W. Kalat, Introduction to Psychology, 3rd ed., Books/Cole Publishing, 1993.

376. D. Kerckhove, *Planetary Mind—Collective Intelligence in the Digital Age*, 1997.

377. P. Levy, *Collective Intelligence*, Plenum Trade, 1997.

378. C. Packer and A.E. Pusey, Divided we fall: Cooperation among lions. *Sci. Am.* **276**, (1997).

379. J.E. Savage, *Models of Computation—Exploring the Power of Computing*, Addison-Wesley, Reading, Mass., 1998.

380. R.J. Sternberg, I.Q. Beyond, Cambridge University Press, New York, 1988.

381. D. Sumpter, Multi-Agent Simulation of Honey Bee Colonies. Homepage: http://www.ma.umist.ac.uk/dsumpter/beesim/Simulation/overview.html

382. T. Szuba and M. Almulla, The computational model of Collective Intelligence suggests that Intelligence (collective version) emerged first, before life on Earth, *BioSP'2000*, Cancun, Mexico.

383. T. Szuba, and A. Stras, On evaluating the inference power of a closed social structures with the help of a Random PROLOG Processor, *PAP'97 "Practical Application of PROLOG"*, London, 21–24 April, 1997.

384. T. Szuba, *A Formal Definition of the Phenomenon of Collective Intelligence and its IQ Measure*, IPPS/SPDP'99, San Juan/Puerto Rico, USA, April 14–16, 1999.

385. T. Szuba and A. Wasiewicz, The idea of consciousness for intelligent machines as the frame for future software construction. *Math. Intell. Models Syst. Simulat.* (1991).

386. N. Tinbergen, Animal in Its World — Field Studies, 1972.

387. N. Tinbergen, *Animal in Its World: Laboratory Experiments and General Papers*, 1976.

388. R. Wehner, Spatial Organization of Foraging Behavior in Individually Searching Desert Ants, in J.M. Pasteels, J-L. Deneubourg eds., *from Individual to Collective Behavior in Social Insects*. Birghaüser Verlag, Basel, 1987.

389. W. Sulis, Collective Intelligenece as a Model for the Unconscious. PSYCHOLOGICAL PERSPECTIVES. Jung Institute of Los Angeles. Spring 1997 Issue: VISIONARIES. 1997.

PUBLICATIONS OF THE RESEARCH GROUPS DIRECTLY INVOLVED IN RESEARCH ON COLLECTIVE INTELLIGENCE

Collective Intelligence Laboratory at McMaster University

(http://www.cas.mcmaster.ca/~sulisw/cilab.html)

Books

W. Suils and A. Combs, (eds.): Nonlinear Dynamics in Human Behavior. Singapore: World Scientific, 1996.

Articles

W. Sulis, Tempered Neural Networks. Proceedings of the International Joint Conference on Neural Networks, 1992.

W. Sulis, Emergent Computation in Tempered Neural Networks 1: Dynamical Automata. Proceedings of WCNN'93, 1993.

W. Sulis, Emergent Computation in Tempered Neural Networks 2: Computation Theory. Proceedings of the WCNN'93, 1993.

W. Sulis, Naturally Occurring Computational Systems. World Futures 39(4) 1993.

W. Sulis, Naturally Occurring Computational Systems. In Chaos Theory In Psychology and the Life Sciences. R. Robertson, A. Combs (eds.). Lawrence Erbaum. New York, 1995.

W. Sulis, Driven Cellular Automata. Lectures on Complex Systems. Lecture Volume VI in the Santa Fe Institute Studies in the Sciences of Complexity. Addison-Wesley, 1995.

W. Sulis, Causality in Naturally Occurring Computational Systems. World Futures 44, 1995.

W. Sulis, Driven Cellular Automata, Adaptation, and the Binding Problem. In Advances in Artificial Life. Lectures Notes in Artificial Intelligence 929. F. Moran, A. Moreno, J.J. Merelo, P. Chacon (eds.). Springer-Verlag. New York, 1995.

W. Sulis, TIGoRs and Neural Codes. In Nonlinear Dynamics in Human Behavior, W. Sulis and A. Combs (Eds.) Singapore: World Scientific, 1996.

W. Sulis, Foundations of Collective Intelligence. Nonlinear Dynamics in Psychology and the Life Sciences, 1(1), 1997.

I. Trofimova, Analysis of behavioral strategies using cellular automaton models. Abstracts of International Psychological Congress. Montreal, 1996.

W. Sulis, Collective Intelligence as a Model for the Unconscious. Jung Institute of Los Angeles. PSYCHOLOGICAL PERSPECTIVES. Spring 1997 Issue: VISIONARIES, 1997.

I. Trofimova, Functional Differentiation in Developmental Systems. Complex Systems. Proceedings of International Conference. Oxford Press, 1998.

I. Trofimova and A.B. Potapov, the definition of parameters for measurement in psychology. In: F.M., 1998.

G. Guindani and Salvadori (eds.): Chaos, Models, and Fractals. Italian University Press. Pavia, Italy, 1998.

I. Trofimova and A. Potapov, W. Sulis, Collective Effects on Individual Behavior: In search of Universality. International Journal of Chaos Theory and Applications. 1998.

NASA Ames Collective Intelligence Group

(http://ic.arc.nasa.gov/ic/projects/collective-intelligence.html)

Publications

K. Tumer and D. Wolpert, Collective Intelligence and Braess' Paradox. In the Proceedings of the 17th National Conference on Artificial Intelligence, Austin, Texas, August 2000.

D. Wolpert, S. Kirshner, C. Merz, and K. Tumer, Adaptivity in Agent-Based Routing for Data Networks," 4th International Conference on Autonomous Agents. Barcelona, Spain, June 2000.

D. Wolpert, and K. Tumer, An Introduction to Collective Intelligence. Tech Report NASA-ARC-IC-99-63. A shorter version of this paper available in: J. M. Bradshaw (ed.), Handbook of Agent Technology, AAAI Press/MIT Press, 1999.

D. Wolpert, K. Wheeler, and K. Tumer, Collective Intelligence for Control of Distributed Dynamical Systems. Europhysics Letters, Vol. 49, No. 6, March 2000.

D. Wolpert, K. Wheeler, and K. Tumer, General Principles of Learning-Based Multi-Agent Systems. 3rd International Conference on Autonomous Agents. Seattle, WA. May 1999.

D. Wolpert, K. Tumer, and J. Frank, Using Collective Intelligence to Route Internet Traffic. Advances in Neural Information Processing Systems-11, Denver, CO, December 1998.

SELECTED INTERNET LOCATIONS[1] USEFUL FOR RESEARCH ON COLLECTIVE INTELLIGENCE

Agent-Based Computational Economics (ACE)

Leigh Tesfatsion
Department of Economics
Iowa State University
http://www.econ.iastate.edu/tesfatsi/ace.htm

UMIST Manchester

David Sumpter
Multi-Agent Simulation of Honey Bee Colonies.
Homepage:
http://www.ma.umist.ac.uk/dsumpter/beesim/Simulation/overview.html

CIlab

Dr. William Sulis
Department of Psychology, McMaster University, Room B114 1280 Main St. W. Hamilton, Ontario, CANADA L8S 4M2:
http://cas.mcmaster.ca/~sulisw/cilab.html

Hewlett-Packard Laboratories, Bristol

Collective intelligence for Network Control
http://www-uk.hpl.hp.com/people/ruud/abc.html

IRIDIA, Université Libre de Bruxelles

Jean-Louis Deneubourg, Marco Dorigo http://iridia.ulb.ac.be/dorigo/

[1] There is high risk of change of given Internet location or even disappearing, due to personal character of some problem oriented locations and inborn dynamics of Internet itself.

Ant Colony Optimisation Links

Marco Dorigo's ACO page: http://iridia.ulb.ac.be/dorigo/ACO/ACO.html
Interaction Lab., Computer Science Department, University of Southern California

Maja J Mataric

http://www-robotics.usc.edu/~maja/

ISAB (The International Society for Adaptive Behavior, Inc.)

Stewart Wilson
http://world.std.com/~sw/

Institute for the Study of Complex Systems Palo Alto,

A. Peter Corning, Ph.D.
The co-operative gene: on the role of synergy in evolution.
http://www.complexsystems.org/

Department of Cybernetics at University of Reading

Kerstin Dautenhahn
Socially Intelligent Agents homepage:
http://homepages.feis.herts.ac.uk/~comqkd/aaai-social.html

Bar-Ilan University

Rina Schwartz
Distributed Artificial Intelligence Home Page
http://www.cs.biu.ac.il/~schwart/DAI/

NASA Ames Research Center MS 269-2 Moffett Field,

CA Computational Sciences Division
Current members of the Collective Intelligence ("Collective INtelligence" (COIN)) effort:
David Wolpert, Ph. D. (Principal Investigator)

Kagan Tumer, Ph. D. (Co-Investigator)
Ann M. Bell, Ph. D.
Joseph Sill, Ph. D.
Chris J. Merz Ph. D.
COIN homepage:
http://ic.arc.nasa.gov/ic/projects/collective–intelligence.html
Collective Intelligence COIN papers:
http://ic.arc.nasa.gov/ic/projects/coin_-pubs.html

The Santa Fe Institute

Chris Langton
The Swarm Corporation
http://www.swarm.com/index.html

TAU — Tel Aviv University

Prof. Eshel Ben-Jacob
Bacterial Cybernetic Group.
http://star.tau.ac.il/~inon/baccyber0

INDEX